Using and Administering Linux: Volume 3

Zero to SysAdmin: Network Services

Second Edition

David Both

Apress®

Using and Administering Linux: Volume 3: Zero to SysAdmin: Network Services

David Both
Raleigh, NC, USA

ISBN-13 (pbk): 978-1-4842-9785-8   ISBN-13 (electronic): 978-1-4842-9786-5
https://doi.org/10.1007/978-1-4842-9786-5

Managing Director, Apress Media LLC: Welmoed Spahr
Acquisitions Editor: James Robinson-Prior
Development Editor: Jim Markham
Editorial Assistant: Gryffin Winkler

Cover image designed by the author

Distributed to the book trade worldwide by Springer Science+Business Media New York, 1 New York Plaza, 1 FDR Dr, New York, NY 10004. Phone 1-800-SPRINGER, fax (201) 348-4505, e-mail orders-ny@springer-sbm.com, or visit www.springeronline.com. Apress Media, LLC is a California LLC and the sole member (owner) is Springer Science + Business Media Finance Inc (SSBM Finance Inc). SSBM Finance Inc is a **Delaware** corporation.

For information on translations, please e-mail booktranslations@springernature.com; for reprint, paperback, or audio rights, please e-mail bookpermissions@springernature.com.

Apress titles may be purchased in bulk for academic, corporate, or promotional use. eBook versions and licenses are also available for most titles. For more information, reference our Print and eBook Bulk Sales web page at http://www.apress.com/bulk-sales.

Any source code or other supplementary material referenced by the author in this book is available to readers on GitHub (https://github.com/Apress). For more detailed information, please visit https://www.apress.com/gp/services/source-code.

Paper in this product is recyclable

This book is dedicated to all

*Linux and open source developers, system administrators,
course developers, and trainers.*

:(){ :|:& };:

Table of Contents

About the Author

David Both is an open source software and GNU/Linux advocate, trainer, writer, and speaker. He has been working with Linux and open source software for more than 25 years and has been working with computers for over 50 years. He is a strong proponent of and evangelist for the "Linux Philosophy for System Administrators."

He worked for IBM for 21 years and, while working as a course development representative in Boca Raton, FL, in 1981, wrote the training course for the first IBM PC. He has taught RHCE classes for Red Hat and has taught classes on Linux ranging from Lunch'n'Learns to full five-day courses.

David's books and articles are a continuation of his desire to pass on his knowledge and to provide mentoring to anyone interested in learning about Linux.

David prefers to purchase the components and build his own computers from scratch to ensure that each new computer meets his exacting specifications. Building his own computers also means not having to pay the Microsoft tax. His latest build is an ASUS TUF X299 motherboard and an Intel i9 CPU with 16 cores (32 CPUs) and 64GB of RAM in a Cooler Master MasterFrame 700.

David is the author of *The Linux Philosophy for SysAdmins* (Apress, 2018) and co-author of *Linux for Small Business Owners* (Apress, 2022) and can be found on Mastodon @linuxgeek46@LinoxRocks.online.

About the Technical Reviewers

Branton Brodie started his Linux journey last year while attending All Things Open 2022. Getting into the IT world was something he wanted to do for a while but didn't know where to start until he went there and saw all the opportunities shown. Linux stood out to him the most, and he is now studying to become a SysAdmin. He enjoys reading about tech and how the future of tech will shape the world around us. He lives in the calming town of Wake Forest, NC.

Seth Kenlon is a Unix and Linux geek, SysAdmin, open source and free culture advocate, music producer, Java and Lua programmer, game designer, and tabletop gamer. He arrived in the computer industry by way of film production.

Acknowledgments

Writing a book – and especially a three-volume second edition – is not a solitary activity, and this massive Linux training course required a team effort much more so than most.

The most important person in this effort has been my awesome wife, Alice, who has been my head cheerleader and best friend throughout. I could not have done this without your support and love. Again!

I owe many thanks to my editors at Apress, James Robinson-Prior and Gryffin Winkler, for seeing the need for a second edition and especially for being supportive as I worked my way through some major restructuring and a significant amount of new material. I especially thank you for your immediate support when I suggested having a student as second technical editor.

Seth Kenlon, my amazing technical reviewer, and I have worked together before on previous books as well as many of the articles I wrote for the now defunct Opensource. com website. I am grateful for his contributions to the technical accuracy of all three volumes of this course. Seth also made some important suggestions that improved the flow and accuracy of this course. I once said that Seth was on the "ragged edge of being brutally honest" in his editorial tasks; he responded that he had been aiming for "completely brutal," but had apparently failed. You still have my ongoing gratitude for the work you do.

I also owe many thanks to Branton Brodie, my second technical editor for all three volumes. Branton and I met as part of his desire to learn about Linux at a time when I was just starting on this second edition. I thought that having a student who wanted to take the course anyway act as a technical editor could provide me with some insight into how students view the course. His contributions have been valuable to my work as I was able to revise descriptions and explanations that made sense to me but not necessarily to anyone who has never been exposed to Linux or system administration.

Of course any remaining errors, omissions, and poor explanations are my responsibility alone.

Introduction

This Linux training course, "Using and Administering Linux – Zero to SysAdmin," is significantly different from other courses. It consists of three volumes. Each of these three volumes is closely connected, and they build upon each other.

This Linux training course differs from others because it is a complete self-study course. You should start at the beginning of Volume 1 and read the text, perform all of the experiments, and do all of the chapter exercises through to the end of Volume 3. If you do this, even if you are starting from zero knowledge about Linux, you can learn the tasks necessary to becoming a Linux system administrator, a SysAdmin.

Another difference this course has over others is that all of the experiments are performed on one or more virtual machines (VMs) in a virtual network. Using the free software VirtualBox, you will create this virtual environment on any reasonably sized host, whether Linux or Windows. In this virtual environment, you are free to experiment on your own, make mistakes that could damage the Linux installation of a hardware host, and still be able to recover completely by restoring the Linux VM host from any one of multiple snapshots. This flexibility to take risks and yet recover easily makes it possible to learn more than would otherwise be possible.

These course materials can also be used as reference materials. I have used my previous course materials for reference for many years, and they have been very useful in that role. I have kept this as one of my goals in this set of materials.

Not all of the review exercises in this course can be answered by simply reviewing the chapter content. For some questions you will need to design your own experiment in order to find a solution. In many cases there will very probably be multiple solutions, and all that produce the correct results will be the "correct" ones.

The Process

The process that goes with this format is just as important as the format of the course – really even more so. The first thing that a course developer must do is generate a list of requirements that define both the structure and the content of the course. Only then can the process of writing the course proceed. In fact, many times I find it helpful to write the review questions and exercises before I create the rest of the content. In many chapters of this course, I have worked in this manner.

These courses present a complete, end-to-end Linux training course for students like you who know before you start that you want to learn to be a Linux system administrator – a SysAdmin. This Linux course will allow you to learn Linux right from the beginning with the objective of becoming a SysAdmin.

Many Linux training courses begin with the assumption that the first course a student should take is one designed to start them as a user. Those courses may discuss the role of root in system administration, but ignore topics that are important to future SysAdmins. Other courses ignore system administration altogether. A typical second course will introduce the student to system administration, while a third may tackle advanced administration topics.

Frankly, this baby step approach did not work well for many of us who are now Linux SysAdmins. We became SysAdmins, in part at least, due to our intense desire to learn as much as possible as quickly as possible. It is also, I think in large part, due to our highly inquisitive natures. We learn a basic command and then start asking questions, experimenting with it to see what its limits are, what breaks it, what using it can break. We explore the man(ual) pages and other documentation to learn the extreme usages to which it might be put. If things don't break by themselves, we break them intentionally to see how they work and to learn how to fix them. We relish our own failures because we learn more from fixing them than we do when things always work as they are supposed to.

In this course we will dive deep into Linux system administration almost from the very beginning. You will learn many of the Linux tools required to use and administer Linux workstations and servers – usually multiple tools that can be applied to each of these tasks. This course contains many experiments to provide you with the kind of hands-on experiences that SysAdmins appreciate. All of these experiments guide you one step at a time into the elegant and beautiful depths of the Linux experience. You will learn that Linux is simple and that simplicity is what makes it both elegant and knowable.

Based on my own years working with Unix and Linux, the course materials contained in these three volumes are designed to introduce you to the practical, daily tasks you will perform as a Linux user and, at the same time, as a Linux system administrator – SysAdmin.

But I don't know everything – that's just not possible. No SysAdmin does. Further, no two SysAdmins know exactly the same things because that, too, is impossible. We have each started with different knowledge and skills; we have different goals; we have different experiences because the systems on which we work have failed in different ways, had different hardware, were embedded in different networks, had different distributions installed, and many other differences. We use different tools and approaches to problem solving because the many different mentors and teachers we had used different sets of tools from each other; we use different Linux distributions; we think differently; and we know different things about the hardware on which Linux runs. Our past is much of what makes us what we are and what defines us as SysAdmins.

So I will show you things in this course – things that I think are important for you to know, things that, in my opinion, will provide you with the skills to use your own curiosity and creativity to find solutions that I would never think of to problems I have never encountered.

I have always found that I learn more from my mistakes than I ever have when things work as they are supposed to. For this reason I suggest that, rather than immediately reverting to an earlier snapshot when you run into trouble, you try to figure out how the problem was created and how best to recover from it. If, after a reasonable period of time, you have not resolved the problem, that would be the point at which reverting to a snapshot would make sense.

What This Course Is Not

This course is not a certification study guide. It is not designed to help you pass a certification test of any type. This course is intended purely to help you become a good or perhaps even great SysAdmin, not to pass a test.

There are a few good certification tests. Red Hat and Cisco certifications are among the best because they are based on the test-taker's ability to perform specific tasks. I am not familiar with any of the other certification tests because I have not taken them. But the courses you can take and books you can purchase to help you pass those tests are designed to help you pass the tests and not to administer a Linux host or network. That does not make them bad – just different from this course.

Content Overview

This quick overview of the contents of each volume should serve as a quick orientation guide if you need to locate specific information. If you are trying to decide whether to purchase this book and its companion volumes, it will give you a good overview of the entire course.

Using and Administering Linux: Volume 1 – Zero to SysAdmin: Getting Started

Chapters 1 through 3 of Volume 1 introduce operating systems in general and Linux in particular and briefly explore the Linux Philosophy for SysAdmins in preparation for the rest of the course.

Chapter 4 then guides you through the use of VirtualBox to create a virtual machine (VM) and a virtual network to use as a test laboratory for performing the many experiments that are used throughout the course. In Chapter 5, you will install the Xfce version of Fedora – a popular and powerful Linux distribution – on the VM. Chapter 6 shows you how to use the Xfce desktop, which will enable you to leverage your growing command-line interface (CLI) expertise as you proceed through the course.

Chapters 7 and 8 will get you started using the Linux command line and introduce you to some of the basic Linux commands and their capabilities. In Chapter 9 you will learn about data streams and the Linux tools used to manipulate them. And in Chapter 10 you will learn a bit about several text editors, which are indispensable to advanced Linux users and system administrators. You will also learn to use the Vim text editor to create and modify the many ASCII plain text files that Linux uses for configuration and administrative programming.

Chapters 11 through 13 start your work as a SysAdmin and take you through some specific tasks such as working as root and installing software updates and new software. Chapters 14 and 15 discuss more terminal emulators and some advanced shell skills. In Chapter 16 you will learn about the sequence of events that take place as the computer boots and Linux starts up. Chapter 17 shows you how to configure your shell to personalize it in ways that can seriously enhance your command-line efficiency.

Finally, Chapters 18 and 19 dive into all things files and filesystems.

1. Introduction

2. Introduction to Operating Systems

Using and Administering Linux: Volume 2 – Zero to SysAdmin: Advanced Topics

Volume 2 of *Using and Administering Linux* introduces you to some incredibly powerful and useful advanced topics that every SysAdmin must know.

In Chapters 20 and 21, you will experience an in-depth exploration of logical volume management (LVM) – and what that even means – as well as the use of file managers to manipulate files and directories. Chapter 22 introduces the concept that, in Linux, everything is a file. You will also learn some fun and interesting uses of the fact that everything is a file.

In Chapter 23 you will learn to use several tools that enable the SysAdmin to manage and monitor running processes. Chapter 24 enables you to experience the power of the special filesystems, such as /proc, which enable us as SysAdmins to monitor and tune the kernel while it is running – without a reboot.

Chapter 25 will introduce you to regular expressions and the power that using them for pattern matching can bring to the command line, while Chapter 26 discusses managing printers and printing from the command line. In Chapter 27 you will use several tools to unlock the secrets of the hardware on which your Linux operating system is running.

Chapters 28 and 29 show you how to do some simple – and not so simple – command-line programming and how to automate various administrative tasks. In Chapter 30 you will learn to use Ansible, a powerful tool that makes automating tasks for thousands of computers just as easy as for one. Chapter 31 discusses the tools you will use to perform repetitive and automated tasks at specific times.

You will begin to learn the details of networking in Chapter 32, and Chapter 33 covers use of the powerful NetworkManager tool.

Chapter 34 introduces the B-Tree Filesystem (BTRFS) and covers its very interesting features. This chapter also informs you why BTRFS is not an appropriate choice for a filesystem in most use cases.

Chapters 35 through 37 allow you to explore systemd, the modern tool for starting Linux at boot time and which is also used to manage system services and tools. Chapter 38 discusses D-Bus and udev and how Linux uses them to treat all devices as plug and play (PnP).

In Chapter 39 you will learn to use and manage traditional log files. You will also learn to configure and use the logwatch facility to assist you with sorting through the many log messages to get to the important ones.

Chapter 40 covers the tasks required to manage users, while Chapter 41 introduces you to some basic tasks needed to manage the firewall. You will use the firewalld command-line tool to create and manage zones to which the network interfaces will be assigned based on various security needs such as internal and external networks.

20. Logical Volume Management (LVM)

21. File Managers

22. Everything Is a File

23. Managing Processes

Using and Administering Linux: Volume 3 – Zero to SysAdmin: Network Services

In Volume 3 of *Using and Administering Linux*, you will start by creating a new VM in the existing virtual network. This new VM will be used as a server for the rest of this course, and it will replace some of the functions performed by the virtual router that is part of our virtual network.

Chapter 42 begins this transformation from simple workstation to server by adding a second network interface card (NIC) to the new VM so that it can act as a firewall and router and then changing its network configuration from Dynamic Host Configuration Protocol (DHCP) to static IP addressing. This includes configuring both NICs so that one is connected to the existing virtual router so as to allow connections to the outside world and so that the other NIC connects to the new "inside" network that will contain the existing VM.

Chapter 43 discusses Domain Name Services (DNS) in detail both from client and server standpoints. You'll learn to use the /etc/hosts file for simple name resolution and then create a simple caching name server. You will then convert the caching name server into a primary name server for your internal network.

In Chapter 44 you will convert the new server into a router using kernel parameters and a simple firewall configuration change.

Chapter 45 shows how to use SSHD to provide secure remote access between Linux hosts. It also provides some interesting insights into using commands remotely and creating a simple command-line program to back up specific directories of a remote host to the local host.

Although we have incorporated security in all aspects of what has already been covered, Chapter 46 covers some additional security topics. This includes physical hardening as well as further hardening of the host to provide enhanced protection from network intrusions.

In Chapter 47 you will learn techniques and strategies for creating backups that use easily available open source tools, which are easy to use for both creating backups and restoring complete filesystems or individual files.

You will learn to install and configure an enterprise-class email server that can detect and block most spam and malware in Chapters 48 through 50. Chapter 51 takes you through setting up a web server, and in Chapter 52 you will set up WordPress, a flexible and powerful content management system.

In Chapter 53 you return to email by setting up a mailing list using Mailman.

Sometimes accessing a desktop remotely is the only way to do some things, so in Chapter 54 you will do just that.

Chapter 55 discusses package management from the other direction by guiding you through the process of creating an RPM package for the distribution of your own scripts and configuration files. Then Chapter 56 guides you through sharing files to both Linux and Windows hosts.

Finally, Chapter 57 will get you started in the right direction because I know you are going to ask, "Where do I go from here?"

42. Server Preparation

43. Name Services

Taking This Course

Although designed primarily as a self-study guide, this course can be used effectively in a classroom environment. This course can also be used very effectively as a reference. Many of the original course materials I wrote for Linux training classes I used to teach as an independent trainer and consultant were valuable to me as references. The experiments became models for performing many tasks and later became the basis for automating many of those same tasks. I have used many of those original experiments in parts of this course, because they are still relevant and provide an excellent reference for many of the tasks I still need to do.

You will see as you proceed through the course that it uses many software programs considered to be older and perhaps obsolete like Sendmail, Procmail, BIND, the Apache web server, and much more. Despite their age, or perhaps because of it, the software I have chosen to run my own systems and servers and to use in this course has been well-proven and is all still in widespread use. I believe that the software we will use in these experiments has properties that make it especially valuable in learning the in-depth details of how Linux and those services work. Once you have learned those details, moving to any other software that performs the same tasks will be relatively easy. In any event, none of that "older" software is anywhere near as difficult or obscure as some people seem to think that it is.

Who Should Take This Course

If you want to learn to be an advanced Linux user and even a SysAdmin, this course is for you. Most SysAdmins have an extremely high level of curiosity and a deep-seated need to learn Linux system administration. We like to take things apart and put them back together again to learn how they work. We enjoy fixing things and are not hesitant about diving in to fix the computer problems that our friends and co-workers bring us.

We want to know what happens when some computer hardware fails, so we might save defective components such as motherboards, RAM, and storage devices. This gives us defective components with which we can run tests. As I write this, I have a known defective hard drive inserted in a hard drive docking station connected to my primary workstation and have been using it to test failure scenarios that will appear in this course.

Most importantly, we do all of this for fun and would continue to do so even if we had no compelling vocational reason for doing so. Our intense curiosity about computer hardware and Linux leads us to collect computers and software like others collect stamps or antiques. Computers are our avocation – our hobby. Some people like boats, sports, travel, coins, stamps, trains, or any of thousands of other things, and they pursue them relentlessly as a hobby. For us – the true SysAdmins – that is what our computers are. That does not mean we are not well-rounded and don't do other things. I like to travel, read, go to museums and concerts, and ride historical trains, and my stamp collection is still there, waiting for me when I decide to take it up again.

In fact, the best SysAdmins, at least the ones I know, are all multifaceted. We are involved in many different things, and I think that is due to our inexhaustible curiosity about pretty much everything. So if you have an insatiable curiosity about Linux and want to learn about it – regardless of your past experience or lack thereof – then this course is most definitely for you.

Who Should Not Take This Course

If you do not have a strong desire to learn about how to use or administer Linux systems, this course is not for you. If all you want – or need – to do is use a couple apps on a Linux computer that someone has put on your desk, this course is not for you. If you have no curiosity about what superpowers lie behind the GUI desktop, this course is not for you.

Why This Course

Someone asked me why I wanted to write this course. My answer is simple – I want to give back to the Linux community. I have had several amazing mentors over the span of my career, and they taught me many things – things I find worth sharing with you along with much that I have learned for myself.

This course – all three volumes of it – started its existence as the slide presentations and lab projects for three Linux courses I created and taught. For a number of reasons, I do not teach those classes anymore. However, I would still like to pass on my knowledge and as many of the tips and tricks I have learned for the administration of Linux as possible. I hope that with this course I can pass on at least some of the guidance and mentoring that I was fortunate enough to have in my own career.

About Fedora Releases

The first edition of this self-study course was originally written for Fedora 29, and we are now up to Fedora 38. As I have worked through the second edition of this course, I have added new materials I thought appropriate and incorporated as many errata corrections as possible.

Where it was necessary, I have also included revised graphics such as screenshots used for illustrative purposes. In many cases the graphics for earlier releases of Fedora are still applicable although the background images and some nonessential visual elements have changed. In those cases I have retained the original graphics.

I have only replaced older graphics with newer ones where necessary to ensure the accuracy and clarity of the illustrated points. Some of the illustrations in this course are from Fedora 29. If you are using later releases of Fedora, such as Fedora 37, 38, or later, the background and other cosmetic elements may be different from Fedora 29.

CHAPTER 42

Server Preparation

Objectives

In this chapter you will

- Create a new VM on which to install Fedora to use as a server, firewall, and router.

- Install the latest version of Fedora on the VM to be used as the server.

- Make a few configuration changes to ensure that the new VM will provide a suitable base to use as a server.

- Set the hostname.

- Change the network configuration to static.

- Verify the virtual network connection between StudentVM1 and StudentVM2, as well as between the VMs and the outside world.

- Define the purpose and functions of DHCP.

- List several of the many network configuration items that DHCP can serve.

- Use DHCP to assign and manage static IP addresses for specific hosts based on the MAC address.

- Configure Chrony for this host to be the Network Time Protocol (NTP) server for the network.

© David Both 2023
D. Both, *Using and Administering Linux: Volume 3*, https://doi.org/10.1007/978-1-4842-9786-5_42

Overview

There are some preparatory tasks that need to be accomplished in order perform the experiments in this third volume of *Using and Administering Linux – Zero to SysAdmin*. Most lab environments use physical machines for training purposes, but in this volume we use at least two Linux hosts in a local network in order to enable a realistic environment for learning about being a SysAdmin.

As we have seen in the previous two volumes of this course, the use of multiple VMs to create a virtual network on a single physical host provides a safe virtual computing and network environment in which to learn by making mistakes.

In Volume 1, you created a VM and a custom virtual network and installed Fedora on it to use in the many experiments encountered in the rest of the course. We now need to create a new VM that we can use as a server for this volume of the course.

In this volume, Volume 3, of the course, I assume that you have completed the previous two volumes. You will not be able to successfully perform the experiments in this volume if you have not completed the first two volumes. This is for two reasons. First, you will probably not have sufficient knowledge to do so, and second, the virtual network and virtual machine created in Volume 1 and changed and modified throughout Volume 2 will not be available or configured correctly to work in this part of the course.

Creating the VM

We first need to create a new VM we will use as our server for the rest of this course and then make some configuration changes. Create the new VM using the specifications listed in Figure 42-1.

Item	Value
VM Name	StudentVM2
Machine folder	/Experiments/
(OS) Type	Linux
Version	The latest Fedora 64-bit Xfce version. At least Fedora 38 or later. It is recommended that you use the most recent version of Fedora Xfce for this VM even if a previous version is being used on StudentVM1.
Memory size	4096MB – The memory size can be changed at any time later so long as the VM is powered off. For now this should be more than enough RAM.
Number of CPUs	4
File location	/Experiments/
(Hard disk) File size	80GB
Hard disk file type	.vdi – The .vdi extension is the VirtualBox Disk Image file format. You could select other formats but this VDI format will be perfect for our needs.
Storage on physical hard disk	Dynamically allocated

***Figure 42-1.** The specifications for the StudentVM2 virtual machine*

Use the VirtualBox Manager to create a new VM using the preceding specifications. If necessary you can review Chapter 5 in Volume 1 for details.

At this point the basic virtual machine has been created, but we need to make a few changes to some of the configuration. Use the VirtualBox Manager **Settings** dialog for StudentVM2 to make these changes:

1. Deselect the **Floppy** disk and then move it down the **Boot Order** to below the **Hard Disk**.

2. If your physical host has 8G of RAM or more, increase the amount of video memory to 128MB. It is neither necessary nor recommended that you enable 2D or 3D video acceleration because it is not needed for this course.

3. Select the **Network** settings page and, on the **Adapter 1** tab, select **NAT Network** in the **Attached to:** field. Because we have created only one NAT network, the StudentNetwork, that network will be selected for us. Click the little blue triangle next to Advanced to view the rest of the configuration for this device. Do not change anything else on this page.

The virtual machine is now configured and ready for us to install Linux.

Installing Linux

Now install the most recent Fedora Linux Xfce version on StudentVM2. The initial configuration for both VMs is exactly the same with only one exception. The hostname for the server VM, StudentVM2, should be studentvm2 in all lowercase.

EXPERIMENT 42-1: INSTALLING FEDORA ON THE SERVER

Using the VirtualBox Manager, insert the ISO image file, Fedora-Xfce-Live-x86_64-38-1.iso – or whatever the current version of the Xfce live image happens to be – into the StudentVM2 virtual machine's storage controller as the IDE secondary master. Then boot the VM and proceed with the installation from the live image using the filesystem configuration shown in Figure 42-2.

Filesystem	Partition	Logical Volume	Filesystem Type	Size (GB)	Label
/boot	Standard		EXT4	1.0	boot
biosboot	Standard		BIOS boot	2.0	
/ (root)	LVM	vg01	EXT4	2.0	root
/usr	LVM	vg01	EXT4	15.0	usr
/home	LVM	vg01	EXT4	2.0	home
/var	LVM	vg01	EXT4	10.0	var
/tmp	LVM	vg01	EXT4	5.0	tmp
Total				**37.00**	

Figure 42-2. *The disk partitions – filesystems – and their sizes*

Tip   When I clicked the "Install to Hard Drive" icon on the desktop, I got a notification that it was an "untrusted application launcher." It is safe to ignore this warning and click the **Launch Anyway** button.

Be sure to use manual filesystem configuration during the installation. If you need a bit of assistance, Volume 1, Chapter 5, of this course contains the details of how to do the complete installation, including creating the filesystems. Just remember to use the correct hostname for this second virtual machine, studentvm2.

Note that we do not initially allocate all of the space in the volume group. However, be sure to create the /boot and biosboot partitions first and then – this is very important – after creating / root, the first filesystem that is part of the LVM system, be sure to alter the configuration of the volume group to use the option "As large as possible," in order to include all of the remaining space on the virtual hard drive in the logical volume. I also suggest changing the volume group name to vg01 to remove the reference to "live."

It is no longer necessary to allocate swap space on the storage drive since Fedora now uses 8GB of Zram for swap space.

Important   Be sure to modify the volume group so that it takes up all of the remaining space on the virtual hard drive after creation of the /boot partition.

Be sure to set the root password and create a non-root user with the name of "student" and set a password for that user before you click the **Start Installation** button. Also, add a check mark to the box labeled "Allow root SSH login with password."

After the Fedora installation has completed, remove the live USB image from the IDE controller and reboot StudentVM2 to verify that it comes up, runs properly, and can ping example.com and StudentVM1.

Personalization and Updates

By this time in this course, you should have enough experience to have some favorite tools that you like to use. I suggest that you take some time right now to install your favorite command-line and desktop tools and personalize StudentVM2.

EXPERIMENT 42-2: PERSONALIZE AND UPDATE THE SERVER

As the root user on StudentVM2, configure the kernel so that it displays all kernel and startup messages. If you need some guidance with this, we did it for StudentVM1 in Volume 1, Chapter 16.

Next, install all current updates. We covered that in Chapter 12, so you may want to go back and refresh your memory.

Perform any additional personalization that you want to both the student and root accounts. This can include setting Bash configuration, installing tools that aren't by default, and more.

Virtual Network Configuration

Using DHCP for network configuration in a traditional environment is good for some hosts, but not for servers. Servers need to set their own network configuration; relying on DHCP can cause changing IP addresses and possibly other information that might lead to the inability of other hosts to find the servers in the network. In a cloud environment, the provider will assign addresses, and you may not be able to depend upon a specific IP address. In this chapter we will use the traditional approach of using static IP addresses in which we have control over all aspects of our environment.

The initial virtual network we have configured for this course provides a virtual router with a DHCP server. So long as we use the virtual DHCP server that is a part of the virtual router, our new server will not receive a static IP address. So we need to change the network configuration of StudentVM2 from DHCP to static.

The objective is for our server, StudentVM2, to become the DHCP server for our new internal virtual network. One underlying reason for this is that the simple DHCP server in the virtual router is not capable of handling some of the configuration settings we will need later on. The other reason is so that you can get some experience with using DHCP. This will also lay the groundwork for installing other services on our server so that we can explore them more fully.

The virtual router provided by VirtualBox when we created StudentVM1 in Volume 1 of this course provides us with the 10.0.2.0/24 address range by default. Now we need an internal virtual network for the internal clients like StudentVM1. The "internal" network is usually called a local network because it is intended to be separate and distinct from the Internet or other networks to which it is connected.

We first create a new "host-only" network and then a new virtual interface card on StudentVM2. A "host-only" network in VirtualBox is one in which the hosts in the network can only connect with each other and not directly to the outside world. The hosts in this network will need a router to access the Internet at large; we will provide that function as we move through this part of the course.

```
EXPERIMENT 42-3: CREATE THE LOCAL NETWORK
```

Use the VirtualBox Manager to create a new network that will be our local network. This is actually quite simple because most of the data is entered by default.

Power down StudentVM2. At the top of the list of VMs, open the **Tools ➤ Network** dialog. Click **Host-only Networks** and then the **Create** button to create a new host network.

The default is to configure the adapter manually, and the required data for IPV4 is already generated and placed in the appropriate locations. Figure 42-3 shows the default configuration for this adapter. There is no need to change anything on this tab.

Configuration item	Value
Configure Adapter Manually	Radio button is checked
IPV4 address	192.168.56.1
IPV4 NetMask	255.255.255.0
IP V6 Address/Mask	May auto fill when **Apply** is pressed.
DHCP Server	Not enabled.

Figure 42-3. *The host network configuration*

Be sure that the Enable Server box is not checked on the DHCP Server tab of the dialog. We don't want two DHCP servers in the network, and this one must be disabled. We will be using vboxnet0 for this course because it is created automatically.

Figure 42-4 shows the completed dialog box, but the IPV6 data fields may be empty. If this is the case, the **Apply** button will be grayed out.

---

[1] Red Hat, Red Hat Enterprise Linux Networking Guide, https://access.redhat.com/documentation/en-us/red_hat_enterprise_linux/7/html/networking_guide/sec-configuring_ip_networking_with_nmcli

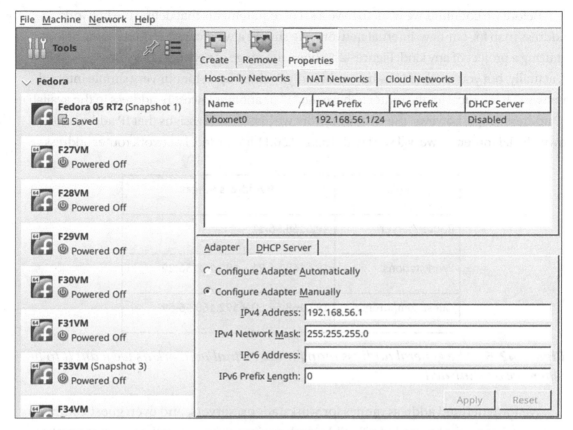

Figure 42-4. *The host network configuration when creating the Virtual Machine*

Click **Apply** – if it is highlighted – to finish creating the new network. Now we can add the new NIC to StudentVM2 and connect it to this network.

Using the VirtualBox Manager, select StudentVM2, which should be powered off. If it is not, do so now. Open the **Settings** dialog for StudentVM2 and select the **Network** tab. Click the **Adapter 2** tab and place a check mark in the **Enable Network Adapter** checkbox.

In the **Attached to** drop-down selection box, click **Host-only Adapter**. Because we have only one network of this type, the **vboxnet0** network is chosen by default. Click the little triangle-shaped twistie next to **Advanced** and check out the rest of the configuration for this new NIC, including the MAC address. Verify that there is a check mark in the **Cable Connected** box.

Click the OK button to complete the addition of this new virtual NIC.

Before we continue, we want to have a set of requirements that define the network address map for our new, internal network. We should always create requirements before starting a project of any kind. Figure 42-5 shows the range of network addresses we – well, I, actually, but you get the idea – have arbitrarily decided upon for our very simple internal network. It is typical for the router to have the "1" or another lowest IP address in the available IP address range; however, the virtual network we just created assigns that IP address to its own virtual router. So we will start with 192.168.56.11 for the local network router address.

Role	IP Address ranges
Router/server	192.168.56.11
Workstations	192.168.56.21 – 192.168.56.29
Guest computers	192.168.56.50 – 192.168.56.59

Figure 42-5. *The general address map for the virtual network as we want it to be when we are finished*

We have defined address ranges for workstations, servers, and even guest computers such as what might be used in a flexible work environment. We will explore more about assigning workstation and guest IP addresses in the "Overview of DHCP" section of this chapter.

But before we can continue, we need to obtain some information about the NICs in our VMs.

EXPERIMENT 42-4: GATHERING INTERFACE DATA

Perform this experiment as root. This experiment obtains the information we need to create our address map. Remember that the MAC addresses will be different for your VMs than they are for mine.

Power on StudentVM2. Log into StudentVM2, open a terminal session, and **su -** to root.

As the root user on StudentVM2, list the NICs installed in StudentVM2 and the associated MAC and IP addresses. Remember that your MAC addresses will be different from mine and the IP addresses – if any – will also be different:

```
[root@studentvm2 ~]# nmcli
enpOs9: connected to Wired connection 3
        "Intel 82540EM"
        ethernet (e1000), 08:00:27:6C:C1:2C, hw, mtu 1500
        ip4 default
        inet4 192.168.0.182/24
        route4 192.168.0.0/24 metric 102
        route4 default via 192.168.0.254 metric 102
        inet6 fe80::1715:719e:37e7:e8de/64
        route6 fe80::/64 metric 1024

lo: connected (externally) to lo
        "lo"
        loopback (unknown), 00:00:00:00:00:00, sw, mtu 65536
        inet4 127.0.0.1/8
        inet6 ::1/128
        route6 ::1/128 metric 256

enpOs3: connecting (getting IP configuration) to Wired connection 1
        "Intel 82540EM"
        ethernet (e1000), 08:00:27:63:57:BE, hw, mtu 1500

enpOs8: connecting (getting IP configuration) to Wired connection 2
        "Intel 82540EM"
        ethernet (e1000), 08:00:27:F8:E1:CF, hw, mtu 1500

DNS configuration:
        servers: 192.168.0.52 8.8.8.8 8.8.4.4
        domains: both.org
        interface: enpOs9

Use "nmcli device show" to get complete information about known devices and
"nmcli connection show" to get an overview on active connection profiles.

Consult nmcli(1) and nmcli-examples(7) manual pages for complete usage
details.
[root@studentvm2 ~]#
```

Note   The enp0s9 interface, like the one on StudentVM1, is one I created to allow me backdoor access to the command line on these VMs. It gives me better access to copy and paste commands and results in both directions. You won't have this device on your VMs.

Remember that we don't really care much about the current IP address, and there aren't any. We will assign IP addresses according to our own plan. What we want from this data is the MAC address that is associated with the NIC name. The MAC address for enp0s3 on my VM is 08:00:27:63:57:BE.

There are four NICs listed here. The first that is not my back door is the local loop, lo. Interface lo stands for "local." This is an internal interface for software clients on the local host (localhost) to talk to server services on the localhost without needing to communicate over the external network. This is one of the incredibly intelligent design points of Linux (and Unix) because programs can talk to other programs through the network interfaces regardless of whether the clients and servers are on the same hosts or remote ones. This really simplifies the work of the developer.

You already know that enp0s3 is the network connection for NIC number 1. We will use this NIC in the 10.0.2.0/24 network as the connection to the outside world.

The enp0s8 NIC is the second network adapter for any VirtualBox VM. This is the NIC we will use for our internal network.

We need to know the IP address of the default gateway router. The preceding data tells us that the IP address for the default gateway to the outside world is 10.0.2.1, which is a best-practice address for the default gateway.

We can also find the MAC addresses of all hosts this host has communicated with. The IP address for the router is on the first line, so the MAC address on that line is for the virtual router:

```
[root@studentvm2 ~]# ip neighbor
10.0.2.1 dev enp0s3 lladdr 52:54:00:12:35:00 STALE
192.168.0.52 dev enp0s9 lladdr e0:d5:5e:a2:de:a4 REACHABLE
192.168.56.21 dev enp0s8 lladdr 08:00:27:01:7d:ad STALE
192.168.0.6 dev enp0s9 lladdr e0:69:95:45:c4:cd STALE
192.168.0.1 dev enp0s9 lladdr b0:6e:bf:3a:43:1f REACHABLE
```

This data allows us to fill in the MAC addresses needed for Figure 42-6.

VirtualBox allows up to four NICs for each virtual machine. The virtual adapters' NIC names are assigned as follows. These names are assigned based on the location of the NIC adapter in the PCI device tree, whether physical or virtual. All of our VMs will have the same PCI device tree, so the adapters will have the same assignments. That is not a problem, and the adapters for one VM will not conflict with the adapters from another:

NIC1: enp0s3

NIC2: enp0s8

NIC3: enp0s9

NIC4: enp0s10

The MAC addresses must be different on each host because that is an identifier that is visible to all the other hosts in the network. Each MAC address must be unique; this is true in both the virtual and physical worlds. The MAC addresses on your virtual NICs will therefore be different from the ones seen in these examples and experiments. Be sure to use the MAC addresses for the NICs on your own experimental configuration.

The IP addresses specified in Figure 42-6 are the ones that we ultimately want to have assigned to the hosts and not any that might be currently assigned. There are many strategies for assigning IP addresses. Each organization and every SysAdmin has their own favored methods. For this course I have arbitrarily decided that servers will be assigned IP addresses in the range from 192.168.56.11 to 192.168.56.19 and that workstations will be in the address range from 192.168.56.21 to 192.168.56.29. These IP addresses will be assigned from lowest to highest in each group.

Hostname	Role	MAC Address	NIC Name	IP Address
Virtual Router	Router	52:54:00:12:35:00	N/A	10.0.2.1
studentvm1	Workstation	08:00:27:01:7D:AD	enp0s3	192.168.56.21
studentvm2	Server	08:00:27:63:57:BE	enp0s3	10.0.2.11
studentvm2	Server	08:00:27:F8:E1:CF	enp0s8	192.168.56.11

Figure 42-6. *The IP address map for the server and the workstation in our internal network*

Now that we have a little bit of a plan, let's configure the network interface cards for StudentVM2. After a new installation, there are no local configuration files available, so the NetworkManager simply looks for a DHCP server and accepts whatever network configuration data is provided. In this chapter we will install the DHCP server package and make the StudentVM2 virtual machine into a DHCP server.

We will use the nmcli (NetworkManager command-line interface) utility to create the static network connection needed by the server. This command creates the network configuration files, and we will look at those files as we proceed through the experiments in this chapter.

Tip   The nmcli command is complex and can be frustrating at first. This is especially true because the available man pages seem to have some discrepancies with the actual command and its options. The best documentation I have found is the RHEL 7 Networking Guide.[1]

The nmcli command has many sub-commands and options. We will only look at a few here, but these will allow us to configure our server with the static IP address specified in Figure 42-6.

EXPERIMENT 42-5: CONFIGURING BOTH NETWORK INTERFACES

This experiment must be performed as root on StudentVM2. It covers configuration for hosts using static IP addresses and other typical configuration parameters. Some default configuration may have been performed by DHCP in which a DHCP server provides all of the data required for network configuration of the host. We need to change that to static configuration in which we provide all of the required configuration parameters.

First, open a root terminal session and make /etc/sysconfig/network-scripts the PWD. List the content of this directory, which should be empty. If it is not, and you are using Fedora 38 or higher,[2] delete any files you find there.

Use the data provided in Figure 42-7 to create an interface configuration file for enp0s3.

---

[2] The requirements for this course specify Fedora 38 or higher, so you should be using at least Fedora 38. Other distributions are not recommended, and you may run into problems if you use them.

Config item	Option name	Value	Description
Network type	type	ethernet	This could also be various types of VPN, or bonded connections. Those options are outside the scope of this course.
Interface name	ifname	enp0s3	This is the name of the interface as displayed by the **nmcli device** command.
Connection name	con-name	enp0s3	This is the name of the connection that will be used in commands. It will be part of the interface configuration file name. I like to keep this name short for ease of typing. I use the NIC name to make identification easy.
IPV4 address	ipv4	10.0.2.11	The static IP-V4 address we assign to this interface.
Gateway IPV4 Address	gw4	10.0.2.1	The default route through the virtual router.
IPV4 DNS servers	ipv4.dns	"10.0.2.1 8.8.8.8"	Up to three DNS server IP addresses, Be sure to use the double quotes.

Figure 42-7. *A list of the information required to configure the enp0s3 network interface*

Enter this command to configure the network interface enp0s3. Then verify the presence and content of the new file ifcfg-enp0s3:

```
[root@studentvm2 ~]# nmcli connection add save yes type ethernet ifname enp0s3
con-name enp0s3 ip4 10.0.2.11/24 gw4 10.0.2.1 ipv4.dns "10.0.2.1 8.8.8.8"
Connection 'enp0s3' (5d4c3d0d-e1a3-4017-bed8-3eb0fa98883c)
successfully added.
```

Ping example.com to ensure that the DNS and gateway configurations are working. I found that this worked fine but it might be necessary to restart NetworkManager to make it take effect.

The following nmcli command creates the interface configuration file for enp0s8 using the data provided in Figure 42-8.

Config item	Option name	Value	Description
Network type	type	ethernet	This could also be various types of VPN, or bonded connections. Those options are outside the scope of this course.
Interface name	ifname	enp0s8	This is the name of the interface as displayed by the **nmcli device** command.
Connection name	con-name	enp0s8	This is the name of the connection that will be used in commands. It will be part of the interface configuration file name. I like to keep this name short for ease of typing. I use the NIC name to make identification easy.
IPV4 address	ipv4	192.168.56.11	The static IP-V4 address we assign to this interface.
Gateway IPV4 Address	gw4	N/A	The default route through the virtual router.
IPV4 DNS servers	ipv4.dns	N/A	Up to three DNS server IP addresses, Be sure to use the double quotes.

Figure 42-8. *A list of the information required to configure the enp0s8 network interface*

Enter this command to configure the network interface enp0s8:

```
[root@studentvm2 ~]# nmcli connection add save yes type ethernet ifname
enp0s8 con-name enp0s8 ip4 192.168.56.11/24
```

Check the connection setup:

```
[root@studentvm2 ~]# nmcli
enp0s3: connected to enp0s3
        "Intel 82540EM"
        ethernet (e1000), 08:00:27:63:57:BE, hw, mtu 1500
        ip4 default
        inet4 10.0.2.11/24
        route4 10.0.2.0/24 metric 100
        route4 default via 10.0.2.1 metric 100
        inet6 fe80::63fb:7087:3813:f549/64
        route6 fe80::/64 metric 1024

enp0s8: connected to enp0s8
        "Intel 82540EM"
        ethernet (e1000), 08:00:27:F8:E1:CF, hw, mtu 1500
        inet4 192.168.56.11/24
        route4 192.168.56.0/24 metric 103
        inet6 fe80::3e67:ef46:a42a:364b/64
        route6 fe80::/64 metric 1024

enp0s9: connected to Wired connection 2
        "Intel 82540EM"
        ethernet (e1000), 08:00:27:6C:C1:2C, hw, mtu 1500
        inet4 192.168.0.182/24
        route4 192.168.0.0/24 metric 102
        route4 default via 192.168.0.254 metric 102
        inet6 fe80::326:45a9:46c5:f95d/64
        route6 fe80::/64 metric 1024

lo: connected (externally) to lo
        "lo"
        loopback (unknown), 00:00:00:00:00:00, sw, mtu 65536
        inet4 127.0.0.1/8
        inet6 ::1/128
        route6 ::1/128 metric 256
```

```
DNS configuration:
        servers: 10.0.2.1 8.8.8.8
        interface: enp0s3

        servers: 192.168.0.52 8.8.8.8 8.8.4.4
        domains: both.org
        interface: enp0s9
```

The results on your VM should be very close to these results. Note that there are some IPV6 entries that were placed there by NetworkManager but that are essentially ignored.

Verify that the two connection configuration files are located in /etc/NetworkManager/system-connections. Check their contents.

Tip   Because the connection configuration files such as /etc/NetworkManager/ system-connections are managed by NetworkManager and the **nmcli** command, it is strongly recommended that you do not edit these files by hand. Use the **nmcli** command to make changes to them.

Now let's do a bit of testing to verify that our new configuration is working properly.

EXPERIMENT 42-6: TESTING THE NETWORK CONFIGURATION

This experiment must be performed as root on StudentVM2. In it we test to ensure that the configuration we have created for NIC enp0s3 is working as expected.

Use the dig or nslookup command to ensure that the DNS resolution is working properly:

```
[root@studentvm2 ~]# dig www.example.com

; <<>> DiG 9.18.13 <<>> www.example.com
;; global options: +cmd
;; Got answer:
;; ->>HEADER<<- opcode: QUERY, status: NOERROR, id: 23266
;; flags: qr rd ra; QUERY: 1, ANSWER: 1, AUTHORITY: 0, ADDITIONAL: 1

;; OPT PSEUDOSECTION:
; EDNS: version: 0, flags:; udp: 65494
```

```
;; QUESTION SECTION:
;www.example.com.                  IN      A

;; ANSWER SECTION:
www.example.com.        86400  IN      A      93.184.216.34

;; Query time: 22 msec
;; SERVER: 127.0.0.53#53(127.0.0.53) (UDP)
;; WHEN: Fri May 26 11:10:27 EDT 2023
;; MSG SIZE  rcvd: 60
```

This tells us the DNS service in the virtual router is working. You may also want to ping an example.com host out on the Internet to verify that you have complete connectivity:

```
[root@studentvm2 ~]# ping www.example.net
PING www.example.net (93.184.216.34) 56(84) bytes of data.
64 bytes from 93.184.216.34 (93.184.216.34): icmp_seq=1 ttl=54 time=28.10 ms
64 bytes from 93.184.216.34 (93.184.216.34): icmp_seq=2 ttl=54 time=51.5 ms
64 bytes from 93.184.216.34 (93.184.216.34): icmp_seq=3 ttl=54 time=40.1 ms
64 bytes from 93.184.216.34 (93.184.216.34): icmp_seq=4 ttl=54 time=117 ms
64 bytes from 93.184.216.34 (93.184.216.34): icmp_seq=5 ttl=54 time=42.5 ms
^C
--- www.example.net ping statistics ---
5 packets transmitted, 5 received, 0% packet loss, time 211ms
rtt min/avg/max/mdev = 28.970/56.009/116.966/31.312 ms
```

The mtr command can show that the current route from the virtual network to the outside world is through the virtual router. This is correct and won't change:

```
[root@studentvm2 ~]# mtr -n example.com
                        My traceroute  [v0.95]
studentvm2 (10.0.2.11) ->
          example.com (93.184.216.34)  2023-05-26T11:22:01-0400
Keys:  Help   Display mode   Restart statistics   Order of fields   quit
                          Packets               Pings
Host                   Loss%   Snt   Last   Avg  Best  Wrst StDev
 1. 10.0.2.1            0.0%    15    0.3   1.3   0.3  13.0   3.3
 2. 192.168.0.254       0.0%    15    0.5   0.5   0.5   0.6   0.0
 3. 45.20.209.46        0.0%    15    1.1   1.3   1.1   2.2   0.3
 4. (waiting for reply
```

```
 5.  99.173.76.162          0.0%   15   3.0    3.0    2.6    3.2    0.1
 6.  (waiting for reply)
 7.  (waiting for reply)
 8.  32.130.16.19           0.0%   15   16.9   13.7   12.3   16.9   1.4
 9.  192.205.32.102         0.0%   14   14.4   16.2   14.2   34.6   5.4
10.  152.195.80.131         0.0%   14   12.9   13.2   12.6   15.9   1.0
11.  93.184.216.34          0.0%   14   13.6   13.6   13.4   14.3   0.2
```

Verify that the first IP address, which is that of the virtual router, is 10.0.2.1. The second router, 192.168.0.254, is the edge router for my local network. Also be sure to test connectivity on StudentVM1. It should still access the Internet via the virtual router.

The domain names example.com, example.org, and example.net are reserved for testing, and we can ping those without interfering with someone's production environment.

Adjusting the Firewall

Our new server uses the default public zone for its firewall rules. This is okay but not ideal as it leaves a few pathways open from the outside world. While this would be fine with most hosts in a private network, this host is designed to be a firewall in order to protect our private network. So for now we will block all network traffic inbound from the outside world.

Before we start, let's define a set of requirements for the zone we want to assign to the outside world:

1. Start by dropping all attempts to connect from the outside. This is a good starting point for the rest of the rules we will need later. By dropping packets instead of responding to them with a message the equivalent of "You are not allowed here," the timeouts prevent the crackers from attacking more frequently. It also gives no indication that there is, in fact, a computer connected to that IP address.

---

[3] We call the hardware a server because it provides services to other hosts in the network, and we also call the services themselves servers. So we talk about specific software functions that provide services to other hosts in the network, such as the DHCP server or the DNS server.

2. We'll use a copy of the drop zone as a starting point. This saves time because we don't need to create our own zone from scratch.

3. Explicitly assign the new zone to the external-facing interface, enp0s3.

4. Leave the public zone as the default zone. This allows us to change the rules for the external zone without changing the local ones and vice versa.

5. Do not assign a zone to the private network interface, enp0s8. We may do that later, but the default public zone is fine for now.

Now we are ready to start.

EXPERIMENT 42-7: ENHANCE THE FIREWALL TO BLOCK THE OUTSIDE WORLD

In this experiment we want to create a new firewall zone that we can use to enhance protection from the outside world. We'll copy the drop zone file as a good starting point for what we ultimately want from our firewall. We'll rename the file though the original will still be in the source directory.

As root on StudentVM2, make /usr/lib/firewalld/zones the PWD. Copy the drop zone to /etc/firewalld/zones directory, changing its name to drop2.xml:

```
[root@studentvm2 zones]# cp drop.xml /etc/firewalld/zones/drop2.xml
```

Make /etc/firewalld/zones the PWD and verify that the file was copied and correctly renamed.

Edit the file and change the short name to "Drop2." We don't need to make any other changes to the file at this time. It should look like this:

```
[root@studentvm2 zones]# cat drop2.xml
<?xml version="1.0" encoding="utf-8"?>
<zone target="DROP">
  <short>Drop2</short>
  <description>Unsolicited incoming network packets are dropped. Incoming
  packets that are related to outgoing network connections are accepted.
  Outgoing network connections are allowed.</description>
  <forward/>
</zone>
```

Reload firewalld to make it aware of the new zone file and assign the enp0s3 interface to the drop2 zone:

```
[root@studentvm2 zones]# firewall-cmd --reload
[root@studentvm2 zones]# firewall-cmd --add-interface=enp0s3 --zone=drop2
--permanent
The interface is under control of NetworkManager, setting zone to 'drop2'.
success
```

Verify the new firewall configuration. Remember that enp0s9 is my back door into the hosts; you won't have that interface on your VM:

```
[root@studentvm2 zones]# firewall-cmd --get-active-zones
drop2
  interfaces: enp0s3
public
  interfaces: enp0s8 enp0s9
```

This change to the firewall provides the greatest possible protection for StudentVM2, which will be our server, from the outside world.

Overview of DHCP

Before we make any further changes in our network, we'll set up the DHCP (Dynamic Host Configuration Protocol) server on our new server.[3] This will give us control over the network configuration data we provide to the hosts in our local network.

The Dynamic Host Configuration Protocol (DHCP) provides a centralized and automated method for configuring hosts when they connect to the network. This reduces the need to configure each network host individually. It is useful for portable devices such as laptops, which might connect as unknown guests. DHCP offers even more advantages when used to manage static IP address assignments for known hosts using the central DHCP database.

The DHCP server uses a database of information created by the SysAdmin. This database is entirely contained in the /etc/dhcp/dhcpd.conf configuration file. Like all well-designed Linux configuration files, it is a simple ASCII plain text file. This means that it is open and knowable and that it can be examined by standard, simple text manipulation tools like cat and grep and modified by any text editor such as Emacs or Vim or a stream editor like sed.

In addition to assigning IP addresses to client hosts, DHCP can also provide host configuration information such as DNS servers, the domain name used for DNS searches, the default gateway, an NTP (Network Time Protocol) server, a server from which a network boot can be performed, and more.

The DHCP client is always installed on Linux clients – certainly at least Fedora-based distros and all the other distros I have tried – because of the very high probability that they will be connected to a network using DHCP rather than with a static configuration.

When a host configured for DHCP is booted, or its NIC is turned up (activated), it sends a broadcast request to the network asking for a DHCP server to respond. The client and the server engage in a bit of conversation, and the server sends the configuration data to the client, which uses it to self-configure its network connection. Hosts may have multiple NICs connected to different networks, and any or all may be configured using DHCP, or one or more of the NICs may be configured using DHCP and one or more NICs may be configured using static configuration. We will keep the setup for this course simple with only a single virtual NIC on each local host other than the firewall.

Installing the DHCP Server

The DHCP server is not installed by default and, like the other servers we'll install during this course, we must install it ourselves. Of course that's the easy part. We also need to configure the DHCP server, and that's a little more complex. We will need to use the network IP address map we created in order to get it set up correctly.

We'll start with installing the DHCP server.

EXPERIMENT 42-8: INSTALL THE DHCP SERVER

This experiment must be performed as root. For now, we will leave StudentVM1 turned off while we get DHCP configured and running. If it is not powered off, do so now. We will first check the installation status of DHCP and then install the DHCP server.

Start StudentVM2 if it is not already running. Log in as the student user, open a terminal session, and **su -** to root. Check to see which DHCP packages are already installed:

```
[root@studentvm2 ~]# dnf list installed dhcp*
Installed Packages
dhcp-client.x86_64          12:4.4.3-2.fc36          @anaconda
```

```
dhcp-common.noarch          12:4.4.3-2.fc36              @anaconda
[root@studentvm2 ~]#
```

This shows the DHCP client has been installed along with libraries and supporting files common to the client, server, and possibly DHCP development packages.

The DHCP server is not installed so we need to install it:

```
[root@studentvm2 ~]# dnf install -y dhcp-server
```

That was easy, and no reboot of the server, StudentVM2, is required.

Configuring the DHCP Server

With the DHCP server installed, the next step is to configure the server. Having more than one DHCP server in the same network can cause problems because one would never know which DHCP server is providing the network configuration data to the client. However, a single DHCP server on one host can listen to multiple networks and provide configuration data to clients in more than one network.

It is possible for DHCP to provide DNS names for the gateway and other servers. For example, the NTP server could use the hostname of that server, such as NTP1, instead of the IP address. Most of the time this would work well, but this configuration might cause problems if the DNS server were to be disabled or if our own server did not exist, such as right at the moment.

The IP addresses specified in Figure 42-9 are the ones that we will assign to the hosts in our internal network. We do not need to assign the IP address for the router because that is configured by the virtual network. I have arbitrarily chosen these IP addresses, and they will be used for the rest of this course.

Hostname	Role	MAC Address	NIC Name	IP Address
studentvm1	Workstation	08:00:27:01:7D:AD	enp0s3	192.168.56.21/24
studentvm2	Server	08:00:27:F8:E1:CF	enp0s8	192.168.56.11/24

Figure 42-9. *The specific IP address map for the server and the workstation in our network*

Before configuring and starting the DHCP server on StudentVM2, we will turn off the DHCP server that is a part of the virtual router.

EXPERIMENT 42-9: CONFIGURE THE DHCP SERVER

In this experiment we create a fairly simple DHCPD configuration file, start the DHCP server, and then test it by determining that StudentVM1 receives the correct network configuration information. Be absolutely certain to use the MAC addresses for the specific hosts in your virtual network.

We will only configure a DHCP server for IPV4. Like the dhcpd.conf file before we modify it, the dhcpd6.conf file has a pointer to a sample configuration file you can use if you need DHCP for IPV6.

Stop DHCP in the Virtual Network

First, we need to turn off the DHCP server in the 10.0.2.0/24 virtual network. As the non-root user on your physical host, turn off the virtual network DHCP server to prevent conflict. Use the VirtualBox Manager and click in the menu bar **File ➤ Preferences** to open the Preferences dialog box. Click the **Network** tab on the left side of the Preferences dialog. Then click **StudentNetwork**.

Remove the check mark from the **Enable DHCP** checkbox. Note that the existing IP address leases will remain in effect until they expire, the client host NICs are turned down and then up again, or the systems are rebooted. We are not turning off the StudentNetwork, just its DHCP server. Click **OK** and then again the **OK** in the Preferences dialog.

Open the Firewall to DHCP

If the firewall on StudentVM2 were blocking DHCP, you would need to add a rule to allow it. Our firewalld public default zone does allow DHCP requests, so we don't need to do anything at this time.

Configure the DHCP Server on StudentVM2

Now we can configure the DHCP server on StudentVM2.

As root, let's look at the existing dhcpd.conf file. Make /etc/dhcp the PWD and then **cat** the dhcpd.conf file to view the content. There is not much there, but it does point to an example file, /usr/share/doc/dhcp-server/dhcpd.conf.example, which you can read in order to understand the main components and syntax of the dhcpd.conf file.

The dhcpd.conf(5) man page also has some excellent descriptions of the various configuration statements that we are likely to need.

Open the dhcpd.conf file in a text editor – I prefer Vim but use whichever editor you prefer – and we will add the statements required for our network in the following steps. Only the five lines shown in the following should exist in this file. We are going to add the lines we need as we proceed through this experiment:

```
#
# DHCP Server Configuration file.
#   see /usr/share/doc/dhcp-server/dhcpd.conf.example
#   see dhcpd.conf(5) man page
#
```

Let's add our required statements to the bottom of the dhcpd.conf file in sections.

This first section contains configuration items that are global – common to all subnets that DHCP is configured to provide for. In our case we have only a single subnet, but we still place these statements in the global section because they are likely to be the same for all subnets. If they were to differ for a given subnet, placing a statement with different values in the subnet declaration would override the global declaration.

These first lines define the name of the domain, example.com, and the default domain name for DNS lookups to search when no domain is explicitly provided. We use example.com because it is explicitly for use in testing. Although this will block the external example.com so we can't use it for testing, we still have the example.net and example.org domains that can be used for external testing:

```
# option definitions common to all supported networks…
# These directives could be placed inside the subnet declaration
# if they are unique to a subnet.
option domain-name "example.com";
option domain-search "example.com";
```

This next line sets the virtual router as the domain name server (DNS). For now be sure to use the IP address of the virtual router for your virtual network. We will change this entry when we add DNS services to our own server:

```
option domain-name-servers 10.0.2.1;
```

Now we set the default lease times in seconds:

```
# All networks get the default lease times
default-lease-time 600;    # 10 minutes
max-lease-time 7200;       # 2 hours
#
```

Next, add these lines, the last of which specifies that this is the authoritative DHCP server for this network. Of course there should never be more than one DHCP server in any network:

```
# If this DHCP server is the official DHCP server for the local
# network, the authoritative directive should be uncommented.
authoritative;
```

Add the declaration for our subnet. We also add a host declaration inside that subnet declaration to provide specific IP address configuration for the StudentVM1 host. Be sure to use the correct MAC address for the host studentvm1 in your setup.

I have included the declarations required for this host to be the NTP server for our private network since we will be setting that up later in this chapter:

```
############################################################
# This is a very basic subnet declaration.                #
############################################################
subnet 192.168.56.0 netmask 255.255.255.0 {
        # default gateway
        option routers              192.168.56.11;
        option subnet-mask          255.255.255.0;

# NTP configuration
        option time-offset          -18000; # Eastern Standard Time
        option ntp-servers          192.168.56.11;

############################################################
# Dynamic allocation range for otherwise unknown hosts    #
############################################################
        range dynamic-bootp 192.168.56.50 192.168.56.59;
############################################################
# Host declaration in the 192.168.56.0/24 subnet.         #
############################################################
        host studentvm1 {
```

```
                        hardware ethernet 08:00:27:01:7D:AD;
                        fixed-address 192.168.56.21;
            }
     }
```

Note that the host declaration has curly braces, {}, around the configuration declarations. The curly braces for the subnet declaration also surround the host declaration because the host declarations need to be inside the subnet declaration.

Be sure to save the file that is now complete enough to test. To test the new DHCP configuration, first start the DHCP service and then configure it to start every time the server is rebooted. Lastly, verify that it is running:

```
[root@studentvm2 ~]# systemctl enable --now dhcpd
Created symlink /etc/systemd/system/multi-user.target.wants/dhcpd.service →
/usr/lib/systemd/system/dhcpd.service.
[root@studentvm2 ~]# systemctl status dhcpd
● dhcpd.service - DHCPv4 Server Daemon
     Loaded: loaded (/usr/lib/systemd/system/dhcpd.service; enabled; preset:
     disabled)
   Drop-In: /usr/lib/systemd/system/service.d
             └─10-timeout-abort.conf
     Active: active (running) since Sun 2023-05-28 15:58:46 EDT; 7s ago
       Docs: man:dhcpd(8)
             man:dhcpd.conf(5)
   Main PID: 1419 (dhcpd)
     Status: "Dispatching packets..."
      Tasks: 1 (limit: 4631)
     Memory: 7.4M
        CPU: 23ms
     CGroup: /system.slice/dhcpd.service
             └─1419 /usr/sbin/dhcpd -f -cf /etc/dhcp/dhcpd.conf -user dhcpd
-group dhcpd --no-pid

May 28 15:58:46 studentvm2 dhcpd[1419]:
May 28 15:58:46 studentvm2 dhcpd[1419]: No subnet declaration for enp0s3
(10.0.2.11).
May 28 15:58:46 studentvm2 dhcpd[1419]: ** Ignoring requests on enp0s3.  If
this is not what
```

```
May 28 15:58:46 studentvm2 dhcpd[1419]:     you want, please write a subnet
declaration
May 28 15:58:46 studentvm2 dhcpd[1419]:     in your dhcpd.conf file for the
network segment
May 28 15:58:46 studentvm2 dhcpd[1419]:     to which interface enp0s3 is
attached. **
May 28 15:58:46 studentvm2 dhcpd[1419]:
May 28 15:58:46 studentvm2 dhcpd[1419]: Sending on    Socket/fallback/
fallback-net
May 28 15:58:46 studentvm2 dhcpd[1419]: Server starting service.
May 28 15:58:46 studentvm2 systemd[1]: Started dhcpd.service - DHCPv4
Server Daemon.
```

You should see no errors from the status command, but you will see a number of statements indicating the DHCP daemon is listening on a specific NIC and the MAC address of the NIC. If this information is not correct, verify that the dhcpd.conf file is correct and try to restart. If there are syntactical errors in your configuration, they will show up in the status report.

Configuring the Client Host

Now that the server is properly configured, the client host, studentvm1, needs to be connected to the new network and the link restarted.

EXPERIMENT 42-10: RECONFIGURE STUDENTVM1

Perform this experiment as root.

If StudentVM1 is running, power it off now. In the VirtualBox Manager, open the Settings dialog for StudentVM1. Go to the **Network** page and ensure that the **Adapter 1** tab is selected. Set the **Attached to:** selection box to **Host-only Adapter**. This connects Adapter 1 to the new internal network we have created and removes it from the original network serviced by the virtual router.

Back in Chapter 33, we used the nmcli command to configure the enp0s3 network interface for a static connection using nmcli, but we now need to revert to DHCP by removing the enp0s3.nmconnection file:

```
# rm -f /etc/NetworkManager/system-connections/enp0s3.nmconnection
```

Restart NetworkManager on StudentVM1:

```
[root@studentvm2 ~]# systemctl restart NetworkManager.service
```

Nothing further will need to be done to obtain an IP address from the newly configured DHCP server. Use nmcli to verify that the network is configured with the correct IP address. Note that the syntax of this command shows all NICs that might be installed, including the lo local loopback device:

```
[root@studentvm1 ~]# nmcli
enp0s3: connected to Wired connection 1
        "Intel 82540EM"
        ethernet (e1000), 08:00:27:01:7D:AD, hw, mtu 1500
        ip4 default
        inet4 192.168.56.21/24
        route4 192.168.56.0/24 metric 100
        route4 default via 192.168.56.1 metric 100
        inet6 fe80::b36b:f81c:21ea:75c0/64
        route6 fe80::/64 metric 1024

lo: unmanaged
        "lo"
        loopback (unknown), 00:00:00:00:00:00, sw, mtu 65536

DNS configuration:
        servers: 10.0.2.1
        domains: example.com
        interface: enp0s3

        servers: 192.168.0.52 8.8.8.8 8.8.4.4
        domains: both.org
        interface: enp0s9
<SNIP>
```

On StudentVM1, verify connectivity to the StudentVM2 server using the ping command. The -c option specifies the number of ping requests to send, in this case 2. We need to specify the IP address of the server because we do not yet have a name server in this private network:

```
[root@studentvm1 ~]# ping 192.168.56.11 -c 2
PING 192.168.56.11 (192.168.56.11) 56(84) bytes of data.
```

```
64 bytes from 192.168.56.11: icmp_seq=1 ttl=64 time=0.448 ms
64 bytes from 192.168.56.11: icmp_seq=2 ttl=64 time=1.54 ms

--- 192.168.56.11 ping statistics ---
2 packets transmitted, 2 received, 0% packet loss, time 1012ms
rtt min/avg/max/mdev = 0.448/0.992/1.536/0.544 ms
[root@studentvm1 ~]#
```

Access to the outside world from StudentVM1 will not be working yet because StudentVM2 is not yet configured as a router. We use example.net for external testing because we have used example.com for our private network:

```
[root@studentvm1 ~]# ping -c2 example.net
PING example.net (93.184.216.34) 56(84) bytes of data.

--- example.net ping statistics ---
2 packets transmitted, 0 received, 100% packet loss, time 1069ms
```

A reboot is not required for either the DHCP client or the server. One configuration change was required on the client, StudentVM1, and simply restarting NetworkManager enabled it to obtain the configuration data from the new DHCP server. Simply turning the interface down and then up again would also work.

Configuring Guest Hosts

Configuring the network settings for guest hosts such as laptops and other mobile devices is also possible with DHCP. This implies that we have no information such as the MAC address for these computers and that we must assign an IP address anyway.

In most cases this usage for DHCP, despite the fact that it was the original intention for DHCP, requires a good bit of trust be afforded to the guest hosts. I personally dislike having guests in my own network, so I usually find a way to set up a second network subnet to which I relegate all guest hosts. This protects my own network and improves security because the guest hosts have no access to it.

There are times when it becomes necessary to include guest computers in a network. The use of DHCP makes that not just possible but also easy. All we need to do is introduce a short stanza into our subnet configuration.

```
┌──────────────────────────────────────────────────────────────┐
│        EXPERIMENT 42-11: CONFIGURING DHCP GUESTS               │
└──────────────────────────────────────────────────────────────┘
```

This experiment must be performed as root.

Insert the following lines at the bottom of the subnet declaration for the 192.168.56.0/24 subnet but outside of any individual host declarations within that subnet. I added it immediately under the option subnet-mask line:

```
#############################################################
# Dynamic allocation range for otherwise unknown hosts     #
#############################################################
        range dynamic-bootp 192.168.56.50 192.168.56.59;
```

Restart the DHCP service to enable this change:

```
[root@studentvm2 ~]# systemctl restart dhcpd
```

Verify that there were no errors during the restart.

To test this DHCP guest allocation, create a brand-new VM, StudentVM3, with a dynamically allocated 120GB hard drive, one or two CPUs, and 4GB of RAM. Be sure the VM used the host-only network adapter, vboxnet0.

Boot to the most recent Fedora live USB image ISO file that you have. After the live image boots, open a terminal session and verify that the network configuration is correct and that the IP address falls within the "guest" host range specified in the declaration:

```
[root@localhost-live ~]# nmcli
enp0s3: connected to Wired connection 1
        "Intel 82540EM"
        ethernet (e1000), 08:00:27:A1:70:2F, hw, mtu 1500
        ip4 default
        inet4 192.168.56.50/24
        route4 192.168.56.0/24 metric 100
        route4 default via 192.168.56.11 metric 100
        inet6 fe80::c028:2889:7051:caeb/64
        route6 fe80::/64 metric 1024

lo: connected (externally) to lo
        "lo"
        loopback (unknown), 00:00:00:00:00:00, sw, mtu 65536
```

```
        inet4 127.0.0.1/8
        inet6 ::1/128
        route6 ::1/128 metric 256
```

DNS configuration:
```
        servers: 10.0.2.1
        domains: example.com
        interface: enp0s3
```

It is not necessary to install Linux on this VM at this time. Just using the live image works fine for this experiment. Ping the other two hosts in our local network – StudentVM1 at IP address 192.168.56.21 and StudentVM2 at 192.168.56.11:

```
[root@localhost-live ~]# ping -c 2 192.168.56.11
PING 192.168.56.11 (192.168.56.11) 56(84) bytes of data.
64 bytes from 192.168.56.11: icmp_seq=1 ttl=64 time=0.566 ms
64 bytes from 192.168.56.11: icmp_seq=2 ttl=64 time=0.559 ms

--- 192.168.56.11 ping statistics ---
2 packets transmitted, 2 received, 0% packet loss, time 1011ms
rtt min/avg/max/mdev = 0.559/0.562/0.566/0.003 ms
[root@localhost-live ~]# ping -c 2 192.168.56.21
PING 192.168.56.21 (192.168.56.21) 56(84) bytes of data.
64 bytes from 192.168.56.21: icmp_seq=1 ttl=64 time=1.20 ms
64 bytes from 192.168.56.21: icmp_seq=2 ttl=64 time=1.38 ms

--- 192.168.56.21 ping statistics ---
2 packets transmitted, 2 received, 0% packet loss, time 1003ms
rtt min/avg/max/mdev = 1.195/1.286/1.378/0.091 ms
```

Tip   I have found that it is sometimes necessary to power off all open VMs and VirtualBox itself before restarting VirtualBox, then StudentVM2, and then the rest of the student VMs in order to reset the VirtualBox DHCP server to off. This behavior is inconsistent, and I have no current explanation for it. Just be aware that it can happen.

After you have finished testing, you can power off the StudentVM3 virtual machine. Do not delete the VM you created for this test.

The Final dhcpd.conf File

The final dhcpd.conf file is shown in Figure 42-10.

```
# DHCP Server Configuration file.
#   see /usr/share/doc/dhcp-server/dhcpd.conf.example
#   see dhcpd.conf(5) man page
#
# option definitions common to all supported networks…
# These directives could be placed inside the subnet declaration
# if they are unique to a subnet.
option domain-name "example.com";
option domain-search "example.com";
option domain-name-servers 10.0.2.1;


# All networks get the default lease times
default-lease-time 600; # 10 minutes
max-lease-time 7200;    # 2 hours
#
# If this DHCP server is the official DHCP server for the local
# network, the authoritative directive should be uncommented.
authoritative;

############################################################
# This is a very basic subnet declaration.                #
############################################################
subnet 192.168.56.0 netmask 255.255.255.0 {
        # default gateway
        option routers                 192.168.56.11;
        option subnet-mask             255.255.255.0;

# NTP configuration
        option time-offset             -18000; # Eastern Standard Time
        option ntp-servers             192.168.56.11;
############################################################
# Dynamic allocation range for otherwise unknown hosts    #
############################################################
        range dynamic-bootp 192.168.56.50 192.168.56.59;
############################################################
# Host declaration in the 192.168.56.0/24 subnet.         #
############################################################
        host studentvm1 {
                hardware ethernet 08:00:27:01:7D:AD;
                fixed-address 192.168.56.21;
        }
}
```

Figure 42-10. *The completed dhcpd.conf file*

Configuring NTP with Chrony

NTP is the Network Time Protocol. We explored the client side of that service in Chapter 31. We will now set up an NTP server on our new VM. That will provide our network with its own reference server while minimizing the load on the main NTP servers.

The nice thing about the Chrony configuration file is that this single file is used to configure the host as both a client and a server. So all we need to do to add a server function to our host – it will always be a client, obtaining its time from a reference server – is to make only a couple changes to the Chrony configuration and then configure the host's firewall to accept NTP requests.

Configuring the NTP Server

The Chrony server requires only a little additional configuration beyond what we did for the NTP client.

EXPERIMENT 42-12: CONFIGURING THE NTP SERVER

Perform this experiment as root on StudentVM2.

Use your favorite editor to modify the /etc/chrony.conf file. Uncomment the line

`# local stratum 10`

This enables the Chrony NTP server to continue to act as if it were connected to a remote reference server if the connection to the Internet fails. Thus, this host can continue to be an NTP server to other hosts in the local network.

Let's restart chronyd and then track how the service is working for a few minutes. We are not yet an NTP server, but we want to test a bit before we go there. Run the following command-line program to initiate this test:

`[root@studentvm2 ~]# systemctl restart chronyd ; watch -n 1 chronyc tracking`

The results should look like this. The watch command runs the chronyc tracking command once every second and allows us to watch changes occur over time:

Tip   It may take a few seconds for the Chrony to locate, connect to, and sync up with the NTP server. Just keep watching.

```
Every 1.0s: chronyc tracking          studentvm2: Mon May 29 14:55:25 2023

Reference ID    : 481E2359 (t1.time.bf1.yahoo.com)
Stratum         : 3
Ref time (UTC)  : Mon May 29 18:55:08 2023
System time     : 0.000079015 seconds fast of NTP time
Last offset     : +0.001016898 seconds
RMS offset      : 0.001016898 seconds
Frequency       : 2211.404 ppm fast
Residual freq   : -1.477 ppm
Skew            : 0.644 ppm
Root delay      : 0.114507250 seconds
Root dispersion : 0.000940076 seconds
Update interval : 2.1 seconds
Leap status     : Normal
```

Synchronizing directly to the Fedora pool machines usually results in synchronization at stratum 2 or 3. This depends upon what stratum the pool server is at. Notice also that, over time, the amount of error will decrease. It should eventually stabilize with a tiny variation about a fairly small range of error. The size of the error depends upon the stratum and other network factors. After a few minutes, use Ctrl+C to break out of the watch loop.

Be sure to watch the **System time** line. This shows the difference between the system hardware time and the NTP time. This difference is reduced slowly so as to prevent problems with internal system timers, cron jobs, and systemd timers. This prevents the possibility of jobs being skipped if the correction were to be made as a single jump.

You can rerun the command-line program to start this over so you can watch it more than once in case you might have missed something.

To make the StudentVM2 host into an NTP server, we need to allow it to listen on the local network. Uncomment the "allow" line to allow hosts in the local network to access our NTP server and set the network IP address to that of our internal network:

```
# Allow NTP client access from local network.
allow 192.168.56.0/24
```

Restart the chronyd.service. Note that the server can listen for requests on any local network to which it is attached. Now restart chronyd.

In order to allow other hosts in your network to access this NTP server, it is necessary to configure the firewall to allow inbound UDP packets on port 123. Note that NTP uses UDP packets and not TCP packets, but this opens both TCP and UDP:

```
[root@studentvm2 ~]# firewall-cmd --permanent --add-service=ntp --zone=public
success
[root@studentvm2 ~]# firewall-cmd --add-service=ntp --zone=public
success
[root@studentvm2 ~]# firewall-cmd --list-services --zone=public
dhcpv6-client mdns ntp ssh
```

At this point this host is an NTP server. We can test it with another host or a VM that has access to the network on which the NTP server is listening.

Configure and Test the NTP Client

We will configure the client, StudentVM1, to use the new NTP server as the preferred server in the /etc/chrony.conf file. Then we will monitor that client using the chronyc tools we have already explored.

EXPERIMENT 42-13: NTP CLIENT TESTING

Perform this experiment as the root user on StudentVM1. Start by viewing the tracking and sources information to determine the current time source and statistics. Your data will be different, but it should look like this:

```
[root@studentvm1 ~]# chronyc -n sources
MS Name/IP address         Stratum Poll Reach LastRx Last sample
===============================================================================
^? 204.17.205.8                 0  10    0      -    +0ns[  +0ns] +/-    0ns
^? 154.16.245.246               0  10    0      -    +0ns[  +0ns] +/-    0ns
^? 69.89.207.99                 0  10    0      -    +0ns[  +0ns] +/-    0ns
^? 72.30.35.88                  0  10    0      -    +0ns[  +0ns] +/-    0ns
^? 162.252.172.49               0  10    0      -    +0ns[  +0ns] +/-    0ns
^? 108.61.73.243                0  10    0      -    +0ns[  +0ns] +/-    0ns
```

```
^? 162.159.200.1              0   10    0     -      +0ns[    +0ns] +/-    0ns
^? 5.161.186.39               0   10    0     -      +0ns[    +0ns] +/-    0ns
^- 192.168.56.11              3   10   377   740   -1889us[-2198us] +/-   49ms
^* 192.168.0.52               4    6   377    19    +110us[ +203us] +/-   12ms
[root@studentvm1 ~]# watch -n 1 chronyc tracking
Reference ID    : A29FC87B (time.cloudflare.com)
Stratum         : 4
Ref time (UTC)  : Sat May 27 01:22:31 2023
System time     : 0.000042382 seconds fast of NTP time
Last offset     : +0.000387692 seconds
RMS offset      : 0.076997802 seconds
Frequency       : 19846.854 ppm slow
Residual freq   : +0.034 ppm
Skew            : 0.167 ppm
Root delay      : 0.021712182 seconds
Root dispersion : 0.002366129 seconds
Update interval : 1036.6 seconds
Leap status     : Normal
```

Keep the tracking command running in one terminal and watch its output as you make the following changes.

Add the following line to the /etc/chrony.conf file on StudentVM1. I usually place this line just above the first pool server statement near the top of the file as shown in the following. There is no special reason for this except that I like to keep the server statements together. It would work just as well at the bottom of the file, and I have done that on several hosts. This configuration file is not sequence-sensitive:

```
server 192.168.56.11 iburst prefer
# Use public servers from the pool.ntp.org project.
# Please consider joining the pool (http://www.pool.ntp.org/join.html).
pool 2.fedora.pool.ntp.org iburst
```

The prefer option marks this as the preferred reference source. As such, this host will always be synchronized with this reference source so long as it is available. You could also use the fully qualified hostname for a remote reference server or the hostname only without the domain name for a local reference time source so long as the search statement is set in the

/etc/resolv.conf file. I prefer the IP address to ensure that the time source is accessible even if DNS is not working. In most environments the server name is probably the better option because NTP will continue to work even if the IP address of the server is changed.

Restart Chrony and continue to observe the chronyc tracking output as it updates every second. The results should eventually sync up to StudentVM2 as the Reference ID server:

```
[root@studentvm1 ~]# chronyc -n sources
MS Name/IP address         Stratum Poll Reach LastRx Last sample
===============================================================================
^* 192.168.56.11                 3   6   177     44   +83us[+1015us] +/-    48ms
^? 198.199.14.69                 0   8     0      -    +0ns[   +0ns] +/-     0ns
^? 129.250.35.250                0   8     0      -    +0ns[   +0ns] +/-     0ns
^? 5.78.62.36                    0   8     0      -    +0ns[   +0ns] +/-     0ns
^? 216.218.254.202               0   8     0      -    +0ns[   +0ns] +/-     0ns
^- 192.168.0.52                  4   6   177     43 +2496us[+2496us] +/-    12ms
[root@studentvm1 ~]# chronyc -n tracking
Reference ID    : C0A8380B (192.168.56.11)
Stratum         : 4
Ref time (UTC)  : Tue May 30 12:33:50 2023
System time     : 0.000008199 seconds slow of NTP time
Last offset     : -0.000005656 seconds
RMS offset      : 0.028415257 seconds
Frequency       : 2709.458 ppm fast
Residual freq   : -0.002 ppm
Skew            : 3.041 ppm
Root delay      : 0.086931512 seconds
Root dispersion : 0.004598102 seconds
Update interval : 64.7 seconds
Leap status     : Normal
```

At this point our StudentVM1 client is using StudentVM2 as its NTP time source. Adding more hosts in our network to use StudentVM2 as the time source is as simple as adding the same line to their chrony.conf files and restarting the Chrony daemon.

Chapter Summary

You now have working DHCP and NTP servers on StudentVM2.

You have finished preparation of StudentVM2 for performing the experiments in the rest of this course and have made some configuration changes to the VM that will be used as the server in our network. You renamed it and set up a static IP configuration. This provided an opportunity to learn a bit about network configuration and use several network management commands.

You also created a network address map that can be used as a guide for assigning IP addresses as we proceed through the rest of this course.

A DHCP server can centralize network configuration management and provide many configuration options to clients. This configuration data includes gateway routers, NTP servers, DNS servers, remote boot servers, and much more. As we continue through this course, we will add configuration items for DNS servers to our DHCP configuration.

You now should have two VMs created using VirtualBox, each with Fedora Xfce installed from the Fedora live USB drive. You have added your favorite command-line tools and personalized the Linux operating system in both VMs to meet your own needs and methods.

Exercises

1. What is the function of DHCP?

2. What five common configuration items are provided by DHCP to Linux hosts?

3. How many name servers can be specified using DHCP?

4. Can servers and routers be specified by name as well as by IP address in the dhcpd.conf file? If so, what problems might arise?

5. Based on the content of the DHCP configuration database we have created in this chapter, what IP address would likely be served to a new VM that booted up on the network?

6. Why is it necessary, or at least a very good idea and a best practice, to use static IP addressing for a server?

7. What function does a network address map serve?

8. Describe the function of the MAC address.

9. Is communication working between StudentVM1 and StudentVM2? Why?

10. How can you tell which DNS server responded to a dig command?

11. What command would you use to determine the DNS names, MAC addresses, and IP addresses of the other hosts in the network with which a given host such as StudentVM2 has been communicating?

12. In case the primary DNS server fails, test whether the second DNS server specified in the interface configuration file for enp0s3 on StudentVM2 is responding.

13. What is the IP address of StudentVM1?

14. How was the IP address set?

CHAPTER 43

Name Services

Objectives

In this chapter you will learn

- To describe the structure and function of Domain Name Services (DNS)

- How to test name services (DNS)

- About the Berkeley Internet Name Domain (BIND)

- How to use the client configuration files

- How to set up a caching name server

- How to configure the iptables firewall for DNS services

- How to create a primary[1] name server from a caching name server including both forward and reverse zones

- How to use several types of records commonly found in zone files

Introducing Domain Name Services

Surfing the Web is fun and easy, but think what it would be like if you had to type in the IP address of every website you wanted to view. For example, locating a website would look like this when you type it in – https://93.184.216.34 – which would be

---

[1] I prefer not to use the common historical terms for the primary and secondary name servers because they have deep racial and gender connotations that I and many others find offensive. Many companies and development organizations are working to change the use of these terms.

© David Both 2023
D. Both, *Using and Administering Linux: Volume 3*, https://doi.org/10.1007/978-1-4842-9786-5_43

nearly impossible for most of us to remember. Of course using bookmarks would help, but suppose your friend tells you about a cool new website and tells you to go to 93.184.216.34. How would you remember that? Telling someone to go to "example.net," for example, is far easier to remember than 54.204.39.132.

The Domain Name Services system provides the database to be used in the translation from human-readable hostnames, such as `www.example.net`, to IP addresses, like 54.204.39.132, so that your Internet-connected computers and other devices can access them. The primary function of the BIND (Berkeley Internet Name Domain) software is that of a domain name resolver, which utilizes that database. There is other name resolver software, but BIND is currently the most widely used DNS software on the Internet. I will use the terms *name server*, *DNS*, and *resolver* pretty much interchangeably throughout this chapter.

Without these name resolver services, it would be nearly impossible to surf the Web as freely and easily as we do. As humans, we tend to do better with names like opensource.org, while computers do much better with numbers like 104.21.84.214. So we need a translation service to convert the names that are easy for us to the IP addresses that are easy for our computers.

Every computer needs its own resolver service so that it can locate hosts in the local network and on the Internet. In this chapter we look at the details of the resolver services on our Linux hosts and learn how to set up a full-fledged name server.

Note   We have not yet configured a router for our new network, so most of these experiments won't work for StudentVM1, which will have no working route to the outside world.

How a Name Search Works

Let's take a look at a simplified example of what happens when a name request for a web page is made by a client service on your computer. For this example, I will use `www.example.net` as the website I want to view in my browser. I also assume that there is a local name server in the network, as is the case with my own network.

Local name resolution will vary a bit depending upon the sequence of entries for the host line in the nsswitch.conf file. External name resolution always works like this regardless of which local resolver is being used:

1. First, I type in the URL or select a bookmark containing that URL. In this case, the URL is `www.example.net`.

2. The browser client, whether it is Opera, Firefox, Chrome, Min, Lynx, Links, or any other browser, sends the request to the operating system.

3. The operating system first checks the /etc/hosts file to see if the hostname is there. If so, the IP address of that entry is returned to the browser. If not, we proceed to the next step. In this case we assume that the name is not in /etc/hosts.

4. The hostname is then sent to the first name server specified in /etc/resolv.conf. In this case the IP address of the first name server is my own internal name server. For this example, my name server does not have the IP address for `www.example.net` cached and must look further afield. So we go on to the next step.

5. The local name server sends the request to a remote name server. This can be one of two destination types, one type of which is a forwarder. A forwarder is simply another name server such as the ones at your Internet Service Provider (ISP) or a public name server such as Google at 8.8.8.8 or 8.8.4.4. The other destination type is that of the top-level root name servers. The root servers don't usually respond with the desired target IP address for `www.example.net`; they respond with the authoritative name server for that domain. The authoritative name servers are the only ones that have the authority to maintain and modify the data for a domain.

6. The local name server is configured to use the root name servers, so the root name server for the .net top-level domain returns the IP address of the authoritative name server for example.net. That IP address could be for any one of the three (at the time of this writing) name servers, ns1.redhat.com, ns2.redhat.com, or ns3.redhat.com.

7. The local name server then sends the query to the authoritative name server, which returns the IP address for `www.example.net`.

8. The browser uses the IP address for `www.example.net` to send a request for a web page, which is downloaded to the browser.

One of the important side effects of this name search is that the results are cached for a period of time by my local name server. That means that the next time I, or anyone in my network, want to access example.net, the IP address is probably already stored in the local cache, which prevents doing another remote lookup.

Top-Level Configuration

Two ASCII plain text files are used to provide the primary configuration for name services. These files have historical origins having been around since the earliest versions of name service resolvers.

NSS and NSSwitch

As its name implies, the NSSwitch – short for Name Service Switch – is used to define the database sources and order in which name service information is obtained. The NSS[2] facility is a tool that is used by a number of services that need name resolver data. Using NSS based on the data in the /etc/nsswitch.conf configuration file, it aids them in locating the appropriate configuration and name resolution sources in a specified sequence.

The sequences listed for each service in this file can be changed and can differ between distributions. They can also be modified to meet local needs. I have never needed to change anything about this file, but it is a good place to start problem determination if there seems to be a problem with name resolution that can't be otherwise explained.

Let's take a look at it.

---

[2] Wikipedia, Name Service Switch, `https://en.wikipedia.org/wiki/Name_Service_Switch`

EXPERIMENT 43-1: THE NSSWITCH.CONF FILE

As root on your StudentVM1 host, display the nsswitch.conf file. Note that some lines are wrapped in the following data stream:

```
[root@studentvm1 etc]# cat nsswitch.conf
# Generated by authselect on Tue Jan 17 21:33:15 2023
# Do not modify this file manually, use authselect instead. Any user changes
will be overwritten.
# You can stop authselect from managing your configuration by calling
'authselect opt-out'.
# See authselect(8) for more details.

# In order of likelihood of use to accelerate lookup.
passwd:      files sss systemd
shadow:      files
group:       files sss systemd
hosts:       files myhostname mdns4_minimal [NOTFOUND=return] resolve
[!UNAVAIL=return] dns
services:    files sss
netgroup:    files sss
automount:   files sss

aliases:     files
ethers:      files
gshadow:     files
networks:    files dns
protocols:   files
publickey:   files
rpc:         files
```

Look at the hosts database entry in the data stream. The first entry is "files," which means that the resolver is to first search the local database. The database isn't explicitly specified here, but it is the /etc/hosts file that we experimented with previously.

Because all of these entries are sequence-sensitive, if an entry is found for a hostname in the /etc/hosts database, that takes precedence over any other, later entries. We will look at the /etc/hosts file in more detail, but by default it contains only generic default names such as localhost and localhost.localdomain.

If a match is not found, the resolver moves on to the next entry, which is "myhostname." This provides name resolution for the locally configured system hostname as contained in the $HOSTNAME environment variable:

```
[root@studentvm1 etc]# echo $HOSTNAME
studentvm1
```

Many tools and applications require a local hostname to function properly, so if the actual hostname is not present in the hosts file, it can be found in this variable. Do you remember setting the hostname during the installation of Fedora? That's where the hostname in this variable comes from. It's hugely important.

The hostnamectl[3] utility can be used to change the hostname as well as to display information about the host. I did this on my primary workstation, but you can also do this on the VM, which is, unfortunately, much less interesting:

```
[root@david ~]# hostnamectl status
     Static hostname: david.both.org
           Icon name: computer-desktop
             Chassis: desktop 🖥
          Machine ID: 0b07292c495a42ee9f5867ebff1ccee2
             Boot ID: 9b59c354f13041878292e84e8a2374f6
    Operating System: Fedora Linux 38 (Thirty Eight)
         CPE OS Name: cpe:/o:fedoraproject:fedora:38
       OS Support End: Tue 2024-05-14
 OS Support Remaining: 11month 1w 6d
              Kernel: Linux 6.2.15-300.fc38.x86_64
        Architecture: x86-64
     Hardware Vendor: ASUSTeK COMPUTER INC.
      Hardware Model: TUF X299 MARK 2
    Firmware Version: 0503
       Firmware Date: Tue 2017-07-11
```

That's a lot of interesting and important information. I especially like the little icon used on the "Chassis" line; it resolves visually a lot better here than in my terminal session. We've seen much of this information in somewhat less readable formats, but there is also information here

---

[3] man 8 nss-myhostname

that I've never seen displayed elsewhere, like the operating system support info. I did notice as I was researching this chapter that the OS support information is not displayed for the VMs.

When used with no arguments, the `hostnamectl` utility displays the same status as the preceding code for the local host. Changing the hostname can be accomplished using this same utility. The new hostname should be the argument:

```
[root@studentvm1 ~]# hostnamectl hostname newhostname
```

This name change is stored in the /etc/hostname file but does not take effect until the next boot. So after changing the name, reboot StudentVM1. Verify that the name has changed after the reboot, then change the name back to studentvm1, and reboot to return it to the original hostname. You could also just edit the /etc/hostname file and reboot.

We're back from the side trip to changing the hostname, and the next entry is mdns4_minimal. This tells nss-resolve to use the Avahi service daemon to use Multicast DNS (mDNS) to locate the host. All of the hosts in the local network must be running the avahi-daemon.service in order to participate in mDNS.

Back in Chapter 36, we disabled Avahi on StudentVM1 as an exercise, so we need to restart it:

```
[root@studentvm1 ~]# systemctl enable --now avahi-daemon.service
Created symlink /etc/systemd/system/dbus-org.freedesktop.Avahi.service →
/usr/lib/systemd/system/avahi-daemon.service.
Created symlink /etc/systemd/system/multi-user.target.wants/avahi-daemon.
service → /usr/lib/systemd/system/avahi-daemon.service.
Created symlink /etc/systemd/system/sockets.target.wants/avahi-daemon.socket
→ /usr/lib/systemd/system/avahi-daemon.socket.
```

This command also enables and starts the avahi-daemon.socket, which listens for connections from other computers requesting mDNS services.

The next thing we find in this list is `[NOTFOUND=return] resolve`. This bit of code instructs nss-resolve[4] to use systemd-resolved[5] to for name resolution. This mode uses the /etc/resolv.conf file.

---

[4] systemd documentation, nss-resolve, `https://systemd.network/nss-resolve.html`

[5] systemd documentation, systemd-resolved.service, `https://systemd.network/systemd-resolved.service.html`

Lastly, at least in Fedora, [!UNAVAIL=return] dns means that if the systemd-resolved is unavailable, then use the historical nss-DNS service for name resolution.

The man page for nsswitch.conf contains information about the other services that use name services. For example, the passwd database is for user passwords.

Experiment 43-1 illustrates the complexity of the current name resolution strategy while also highlighting the flexibility available to the SysAdmin in aid of supporting local needs for name resolution. We'll explore more about name resolution and the rest of these files as we continue through this chapter.

resolv.conf

We start by exploring the /etc/resolv.conf file because it is the key to determining exactly how the systemd-resolved.service works.

Historical Usage

This file used to be an ASCII plain text file that contained a list of up to three domain name servers that would be used to perform hostname resolution into IP addresses. It still can be used that way, but that would bypass systemd-resolved. Of course that might be a desired outcome as it was for me when NetworkManager took over this service and then when systemd-resolved was first introduced and had a few problems. It all works fine now, so I haven't needed to do that for a few years.

The resolv.conf file also contains the domain name to search when a fully qualified domain name (FQDN) isn't appended to the hostname. For example, a fully qualified domain name would be host1.example.com. This can be searched without a problem. But suppose I just use a hostname line host1 and not the domain name. In that case the domain name specified for searches is appended to the hostname.

A typical /etc/resolv.conf file used to look like that in Figure 43-1. It is a link in /etc to the /run/NetworkManager/resolv.conf and contains the search domain as well as the IP addresses of three name servers.

```
[root@david etc]# ll resolv.conf
lrwxrwxrwx 1 root root 31 Jun  1 09:07 resolv.conf ->
/run/NetworkManager/resolv.conf

[root@david etc]# cat resolv.conf
# Generated by NetworkManager
search both.org
nameserver 192.168.0.52
nameserver 8.8.8.8
nameserver 8.8.4.4
[root@david etc]#
```

Figure 43-1. *A typical /etc/resolv.conf file prior to the advent of systemd-resolved*

The first name server in the list is my internal name server. The second and third are fallback external name servers. I use Google name servers because I trust them more than my ISP's, whichever ISP I have been using at a given time. I have had many disruptions to my Internet service due to nonresponsive, poorly configured name servers that were not updated in a timely manner. This is one of the reasons I decided to set up my own internal name server. We'll set one up for our network later in this chapter.

Current Usage

The current use of /etc/resolv.conf is as a symbolic link (symlink) to a stub file, /run/systemd/resolve/stub-resolv.conf, or to /run/systemd/resolve/resolv.conf. The file linked determines how systemd-resolved is supposed to deal with name service resolution requests. The default setup is for /etc/resolv.conf to link to /run/systemd/resolve/stub-resolv.conf, which enables use of systemd-resolved although the systemd-resolved.service must also be up and running.

EXPERIMENT 43-2: RESOLV.CONF

Let's start by looking at /etc/resolv.conf. As you can see, it is a link that points to /run/systemd/ resolve/stub-resolv.conf:

```
[root@studentvm1 ~]# cd /etc ; ll resolv.conf ; cat resolv.conf
lrwxrwxrwx. 1 root root 39 Nov  5  2022 resolv.conf -> ../run/systemd/
resolve/stub-resolv.conf
# This is /run/systemd/resolve/stub-resolv.conf managed by man:systemd-
resolved(8).
# Do not edit.
#
# This file might be symlinked as /etc/resolv.conf. If you're looking at
# /etc/resolv.conf and seeing this text, you have followed the symlink.
#
# This is a dynamic resolv.conf file for connecting local clients to the
# internal DNS stub resolver of systemd-resolved. This file lists all
# configured search domains.
#
# Run "resolvectl status" to see details about the uplink DNS servers
# currently in use.
#
# Third party programs should typically not access this file directly,
but only
# through the symlink at /etc/resolv.conf. To manage man:resolv.conf(5) in a
# different way, replace this symlink by a static file or a different symlink.
#
# See man:systemd-resolved.service(8) for details about the supported modes of
# operation for /etc/resolv.conf.

nameserver 127.0.0.53
options edns0 trust-ad
search example.com
[root@studentvm1 etc]#
```

The nameserver line in this file points to an IP address that has been designated to represent the local hosts resolver. In this address, 127.0.0.53, the last octet, 53, is the same number as the standard DNS port of 53.

systemd-resolved.service

The systemd-resolved.service provides name resolution services for modern Fedora and other distributions. It works with and is a requirement for Multicast DNS (mDNS). We'll explore mDNS in this chapter, but for now let's just take a quick look at the service itself.

EXPERIMENT 43-3: SYSTEMD-RESOLVED.SERVICE

The systemd resolver can be started, restarted, and stopped, as well as having its status checked, by using the systemctl command like the other systemd services. Check its current status; it should be running:

```
[root@studentvm2 ~]# systemctl status systemd-resolved.service
● systemd-resolved.service - Network Name Resolution
     Loaded: loaded (/usr/lib/systemd/system/systemd-resolved.service;
     enabled; preset: >
    Drop-In: /usr/lib/systemd/system/service.d
             └─10-timeout-abort.conf
     Active: active (running) since Tue 2023-05-30 15:51:08 EDT; 18h ago
       Docs: man:systemd-resolved.service(8)
             man:org.freedesktop.resolve1(5)
             https://www.freedesktop.org/wiki/Software/systemd/writing-
             network-configura>
             https://www.freedesktop.org/wiki/Software/systemd/writing-
             resolver-clients
   Main PID: 820 (systemd-resolve)
     Status: "Processing requests..."
      Tasks: 1 (limit: 4631)
     Memory: 8.2M
        CPU: 300ms
     CGroup: /system.slice/systemd-resolved.service
             └─820 /usr/lib/systemd/systemd-resolved

May 30 15:51:08 studentvm2 systemd[1]: Starting systemd-resolved.service -
Network Name >
May 30 15:51:08 studentvm2 systemd-resolved[820]: Positive Trust Anchors:
May 30 15:51:08 studentvm2 systemd-resolved[820]: . IN DS 20326 8 2
e06d44b80b8f1d39a95c>
```

```
May 30 15:51:08 studentvm2 systemd-resolved[820]: Negative trust anchors:
home.arpa 10.i>
May 30 15:51:08 studentvm2 systemd-resolved[820]: Using system hostname
'studentvm2'.
May 30 15:51:08 studentvm2 systemd[1]: Started systemd-resolved.service -
Network Name R>
May 30 15:51:20 studentvm2 systemd-resolved[820]: enpOs3: Bus client set
default route s>
May 30 15:51:20 studentvm2 systemd-resolved[820]: enpOs3: Bus client set DNS
server list
```

Other functionality for the systemd resolver is managed with the resolvectl command, which we will look at later in this chapter.

Name Service Strategies

There are currently three strategies available for use in resolving domain names into IP addresses. Each has its own tools, advantages, and best use cases. Two of these tools require work on the part of the SysAdmin. One, though, requiring almost no administrative work, is quite chatty and creates a significant amount of network traffic.

We'll explore all three strategies in this section, the /etc/hosts file, Multicast DNS, and nss-DNS.

The /etc/hosts File

The /etc/hosts[6] file is an ASCII text file that can list the IP addresses of all hosts in the local network and is the first tool used for local network name resolution.

In small networks the /etc/hosts file on each host can be used as a simple local name resolver. The SysAdmin can add and manage entries in the hosts file. Maintaining copies of this file on several hosts can become very time-consuming, and errors can cause much confusion and wasted time before they are found. Although the hosts file can have non-local domains such as www.example.net added to it, if the IP addresses can be discovered, it is a labor-intensive tool best suited for use in small local networks.

---

[6]Wikipedia, hosts (file), https://en.wikipedia.org/wiki/Hosts_(file)

A default hosts file is always present, but it would normally contain only the lines needed to enable internal services and commands to translate the localhost hostname to IPV4 address 127.0.0.1 and IPV6 address ::1 – this is an explicitly defined standard to enable Linux services and commands to deal with the local host.

EXPERIMENT 43-4: USING /ETC/HOSTS

Perform this experiment as root on StudentVM1. In this experiment you will see the simple /etc/hosts file on your VM and then add some entries for the local network to make it easier to communicate with other local hosts.

Open the /etc/hosts file in an editor. It will look like this, with only a set of default entries:

```
# Loopback entries; do not change.
# For historical reasons, localhost precedes localhost.localdomain:
127.0.0.1    localhost localhost.localdomain localhost4 localhost4.
localdomain4
::1          localhost localhost.localdomain localhost6 localhost6.
localdomain6
# See hosts(5) for proper format and other examples:
# 192.168.1.10 foo.mydomain.org foo
# 192.168.1.13 bar.mydomain.org bar
```

Make a backup copy of the /etc/hosts file and store it in /root. Try to ping studentvm2 before we change anything:

```
[root@studentvm1 ~]# ping -c2 studentvm2
ping: studentvm2: Name or service not known
```

This result shows that there is no resolution from the studentvm2 hostname to an IP address. Now edit the /etc/hosts file on StudentVM1 so that it looks like this:

```
# Loopback entries; do not change.
# For historical reasons, localhost precedes localhost.localdomain:
127.0.0.1    localhost localhost.localdomain localhost4 localhost4.
localdomain4
::1          localhost localhost.localdomain localhost6 localhost6.
localdomain6
# See hosts(5) for proper format and other examples:
```

```
# 192.168.1.10 foo.mydomain.org foo
# 192.168.1.13 bar.mydomain.org bar

# Student hosts
192.168.56.11          router server studentvm2
192.168.56.21          workstation1 ws1 studentvm1
192.168.56.22          workstation2 ws2
192.168.56.23          workstation3 ws3
192.168.56.24          workstation4 ws4
192.168.56.25          workstation5 ws5
```

Notice that IP addresses can have multiple hostnames associated with them. Only a single host can be assigned a specific address, so these hostnames are aliases and all point to the same host. This can be a way to maintain backward compatibility with previous naming strategies, for example. For illustrative purposes we have also added some hostnames and IP addresses that are not actually present in our network.

Let's test the /etc/hosts file:

```
[root@studentvm1 ~]# ping -c2 server
PING router (192.168.56.11) 56(84) bytes of data.
64 bytes from router (192.168.56.11): icmp_seq=1 ttl=64 time=0.521 ms
64 bytes from router (192.168.56.11): icmp_seq=2 ttl=64 time=0.492 ms

--- router ping statistics ---
2 packets transmitted, 2 received, 0% packet loss, time 1048ms
rtt min/avg/max/mdev = 0.492/0.506/0.521/0.014 ms
[root@studentvm1 ~]# ping -c2 router
PING router (192.168.56.11) 56(84) bytes of data.
64 bytes from router (192.168.56.11): icmp_seq=1 ttl=64 time=0.591 ms
64 bytes from router (192.168.56.11): icmp_seq=2 ttl=64 time=1.71 ms

--- router ping statistics ---
2 packets transmitted, 2 received, 0% packet loss, time 1101ms
rtt min/avg/max/mdev = 0.591/1.149/1.708/0.558 ms
[root@studentvm1 ~]# ping -c2 workstation1
PING workstation1 (192.168.56.21) 56(84) bytes of data.
64 bytes from workstation1 (192.168.56.21): icmp_seq=1 ttl=64 time=0.062 ms
64 bytes from workstation1 (192.168.56.21): icmp_seq=2 ttl=64 time=0.119 ms
```

```
--- workstation1 ping statistics ---
2 packets transmitted, 2 received, 0% packet loss, time 1029ms
rtt min/avg/max/mdev = 0.062/0.090/0.119/0.028 ms
[root@studentvm1 ~]# ping -c2 ws1
PING workstation1 (192.168.56.21) 56(84) bytes of data.
64 bytes from workstation1 (192.168.56.21): icmp_seq=1 ttl=64 time=0.061 ms
64 bytes from workstation1 (192.168.56.21): icmp_seq=2 ttl=64 time=0.083 ms

--- workstation1 ping statistics ---
2 packets transmitted, 2 received, 0% packet loss, time 1086ms
rtt min/avg/max/mdev = 0.061/0.072/0.083/0.011 ms
```

Try pinging the hosts that don't exist:

```
[root@studentvm1 ~]# ping -c2 ws4
PING workstation4 (192.168.56.24) 56(84) bytes of data.
From workstation1 (192.168.56.21) icmp_seq=1 Destination Host Unreachable
From workstation1 (192.168.56.21) icmp_seq=2 Destination Host Unreachable

--- workstation4 ping statistics ---
2 packets transmitted, 0 received, +2 errors, 100% packet loss, time 1050ms
pipe 2
```

In the second part of this experiment, we pinged the same host – at IP address 192.168.56.11 – using the hostnames of server and router. Both of these hostnames were correctly resolved to the IP address of 192.168.56.11.

Comment out the lines you added to /etc/hosts by prepending a # character to each line. This is necessary so that the /etc/hosts file will not resolve the hosts we will be testing with mDNS and BIND.

I used the /etc/hosts file to manage name services for my network for several years. It ultimately became too much trouble to maintain even with only the 8–12 physical computers and a similar number of VMs I normally have operational. As a result I converted to running my own BIND name server to resolve both internal and external hostnames.

Most networks of any size require centralized management with name service software such as BIND. However, smaller local networks can use mDNS for hands-free resolver services.

mDNS

Multicast DNS (mDNS)[7] is a relatively new addition to name service resolution. Intended to provide name resolution for local networks that have no internal, central name resolver, mDNS requires no user intervention. In addition to automatic discovery of local hosts, it also uses more traditional name services for access to the Internet.

This hands-off approach means that even with an internal network consisting of a moderate number of hosts, it requires no user intervention. It is implemented via the avahi package, which is installed during the initial Fedora installation.

The cost of this level of automation for local host discovery is a significant amount of network traffic from each host that is intended to discover other hosts in the network. This type of chatty protocol sucks up network bandwidth, uses host system resources, and is not fast relative to the more traditional nss-DNS protocols.

How It Works

Let's start with two comparative definitions.

Multicast services like mDNS send out broadcast (multicast) packets[8] that are received and examined by every host in the network. The packet is a request to the computer with the hostname it wants to communicate with to respond with its IP address so the requesting computer can send further packets directly to that host. Since only one computer (hopefully) has that hostname, only that computer will respond with its IP address, and the requesting host enters that hostname/IP address into its local database. Other computers in the network that use mDNS can also add that data to their own mDNS databases. With mDNS each host keeps its own database. Entries in the database have a TTL (Time to Live), so they expire. This means that the host must make another mDNS broadcast request to the network in order to obtain that IP address again.

Unicast services like nss-DNS use a single server that maintains the entire database. If a host needs the IP address of another host in the network, it sends a unicast packet only to the name server requesting the IP address from it. The name server responds only to the requesting host with a packet containing that IP address.

---

[7] Wikipedia, Multicast DNS, https://en.wikipedia.org/wiki/Multicast_DNS
[8] Wikipedia, IP multicast, https://en.wikipedia.org/wiki/IP_multicast

The mDNS protocols require that the systemd-resolved.service be running on all hosts. The `resolvectl` command can be used to view and provide a little management of the state of the systemd-resolved.service.

EXPERIMENT 43-5: THE RESOLVECTL COMMAND

Perform this experiment as root on StudentVM2. This first command returns the DNS status of all network interfaces:

```
[root@studentvm2 etc]# resolvectl status
Global
        Protocols: LLMNR=resolve -mDNS -DNSOverTLS DNSSEC=no/unsupported
  resolv.conf mode: stub

Link 2 (enp0s3)
    Current Scopes: DNS LLMNR/IPv4 LLMNR/IPv6
        Protocols: +DefaultRoute LLMNR=resolve -mDNS -DNSOverTLS DNSSEC=no/
        unsupported
Current DNS Server: 10.0.2.1
        DNS Servers: 10.0.2.1 8.8.8.8
```

This command can be used to resolve an FQDN to an IP address:

```
[root@studentvm2 etc]# resolvectl query www.example.net
www.example.net: 93.184.216.34                    -- link: enp0s3
                 2606:2800:220:1:248:1893:25c8:1946 -- link: enp0s3

-- Information acquired via protocol DNS in 2.2ms.
-- Data is authenticated: no; Data was acquired via local or encrypted
transport: no
-- Data from: network
```

Of course if you are using these commands, you probably need to migrate to nss-DNS.

---

mDNS Performance

After several not-very-scientific experiments involving the `time` command, I have found that mDNS is noticeably slower than using historical DNS services, especially in comparison with a network that provides its own name servers. My experiments show that mDNS can take as much as five times as long as historical name services. Of course we're only talking about hundredths of a second difference, but that can be important in some situations.

Delays can be especially noticeable to users accessing websites with a lot of external links that need to be resolved such as found on large, complex, commercial websites. Using ad blockers can help by simply not attempting to load from external addresses that are known advertising sources. However, in the ongoing battle between suppliers of ads and ad blockers, the latest strategy is to pop up a dialog that informs you to unblock ads or subscribe to the service.

nss-DNS

This is the historical name service database and resolver combination. The NSS resolver performs the client tasks of requesting IP addresses from the global Domain Name Services distributed database.

The DNS Database

The DNS system is dependent upon its database to perform lookups on hostnames to locate the correct IP address. The DNS database is a general-purpose distributed, hierarchical, replicated database. It also defines the structure of hostnames used on the Internet, properly called a fully qualified domain name (FQDN).

FQDNs consist of complete hostnames such as hornet.example.com and studentvm2.example.com. FQDNs break down into three parts:

1. The top-level domain names (TLDNs) such as .com, .net, .biz, .org, .info, .edu, and so on provide the last segment of an FQDN. All TLDNs are managed on the root name servers. Aside from the country top-level domains such as .us, .uk, and so on, there were originally only a few main top-level domains. As of February 2017, there were 1,528 top-level domains.

2. The second-level domain name is always immediately to the left of the top-level domain when specifying a hostname or URL. So names like redhat.com, example.net, getfedora.org, and example. com provide the organizational address portion of the FQDN.

3. The third level of the FQDN is the hostname portion of the name. So the FQDN of a specific host in a network would be something like host1.example.com.

Figure 43-2 shows a simplified diagram of the DNS database hierarchy. The "top" level, which is represented by a single dot (.), has no real physical existence. It is a device for use in DNS zone file configuration to enable an explicit end stop for domain names. A bit more on this later when we create zone files for our own name server.

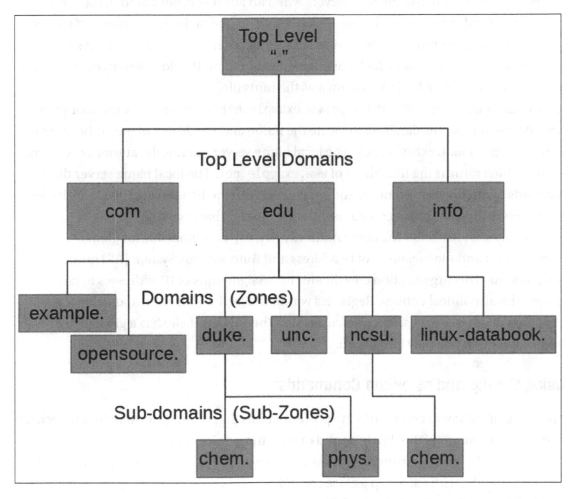

Figure 43-2. *A very simplified representation of the DNS database hierarchical structure*

The true top level consists of the root name servers. These are a limited number of servers that maintain the top-level DNS databases. The root level may contain the IP addresses for some domains, and the root servers will directly provide those IP addresses where they are available. In other cases the root servers provide the IP address of the authoritative server for the desired domain.

For example, assume we want to browse `www.example.net`. Our browser makes the request of the local name server, which does not contain that IP address. My local name server is configured to use the root servers when an address is not found in the local cache, so it sends the request for `www.example.net` to one of the root servers. Of course the local name server must know how to locate the root name servers, so it uses the /var/named/named.ca file, which contains the names and IP addresses of the root name servers. The named.ca file is also known as the hints file.

In this example, the IP address for `www.example.net` is not stored by the root servers. The root server uses its database to locate the name and IP address of the authoritative name server for `www.example.net`. The local name server queries the authoritative name server, which returns the IP address of `www.example.net`. The local name server then responds to the browser's request and provides it with the IP address. The authoritative name server for example.net contains the zone files for that domain.

The Internet Assigned Numbers Authority (IANA)[9] is responsible for global coordination and management of IP address and Autonomous System (AS) number assignments. This organization coordinates the assignments of IP addresses to large geographical-political entities. Registries within those divisions are responsible for assigning addresses to customers such as ISPs. The IANA website has a great deal of information that you may find useful.

Using the dig and nslookup Commands

The `dig` and nslookup commands are powerful tools that return information and records about a host from the DNS database and display the results in four main sections. The `dig` command is one of the most important tools we have in our network toolbox, and I use it frequently, with nslookup a close second.

---

[9] Internet Assigned Numbers Authority (IANA), `www.iana.org/`

EXPERIMENT 43-6: THE DIG AND NSLOOKUP COMMANDS

Perform this experiment as root. Use the dig command to obtain DNS information about the example.net domain. I already know that this will work because the example domains all have records that refer to the domain as a whole rather than merely to a single host:

```
[root@studentvm2 ~]# dig example.net

; <<>> DiG 9.18.13 <<>> example.net
;; global options: +cmd
;; Got answer:
;; ->>HEADER<<- opcode: QUERY, status: NOERROR, id: 17105
;; flags: qr rd ra; QUERY: 1, ANSWER: 1, AUTHORITY: 0, ADDITIONAL: 6

;; OPT PSEUDOSECTION:
; EDNS: version: 0, flags:; udp: 65494
;; QUESTION SECTION:
;example.net.                  IN      A

;; ANSWER SECTION:
example.net.           512    IN      A      93.184.216.34

;; ADDITIONAL SECTION:
example.net.           512    IN      MX     0 .
example.net.           512    IN      NS     b.iana-servers.net.
example.net.           512    IN      SOA    ns.icann.org.    noc.dns.icann.
org. 2022091282 7200 3600 1209600 3600
example.net.           512    IN      NS     a.iana-servers.net.
a.iana-servers.net.    512    IN      A      199.43.135.53

;; Query time: 0 msec
;; SERVER: 127.0.0.53#53(127.0.0.53) (UDP)
;; WHEN: Sun Jun 04 16:10:43 EDT 2023
;; MSG SIZE  rcvd: 188
```

This result is the A record that defines the IP address of the domain. If you use "www.example.net", the result will be the same. This shows the basic information we need, but there is much more lurking beneath the surface.

Note that the server IP address of 127.0.0.53 near the bottom of these results indicates that systemd-resolved.service is the active resolver. Refer to the results of this experiment as you read the descriptions of these sections in the following.

Interpreting dig Command Results

QUESTION: The first section of specific interest in Experiment 43-6 is the QUESTION section. For our example, it states that we are looking for the A record of "`www.example.net.`". If no other record type is explicitly requested in the command, the A record is assumed. Notice the dot at the end of the top-level domain name. This explicitly indicates that .com is the final domain name component in the hostname.

ANSWER: This section shows a single entry, an A record. A records are the primary name resolver records, and there must be an A record for each host, which contains the IP address. This section might also contain a CNAME, which stands for Canonical Name, record, and this record type is an alias for the A record and points to it. It is not typical practice to use "www" as the hostname for a web server. It is common to see a CNAME record that points to the A record of the FQDN. It is possible to have a record that applies to the domain as a whole such as simply example.net – however in this case it is an A record.

ADDITIONAL: This section lists the authoritative name servers for the example.net domain along with other records such as MX, the mail server, and SOA, which is the Start of Authority record. It also displays the top-level name server and its IP address.

Following the ADDITIONAL section, you can find some additional interesting information, including the IP address of the server that returned the information shown in the results. In this case it was the internal resolver, but the data was retrieved from the authoritative server for the example.net domain.

EXPERIMENT 43-7: GETTING THE REST

Experiment 43-6 showed us the basic information we asked for and allowed us to interpret the sections in the response. But there is much more information available.

Next, use the any argument to extract all of the records of any type for this domain. There is a lot more information here:

```
[root@studentvm2 ~]# dig any example.net

; <<>> DiG 9.18.13 <<>> any example.net
;; global options: +cmd
;; Got answer:
;; ->>HEADER<<- opcode: QUERY, status: NOERROR, id: 55633
;; flags: qr rd ra; QUERY: 1, ANSWER: 10, AUTHORITY: 0, ADDITIONAL: 5

;; OPT PSEUDOSECTION:
; EDNS: version: 0, flags:; udp: 65494
;; QUESTION SECTION:
;example.net.                    IN      ANY

;; ANSWER SECTION:
example.net.            86225   IN      A        93.184.216.34
example.net.            3425    IN      DNSKEY   256 3 13 TNz9N+iigsi9eUs4/
hX0Nl1vrpq5ytXieZhsF20aO2gm8D/nKqbVNRAR 9cpazxhLNpmQqoOJgMh1fBrD5/1jKg==
example.net.            3425    IN      DNSKEY   256 3 13 Q3GWFUzbgehRlB+Quixs
MM53g9v2SKZt6yYRzelVA1qeGmPramIv3KHX tmrLOXwsIjYL1z17Noppj+DxBQOH5Q==
example.net.            3425    IN      DNSKEY   257 3 13 UClVyPIUG66JvAgbsjvu
TL4/66/6SOknnEJ3LqxhnUNvVAjVKrtQmKsb aBrIVBzcvqcIzP1khIyZH88U9POMMg==
example.net.            86224   IN      DS       29511 13 2
306BAFA02D6A3CBBB182E53ECE8AF3D4141978A030F065971BDB076F 4DD6C0AF
example.net.            172624  IN      NS       b.iana-servers.net.
example.net.            172624  IN      NS       a.iana-servers.net.
example.net.            86400   IN      RRSIG    A 13 2
86400 20230611165621 20230521074947 9502 example.net.
8UDxtj45gdOUsx4a8fbfZSMqWDaHcMb2fxM3Cl74eoiwWSlv4ba4jF5h BM/
hDZwDavIpAQaaUajT53clRExjVg==
example.net.            3425    IN      RRSIG    DNSKEY 13 2 3600
20230611174757 20230521074947 29511 example.net. XVOKKLQoANPG2Cz+sjh8yydNLCUi
tvnbOo9VW/zptakQZTl8BSwKrOr9 t2XaMn4ocFVzzuXcj5Dm7qjtROCvKg==
example.net.            86224   IN      RRSIG    DS 8 2 86400 20230611070612
20230604055612 27554 net. hS6RaHJ+1qOyhaCTtIPcZDaqpACVmOCh9arIfzqYEu
yevG+sR9g/7XsY lWLTXCkE2MK6NjdTJS9lv+uKAc7foxjzDvOG8kEyIDRiEgedBLggl
zAr y2+9q5N/LAXjE1ZMP5JwKoTcux3GauYUDA7d+uvY8bzCstO58jJX9QHP Vhrv1a/
VbCy7x6kZIraQywMxqXPO8QUBf1V/bEqM2VSt6w==

;; ADDITIONAL SECTION:
a.iana-servers.net.     57903   IN      A        199.43.135.53
```

```
b.iana-servers.net.      57903    IN        A         199.43.133.53
a.iana-servers.net.      57903    IN        AAAA      2001:500:8f::53
b.iana-servers.net.      57903    IN        AAAA      2001:500:8d::53

;; Query time: 25 msec
;; SERVER: 127.0.0.53#53(127.0.0.53) (TCP)
;; WHEN: Sun Jun 04 15:22:11 EDT 2023
;; MSG SIZE  rcvd: 886
```

Advanced dig Command Results

Experiment 43-7 shows all of the DNS records associated with the example.net domain. This includes many additional records in the ANSWER section and both IPV4 and IPV6 server entries in the ADDITIONAL section.

Common DNS Record Types

There are a number of different DNS record types, and I want to introduce some of the more common ones here. Later in this chapter, you will create your own name server using BIND and will use many of these record types. These record types are used in the zone files that comprise the DNS database. One common field in all of these records is "IN", which specifies that these are INternet records. You can find a complete list of DNS record types at Wikipedia.[10]

I will make the assertion in this discussion that studentvm2.example.com is the BIND name server, which is why its hostname appears in these records. The example. com domain is a valid domain and is used for testing purposes on the Internet. It can also be used for internal testing, and we will be doing that later in this chapter. Therefore, the sample listings in the following figures will use example.com for the domain name.

SOA

SOA is the Start of Authority record.[11] It is the first record in any forward or reverse zone file, and it identifies this as the authoritative source for the domain it describes. It also specifies certain functional parameters. A typical SOA record looks like the sample here:

---

[10] Wikipedia, List of DNS record types, https://en.wikipedia.org/wiki/List_of_DNS_record_types
[11] The Network Encyclopedia, Start of Authority (SOA) record, www.thenetworkencyclopedia.com/entry/start-of-authority-soa-record/

```
@   IN SOA  studentvm2.example.com   root.studentvm2.example.com. (
                        2018101501      ; serial
                        1D              ; refresh
                        1H              ; retry
                        1W              ; expire
                        3H )            ; minimum
```

The first line of the SOA record contains the name of the server for the zone and the zone administrator, in this case root.

The second line is a serial number. In this example I use the date in YYYYMMDDXX format where XX is a counter for 00 to 99. The serial number in the SOA record represents the first version of this file on October 15, 2018. This format ensures that all changes to the serial number are incremented in a numerically sequential manner. That is important because secondary name servers only replicate from the primary server when the serial number of the zone file on the primary is greater than the serial number on the secondary. Be sure to increment the serial number when you make changes, or the secondary server will not sync up with the modified data.

The rest of the SOA record consists of various times that secondary servers should perform a refresh from the primary and wait for retries if the first refresh fails. It also defines the amount of time before the zone's authoritative status expires.

Times all used to be specified in seconds, but recent versions of BIND allow other options defined with W=week, D=day, H=hour, and M=minute. Seconds are assumed if no other specifier is used.

$ORIGIN

The $ORIGIN record is like a variable assignment. The value of this variable is appended by the BIND program to any hostname in an A or PTR record that does not end in a period (.) in order to create the FQDN for that host. This makes for less typing because the zone administrator only has to type the hostname portion and not the fully qualified domain name (FQDN) for each record:

```
$ORIGIN         example.com.
```

The @ symbol is used as a shortcut for this variable, and any occurrence of @ in the file is replaced by the value of $ORIGIN.

NS

The NS record specifies the authoritative name server for the zone. Note that both names in this record end with periods so that ".example.com" does not get appended to them. This record will usually point to the local host – which is also the name server – by its fully qualified domain name:

```
example.com.            IN    NS      studentvm2.example.com.
```

Note that the host, studentvm2.example.com, must also have an A record in the zone. The A record can point to the external IP address of the host or to the localhost address, 127.0.0.1.

A

The A record is the Address record type that specifies the relationship between the hostname and the IP address assigned to that host. In the following example, the host studentvm2 has IP address 192.168.56.1. Note that the value of $ORIGIN is appended to the name studentvm2 because studentvm2 is not an FQDN and does not have a terminating period in this record:

```
studentvm2              IN    A       192.168.56.1
```

The A record is the most common type of DNS database record.

AAAA

The AAAA records are used for IPV6 addresses in the DNS system. They perform exactly the same function as A records do for IPV4 addresses.

CNAME

The CNAME record is an alias for the name in the A record for a host. For example, the hostname studentvm2.example.com might serve as both the web server and the mail server. So there would be one A record and possibly two or three CNAME records as shown in the following:

```
studentvm2    IN    A        192.168.56.1
server        IN    CNAME    studentvm2
www           IN    CNAME    studentvm2
mail          IN    CNAME    studentvm2
```

It is good practice to have the A record contain the true hostname of the host. All of the other alias hostnames can be set using CNAME records. It is possible to have multiple A records, each with a different hostname, point to the same IP address, but this is not a good practice because it requires more work if the host's IP address is changed. The lazy SysAdmin types as little as possible and keeps things like configuration files as simple as possible.

DNSKEY

These records contain the public signing key for the DNS record and are used to determine the authenticity of the received data. This helps prevent DNS man-in-the-middle attacks, which are used by crackers to redirect your connections, especially web browsers, to malicious servers that will attempt to steal or phish for identity or financial data. They can also be used to reroute email through rogue email servers. These records are part of the implementation of DNSSEC, the DNS security protocol.

DS

This is a Delegation Signer record, which provides authorization (trust) for secondary servers as part of DNSSEC.

MX

The MX record defines the Mail eXchanger, that is, the mail server for the domain example.com. Notice that it points to the CNAME record for the server in the preceding example. Note that both example.com names in the MX record terminate with a dot so that example.com is not appended to the names:

```
; Mail server MX record
example.com.            IN     MX     10     mail.example.com.
```

Domains may have multiple mail servers defined. The number "10" in the preceding MX record is a priority value. Other servers may have the same priority or different ones. The lower numbers define higher priorities. So if all mail servers have the same priority, they would be used in round-robin fashion. If they have different priorities, the mail delivery would first be attempted to the mail server with the highest priority – the lowest number – and if that mail server did not respond, delivery would be attempted to the mail server with the next highest priority.

PTR

The PTR records are to provide for reverse lookups. This is when you already know the IP address and need to know the fully qualified hostname. For example, many mail servers do a reverse lookup on the alleged IP address of a sending mail server to verify that the name and IP address given in the email headers match. PTR records are located in reverse zone files. Reverse lookups can also be used when attempting to determine the source of suspect network packets.

Be aware that not all hosts have PTR records. Most ISPs create and manage the PTR records for home and small business accounts, so reverse lookups may not provide the needed information. For example, I use Spectrum business class for my Internet connection. I use Google Domains to manage my several external domains including both.org, linux-databook.info, and mtc-llc.net. Google Domains does allow me to create PTR records, but my ISP has already created an authoritative PTR record for my external IP address. I have not taken much time to explore whether this can be changed or not, but early experiments indicate not.

RRSIG

This is another DNSSEC record type. It contains a signature for a group of DNS records with the same name and type.

Other Records

There are other types of records that you may encounter in the DNS database. One type, the TXT records, is used to record comments about the zone or hosts in the DNS database. TXT records can also be used for DNS security. The rest of the DNS record types are outside the scope of this chapter.

Using BIND

BIND is the Berkeley Internet Name Daemon (Domain). It is used to centrally manage name services, generally in medium and large environments. It can, however, be used very successfully in smaller environments as well. Configuring BIND requires editing a number of files. The BIND configuration can be very picky about syntax, and I have found that some syntactical elements that should work apparently do not.

We will first configure a simple caching name server and then add the necessary configuration components to convert it into a primary name server. We will also configure the DHCP server for client-side DNS configuration.

Preparation

A caching name server cannot replace our use of /etc/hosts to resolve hostnames in the internal network. Compared with using an ISP or another public name server, however, a caching name server can improve both reliability and performance when resolving external names that are commonly used, such as www.cnn.com. I have experienced loss of DNS services from my ISP many times and have found my own name server is far more reliable than most ISPs. The best part is that setting up a caching name server is quite easy. It is also the first step in creating a primary name server that we can use for name resolution inside our own network.

EXPERIMENT 43-8: INSTALLING BIND

This experiment must be performed as root. Install the following BIND RPMs on the studentvm2 host: bind, bind-chroot, and bind-utils:

```
[root@studentvm2 ~]# dnf -y install bind bind-chroot bind-utils
```

To enable the StudentVM2 host to use itself as a caching name server, we must change the content of the system connection files.

Make /etc the PWD. Disable the systemd resolver:

```
[root@studentvm2 etc]# systemctl disable --now systemd-resolved.service
Removed "/etc/systemd/system/dbus-org.freedesktop.resolve1.service".
Removed "/etc/systemd/system/sysinit.target.wants/systemd-resolved.service".
```

Disable the Avahi daemon:

```
[root@studentvm2 etc]# systemctl disable --now avahi-daemon.service
Removed "/etc/systemd/system/sockets.target.wants/avahi-daemon.socket".
Removed "/etc/systemd/system/multi-user.target.wants/avahi-daemon.service".
Removed "/etc/systemd/system/dbus-org.freedesktop.Avahi.service".
Warning: Stopping avahi-daemon.service, but it can still be activated by:
  avahi-daemon.socket
[root@studentvm2 etc]# systemctl disable --now avahi-daemon.socket
```

Remove the existing /etc/resolv.conf link. NetworkManager will create a new /etc/resolv.conf file the next time it is restarted:

```
[root@studentvm2 etc]# rm -f resolv.conf
```

Tip   Although we used the nmcli command to create these nmconnection files, we can edit them directly using our favorite text editors. I find this to be more efficient than searching for the correct commands.

Edit the enp0s3.nmconnection file. Do not change anything except the highlighted lines. Everything else should remain the same. Note the second IP address in the IPV4 section, which defines the IP address of the default gateway router. If there is a dns= line, delete it. Your UUID line will be different, so be sure to not change it:

```
[connection]
id=enp0s3
uuid=176b534b-9e96-4453-892e-9569443ce056
type=ethernet
interface-name=enp0s3
timestamp=1685360872
zone=drop2

[ethernet]

[ipv4]
address1=10.0.2.11/24
gateway=10.0.2.1
method=manual

[ipv6]
addr-gen-mode=default
method=auto

[proxy]
```

Now change the enp0s8.nmconnection file. This one will be just a little different. We keep the dns= line but change it as shown. On my StudentVM2 host, the dns line was not present in this file, so I had to add it. Notice that we are using the host's IP external address rather than the internal one, 127.0.0.1:

```
[connection]
id=enp0s8
uuid=ccd54263-79df-4243-8049-11a49de3b15b
type=ethernet
interface-name=enp0s8

[ethernet]

[ipv4]
address1=192.168.56.11/24
search=example.com
domain=example.com
method=manual

[ipv6]
addr-gen-mode=default
method=auto

[proxy]
```

The search and domain entries in the ipv4 section indicate which domain to search when doing a lookup with the nslookup utility or when using the ping command with only the hostname and no domain name.

The man pages nm-settings(5) and nm-settings-keyfile(5) list many (but not all) of the configuration properties that can be used in the nmconnection files.

Restart NetworkManager to activate these changes:

```
[root@studentvm2 etc]# systemctl restart NetworkManager
```

And do a bit of checking to ensure that the server is working as we expect:

```
[root@studentvm2 ~]# nmcli
enp0s3: connected to enp0s3
        "Intel 82540EM"
        ethernet (e1000), 08:00:27:63:57:BE, hw, mtu 1500
        ip4 default
        inet4 10.0.2.11/24
        route4 default via 10.0.2.1 metric 100
        route4 10.0.2.0/24 metric 100
        inet6 fe80::63fb:7087:3813:f549/64
        route6 fe80::/64 metric 1024
```

```
enp0s8: connected to enp0s8
        "Intel 82540EM"
        ethernet (e1000), 08:00:27:F8:E1:CF, hw, mtu 1500
        inet4 192.168.56.11/24
        route4 192.168.56.0/24 metric 101
        inet6 fe80::3e67:ef46:a42a:364b/64
        route6 fe80::/64 metric 1024

lo: connected (externally) to lo
        "lo"
        loopback (unknown), 00:00:00:00:00:00, sw, mtu 65536
        inet4 127.0.0.1/8
        inet6 ::1/128
        route6 ::1/128 metric 256

<SNIP>
[root@studentvm2 etc]# cat resolv.conf
# Generated by NetworkManager
search example.com
domain example.com
nameserver 192.168.56.11
nameserver 8.8.8.8
nameserver 8.8.4.4
```

Don't forget that /etc/resolv.conf is regenerated by NetworkManager every time it is restarted and on every boot.

We have now prepared our server so that it can be configured as a caching name server. At the moment name resolution does not work, so we can't connect to the outside world.

Setting Up the Caching Name Server

Now we will set up our name server in its most basic configuration, that of a caching name server. That means it will be able to resolve names to IP addresses for hosts on the Internet such as www.example.net.

It is necessary to make a couple modifications to the /etc/named.conf file.

Note   The named.conf file is very particular about syntax and especially punctuation. Semicolons are used to delineate the end of an entry and the end of a stanza as well as the end of a line. Be sure to add them in correctly as shown in the samples.

EXPERIMENT 43-9: SETTING UP THE CACHING NAME SERVER

This experiment must be performed as root. In this experiment we alter the default /etc/ named.conf file to create our caching name server. The lines that need to be changed are highlighted in bold. I have removed some comment lines from the version of named.conf shown here to save some space.

By default, BIND refers to the Internet's root name servers to locate the authoritative name servers for a domain. It is possible to specify other servers that are called "forwarders" to which the local instance of BIND will send requests instead of the root servers. This does increase the possibility of DNS hijacking, but let's do that first to see how it works. We'll change it back later.

Add the IP address of your local student host to the "listen-on port 53" line. This enables named to listen on the external IP address of your host so that other computers can use it as a name server as well.

Add a "forwarders" line as shown in the following. This tells your caching DNS server where to obtain IP addresses when they are not already cached locally. The IP address listed there is for the virtual router and DNS server of the virtual network. You could use your local ISP or OpenDNS or some other public name server as your forwarder.

It is not necessary to define any forwarders at all. By default BIND will use the Internet root servers as defined in the file /var/named/named.ca to locate the authoritative name servers for domains if no forwarders are defined. However, for this part of the exercise, you will define two forwarders in /etc/named.conf. We will use the virtual router/name server of our virtual network with IP address 192.168.56.1 and one of the Google public name servers at IP address 8.8.8.8.

Comment out the IPV6 line as we are not using IPV6 in the test environment:

```
//
// named.conf
// Provided by Red Hat bind package to configure the ISC BIND named(8) DNS
// server as a caching only name server (as a localhost DNS resolver only).
// See /usr/share/doc/bind*/sample/ for example named configuration files.
//
//
options {
        listen-on port 53 { 127.0.0.1; 192.168.56.11; };
//      listen-on-v6 port 53 { ::1; };
        forwarders { 8.8.8.8; 8.8.4.4; };
        directory       "/var/named";
        dump-file       "/var/named/data/cache_dump.db";
        statistics-file "/var/named/data/named_stats.txt";
        memstatistics-file "/var/named/data/named_mem_stats.txt";
        secroots-file   "/var/named/data/named.secroots";
        recursing-file  "/var/named/data/named.recursing";
        allow-query     { localhost; 192.168.56.0/24; };
        recursion yes;

        dnssec-enable yes;
        dnssec-validation yes;
        dnssec-lookaside auto;

        /* Path to ISC DLV key */
        bindkeys-file "/etc/named.iscdlv.key";

        managed-keys-directory "/var/named/dynamic";
        pid-file "/run/named/named.pid";
        session-keyfile "/run/named/session.key";

        /* https://fedoraproject.org/wiki/Changes/CryptoPolicy */
        include "/etc/crypto-policies/back-ends/bind.config";
};
logging {
        channel default_debug {
                file "data/named.run";
                severity dynamic;
        };
};
```

```
zone "." IN {
        type hint;
        file "named.ca";
};
include "/etc/named.rfc1912.zones";
include "/etc/named.root.key";
```

Also add the local network address in CIDR format, 192.168.56.0/24, to the **allow-query** line. This line specifies the network(s) from which DNS queries will be accepted by this DNS server. Multiple networks can be specified.

Keep the named.conf file open in your editor as you will be making several changes to it during the rest of this chapter.

Configuring the Firewall for DNS

The default public zone of the firewall on your student host currently blocks everything except Secure Shell (SSH). The firewall must be configured to allow UDP and TCP packets inbound on your name server in order for other hosts to use it for name resolution.

EXPERIMENT 43-10: CONFIGURE THE FIREWALL FOR DNS

This experiment must be performed as root on StudentVM2. We will only open the internal network on enp0s8, which is in the public zone:

```
[root@studentvm2 etc]# firewall-cmd –add-service=dns --zone=public --permanent
success
[root@studentvm2 etc]# firewall-cmd --add-service=dns --zone=public
success
[root@studentvm2 system-connections]# firewall-cmd --list-services --zone=public
dhcpv6-client dns mdns ntp ssh
[root@studentvm2 system-connections]# firewall-cmd --list-services --zone=
public --permanent
dhcpv6-client dns mdns ntp ssh
```

The firewall will now accept DNS queries from other hosts in our internal network.

Start the Name Service

Now we start the named service and configure it to start at every boot. Name resolution for external hosts will work after we do this.

EXPERIMENT 43-11: START THE NAMED SERVICE

As root on StudentVM2, run the following command to enable and start the named service:

```
[root@studentvm2 ~]# systemctl enable --now named.service
Created symlink /etc/systemd/system/multi-user.target.wants/named.service →
/usr/lib/systemd/system/named.service.
```

The named resolver service is now up and ready for local testing.

To test your caching name server, use the dig command to obtain the IP address(es) for some common Internet websites, such as CNN, Wired, and any others you like. Notice that the results should now show your host as the responding server rather than the virtual router or the Google name server.

Note that on the first attempt, the responding server might be one of the upstream resolvers because your host as client may have timed out waiting for the result from your host as DNS server. Additional attempts will be resolved from the cache of your host as DNS server.

EXPERIMENT 43-12: TEST NAMED

This experiment can be performed as either the root or student user on StudentVM2. The PWD doesn't matter for this experiment:

```
[student@studentvm2 ~]$ dig www.redhat.com

; <<>> DiG 9.18.15 <<>> www.redhat.com
;; global options: +cmd
;; Got answer:
;; ->>HEADER<<- opcode: QUERY, status: NOERROR, id: 21530
;; flags: qr rd ra; QUERY: 1, ANSWER: 4, AUTHORITY: 0, ADDITIONAL: 1

;; OPT PSEUDOSECTION:
```

```
; EDNS: version: 0, flags:; udp: 1232
; COOKIE: 7c5e27d706c301ed0100000064806cc4de6882c3e5d54b58 (good)
;; QUESTION SECTION:
;www.redhat.com.                         IN      A

;; ANSWER SECTION:
www.redhat.com.         1618    IN      CNAME   ds-www.redhat.com.
edgekey.net.
ds-www.redhat.com.edgekey.net. 21600 IN CNAME    ds-www.redhat.com.edgekey.
net.globalredir.akadns.net.
ds-www.redhat.com.edgekey.net.globalredir.akadns.net. 3600 IN CNAME e3396.
dscx.akamaiedge.net.
e3396.dscx.akamaiedge.net. 20   IN      A       104.86.87.87

;; Query time: 261 msec
;; SERVER: 192.168.56.11#53(192.168.56.11) (UDP)
;; WHEN: Wed Jun 07 07:40:52 EDT 2023
;; MSG SIZE  rcvd: 235
;; WHEN: Tue Jun 06 13:08:55 EDT 2023
;; MSG SIZE  rcvd: 235
```

The important bit of data for us in this result is that the responding server (located near the bottom of the output) is 192.168.56.11, which is the IP address of our new caching DNS server. The #53 indicates the number of the DNS port.

The local caching server does not respond immediately the first time a new domain name is resolved. This delay, usually a few hundred milliseconds, should be very small and is the result of having to query the forwarder for the information. After that, query times should be minimal as the server can return data that's already in the cache instead of having to look it up every time.

The fact that the data is indicated to be non-authoritative is the result of using forwarders. This is not a problem and does not affect the results or speed of queries from application programs and utilities. The dig command is intended to provide data that can be used by a SysAdmin for use in problem determination when there is an issue of some type. You should also be aware that different servers and forwarders may produce different amounts of data in the AUTHORITY and ADDITIONAL sections of the dig output.

Do some additional queries using both dig and nslookup to further verify the results from our server.

We are not quite finished. The caching name server is working as we expect it to, but we do need to ensure that hosts configured by DHCP services now have the correct IP address for our new name server.

Reconfiguring DHCP

This step is important so that hosts being booted on our virtual network are served the correct IP address for the name server. We do not need to turn off the name server in the virtual router, and we do not want to do that anyway because we are using it as a forwarder. Also, I have not found a way to turn off DNS services on the virtual router.

EXPERIMENT 43-13: RECONFIGURE DHCP FOR THE CORRECT NAME SERVER

Perform this experiment as root. In this experiment we change the DNS server to the new one we just created. We will leave the DNS server in the virtual router as an alternative in case our primary name server fails.

On StudentVM2, change the "option domain-name-servers" line in the dhcpd.conf configuration file. This is line 11 in my file:

```
option domain-name-servers 192.168.56.11, 8.8.8.8, 8.8.4.4;
```

Now restart the DHCPD service:

```
[root@studentvm2 ~]# systemctl restart dhcpd
```
Now we can reconfigure studentVM1.

We need to stop the systemd resolver on StudentVM1, delete /etc/resolv.conf, and restart NetworkManager:

```
[root@studentvm1 etc]# systemctl disable --now systemd-resolved.service
[root@studentvm1 etc]# rm -f resolv.conf
[root@studentvm1 etc]# systemctl restart NetworkManager
[root@studentvm1 etc]# ll resolv.conf
-rw-r--r-- 1 root root 286 Jun  6 13:33 resolv.conf
[root@studentvm1 etc]# cat resolv.conf
# Generated by NetworkManager
search example.com both.org
nameserver 192.168.56.11
```

```
nameserver 8.8.8.8
nameserver 8.8.4.4
```

Verify that the resolver is working. Be sure to check the server line in the return data:

```
[root@studentvm1 ~]# dig example.net
```

It shows the name data for example.net, and it also proves that the resolver used to obtain this data is our own name server. Try some additional lookups for additional testing and verification.

Although StudentVM1 can now resolve FQDNs, the StudentVM2 server has not yet been configured as a router, so we have some work to do before StudentVM1 can browse the Web. After we finish some additional work with our name server in this chapter, we'll make StudentVM2 into a router in the next chapter.

Using the Top-Level DNS Servers

We could continue to use the forwarders as the source of our DNS information. Forwarders are not a bad thing, and they are very useful in many environments. The problem is that most forwarders are configured to be the DNS servers of the ISP providing the Internet connection. My personal experience is that some ISP's DNS reliability is significantly less than stellar. For a while I used public DNS servers to test them, including Google public DNS, which is reliable, fast, and not censored. Some other public DNS systems are censored or redirect you to places you did not intend and subject you to things like advertisements or pages flogging domains for sale.

I decided years ago to use my own DNS server and that I would also use the top-level DNS servers rather than forwarders. One reason for this is that the top-level servers reflect database record changes much faster than down-level servers. As a SysAdmin I find this helpful when I make changes for my own domains. I also use the top-level servers as a learning experience so that I can more fully understand how to manage that environment for my networks and others.

A really good forwarder is perfectly fine, but let's now use the top-level servers.

```
┌──────────────────────────────────────────────────────────────────────┐
│        EXPERIMENT 43-14: DISABLE USE OF DNS FORWARDERS                  │
└──────────────────────────────────────────────────────────────────────┘
```

Perform this experiment as root on StudentVM2. Here we comment out the forwarders line in named.conf in order to use the DNS top-level name servers. Use the double forward slash (//) to comment out the forwarders line in /etc/named.conf:

```
//        forwarders { 8.8.8.8; 8.8.4.4; };
```

Restart named on StudentVM2:

```
[root@studentvm2 etc]# systemctl restart named
```

Test this change on StudentVM1:

```
[root@studentvm1 ~]# dig www.redhat.com
```

There was almost certainly a small but possibly noticeable delay in getting the return data because of the fact we restarted the named service, which flushed the cache. Additional searches on the same name will return much faster because the data is now cached. Notice the difference in the output data. Leave named.conf open in your editor because we will be making more changes to it in this chapter.

Creating a Primary Name Server

Once a caching name server has been created, it is not too difficult to convert it into a full-fledged primary name server. We need to change named.conf again and create a couple new files. We will create a domain called example.com, which is a valid public domain name reserved for testing labs and classes.

With the proper configuration, name servers can also perform reverse lookups to convert IP addresses into hostnames. The two new files we will create are the forward and reverse zone files. They will be located in the /var/named directory. Remember that this location is specified by the "directory" directive in the named.conf configuration file.

Creating the Forward Zone File

The forward zone files are the name database files that are used to cross-reference hostnames with their assigned IP addresses. Each zone file contains the database for a single domain. Each host has at least one A record entry in the zone file with the name of the host and its IP address. Each host may also have one or more CNAME records that provide aliases for the primary hostname.

We are going to create a simple zone file for our example.com domain. This will be our local test instance of the example.com domain and not the public instance.

EXPERIMENT 43-15: CREATE THE FORWARD ZONE FILE

This experiment must be performed as root on studentvm2. Create a basic forward zone file, /var/named/example.com.zone, and add the following content to it. We will be using lines taken almost directly from the "Common DNS Record Types" section earlier in this chapter:

```
; Authoritative data for example.com zone
;
$TTL 1D
@   IN SOA  studentvm2.example.com   root.studentvm2.example.com. (
                                2023060701      ; serial
                                1D              ; refresh
                                1H              ; retry
                                1W              ; expire
                                3H )            ; minimum

$ORIGIN       example.com.
example.com.    IN    NS      studentvm2.example.com.
router          IN    A       192.168.56.1
studentvm2      IN    A       192.168.56.1
studentvm1      IN    A       192.168.56.21
studentvm3      IN    A       192.168.56.22
studentvm4      IN    A       192.168.56.23
```

These entries will give you a few hostnames to experiment with even though some do not exist in the virtual network. Be sure to use today's date and a sequence number for the serial number.

Adding the Forward Zone File to named.conf

Before your DNS server will work, however, you need to create an entry in /etc/named.
conf that will point to your new zone file.

EXPERIMENT 43-16: ADD THE FORWARD ZONE FILE TO NAMED.CONF

As root on StudentVM2, add the following lines below the entry for the top-level hints
zone – zone "." IN:

```
zone "example.com" IN {
        type master;
        file "example.com.zone";
};
```

Now restart the named service:

[root@studentvm2 named]# **systemctl restart named**

Test your name server by using the dig and nslookup commands to obtain the IP addresses
for the hosts you have configured in the forward zone file. Note that the host does not have to
exist in the network for the dig and nslookup commands to return an IP address:

[root@studentvm2 named]# **dig studentvm1.example.com**

```
; <<>> DiG 9.18.15 <<>> studentvm1.example.com
;; global options: +cmd
;; Got answer:
;; ->>HEADER<<- opcode: QUERY, status: NOERROR, id: 18413
;; flags: qr aa rd ra; QUERY: 1, ANSWER: 1, AUTHORITY: 0, ADDITIONAL: 1

;; OPT PSEUDOSECTION:
; EDNS: version: 0, flags:; udp: 1232
; COOKIE: 3595a06b9055c18d01000000648074315d66d8810bd923b9 (good)
;; QUESTION SECTION:
;studentvm1.example.com.               IN      A

;; ANSWER SECTION:
studentvm1.example.com. 86400   IN      A       192.168.56.21
```

```
;; Query time: O msec
;; SERVER: 192.168.56.11#53(192.168.56.11) (UDP)
;; WHEN: Wed Jun 07 08:12:33 EDT 2023
;; MSG SIZE  rcvd: 95
```

Ping the router and the studentvm1 host. Also ping some external hosts to verify that external name services are still working as expected. You can use the example.org domain for this because we have used example.com for our test domain.

Be aware that it is necessary to use the FQDN for the dig command but not for the nslookup command so long as the domain and search entries are provided in the /etc/resolv.conf file. Ping one of the hosts that does exist, such as the studentvm1 host. Notice that it is not necessary to use the FQDN for this command.

Our name server is up and responding to requests, but there is more to do.

Adding CNAME Records

Now we will add some CNAME records; these are like aliases. These records can be added almost anywhere after the name server (NS) line in the zone file, but I like to keep them with the A record to which they point, which makes it easier to find related records. The following example.com.zone file is what yours should look like when you have finished adding the CNAME entries.

EXPERIMENT 43-17: ADD CNAME RECORDS

As the root user on the name server, add the CNAME records to the forward zone file as shown in the following. Be sure to set ownership of the zone file to root.named and increment the serial number:

```
; Authoritative data for example.com zone
;
$TTL 1D
@   IN SOA  studentvm2.example.com   root.studentvm2.example.com. (
                                2018122802      ; serial
                                1D              ; refresh
```

```
                                      1H                ; retry
                                      1W                ; expire
                                      3H )               ; minimum

$ORIGIN          example.com.
example.com.     IN    NS        studentvm2.example.com.
router           IN    A         192.168.56.1
studentvm2       IN    A         192.168.56.1
server           IN    CNAME     studentvm2
studentvm1       IN    A         192.168.56.21
workstation1     IN    CNAME     studentvm1
ws1              IN    CNAME     studentvm1
wkst1            IN    CNAME     ws1
studentvm3       IN    A         192.168.56.22
studentvm4       IN    A         192.168.56.23
```

Note that some of the CNAME records ultimately point to the same host IP address for the studentvm1 host. CNAME records can be nested to as many levels as necessary, but it tends to complicate things when there are too many levels of indirection.

This time, instead of doing a complete restart of the named service, we will use the "reload," which causes the named service to reload all of its configuration files. This is usually faster than a restart and can prevent interruptions to the service. Test these CNAME entries using dig and nslookup:

```
[root@studentvm2 etc]# systemctl reload named
```

Be sure to perform a lookup on wkst1.example.com and examine the answer lines in the results. You should be able to see the CNAME and A record trail from the CNAME you requested to the A record. This is especially apparent when using the dig command:

```
[root@studentvm2 etc]# dig wkst1.example.com
; <<>> DiG 9.18.15 <<>> wkst1.example.com
;; global options: +cmd
;; Got answer:
;; ->>HEADER<<- opcode: QUERY, status: NOERROR, id: 10847
;; flags: qr aa rd ra; QUERY: 1, ANSWER: 3, AUTHORITY: 0, ADDITIONAL: 1

;; OPT PSEUDOSECTION:
; EDNS: version: 0, flags:; udp: 1232
```

```
; COOKIE: ae98d044c1bc7c6f010000006480b4cd8a714fd8a5362de7 (good)
;; QUESTION SECTION:
;wkst1.example.com.                 IN      A

;; ANSWER SECTION:
wkst1.example.com.       86400   IN      CNAME   ws1.example.com.
ws1.example.com.         86400   IN      CNAME   studentvm1.example.com.
studentvm1.example.com. 86400   IN      A       192.168.56.21

;; Query time: 0 msec
;; SERVER: 192.168.56.11#53(192.168.56.11) (UDP)
;; WHEN: Wed Jun 07 12:48:13 EDT 2023
;; MSG SIZE  rcvd: 133
```

Also use the ping command with these CNAME aliases to verify that the end result is a correct ping response:

```
[root@studentvm2 etc]# ping -c2 wkst1
PING studentvm1.example.com (192.168.56.21) 56(84) bytes of data.
64 bytes from 192.168.56.21 (192.168.56.21): icmp_seq=1 ttl=64 time=2.15 ms
64 bytes from 192.168.56.21 (192.168.56.21): icmp_seq=2 ttl=64 time=2.22 ms

--- studentvm1.example.com ping statistics ---
2 packets transmitted, 2 received, 0% packet loss, time 1011ms
rtt min/avg/max/mdev = 2.151/2.184/2.217/0.033 ms
```

Be sure to use ping or mtr to verify that external name services still work.

Our name server is now working as expected but only to resolve IP addresses from a hostname.

Creating the Reverse Zone File

A reverse zone for your domain will provide the ability to do reverse lookups. Many organizations do not do these internally, but reverse lookups can be helpful in doing problem determination. Many spam-fighting configurations such as SpamAssassin look for reverse lookups to verify valid email servers.

```
┌────────────────────────────────────────────────────────────────┐
│         EXPERIMENT 43-18: CREATE THE REVERSE ZONE FILE           │
└────────────────────────────────────────────────────────────────┘
```

Create the reverse zone file, /var/named/example.com.rev, and add the following contents. This file name uses current naming conventions for reverse zone files. Use an appropriate serial number. Be sure to set ownership of the zone file to root.named:

```
; reverse mapping for example.com zone
;
$TTL 1D
@        IN SOA   studentvm2.example.com.    root.studentvm2.example.com. (
                                             2018122801      ; serial
                                             1D              ; refresh
                                             1H              ; retry
                                             1W              ; expire
                                             3H )            ; minimum

@        IN      NS      studentvm2.example.com.
1        IN      PTR     router.example.com.
11       IN      PTR     studentvm2.example.com.
21       IN      PTR     studentvm1.example.com.
```

You could also name your reverse zone file /var/named/25.168.192.in-addr.arpa, which follows older conventions. You can actually name it anything you want because you will point to it explicitly in the named.conf file, but using one of the two conventions will make it easier for others to follow your work.

The serial numbers for the named.conf file and the forward and reverse zones do not need to be the same. It is important to remember to update the serial number of any given file every time its content is altered. This does provide a way to determine the last time a file was modified if you use the same numbering strategy that I do. It is also critical in an environment where the primary server updates secondary name servers when the primary is changed.

Adding the Reverse Zone to named.conf

We need to add a stanza for the reverse zone file to named.conf to complete the reverse lookup function.

```
EXPERIMENT 43-19: ADD THE REVERSE ZONE TO NAMED.CONF
```

Add the following stanza to the /etc/named.conf file to point to the new reverse zone. I always add the reverse zone stanza after the forward zone:

```
zone        "56.168.192.in-addr.arpa" IN {
    type master;
    file "example.com.rev";
};
```

Now reload named and test your reverse zone. The -x option specifies that we are requesting a reverse lookup. Appending .service to the service name is optional in most current Linux distros that use systemd. It was a requirement in early versions:

```
[root@studentvm2 ~]# systemctl reload named.service
[root@studentvm2 ~]# dig -x 192.168.56.21

; <<>> DiG 9.18.15 <<>> -x 192.168.56.21
;; global options: +cmd
;; Got answer:
;; ->>HEADER<<- opcode: QUERY, status: NOERROR, id: 24095
;; flags: qr aa rd ra; QUERY: 1, ANSWER: 1, AUTHORITY: 0, ADDITIONAL: 1

;; OPT PSEUDOSECTION:
; EDNS: version: 0, flags:; udp: 1232
; COOKIE: f5b59c3b8c70b132010000006480b950dcf72623ab040064 (good)
;; QUESTION SECTION:
;21.56.168.192.in-addr.arpa.     IN      PTR

;; ANSWER SECTION:
21.56.168.192.in-addr.arpa. 86400 IN    PTR     studentvm1.example.com.

;; Query time: 0 msec
;; SERVER: 192.168.56.11#53(192.168.56.11) (UDP)
;; WHEN: Wed Jun 07 13:07:29 EDT 2023
;; MSG SIZE  rcvd: 119

[root@studentvm2 named]#
```

Now let's see what the status of a working name server looks like:

```
[root@studentvm2 ~]# systemctl status named
● named.service - Berkeley Internet Name Domain (DNS)
     Loaded: loaded (/usr/lib/systemd/system/named.service; enabled; preset:
     disabled)
    Drop-In: /usr/lib/systemd/system/service.d
             └─10-timeout-abort.conf
     Active: active (running) since Wed 2023-06-07 13:06:44 EDT; 2min 4s ago
    Process: 10520 ExecStartPre=/bin/bash -c if [ ! "$DISABLE_ZONE_CHECKING"
    == "yes" ]; then /usr/bin/named-checkconf -z "$NAMEDC>
    Process: 10522 ExecStart=/usr/sbin/named -u named -c ${NAMEDCONF}
    $OPTIONS (code=exited, status=0/SUCCESS)
   Main PID: 10523 (named)
      Tasks: 10 (limit: 4634)
     Memory: 7.6M
        CPU: 134ms
     CGroup: /system.slice/named.service
             └─10523 /usr/sbin/named -u named -c /etc/named.conf

Jun 07 13:06:44 studentvm2 named[10523]: network unreachable resolving
'./DNSKEY/IN': 2001:500:1::53#53
Jun 07 13:06:44 studentvm2 named[10523]: network unreachable resolving
'./NS/IN': 2001:500:1::53#53
Jun 07 13:06:44 studentvm2 named[10523]: network unreachable resolving
'./DNSKEY/IN': 2001:7fe::53#53
Jun 07 13:06:44 studentvm2 named[10523]: network unreachable resolving
'./NS/IN': 2001:7fe::53#53
Jun 07 13:06:44 studentvm2 named[10523]: network unreachable resolving
'./DNSKEY/IN': 2001:503:ba3e::2:30#53
Jun 07 13:06:44 studentvm2 named[10523]: network unreachable resolving
'./NS/IN': 2001:503:ba3e::2:30#53
Jun 07 13:06:44 studentvm2 named[10523]: network unreachable resolving
'./DNSKEY/IN': 2001:7fd::1#53
Jun 07 13:06:44 studentvm2 named[10523]: network unreachable resolving
'./DNSKEY/IN': 2001:500:a8::e#53
```

```
Jun 07 13:06:44 studentvm2 named[10523]: managed-keys-zone: Key 20326 for
zone . is now trusted (acceptance timer complete)
Jun 07 13:06:45 studentvm2 named[10523]: resolver priming query
complete: success
```

The lines indicating that a network is unreachable refer to the IPV6 network, which we have not activated.

Perform some additional testing at your own discretion to ensure that the reverse lookup is working. Be sure to test the name services from StudentVM1 too.

At this point you have a working name server using BIND. Do not turn it off or disable it. You will use your own name server for the rest of these experiments, and you will be adding some entries to it.

Automating BIND Administration

The BIND name database server does require hands-on by the SysAdmin in networks that change frequently. However, the task of updating the named zone files can be automated.

During my time at Cisco, my official job was as a Linux tester, but part of my job was assistant lab manager. In that part of my job, Bruce,[12] the lab manager, and I would need to install new servers and remove old ones on a regular basis. Some days we were able to completely install and configure as many as six new Linux hosts per day between the two of us. This included unboxing, racking, cabling, etc.

Chapter Summary

Domain Name Services is a very important part of making the Internet easily accessible. It binds the myriad disparate hosts connected to the Internet into a cohesive unit that makes it possible to communicate with the far reaches of the planet with ease. It has a complex distributed database structure that is perhaps even unknowable in its totality, yet which can be rapidly searched by any connected device to locate the IP address of any other device that has an entry in that database.

---

[12] Yes, BRuce is the correct spelling.

We've explored the three main resolver tools and tried all three of them.

We started with the /etc/hosts file that requires a simple but high-maintenance file on all local hosts.

For small networks, including those with as few as one or two hosts, mDNS is a viable option that requires no administrative effort and that is the default resolver in modern versions of Fedora. However, its performance is less than that of the standard resolver nss-DNS. mDNS also generates a lot of network traffic, and its chattiness can be an issue in some networks.

If you are a system administrator on a network of almost any size, you will find it helpful to know how to build your own name server as we did in this chapter. A traditional name server using a tool like BIND provides the most efficient name service in terms of performance; however, it does require some administrative work to keep it current when local hosts are being added and deleted on a regular basis. It is pretty much hands-off in a stable network environment.

Exercises

Perform these exercises to complete this chapter:

1. Why do local networks and the Internet need name services?

2. What is the sequence of events that will take place in order to obtain the IP address for a host in our own network if we enter the command ping router? Assume the setup is identical to the one that we have created in this course.

3. What difference is there – if any – if we use the command ping router.example.com?

4. What IP (V4) address is associated with the name localhost?

5. Is a reverse zone required for DNS services to work for forward lookups?

6. How is it possible for organizations to use DNS to redirect – not block – web browsing to one or more outside websites?

7. Can a single name server provide name services for more than one domain such that it can be the authoritative name server for both example.com and example.org – for example?

CHAPTER 44

Routing

Objectives

In this chapter you will learn

- To define the function of a router
- To configure a Linux host as a router
- To configure the router firewall to support routing functions
- To understand and create entries for a routing table

Introduction

At first glance routing and firewalls might seem to have little to do with each other, but they are very closely entwined. Both are found at the edges of networks, and they work together to perform routing.

Routing is the task of ensuring that packets get routed to their specified destination. Every computer attached to a network requires some type of routing instructions for network TCP/IP packets when they leave the local host. This is usually very straightforward because most network environments are very simple and there are only two options for departing packets. All packets are sent either to a device in the local network or to some remote network via a router that may also be known as the default gateway. Multiple routers may be in use in a network, but only one router can be the default gateway.

Let's be sure to define the "local" network as the logical and usually also the physical network in which the local host resides. Logically that means the local subnet in which the host is assigned one of the ranges of the local subnet's IP addresses. Physically that means the host is connected to one or more switches that are also connected to the rest of the local network.

© David Both 2023

D. Both, *Using and Administering Linux: Volume 3*, https://doi.org/10.1007/978-1-4842-9786-5_44

A firewall is responsible for protecting the firewall host and the internal network from network-based attacks of many kinds. Firewalls are also used to aid in router implementation by providing a mechanism to route packets from one network interface on the router host to another network interface.

In this chapter we will look at routing on a workstation, StudentVM1, that is not used as a router. We will then convert our server, StudentVM2, into a router and change the DHCP configuration to use it as the router for the virtual network. Of course, the packets must still pass through the virtual router to get to the outside world. This is a common enough situation in many networks, and we will explore that too.

We are also going to install Fail2Ban again, which is a tool for dynamically blocking IP addresses that are making attempts to crack into our systems. We did this on host StudentVM1 in Volume 2, Chapter 41, but we also need to ensure that it is done on StudentVM2. It will be a good review.

Every device in a network that will connect to another network such as the Internet or other internal networks needs to have its own routing table. By default, Fedora creates a routing table on every device on which it is installed.

If the network uses a static configuration, the IP address of the default gateway is defined during that configuration and is stored in the nmconnection file for that interface. Fedora does not allow static configuration during the initial installation from the live image, so it would need to be done later, as we did in the first book of this course.

If DHCP is used to configure the host, no nmconnection file is required because the IP address of the default gateway is provided to the host at each boot. We have already configured DHCP to provide the appropriate information including the list of name servers and the default gateway to DHCP client hosts inside our network. The only thing we have left to do to complete our network configuration is to convert StudentVM2, the server, into a router.

Routing on a Workstation

Let's start by looking at routing packets on a workstation, which is usually pretty straightforward. Packets go either to another device in the local network segment, or they go to a device in another network. In the latter case, the network packets must be sent to a router in order to be sent to the correct network. There is usually only a single router for a network segment because the local network is only connected to a single external network.

The logic used to determine routing is simple:

1. If the destination host is in the local network, send the data directly to the destination host.

2. If the destination host is in a remote network that is reachable via a local gateway listed in the routing table, send it to the explicitly defined gateway.

3. If the destination host is in a remote network and there is no other entry that defines a route to that host, send the data to the default gateway.

These rules mean that if all else fails because there is no match, send the packet to the default gateway. So let's look at the simple scenario of our StudentVM1 host.

EXPERIMENT 44-1: ROUTING ON A SIMPLE WORKSTATION

Perform this experiment as the root user on the StudentVM1 host. Look at the current route information:

```
[root@studentvm1 ~]# ip route
default via 192.168.56.11 dev enp0s3 proto dhcp src 192.168.56.21 metric 100
192.168.56.0/24 dev enp0s3 proto kernel scope link src 192.168.56.21
metric 100
```

The default route set on StudentVM1 is that of the router we just created and configured on StudentVM2. It was provided with the other network configuration data by the DHCP server on StudentVM2.

This is a trivial and common routing configuration with only a single default gateway. It means that any packet that has a destination outside the local network, 192.168.56.0/24, will be sent to the default router from where it will be routed onward, perhaps through several more routers, to its final destination – as soon as we get our router working.

Creating a Router

Let's make a Linux router out of the StudentVM2 host. We have previously configured our original network to match the default defined by the virtual network router as generated by VirtualBox. Both of our hosts used the virtual router as the default gateway. We want StudentVM1 and any other hosts inside our 192.168.56.0/24 network to use the StudentVM2 router as the default gateway while it, in turn, uses the virtual router as its default gateway in the 10.0.2.0/24 network.

We have already created a host-only network for this internal network, and VirtualBox automatically selects the IP address range of 192.168.56.0/24. We could change this but there is really no need to do so. The use of the 192.168.56.0/24 address range also is different enough from the 10.0.2.0/24 address range to ensure that we are less likely to be confused about which network we are working with.

Our new network configuration looks like Figure 44-1. This is a very common configuration for many networks. The ISP supplies the external modem/router to the outside world, and the organization maintains its own internal firewall and router to provide security and isolation from the Internet or other external networks.

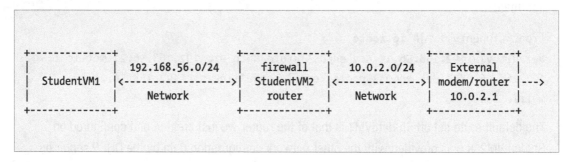

Figure 44-1. *The new network configuration*

To make recovery easier, let's make snapshots of both virtual machines.

EXPERIMENT 44-2: MAKE SNAPSHOTS OF THE VMS

Make new snapshots of both student VMs.

As I was preparing this chapter, I made some mistakes and tried some things that didn't work. So it was very helpful to be able to revert to the snapshots of both hosts that I made before I started working on this chapter. If you don't need them, that's great. If you do need them, you'll be glad you made them.

It's so much easier to be able to revert to a snapshot than it is to undo everything you did. I can't always even remember everything I changed especially when I am just experimenting to satisfy my own curiosity.

Setting Up the Router

There are two things that we need to do to create our Linux router. We need to tell the Linux kernel that it should act as a router, and we need to reconfigure the firewall so that it can route packets between the appropriate network interfaces.

Kernel Configuration

Configuring the kernel to support routing is trivial. Really! We do not need to recompile the kernel, and we do not even need to reboot. We only need to turn on packet forwarding, which allows packets to be accepted on one network interface and sent back out on another. Keeping packet forwarding turned off when it is not required is a smart security precaution.

EXPERIMENT 44-3: CONFIGURING THE KERNEL

Perform this experiment as the root user on StudentVM2. We will turn on packet forwarding and set that up so that it is permanent.

First, let's set packet forwarding on in the /proc filesystem. We could do this with the sysctl command, but that would not really show you how simple and easy it really is.

Make /proc/sys/net/ipv4 the PWD. List the files in this directory. Check the current value of the file ip_forward. It should contain the number 0. To turn on packet forwarding for IPV4, overwrite the content of the ip_forward file with the number 1:

```
[root@studentvm2 ipv4]# echo 1 > ip_forward ; cat ip_forward
1
```

Testing this does not result in complete success but does show a change in the error message. Do this bit as root on StudentVM1. The reply indicates that StudentVM2 is now working differently. It is now a router, but it is rejecting these packets because there is not an appropriate rule in the firewall:

```
[root@studentvm1 ~]# ping -c2 example.org
PING example.org (93.184.216.34) 56(84) bytes of data.

--- example.org ping statistics ---
2 packets transmitted, 0 received, 100% packet loss, time 57ms
```

We have set IP forwarding on but it is not permanent. The value of this file will return to 0 at the next reboot. To make this change permanent, we need to add a new file to the /etc/sysctl.d/ directory.

Although the /etc/sysctl.conf file still exists, it is no longer used to set kernel parameters. Rather, all kernel parameters are now set using files in /etc/sysctl.d. There is no naming convention for the files stored in this directory except that they all be prepended with a two-digit number, which will define the sorted order in which the files are acted upon. Back on StudentVM2, create a new file named 50-network.conf[1] in the /etc/sysctl.d directory and add the following content to it:

```
# Controls IP packet forwarding
net.ipv4.ip_forward = 1
```

This file will now be read at each boot.

Notice that the file name contains a partial path indicating the location of the file referred to by this statement. The base path is proc/sys/ and the separators are dots (.) instead of slashes (/).

Save the new file. The default permissions are fine.

We explored the /proc filesystem in some detail in Chapter 24 of Volume 2.

---

[1] I arbitrarily chose the number 50 for this file. The number used should be irrelevant – at least for our purposes.

Firewall State

Before we make any changes to the firewall, let's take a quick look at its current state. This allows us to take a quick inventory of the original state of things so we can revert if necessary.

EXPERIMENT 44-4: CURRENT FIREWALL STATE

Perform this experiment as root on StudentVM2. Your firewall should look like this before starting:

```
[root@studentvm2 ~]# firewall-cmd --get-active-zones
drop2
  interfaces: enp0s3
public
  interfaces: enp0s8
[root@studentvm2 ~]# firewall-cmd --list-all
public (active)
  target: default
  icmp-block-inversion: no
  interfaces: enp0s8 enp0s9
  sources:
  services: dhcpv6-client dns mdns ntp ssh
  ports:
  protocols:
  forward: yes
  masquerade: no
  forward-ports:
  source-ports:
  icmp-blocks:
  rich rules:
[root@studentvm2 ~]# firewall-cmd --list-all --zone=drop2
drop2 (active)
  target: DROP
  icmp-block-inversion: no
  interfaces: enp0s3
  sources:
```

```
    services:
    ports:
    protocols:
    forward: yes
    masquerade: no
    forward-ports:
    source-ports:
    icmp-blocks:
    rich rules:
  [root@studentvm2 ~]#
```

Firewall Requirements

The final step in creating a router on StudentVM2 is configuring the firewall on StudentVM2 so that it will forward all packets addressed to the Internet outside our local network to be routed through our firewall/router to the appropriate destination.

Our extremely secure drop2 zone won't work on the router for this because the default is to drop all incoming packets. The internal zone won't work either because it still blocks too many packets that need to be sent to the outside world. Remember that the internal zone has only a short list of services that are allowed past the firewall and all the rest are blocked by default.

We will change the zone for enp0s8, the private internal network, to trusted, which uses "ACCEPT" for the target. This accepts all packets incoming from the internal private network and blocks nothing. The trusted zone already has forward set to yes but masquerade is set to no. The trusted zone is just that – all of the hosts in the trusted zone are considered to be trusted and not a threat to the server.

Zones

Before we configure our firewall to act as the router for our internal network, it's helpful to understand more about zones and some of the strategies involved in using firewalld zones for security.

You'll recall that the firewall is composed of rules that are interpreted by the netfilter modules in the Linux kernel. Netfilter is the Linux kernel's enforcement mechanism for firewall rules regardless of how those rules are created. There are multiple tools that can be used to create and organize rule sets. Among those tools are firewalld, the old but still viable iptables, the very old ipchains, and the newer nftables. These tools each work with different user interfaces that organize and manage the rule sets using different conceptual models, such as zones or tables, but they all create rule sets that are enforced by the Linux kernel's netfilter modules.

The zones used by firewalld are arbitrary logical constructs of rules that have been collected into a single entity for ease of use. They exist as zone files, and any single zone can be applied to any network interface on a Linux host. One zone can be assigned to all network interfaces, or each interface can be assigned a different zone. Only one zone can be assigned to a given network interface at one time.

Zones are not part of the network. Zones are logical constructs that exist only within the computer hosts. They provide a method and terminology for the SysAdmin to think about the networks to which the computers are connected.

firewalld has nine predefined zones that can be used as is or modified to meet local needs. Figure 44-2 – which you first encountered as Figure 41-2 – lists the predefined firewalld zones and a short description of each.

Zone	Description
drop	Any incoming network packets are dropped, there is no reply. Only outgoing network connections are possible.
block	Any incoming network connections are rejected with an icmp-host-prohibited message for IPv4 and icmp6-adm-prohibited for IPv6. Only network connections initiated within this system are possible.
public	For use in public areas such as coffee shops. You do not trust the other computers on networks to not harm your computer. Only selected incoming connections are accepted.
external	For use on external networks with IPv4 masquerading enabled especially for routers. You do not trust the other computers on networks to not harm your computer. Only selected incoming connections are accepted.
dmz	For computers in your demilitarized zone that are publicly-accessible with limited access to your internal network. Only selected incoming connections are accepted.
work	For computers in your demilitarized zone that are publicly-accessible with limited access to your internal network. Only selected incoming connections are accepted.
home	For use in home areas. You mostly trust the other computers on networks to not harm your computer. Only selected incoming connections are accepted.
internal	For use on internal networks. You mostly trust the other computers on the networks to not harm your computer. Only selected incoming connections are accepted.
trusted	All network connections are accepted.

Figure 44-2. *The default firewalld zones*

You have also had the opportunity in Chapter 41 to create new zones and to modify existing ones. These zones define how the computer treats incoming TCP/IP data packets on the interfaces to which they are assigned.

Zoning Strategy

Our objective is to use these zones to protect our StudentVM2 server/firewall from malicious attacks from the Internet while also allowing outbound packets from our network to reach the Internet so that our host can access the Internet. For now we want to ensure that nothing enters from the Internet unless the hosts in our private network have requested it. In later chapters we will explore how to modify the firewall to allow email to be sent to us and to allow access from the Internet to a website we will create on our server.

Experiment 44-4 shows the current state of the firewalld firewall.

The enp0s3 interface connects StudentVM2, the host we are using as the firewall, to the Internet through the 10.0.2.0/24 virtual network. It currently is assigned the drop2 zone that you created earlier. This zone drops all attempted connections from the Internet and allows no incoming new connections at all. Like most zones, it will allow routing of all packets from the StudentVM2 host to pass through to the Internet. We will not change this zone because it provides the highest level of protection from the outside world while allowing us to initiate connections from inside to the Internet.

The enp0s8 interface connects the StudentVM2 host to our internal private network. We have already configured the kernel so that it will allow packet routing from one interface to another, so now we need to assign enp0s8 to a zone that allows all packets from the private network to pass through on their way into our router where they will be routed to the target host via the Internet. We will change the zone assigned to enp0s8 to the trusted zone, which does exactly that.

About the Trusted Zone

In Experiment 44-4 we looked at the configuration of the active zones, but let's look at the configuration of the trusted zone. This zone will be used on the enp0s8 interface to our private network.

EXPERIMENT 44-5: EXPLORING THE TRUSTED ZONE

Perform this experiment as the root user on StudentVM2, our firewall host:

```
[root@studentvm2 etc]# firewall-cmd --list-all --zone=trusted
trusted (active)
  target: ACCEPT
  icmp-block-inversion: no
  interfaces:
  sources:
  services:
  ports:
  protocols:
  forward: yes
  masquerade: no
  forward-ports:
  source-ports:
  icmp-blocks:
  rich rules:
[root@studentvm2 etc]#
```

The ACCEPT target in this zone is one of its important attributes. This means that we don't need to explicitly allow individual services to access from the network being filtered by this zone. It allows all packets to enter.

It is already set up to allow packet forwarding, which is also what we need. It is not necessary to specify the ports and services allowed in because all are allowed by the ACCEPT target.

At the moment no interfaces have been assigned to the trusted zone.

The bottom line for this zone is that, when it has been applied to the enp0s8 interface, it will allow all packets from the internal network to pass through and it will route them to the enp0s3 interface where they will be sent to the Internet for further routing to their destinations. Packets returning from those destinations will be allowed back through the network interface to the hosts from which the requests originated.

Adapting the Firewall

Now that you understand a little more about zones and how they are used, and more specifically the trusted zone and why we need it for this use case, it's time to configure the firewall for its role in our router configuration.

EXPERIMENT 44-6: CONFIGURING THE FIREWALL

Start this experiment as root on StudentVM2. Be sure to note where you need to change from one VM to the other as we'll switch back and forth a few times.

First, assign the trusted zone to interface enp0s8 on StudentVM2:

```
[root@studentvm2 ~]# firewall-cmd --change-interface=enp0s8 --zone=trusted
success
[root@studentvm2 ~]# firewall-cmd --permanent --change-interface=enp0s8 --zone=
trusted
The interface is under control of NetworkManager, setting zone to 'trusted'.
success
```

And test from StudentVM2 to ensure that it is working as it should:

```
[root@studentvm2 etc]# ping -c2 example.net
PING example.net (93.184.216.34) 56(84) bytes of data.
64 bytes from 93.184.216.34: icmp_seq=1 ttl=50 time=13.2 ms
64 bytes from 93.184.216.34: icmp_seq=2 ttl=50 time=13.3 ms

--- example.net ping statistics ---
2 packets transmitted, 2 received, 0% packet loss, time 1461ms
rtt min/avg/max/mdev = 13.210/13.241/13.273/0.031 ms
```

Now perform a quick test from StudentVM1:

```
[root@studentvm1 ~]# ping -c2 example.net
PING example.net (93.184.216.34) 56(84) bytes of data.
64 bytes from 93.184.216.34 (93.184.216.34): icmp_seq=1 ttl=50 time=13.5 ms
64 bytes from 93.184.216.34: icmp_seq=2 ttl=50 time=13.6 ms

--- example.net ping statistics ---
2 packets transmitted, 2 received, 0% packet loss, time 1428ms
```

```
rtt min/avg/max/mdev = 13.491/13.546/13.601/0.055 ms
[root@studentvm1 ~]#
```

Be sure to verify that the IP address is the external one shown here and not on our internal network. This shows that the name server is working as it should and that the router is functioning properly.

There are a couple interesting tools that can be used to help us test network functionality from the command line. This is quite useful on hosts with no GUI desktop installed. The links and lynx programs are web browsers that have text-mode user interfaces, so they can run in a terminal session. They're especially useful when working as root because root is configured to not have access to the GUI desktop as a security precaution; it prevents users from doing everything as root.

Let's install them:

```
[root@studentvm1 ~]# dnf -y install lynx links
```

The fact that these tools install on StudentVM1 indicates that the router configuration on StudentVM2 is working properly. Using lynx we can view web pages:

```
[root@studentvm1 ~]# lynx www.example.net
```

The result looks like Figure 44-3.

```
Example Domain
This domain is for use in illustrative examples in documents. You may use this
domain in literature without prior coordination or asking for permission.

   More information...




Commands: Use arrow keys to move, '?' for help, 'q' to quit, '<-' to go back.
  Arrow keys: Up and Down to move.  Right to follow a link; Left to go back.
  H)elp O)ptions P)rint G)o M)ain screen Q)uit /=search [delete]=history list
```

Figure 44-3. Using lynx to view a web page in a terminal session

Press Enter to begin exploring this website. Use the command list at the bottom of the screen to explore the website a little. The selected item is highlighted in yellow on black. It's not necessary to spend a lot of tine with this because I'm just showing it to you as an example of a text-mode tool that can be used for testing if necessary.

Now open the Firefox web browser on the StudentVM1 desktop and enter www.example.net on the URL line. You should see the simple web page. This reverifies that our router is working as it should.

Network Routing

Your network's default gateway is rarely the final destination for packets. As its name suggests, a gateway router is usually a literal gateway to other networks. We can trace the routes packets might take through our own router and beyond to arrive at a specific destination.

EXPERIMENT 44-7: USING MTR TO TRACE A ROUTE

This experiment can be performed as the student user on the StudentVM1 host. In this experiment we will discover the list of all the routers through which packets travel to a destination and some interesting metrics pertaining to that.

My preferred tool for this is mtr. This tool started out as Matt's traceroute because Matt wrote it and it was designed as a dynamic replacement for the old traceroute tool. Because Matt no longer maintains this and someone else has taken over, it is now referred to as "my traceroute."

The -r option places mtr into report mode, which leaves the result on the screen so it can be viewed or copy-and-pasted into this book. The -n option causes it to display IP addresses instead of using DNS to find the hostnames for each IP. The -c5 option causes mtr to send a maximum count of five ICMP packets:

```
[root@studentvm1 ~]# mtr -r -n -c5 example.net
Start: 2023-06-13T21:28:49-0400
HOST: studentvm1              Loss%   Snt   Last   Avg  Best  Wrst StDev
  1.|-- 10.0.2.1              0.0%      5    0.2   0.4   0.2   0.7   0.2
  2.|-- 192.168.0.254         0.0%      5    0.5   0.5   0.5   0.5   0.0
```

```
 3.|-- 45.20.209.46          0.0%    5    1.1   1.1   1.1   1.2   0.0
 4.|-- ???                  100.0    5    0.0   0.0   0.0   0.0   0.0
 5.|-- 99.173.76.162          0.0%    5    3.0   2.9   2.8   3.0   0.0
 6.|-- ???                  100.0    5    0.0   0.0   0.0   0.0   0.0
 7.|-- ???                  100.0    5    0.0   0.0   0.0   0.0   0.0
 8.|-- 32.130.16.19           0.0%    5   13.4  13.9  13.3  15.6   0.9
 9.|-- 192.205.32.102         0.0%    5   15.4  16.6  14.0  19.2   2.2
10.|-- 152.195.80.131         0.0%    5   12.7  18.1  12.4  39.8  12.2
11.|-- 93.184.216.34          0.0%    5   13.5  13.4  13.3  13.5   0.1
[root@studentvm1 ~]#
```

Now use this form to view the results dynamically without limiting the number of pings sent:

```
[root@studentvm1 ~]# mtr -n example.net
```

```
                          My traceroute  [v0.92]
studentvm1
(10.0.2.21)                             2019-06-21T14:38:21-0400
Keys:  Help    Display mode   Restart statistics   Order of fields    quit
                                        Packets                  Pings
Host                            Loss%   Snt   Last   Avg  Best  Wrst StDev
 1. 10.0.2.1                     0.0%   25    0.3   0.3   0.2   0.4   0.1
 2. 192.168.0.254                0.0%   25    0.5   0.6   0.4   0.9   0.1
 3. 24.199.159.57                0.0%   25    3.7   6.3   2.1  13.4   3.4
 4. 142.254.207.205              0.0%   25   69.3  23.6  12.0  69.3  11.9
 5. 174.111.105.178              0.0%   25   25.3  24.0  12.6  38.9   6.5
 6. 24.25.62.106                 0.0%   25   28.1  24.9  17.7  36.4   4.5
 7. 24.93.64.186                 0.0%   25   30.4  43.3  26.5 161.2  29.0
 8. 66.109.6.34                  8.3%   24   35.5  47.8  27.5 158.8  30.9
 9. 152.195.80.196               0.0%   24   45.7  45.7  26.1 156.3  30.5
10. 152.195.80.131               0.0%   24   37.3  56.8  27.4 238.1  50.8
11. 93.184.216.34          0.0%   24   32.3  43.0  26.4 142.0  26.9
```

This is a dynamic display and it keeps checking the route until you press **q** to quit. Because of this, mtr can display statistics for each hop along the way to the destination including response times and packet loss at each intermediate router along the way.

Another thing you might see for any given hop number (the sequential numbers down the left side of the display) is multiple routers indicating that the path to the remote host is not always through the same sequence of routers.

Note the packet loss at hop 8. Although this could indicate a problem, it is more likely that the router is discarding unimportant packets such as ICMP if the router is heavily loaded. If you try this at another time, the packet loss will probably be zero.

If you are actually having problems connecting with a site and mtr indicates a high packet loss, that could be the source of the problem. The only thing to be done is to report this to your ISP.

Complex Routing

It is possible to add more complexity to our router. We won't actually do that, but this short section examines what that might look like.

The routing table shown using the old and newer commands in Figure 44-4 is a bit more complex because it belongs to a Linux host acting as a router that connects to three networks, one of which leads to the Internet. The local networks, 192.168.0.0/24 on interface enp6s0 and 192.168.10.0/24 on enp4s0, each have entries in the table, as well as the default route that leads to the rest of the world on enp2s0.

```
[root@wally1 ~]# ip route
default via 24.199.159.57 dev enp2s0 proto static metric 103
24.199.159.56/29 dev enp2s0 proto kernel scope link src 24.199.159.59 metric 103
192.168.0.0/24 dev enp6s0 proto kernel scope link src 192.168.0.254 metric 102
192.168.10.0/24 dev enp4s0 proto kernel scope link src 192.168.10.1 metric 104

[root@wally1 ~]# route -n
Kernel IP routing table
Destination     Gateway         Genmask         Flags Metric Ref    Use Iface
0.0.0.0         24.199.159.57   0.0.0.0         UG    103    0        0 enp2s0
24.199.159.56   0.0.0.0         255.255.255.248 U     103    0        0 enp2s0
192.168.0.0     0.0.0.0         255.255.255.0   U     102    0        0 enp6s0
192.168.10.0    0.0.0.0         255.255.255.0   U     104    0        0 enp4s0
[root@wally1 ~]#
```

Figure 44-4. *A more complex routing table from my own network router*

Note that there is still only one default gateway, and that is on interface enp2s0, which connects the host to the Internet.

Of course it is also necessary to have appropriate rules in the firewall to allow routing.

Fail2Ban

A great firewall is one that can adapt as the threats change. I needed something like that to stem the large number of attacks via SSH I had been experiencing a few years ago. After a good bit of exploring and research, I found Fail2Ban, an open source software that automates what I was previously doing by hand and adds repeat offenders to a blocklist in firewalls. The best part is that it integrates nicely with firewalld.

Fail2Ban has a complex series of configurable matching rules and separate actions that can be taken when attempts are made to crack into a system. It has rules for many types of attacks that include web, email, and many other services that might have vulnerabilities. Fail2Ban works by detecting attacks and then adding a rule to the firewall that will block further attempts from that specific, single IP address for a specified and configurable amount of time. After the time has expired, it removes the blocking rule.

Let's install Fail2Ban and see how it works.

EXPERIMENT 44-8: FAIL2BAN

Perform this experiment as the root user on StudentVM2. First, install Fail2Ban. This only takes a minute or so and does not require a reboot. The installation includes the firewalld interface to Fail2Ban:

```
[root@studentvm1 ~]# dnf -y install fail2ban
```

Fail2Ban is not started as a part of the installation, so we will need to do so after we perform a bit of configuration. Make /etc/fail2ban the PWD and list the files there. The jail.conf file is the main configuration file, but it is not used for most configuration because it might get overwritten during an update. We will create a jail.local file in the same directory. Any settings defined in jail.local will override ones set in jail.conf.

Copy jail.conf to jail.local. Edit the jail.local file and ignore or remove the comment near the beginning that tells you not to modify this file. It is, after all, the file we will be modifying.

Find the line **# ignoreself = true**, which should be line 87. Remove the comment hash, and change it to **ignoreself = false**. We do this so that Fail2Ban will not ignore failed login attempts from the localhost. It should be changed back to true after finishing this chapter.

Scroll down to the line **bantime = 10m** (line 101) and change that to one minute (1m). Since we have no other hosts to test from, we will test using the localhost or StudentVM1. Yes, you can easily test the same host you're working on even if it's the only host you have available. We do not want either host banned for long so that we can resume experiments quickly. In the real world, I would set this to several hours so that the crackers cannot get more attempts for a long time.

Change **maxretry = 5** to 2. This is the maximum number of retries allowed after any type of failed attempt. Two retries are a good number for experimental purposes. I normally set this to three because anyone failing three retries to get into my systems using SSH does not belong there.

We could also change both of these configuration options in the [sshd] filter section, which would limit them to sshd, while the global settings we just changed apply to all filters.

Read the comments for the other miscellaneous options in this section of the file and then scroll down to the [sshd] section in JAILS.

Add the highlighted line that enables the sshd jail. The documentation is not clear about needing to add this line. In previous versions the line was **enabled = false**, so it was clear that changing false to true would enable the sshd jail:

```
[sshd]

# To use more aggressive sshd modes set filter parameter "mode" in
jail.local:
# normal (default), ddos, extra or aggressive (combines all).
# See "tests/files/logs/sshd" or "filter.d/sshd.conf" for usage example and
details.
enabled = true
#mode    = normal
port    = ssh
logpath = %(sshd_log)s
backend = %(sshd_backend)s
```

Do not enable Fail2Ban, but start it:

```
[root@studentvm1 ~]# systemctl start fail2ban.service
```

Now ssh to localhost and log in using a bad user account or password on a good user account. It takes three failed attempts to log in, not three failed password entries. After three failed login attempts, the following error message is displayed:

```
[student@studentvm1 ~]$ ssh localhost
<snip>
ssh: connect to host localhost port 22: Connection refused
```

This means that the sshd jail is working. Look at the iptables firewall rules. Remember that these Fail2Ban rules are stored in memory and are not permanent. The rejection rules are removed after one minute, so if you don't see that line, force the failed logins again.

The following output shows that the rules are actually interpreted by nftables. List the nftables rules and page to the bottom to find the following entries:

```
[root@studentvm1 ~]# nft list ruleset | less
table ip6 filter {
        chain INPUT {
                type filter hook input priority filter; policy accept;
                meta l4proto tcp tcp dport 22 counter packets 68 bytes 11059
                jump f2b-sshd
        }

        chain f2b-sshd {
                ip6 saddr ::1 counter packets 4 bytes 320 reject
                counter packets 54 bytes 9939 return
        }
}
table ip filter {
        chain INPUT {
                type filter hook input priority filter; policy accept;
                meta l4proto tcp tcp dport 22 counter packets 62 bytes 9339
                jump f2b-sshd
        }

        chain f2b-sshd {
                ip saddr 127.0.0.1 counter packets 2 bytes 120 reject
                counter packets 54 bytes 8859 return
        }
}
```

Now let's look at a couple log files. In /var/log, first look at /var/log/secure. You should see a number of entries indicating failed passwords. These are the log entries checked by Fail2Ban for failures.

Look at the /var/log/fail2ban.log file. This log file shows the times that triggering entries were found in the secure log and the ban and unban actions taken to protect the system.

After the one-minute ban time has expired, try to log in from the localhost again to verify that you can do so. This time use the correct password:

```
[root@studentvm2 ~]# ssh localhost
root@localhost's password:
Last failed login: Wed Jun 14 14:15:10 EDT 2023 from ::1 on ssh:notty
```

There were 2 failed login attempts since the last successful login.

```
Last login: Tue Jun 13 14:36:51 2023 from 192.168.0.1
[root@studentvm2 ~]# exit
logout
Connection to localhost closed.
[root@studentvm2 ~]#
```

Be aware that the f2b-sshd chain entries do not appear in the iptables rule set until the first time a ban is triggered. Once there, the first and last lines of the chain are not deleted, but the lines rejecting specific IP addresses are removed as they time out. It took me a bit of work to figure out this bit.

The installation of Fail2Ban installs the configuration files needed for logwatch to report on Fail2Ban activity. It is possible to create your own filters and actions for Fail2Ban, but that is beyond the scope of this course.

Be sure to look at the various jails in the fail2ban.local file. There are many different events that can trigger Fail2Ban to ban source IP addresses from access to a particular port or service.

Cleanup

Change **ignoreself = false** back to **ignoreself = true**. We do this so that Fail2Ban will ignore failed login attempts from the localhost. Also set **maxretry = 5**.

This is the default configuration.

Chapter Summary

In this chapter we converted the StudentVM2 host into a router. To accomplish that we configured the kernel to perform IP forwarding, which is the functional basis for routing. We set the internal network interface, enp0s8, to the trusted zone and then tested the results. We also installed Fail2Ban on the firewall/router, StudentVM2, to provide the maximum amount of protection for our entire network. And – of course – we tested the results.

Creating a router out of a host with two or more network interfaces is an easy one you know how.

You should ignore most of the websites returned when you search the Internet about using firewalld to create a Linux router. Most of that information is incorrect or needlessly complex. We will add some complexity to our router as we add services that are intended to be accessed from the Internet like a local email server and a website, but that complexity is not needed in many environments where we only want to access the Internet.

Exercises

1. Why is a router required when connecting two networks?

2. What is the function of the default router?

3. Can there be more than one router on a network segment?

4. Can there be more than one default router on a network segment?

5. Why did we use the domain example.org instead of example.com in Experiment 44-7?

6. Before StudentVM2 is made into a router, why do DNS queries from StudentVM2 regarding external hosts, such as example.org and cnn.com, return the correct responses?

7. List the routers between your StudentVM1 host and `www.apress.com`. Do the same for `www.both.org`. Are any of the routers dropping packets? Can you tell in what cities or countries the routers are located?

CHAPTER 45

Remote Access with SSH

Objectives

In this chapter you will learn

- How SSH works to create and maintain secure connections

- Advanced SSH usage and techniques

- How to use SSH for secure file transfers

- How to use SSH to perform remote command execution

- How to generate and use public/private key pairs (PPKPs) for authentication

- To use X-forwarding to run GUI programs on the remote host so that the windows of their GUI interface are displayed on the local host

- An easy and elegant way to perform a centralized backup of remote hosts

Introduction

SSH is an important mechanism for secure connections between Linux hosts. SSH is a software-based virtual private network (VPN) tool that can create a secure VPN whenever needed. It can be used to securely log into any remote host so long as you have proper credentials, and it can be used to enhance tools such as `tar` and other backup programs like `rsync` so that remote hosts can be easily backed up to a local system. The `scp` (secure copy) program uses the SSH encrypted tunnel to copy files between a remote host and a local one.

© David Both 2023
D. Both, *Using and Administering Linux: Volume 3*, https://doi.org/10.1007/978-1-4842-9786-5_45

We looked at using Secure Shell (SSH) in Volume 2, Chapter 30, of this course when we set up Ansible. We set up the SSH server and used it to connect itself to the localhost for testing automated updates with Ansible. In this chapter we will explore SSH in more depth and use it to communicate between two separate VM hosts. We will also use public/private key pairs for authentication that is more secure than using passwords.

The name Secure Shell is misleading. SSH is not a shell; it is only a set of connection protocols that enables secure, encrypted links between two computers. An SSH login to a remote host uses the default shell of the user on the remote host. In most cases this would be Bash, but some users prefer other shells and have designated them as their default shell. Whichever shell they use as their default will be the shell used for the SSH connection.

SSH provides three important properties:

1. It provides reliable authentication for the identities of the hosts as well as the users. It ensures that the hosts and users are whom they claim to be.

2. It encrypts the communication between the hosts, including the transmission of any login ID and password or public/private key pairs (PPKPs).

3. It ensures the integrity of the transmissions and can detect and notify the user if data is missing, added, or changed.

Using SSH for inter-host communications is an excellent security precaution and can prevent data that is transmitted over any part of a public network from being intercepted, blocked, or altered. As with all security tools, SSH is not the complete solution, and other security precautions must also be taken. But SSH ensures secure communications can be easily accomplished.

Tip   This chapter is about using individual GUI applications on a remote computer. In Chapter 54 of this volume, we will explore the TigerVNC remote desktop access tool, which allows remote sharing of a complete desktop.

Starting the SSH Server

We have already started the SSH server on StudentVM1, but we need to start it on StudentVM2, also. Any Linux host can be an SSH server, and it makes sense to do so in order to facilitate easy communications and the ability to work on remote hosts.

EXPERIMENT 45-1: STARTING SSHD ON STUDENTVM2

Start this experiment as the root user on StudentVM2. Start the SSHD server daemon and enable it so it will start on boot. The default SSHD configuration is perfect for our needs, and it allows direct login by the root user. In a real-world environment, we would most likely change that so that direct root logins would be disallowed:

```
[root@studentvm2 ~]# systemctl start sshd ; systemctl enable sshd
Created symlink /etc/systemd/system/multi-user.target.wants/sshd.service →
/usr/lib/systemd/system/sshd.service.
[root@studentvm2 ~]#
```

That was easy, and our StudentVM2 host is now ready for us to try out an SSH connection. In a terminal session as the student user on StudentVM1, ssh to StudentVM2:

```
[student@studentvm1 ~]$ ssh studentvm2
The authenticity of host 'studentvm2 (192.168.56.1)' can't be established.
ECDSA key fingerprint is SHA256:NDM/B5L3eRJaalex6IOUdnJsE1smOSiQNWgaI8BwcVs.
Are you sure you want to continue connecting (yes/no)? yes
Warning: Permanently added 'studentvm2,192.168.56.1' (ECDSA) to the list of
known hosts.
Password: <Enter the password for student1 on StudentVM2>
[student@studentvm2 ~]$
```

The first time an SSH connection is made to any host, the authenticity message is displayed along with the fingerprint of the private key of the remote host. In a very security-conscious environment, we would have already received a copy of the remote host's key fingerprint. This allows comparison so that we know we are connecting to the correct remote host. This is not the security key; it is a fingerprint that is unique to that host's private key. It is impossible to reconstruct the original private key from which the fingerprint was generated, which prevents it being used to crack into the remote host.

You must type "**yes**" – the full word – in order to continue the login. Then you must enter the password for the remote host.

Now let's look at the /home/student/.ssh directory. Then look at the contents of the ~/.ssh/known_hosts file on StudentVM1. You should see the public host key for the remote host, StudentVM2. This file is created on the local host, the one we are connecting from, and not on the remote host, the one we are connecting to. Each host we connect to will have a unique signature of its own in our known_hosts file to identify it for future connections:

```
[student@studentvm1 ~]$ cat .ssh/known_hosts
localhost ssh-ed25519 AAAAC3NzaC1lZDI1NTE5AAAAIBLOJ/wd2RJpsu2fPKOEPzFq6dCnT-
Fk3/m3U716SD2BY
studentvm2 ssh-ed25519 AAAAC3NzaC1lZDI1NTE5AAAAIFm+TnU+D2+OOiGkcgp47LvEN9ZQ3
yKU8l2nuAMeXI6D
studentvm2 ssh-rsa
<SNIP>
uKMVvVC3DliZZ+GEkXd2U4vsmDhtOfXH1RcnPJPBM9xPP32dhfg9Zwprwra1VJxa9icecmZbglvJj
ORUgvvFp/PHZxHFVkGWKZ7ywoojFTOeFjROxc=
studentvm2 ecdsa-sha2-nistp256 AAAAE2VjZHNhLXNoYTItbmlzdHAyNTYAAAAIbmlzdHAyNT
YAAABBBPOZ9+hEe2P3P5475c3hS45C73w52eoN/9R/dkO724/qYZ9dzNSB6yl+jH35BTIRGtzbqhn
oaKTBqCTBLAQdG/c=
[student@studentvm1 ~]$
```

After accepting this key during the first connection to the remote host, the connections initialize a little faster because the two computers now know each other and can identify themselves via the keys.

The host keys are stored in /etc/ssh along with the SSH client and server configuration files. List the contents of that directory to view the various key files.

Now, as the root user on StudentVM1, connect to StudentVM2 and verify that connection works as well.

Type **exit** to disconnect from all SSH connections between the two VMs.

Now we know that the SSH server on StudentVM2 is working as it should and can accept connections from remote hosts. But there is so much more.

How SSH Works – Briefly

Let's look briefly at the sequence of events that take place when an SSH connection is made between hosts:

1. On StudentVM1 you enter the `ssh studentvm2` command.

2. The local host establishes an unencrypted TCP connection to the remote host.

3. The remote host responds with its own public key to the local host, which compares it to the one for that host in ~/.ssh/known_ hosts. This authenticates the remote host. It does not authenticate the user.

4. The two hosts negotiate the encryption algorithm to use and start it so that all further communications are performed through the encrypted channel.

5. The local host prompts the user for their password and sends it to the remote server over the encrypted channel.

6. The remote server verifies the password is correct and permits the login to proceed.

7. The remote host launches the user's default shell – usually Bash.

If no user is specified as a part of the ssh command in user@host format, the user ID issuing the command is assumed by SSH to be the user ID to connect with on the remote host.

As an alternative to using passwords, a public/private key pair (PPKP) could be used. The details of this will be covered later in this chapter. The PPKP may also use an arbitrarily long optional passphrase for an additional level of security.

SSH can multiplex many different concurrent channels over the single authenticated connection. This allows tunneling of login sessions and TCP forwarding so that other protocols, such as the X Window System, that are not normally encrypted can use this encrypted channel.

SSH today is normally implemented with OpenSSH.[1] Until September of 2000, SSH was encumbered with patents and other proprietary restrictions, but those all expired at that time. There are still commercial versions of SSH available, but there is no reason to use them on Linux. Fedora and at least some other distributions I have tried install both the client and server by default and allow root access by default.

Public/Private Key Pairs

PPKPs are used to enhance security by – mostly – removing the need for passwords to initiate SSH connections to a remote host. For the user, this is more secure because it eliminates the need to memorize and the temptation to write down long and complex but good passwords.

Each host already has a PPKP that was generated during first boot after install. Those key host pairs are stored in the /etc/ssh directory. The host's public key is swapped at the first SSH connection during the initial handshaking protocols. These host keys are used to positively identify the hosts to each other and are used to launch the initial encryption of the connection so that the authentication sequences are secure.

How PPKPs Work

Suppose that I want to send you encrypted messages that only you – and others with the public key – can read. I need to be able to encrypt it, and you need to be able to decrypt it. Cryptology texts are full of ways to do this that involve various types of keys and varying levels of security. Shared keys are fine until the key is compromised. I may not know that the key we share has been compromised and will keep sending messages that can be intercepted and read by the very people I might want to keep them from.

The use of public/private key pairs resolves this problem in a very elegant and secure manner. The key (if you will pardon the pun) is that the public key is the only one that can decrypt messages encrypted by the private key and the private key is the only one that can decrypt messages encrypted with the public key. I had to think about that for a few minutes when I first heard it:

---

[1]OpenSSH, www.openssh.com.

1. Create a public/private key pair.

2. Send the public key to the remote computer, which will be decrypting my messages and encrypting the reply messages back to me.

3. Encrypt messages with the private key and send them to the remote computer.

4. The encrypted message is decrypted by the remote computer using the public key.

5. To respond, the remote computer encrypts the message using the public key from my host and sends it to my host.

6. The message encrypted by the public key is decrypted on the local host using the private key.

Of course these messages are the data contained in the TCP packets sent between the computers. This PPKP solution can also work for entire emails or other types of messages to keep them secure.

There are some interesting implications from all this. First, anyone who has the public key can decrypt the messages (data packets) that I send. Therefore, I can send my one public key to many different computers and then use SSH to connect to them all using the single private key. I do not need a separate set of keys for each computer.

Another inference that we can make is that anyone with the public key can send me messages. However, only I can initiate a conversation by using the private key. If another host wishes to initiate a conversation, they must create a PPKP and send a copy of their public key to me. So someone cannot just obtain a copy of my public key and then use it to initiate encrypted connections to my host computer.

I could send my public key to the user of the host on the other end in an email, and the user at that end could then append it to their ~/.ssh/authorized_keys file. However, there is a tool that I can use to install my public key on the remote host so long as I have the password of the user account with which I want to communicate. Therefore, without the cooperation of a friendly user at the remote host, or already having my own user account and password, I cannot just push my public key across the network and log into any random remote host.

This is all very nice and secure, which is, of course, the intention.

So I am limited to SSH connections to remote hosts on which I have an account and know the original password. This reduces to the student user (or the root user) having an account on both StudentVM1 and StudentVM2 and sending the public key from one host to another.

EXPERIMENT 45-2: GENERATING AND USING A PPKP

Perform this experiment as the student user on both StudentVM1 and StudentVM2 hosts.

On the StudentVM1 host as the student user, use the following command to create a public/private key pair. The -b 2048 option generates a key that is 2048 bits in length; the minimum allowable length is 1024 bits. By default it will generate an RSA key, but we could also specify other key types. RSA is considered to be very secure, so we will use RSA. We will press **Enter** to respond to all inquiries so as to take all of the defaults:

```
[student@studentvm1 ~]$ ssh-keygen -b 2048
Generating public/private rsa key pair.
Enter file in which to save the key (/home/student/.ssh/id_rsa): <Enter>
Enter passphrase (empty for no passphrase): <Enter>
Enter same passphrase again: <Enter>
Your identification has been saved in /home/student/.ssh/id_rsa.
Your public key has been saved in /home/student/.ssh/id_rsa.pub.
The key fingerprint is:
SHA256:y/y5kKXhcebO93iLg3XhOZGIqFBsEZSTXi3cdKh22fY student@studentvm1
The key's randomart image is:
+---[RSA 2048]----+
|      +=* =.o.. .|
|      . * = =.. o |
|      + + o o   o|
|       o o o o o.|
|        S * . o o|
|        + % . . E |
|        O . + o  |
|         o o o.o.|
|          +. .ooo|
+----[SHA256]-----+
[student@studentvm1 ~]$
```

The host key's fingerprint and/or the randomart image can be used to verify the validity of a public key for the host. It cannot be used to recreate the original public or private key, and it cannot be used for communication. It is used only to verify the validity of the key.

Now that we have generated our key pair, look again at the contents of the ~/.ssh directory for the student user on StudentVM1. You should see two new files, id_rsa, which is the private key, and id_rsa.pub, which is the public key. The .pub extension kind of gives that away.

These days it is not necessary to send our public keys via email or other off-network types of delivery. We have a nice tool for that. Do this as the student user on StudentVM1:

```
[student@studentvm1 ~]$ ssh-copy-id studentvm2
/usr/bin/ssh-copy-id: INFO: Source of key(s) to be installed: "/home/
student/.ssh/id_rsa.pub"
The authenticity of host 'studentvm2 (10.0.2.11)' can't be established.
ECDSA key fingerprint is SHA256:NDM/B5L3eRJaalex6IOUdnJsE1smOSiQNWgaI8BwcVs.
Are you sure you want to continue connecting (yes/no)? yes
/usr/bin/ssh-copy-id: INFO: attempting to log in with the new key(s), to
filter out any that are already installed
/usr/bin/ssh-copy-id: INFO: 1 key(s) remain to be installed -- if you are
prompted now it is to install the new keys
Password: <Enter password of the user on the remote host>
Running /home/student/.bashrc
Running /etc/bashrc

Number of key(s) added: 1

Now try logging into the machine, with:    "ssh 'studentvm2'"
and check to make sure that only the key(s) you wanted were added.
```

As the student user on StudentVM1, open a terminal session and ssh to StudentVM2. Verify that you are logged into the StudentVM2 host.

You should do some simple tests on the remote host like listing files and so on. Let's copy a file from StudentVM1 to StudentVM2.

As the student user on StudentVM1, open a new terminal session if necessary. If you did the experiments in Volume 1 of this course, there should be several files and directories in the student user's home directory, one of which should be random.txt. If you do not have this file, create it:

```
[student@studentvm1 ~]$ dd if=/dev/urandom of=random.txt bs=512 count=500
500+0 records in
500+0 records out
256000 bytes (256 kB, 250 KiB) copied, 0.00304606 s, 84.0 MB/s
[student@studentvm1 ~]$ ll rand*
-rw-rw-r-- 1 student student 256000 Jun 18 14:50 random.txt
```

Now we can copy this file to the remote host. We use ~, which expands to the home directory of the student user on the remote host. We could also have used `pwd` to specify the PWD, which just happens to be the student user's home directory at this moment:

```
[student@studentvm1 ~]$ scp random.txt studentvm2:~
[student@studentvm1 ~]$
```

Use the terminal session on StudentVM1 that is logged into the student user on StudentVM2 by SSH to verify that the file has been copied to StudentVM2. There is a possibility that it has not been copied. If the random.txt file is not present in the student user's home directory on StudentVM2, it is likely the unintended consequence of the echo statements we added to various Bash configuration files. Even if you did not encounter this problem, be aware that disruption of the expected protocol stream by added comments like this can cause SSH and Secure CoPy (SCP) to fail without an error.

To fix this, locate and edit all of the Bash configuration files for root and the student user. Comment out the echo statements that indicate the name of the running scripts. Do this on both hosts:

1. ~/.bashrc

2. ~/.bash_profile

3. /etc/bashrc

4. /etc/profile

5. /etc/profile.d/myBashConfig.sh

Then try the copy again. It should work now. Be sure to verify. Now exit the SSH session from StudentVM1 to StudentVM2, if it is still open:

```
[student@studentvm2 ~]$ exit
logout
Connection to studentvm2 closed.
[student@studentvm1 ~]$
```

Create a PPKP for the root user on StudentVM1 and copy the public key to StudentVM2. Also create PPKPs for both the root and student users on the StudentVM2 host and copy them to StudentVM1. This sets up a situation where users can SSH easily from one host to another.

Now, as the student user on StudentVM2, copy your public key to the student1 account on the StudentVM1 host. That account should already exist; create it if it does not. Now SSH from student on StudentVM2 to student1 on StudentVM1. Notice that the key fingerprint here matches that of the key we saw previously because this is the fingerprint of the host key for the StudentVM1 host and not the fingerprint of the user key:

```
[student@studentvm2 ~]$ ssh-copy-id student1@studentvm1
/usr/bin/ssh-copy-id: INFO: Source of key(s) to be installed: "/home/
student/.ssh/id_rsa.pub"
The authenticity of host 'studentvm1 (192.168.0.181)' can't be established.
ECDSA key fingerprint is SHA256:NDM/B5L3eRJaalex6IOUdnJsE1smOSiQNWgaI8BwcVs.
Are you sure you want to continue connecting (yes/no)? yes
/usr/bin/ssh-copy-id: INFO: attempting to log in with the new key(s), to
filter out any that are already installed
/usr/bin/ssh-copy-id: INFO: 1 key(s) remain to be installed -- if you are
prompted now it is to install the new keys
student1@studentvm1's password: <Enter password for student1 on StudentVM1>

Number of key(s) added: 1

Now try logging into the machine, with:   "ssh 'student1@studentvm1'"
and check to make sure that only the key(s) you wanted were added.

[student@studentvm2 ~]$
```

Now SSH from the student account on StudentVM2 to the student1 account on StudentVM1. Run a couple simple tests to verify the host and user account ID. Then exit from the SSH connection:

```
[student@studentvm2 ~]$ ssh student1@studentvm1
Last login: Thu May 30 14:39:56 2019 from 10.0.2.11
[student1@studentvm1 ~]$ pwd
/home/student1
[student1@studentvm1 ~]$ hostname
studentvm1
[student1@studentvm1 ~]$ whoami
student1 pts/4       2019-06-20 08:12 (192.168.0.182)
[student1@studentvm1 ~]$ exit
```

Even without a passphrase, using a PPKP is more secure than a basic SSH connection using a password.

X-Forwarding

We now have SSH working and tested, so there's more fun stuff ahead. Let's start by running a GUI program on the remote host with the display of the program's window on the local host. Most GUI desktop systems use the Wayland[2] windowing system or the X Window System,[3] a.k.a. X, as their underlying windowing engines. X-forwarding works in either event because they both use the same protocols.

EXPERIMENT 45-3: USING REMOTE GUI PROGRAMS VIA X-FORWARDING

Perform this experiment as the student user on the StudentVM1 host.

First, ssh from StudentVM1 to StudentVM2 using the -X (uppercase) option to specify the use of X-forwarding. If you see a message regarding the Xauthority file, it is normal at this stage, and the file will be created if necessary:

---

[2]Wikipedia, Wayland, https://en.wikipedia.org/wiki/Wayland_(display_server_protocol)
[3]Wikipedia, X Window System, https://en.wikipedia.org/wiki/X_Window_System

```
[student@studentvm1 ~]$ ssh -X studentvm2
Last login: Wed Jun 19 08:31:28 2019 from 10.0.2.21
/usr/bin/xauth:   file /home/student/.Xauthority does not exist
[student@studentvm2 ~]$ thunar &
[1] 2683
[student@studentvm2 ~]$
```

The result of this is shown Figure 45-1 as a screen capture of the StudentVM1 host desktop. It shows the effects of using X-forwarding via SSH to display the Thunar file manager running on StudentVM2 on the desktop of StudentVM1. Navigate around the directory structure on StudentVM2 for a bit.

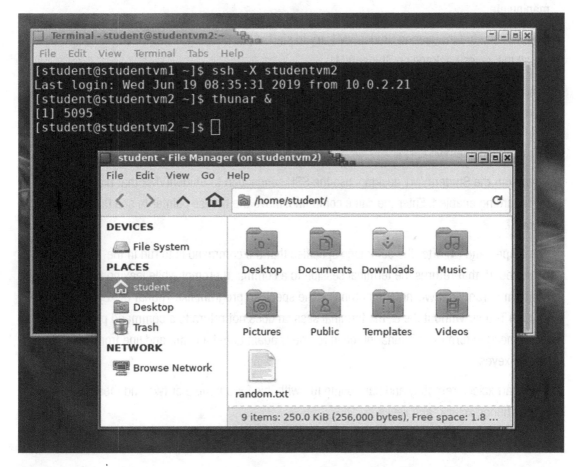

Figure 45-1. *Using X-forwarding via SSH to display the Thunar file manager running on StudentVM2 in a window on the desktop of StudentVM1*

Now install some fun and interesting Xorg programs. As root on StudentVM2, install the xeyes (X eyes) and xclock packages on StudentVM2 but not StudentVM1:

```
[root@studentvm2 ~]# dnf -y install xeyes xclock
```

As the student user on StudentVM2, try out the xeyes program:

```
[student@studentvm2 ~]$ xeyes &
[1] 23848
[student@studentvm2 ~]$
```

Kill this instance of xeyes using the window buttons at the top of the Xfce desktop. The xeyes program must be moved or closed from the application bar because it has no window frame to manipulate.

Now, as the student user on StudentVM1, try to start xeyes (X eyes). It fails because we did not install the xeyes package on StudentVM1:

```
[student@studentvm1 ~]$ xeyes &
-bash: xeyes: command not found
[1]+  Exit 127                xeyes
[student@studentvm1 ~]$
```

Now, from the StudentVM1 desktop, use the SSH connection to StudentVM2 that has X-forwarding enabled. Enter the same command. Move the mouse pointer to see the eyes follow it.

The ampersand (&) after the command specifies that the command is to run in the background; that returns the terminal session to a command prompt while leaving the GUI program to run. That will not affect running the specified program like Thunar or xeyes, but if you run Thunar without the &, the terminal session does not return to a command prompt. You would need to terminate Thunar or log in remotely again to get a command line from which to launch xeyes.

Now start xclock remotely and have some fun with this for a minute or two and then close down Thunar, xclock, and xeyes.

This capability can be both fun and useful.

The X Window System

Because X-forwarding over SSH is a client/server type of operation, let's look at the details a little more closely.

Tip   Although some people call it X Windows or X-Windows, to be technically and legally correct, it should be called the "X Window System" or just "X."

It seems pretty clear that a standard SSH connection takes place from the client on the local host to a server on the remote host. We have, in fact, done that over the course of these experiments. But is that also true of X-forwarding over SSH?

To understand this we need to know more about the X Window System.[4] Wikipedia has a rather old article describing the X Window System and some of its history. The short version is that the X Window System is a windowing system for Unix-like operating systems such as Linux. X does not do anything other than provide the primitive graphical tools to create and manipulate windows and objects on a bit-mapped display. It does not impose any aspect of the user interface such as how it looks or how users and application programs can interact with it.

The X Window System uses a client-server model, which separates the applications and their requests from the server functions that fulfill those requests. This allows X to be versatile and creates the basis for X-forwarding. However, it is necessary to think about the client-server model from the perspective of the application rather than of the user, which is how we normally think of it. Let's do this thinking about the way we did it in Experiment 45-3 where we used SSH from the local host, StudentVM1, to connect to the remote host, StudentVM2, and then started applications running on StudentVM2 with the applications' windows displayed on StudentVM1:

1.   We use the mouse on StudentVM1 to select a folder in Thunar.

2.   Thunar, running on StudentVM2, opens the folder and generates a series of graphical commands that cause the redrawing of the Thunar window. This is a client request to the X server.

---

[4]Wikipedia, X Window System, https://en.wikipedia.org/wiki/X_Window_System

3. Those commands are sent to StudentVM1 where the X server translates them into the new images in the Thunar window. This is the X server fulfilling the request from the client.

Most of the time, the server and the client are located on the same host, but they can be located on different hosts as seen in the preceding experiment. This is only possible because the client and server functions are separate.

Remote Commands

Although using SSH to perform remote commands may sound like logging into a remote computer using SSH and then typing in commands on the remote Bash shell, there is a significant difference. And that little difference is what makes SSH such a powerful tool. Let's start with a simple task like checking the contents of a directory on the remote host.

EXPERIMENT 45-4: EXPLORING REMOTE COMMANDS

Perform this experiment as the student user on StudentVM1. Our objective is to determine the contents of the student user's home directory on the remote host.

As the student user on the StudentVM1 host, run the following command. This can only be accomplished without using a password if a PPKP is in place.

The quotes are used to delimit the command being sent to the remote host but can actually be dispensed with for simple commands like this. For more complex commands, such as we will see further along in this experiment, they are quite useful and necessary:

```
[student@studentvm1 ~]$ ssh studentvm2 "ls -l"
total 284
drwxr-xr-x. 2 student student    4096 Dec 24 08:19 Desktop
drwxr-xr-x. 2 student student    4096 Dec 22 13:15 Documents
drwxr-xr-x. 2 student student    4096 Dec 22 13:15 Downloads
drwxr-xr-x. 2 student student    4096 Dec 22 13:15 Music
drwxr-xr-x. 2 student student    4096 Dec 22 13:15 Pictures
drwxr-xr-x. 2 student student    4096 Dec 22 13:15 Public
```

```
-rw-rw-r--. 1 student student 256000 Jun 19 08:16 random.txt
drwxr-xr-x. 2 student student   4096 Dec 22 13:15 Templates
drwxr-xr-x. 2 student student   4096 Dec 22 13:15 Videos
```

Now a bit more fun with this:

```
[student@studentvm1 ~]$ ssh studentvm2 "cp random.txt textfile.txt ; ls -l"
total 536
drwxr-xr-x. 2 student student   4096 Dec 24 08:19 Desktop
drwxr-xr-x. 2 student student   4096 Dec 22 13:15 Documents
drwxr-xr-x. 2 student student   4096 Dec 22 13:15 Downloads
drwxr-xr-x. 2 student student   4096 Dec 22 13:15 Music
drwxr-xr-x. 2 student student   4096 Dec 22 13:15 Pictures
drwxr-xr-x. 2 student student   4096 Dec 22 13:15 Public
-rw-rw-r--. 1 student student 256000 Jun 19 08:16 random.txt
drwxr-xr-x. 2 student student   4096 Dec 22 13:15 Templates
-rw-rw-r--. 1 student student 256000 Jun 20 08:22 textfile.txt
drwxr-xr-x. 2 student student   4096 Dec 22 13:15 Videos
[student@studentvm1 ~]$
```

So that works as we expect. But try the same command without quotes. You will see that the remote command ends at the semicolon that the local shell uses to delimit the final command. The quotes are required so that the shell can properly send the entire command to the remote host.

Tip Bash shell aliases such as the ll command are not available when using remote commands. So be careful when using scripts containing remote commands to not use command aliases.

Remote Backups

The term "remote backups" may be a bit misleading, even with what we now know about running commands remotely. For many years I used a script to perform backups on my main workstation and several remote hosts. I used remote commands to perform the remote backups to the local workstation.

Making backups of remote hosts is much easier than you might think.

EXPERIMENT 45-5: BACK UP A REMOTE HOST TO THE LOCAL HOST

Perform this experiment as the root user on StudentVM1. We start with the simple task
of creating a backup of the StudentVM2 remote host with the resulting backup stored on
StudentVM2. We will make a backup of /home, /root, and /etc and store the backup tarball in
studentvm2://tmp:

```
[root@studentvm1 ~]# ssh studentvm2 "tar -cvf /tmp/studentvm2.tgz /home /etc
/root ; ls -l /tmp "
```

Now verify that the tarball /tmp/studentvm2.tgz contains the files we expect. But do it from
StudentVM1.

Now let's look at something and try to make a bit of sense from it:

```
[root@studentvm1 ~]# ssh studentvm2 "tar -c /home /etc /root"
```

Do you see what happened? The data stream from the tar command that was executed on the
remote host, StudentVM2, is sent across the SSH connection to the standard out (STDOUT) of
the terminal session on the local host, StudentVM1. So now we have the data stream from a
remote host here on our local host just waiting to be piped or redirected – on our local host.

Got it yet? Note where we place the closing quote in this simple command-line program:

```
[root@studentvm1 ~]# ssh studentvm2 "tar -cz /home /etc /root" > /tmp/
studentvm2.tgz ; ls -l /tmp
tar: Removing leading `/' from member names
tar: Removing leading `/' from hard link targets
total 287352
<snip>
-rw-r--r--  1 root     root      6259259 Jun 20 08:57 studentvm2.tgz
<snip>
```

We used an SSH tunnel with a remote tar command to create a stream consisting of the backup data from the remote host. That data stream is sent across the SSH tunnel to STDOUT on the local host where it can be used with other commands through pipes or redirected to a file.

We have now performed a backup of a remote host and stored the backup file on the local host, all with a simple command-line program.

Once I had created an easy and elegant method for creating backups of remote hosts using **tar** and SSH, the next step for me was to create a script that would perform that same backup on several hosts and then set up a cron job or a systemd timer to do those backups every night.

Chapter Summary

SSH uses two levels of authentication: first, authenticating the hosts themselves and then user authentication. It encrypts the entire session including the authentication and all of the data transmission. SSH is very secure and can be used to transmit data securely over public networks.

SSH features such as remote command execution and data stream transmission over the encrypted connection enable powerful solutions for things like backups using simple tools like **tar**. SSH also provides X-forwarding so that we can run graphical programs on the remote host with their windows on our local host.

Exercises

Perform the following exercises to complete this chapter:

1. What are the permissions on the ~/.ssh/id_rsa file? Why?

2. What are the permissions on the ~/.ssh/id_rsa.pub file? Why?

3. The StudentVM1 host should have several user accounts including one named "student1." If it does not, create that account. As the student1 user on StudentVM1, create a PPKP and copy the public key to the student (*not* student1) account on StudentVM2. SSH to the student account on the StudentVM2 host.

4. You should already have created PPKPs for both root and the student user on both hosts, StudentVM1 and StudentVM2. Copy the public key of the student user on StudentVM1 to the root account of StudentVM2. As the student user on StudentVM1, SSH to root at StudentVM2.

5. Suppose you, as the student user, have created a PPKP and copied the public key to the remote host using your password. A few days or weeks later, as is the policy, you change the password on both the local and remote hosts. Can you still log into the remote host using the PPKP?

6. Write a Bash script on StudentVM1 to back up the /home, /root, and /etc of it and to also back up /home, /root, /etc, and /var of the StudentVM2 host.

7. After you have tested the backup script from the previous exercise, create a cron job or systemd timer to run the script every morning at 02:00 a.m.

8. When using X-forwarding over SSH, which host is the X server?

9. When using X-forwarding over SSH, which host is the X client?

10. Why does it take so much longer when you display the backup data stream than it does to create the backup file from it?

Nope! The answer is not in the text. You'll need to think about this one and perhaps devise some experiments to prove your hypothesis.

CHAPTER 46

Security

Objectives

In this chapter you will learn

- Advanced security tools and techniques
- How to enhance security for DNS using chroot
- To modify kernel parameters to enhance network security
- Advanced backup techniques
- The use of ClamAV to check for viruses
- To configure basic intrusion detection using Tripwire
- To detect root kits using Rootkit Hunter and chkrootkit
- To use SELinux to prevent crackers from modifying critical system files
- To describe the full scope of Linux security
- To identify and implement additional aspects of password security
- To use the firewalld firewall to manage access to the host on SSH and Telnet ports
- To use tcpdump to monitor the plain text data of a Telnet conversation
- To enable the SSHD server and use tcpdump to verify that the conversation is encrypted
- To describe Pluggable Authentication Modules (PAM) authentication
- To take some basic steps to improve security of any Linux host

© David Both 2023
D. Both, *Using and Administering Linux: Volume 3*, https://doi.org/10.1007/978-1-4842-9786-5_46

Introduction

The Linux operating system is intentionally designed to be a very secure operating system. It provides a secure environment in which to work and store files. However, good security by its very nature can be more than just a bit obtrusive. We have already had discussions about security in many sections of this course. This is because security must be an integral component of everything we do as SysAdmins. The security of our systems and the data on them must be a major consideration if not the prime consideration in everything we do.

Any device connected to the Internet is subject to attack, and no operating system, even Linux, is completely free of exploitable flaws. Linux just happens to be more secure than other operating systems and, when it is breached, is less vulnerable to widespread damage.

There are only four rules required to achieve complete and unbreakable security:

1. The computer must be locked in a blast-proof room to prevent both unauthorized physical access and destruction of the computer and its contents.

2. It must be inside a Faraday cage[1] to prevent its own radio frequency emissions from escaping to be captured by "the bad people." This would also protect the host against an EMP[2] blast but assumes a power source completely within the confines of the cage.

3. It must have a 100% air gap – that is, it must not be connected to any network and especially not to the Internet. This includes all hard-wired and wireless connections such as Wi-Fi, Bluetooth, infrared, and anything else that transmits data outside of the computer.

4. It must be turned off, and the rest of the rules don't count.

---

[1] Wikipedia, Faraday cage, https://en.wikipedia.org/wiki/Faraday_cage
[2] Electromagnetic Pulse. Wikipedia, https://en.wikipedia.org/wiki/Electromagnetic_pulse

Yes, that is a geek joke but only because of the truth embedded in it. Unfortunately, implementing these rules would mean the computer is unusable even for its intended purpose. That, in turn, means that any computer that is turned on is vulnerable to cracking. A cracker is the correct name for a hacker with evil intent. Hackers – the good people who hack, that is, work on, hardware and code – are the ones who gave us things like free and open source tools like Linux and the many applications that run on it. So we must use our computers in an imperfect and unsafe environment at all times.

Security is not an afterthought that is appended to the end of a book – it is something that must be considered as a part of all we do as SysAdmins. We have already enabled and used various types of security throughout this course. In this chapter we will look at some additional security considerations.

Security by Obscurity

Most computers are connected to the Internet through, first, a wireless or wired router and then the router/modem supplied by the Internet Service Provider, or ISP. This would seem to provide a couple layers of security and obscurity between the computer and the Internet. Our small office/home office (SOHO) or other small organization and personal home computers are definitely not too small or insignificant to attract the attention of the crackers. We cannot count on any amount of relative obscurity to protect us from the crackers just because there are surely more lucrative and much larger and important targets available.

In fact the worst assumption we can make is that some level of obscurity can protect our computers. Some small businesses I have worked with, including my own systems, are constantly subjected to attempts to crack into their firewall servers, hundreds of attempts per day and thousands per month. And that is *after* I have instituted measures to reduce the total number of attacks. Every computer and device that is connected to any network – and especially the Internet – is a target.

There are a number of measures that can be instituted to protect our computers, but they will never be impervious. And we must exercise care in the way we use the Web and deal with spam email.

There are some good websites with information on how to protect ourselves online. Although I cannot verify all of the information on them, there is one I especially like, Get Safe Online.[3] It even has a section on safe Linux use. They don't sell anything. They don't even require an account or for us to log in to access the information there.

What Is Security?

Security is about far more than simply preventing unwanted people from logging into our Linux computers. Although good passwords and other security measures are helpful and can help prevent that type of security vulnerability, they are the response to only one part of the security problem. There are many aspects to security, and it is important to understand that fact as well as to know the things that we are using various security protocols to protect.

So what are the things we are trying to protect? Not surprisingly, a large part of security is designed to protect our data but perhaps in ways and for reasons you have not previously considered.

Data Protection

There are three major considerations to data protection, and different tools and strategies apply to each:

First, we want to protect our data from loss in the sense that it needs to be available to us. We need to be able to have access to it. So this is about ensuring that the data will not be destroyed or lost so that it is no longer available. As a business owner, loss of my financial records in a fire or natural disaster would be a disaster for my company, and that might be impossible to recover from. This is about the accessibility of our data in order to ensure the continuity of our business.

Second, we want to protect our data from unauthorized access. We need to ensure that our company and personal data is not available to someone who might use it to steal our identity or to steal money from us. In the case of many organizations, that data might contain information that a competitor could use to gain advantage over us. This is about the confidentiality of our data.

---

[3] Get Safe Online, `https://www.getsafeonline.org/`

Third, we want to ensure that our data is safe from unauthorized changes or corruption, perhaps by malware or a disgruntled employee or one who is simply a thief. And we also want to ensure that we are not blocked from access to our own data by malware such as ransomware, which would encrypt the data and keep us from accessing it until the ransom is paid. This is about ensuring the integrity of our data.

It's not just about keeping the data safe, but knowing for a fact that the data was kept safe from espionage or destruction or corruption.

Security Vectors

Security attack and danger vectors are many and varied. These vectors are all classifiable into five major categories: self-inflicted, environmental, physical, network, and software vulnerabilities. Although we will list a number of common security vulnerabilities of different types, I have no intention of exploring all the responses to these problems here. There are some things that can be done, in addition to some of the obvious ones hinted at in this section, and we will explore those later in this chapter.

In case you have not figured it out yet, this is where I try to scare you enough to apply some common sense and freely available open source tools to improving the security of your Linux systems.

Self-Inflicted Problems

Self-inflicted data loss comes in many forms, the most common form being the semi-intentional erasure of one or more important files or directories.

Sometimes erasing needed files is accidental. I just erase a bunch of old files in a directory, and it turns out later that one or two are still needed. More often, for me at least, I actually look at the files and decide they are no longer needed. A day or two or a week after I delete them, it turns out that I still need at least some of the files I just deleted. I have also made significant changes to a file and saved it. Once again I find at some time later I made changes and especially deletions that I should not have. Clearly it is necessary to pay attention when deleting files or making changes to them. That still won't keep us from deleting data we may need later.

On other occasions I have been working on the back side of a computer rack and accidentally pulled the power plug – or plugs if there were redundant power supplies – from the wrong computer. Although storage devices and journaling filesystems can generally withstand a power loss, it still happens. In a somewhat less stringent environment than a data center, I have managed to accidentally kick a power cable out of the wall.

This category also includes things like using poor passwords that can be easily cracked and leaving a USB drive with critical data stored on it in an accessible location. Leaving a laptop unattended in a public place like a coffee shop and using unencrypted wireless links are also common points of data loss.

Environmental Problems

Environmental issues that can affect the security of computer systems are usually not considered as potential problems or at least are misunderstood by most people. When we use the word *environmental*, we tend to think in terms of electrical power backup units, cooling the data center so the computers will be cool, and so on. But there is so much more that many of us don't think about. I was fortunate that I learned about environmental issues early in my career at IBM.

Power failures can occur for many reasons. This includes momentary power failures that can shut down the computer just as irrevocably as longer ones. Regardless of the reason for the power failure, there is the danger of losing data especially from documents that have not been saved. Modern storage devices and filesystems employ strategies that help minimize the probabilities of data loss, but it still happens.

Grounding – actually the lack thereof or improper grounding – can be a serious issue. Good grounding is essential for the proper electronic operation and functional stability of computers.

Electromagnetic interference, EMI, is various types of electromagnetic radiation from many different sources. This radiation can interfere with the correct operation of any electronic device including computers. Lightning, static electricity, microwaves, old CRT displays, military radar systems, radio frequency bursts on a ground line – all of these and more can cause problems. Good grounding can reduce the effects of all of these types of EMI. But that does not make our computers completely immune to the effects of strong EMI fields.

Hard drive failures also cause data loss. The most common failures in today's computers are devices that have moving mechanical components. Leading the frequency list are cooling fans, and storage devices are a close second. Modern storage devices have SMART capabilities that enable predictive failure analysis. Linux can monitor these drives and send an email to root indicating that failure is imminent. Do not ignore those emails because replacing a hard drive before it fails is less trouble than replacing one after it fails and then hoping the backups are up to date.

Modern computers are well protected against many aspects of environmental problems. All we need to do is to ensure that we use battery backup units, which are also known as Uninterruptible Power Supplies (UPS), and that they are plugged into properly grounded outlets. Things can still happen, but this will minimize the possibilities.

Physical Attacks

Physical security is about protecting the hardware from various types of harm. Although we tend to think in terms of keeping bad people away from the hardware on which we run our systems, we also need to consider disaster scenarios as a major part of our planning.

Disgruntled employees can maliciously destroy data. Proper security procedures can mitigate this type of threat, but backups are still handy.

Common theft is also a way to lose data. Soon after we moved to Raleigh, NC, in 1993, there was a series of articles in the local paper and TV that covered the tribulations of a scientist at one of our better-known universities. This scientist kept all of his data on a single computer. He did have a backup – to another hard drive on that same computer. When the computer was stolen from his office, all of his experimental data went missing as well and, as far as I know, it was never recovered.

Natural disasters occur. Fire, flood, hurricanes, tornadoes, mud slides, tsunamis, and so many more kinds of disasters can destroy computers and locally stored backups as well. I can guarantee that, even if I have a good backup, I will never take the time during a fire, tornado, or natural disaster that places me in imminent danger to save the backups.

Back up everything – frequently. And keep the most recent backups someplace off-site. I store my backups in a safe deposit box at my credit union. If my home office is devastated by a disaster, I can rebuild from my backups.

Network Attacks

Attacks via networks, both local and the Internet, are common and can be extremely dangerous. These attacks can take many forms ranging from direct attacks from the Internet against firewalls and servers to indirect attacks in which malware is introduced into a host by some stealthy means such as hiding in a downloaded file, an email, or a click-bait link on a website.

This type of attack does not require direct physical access to your computers. Rather, they come through your connections to the outside world.

Scripted attacks are generally used by so-called script kiddies. This derogatory term is used because they are not usually smart or determined enough to create the attack scripts themselves so they purchase them from those who are – yes, that is a lucrative business. The scripts they use are simple brute-force remote login attempts. Their malicious attacks are useless against today's well-protected Linux hosts because most distributions are well hardened at installation and do not have the SSH server up and running, so this type of attack is fruitless when SSH is not available for a connection.

These attacks usually consist of automated dictionary probes against a large number of remote hosts, usually those on a specific network address range, rather than against a specific single host or organization.

Malware is a very generic term for software that can be used for various malicious purposes including destroying or deleting your data.

Ransomware is a specific form of malware that encrypts your data and holds it for ransom. If you pay the ransom, you may get the key that will allow you to decrypt your data – if you are lucky.

Drive-by malware is a malicious link in an apparently innocuous advertisement on an otherwise legitimate web page. You do not even need to click this link for your computer to be infected.

Targeted login attempts are aimed directly at you or your organization. These are like script kiddie attacks but with you as the main target. These attacks are usually carried out by someone or some group with a specific reason to target you. If someone targets you specifically and really wants to crack into your system, they will be able to do so, given enough time and even the smallest amount of carelessness on your part.

Always keep systems up to date so that the latest security patches are installed. Ensure that good firewalls are in place and properly configured. And check frequently for evidence of break-ins.

Software Vulnerabilities

Many attacks on connected computers are aided and abetted by vulnerabilities in the host's software. These vulnerabilities are exploited by the attackers and can be leveraged to install malware of various types. However, just because a vulnerability exists does not mean that an exploit is available to take advantage of it.

Always install the latest updates to ensure that the software is as secure as possible.

Linux and Security

So did that scare you? It should have.

But the good news is that Linux in general is very secure, and so is Fedora especially when SELinux is set to enforcing. Linux is very secure immediately upon installation. There are only a couple minor services running that do not need to run, but none provide external access from the Internet. The remaining ones can be easily turned off. Unneeded services can be an access point for a cracker. In our study of systemd, we turned off the pcscd service for this very reason.

Fedora has an excellent firewall in place, and the one service I use in all of my Linux hosts, the SSH server for secure logins to and from remote hosts, is configured only for outbound connections. The inbound SSHD server is disabled.

Login Security

Login security – ensuring that only authorized users have access to log in and use the system's resources – is the first line of defense. Generating and using secure passwords is the main tool we have to provide this security, whether a local or remote login. But it seems a bit silly for me to write an entire section on password security when the passwd(1) man page already has an excellent section on just that. So here it is, directly from the passwd man page:

Remember the following two principles

Protect your password.

Don't write down your password – memorize it. In particular, don't write it down and leave it anywhere, and don't place it in an unencrypted file! Use unrelated passwords for systems controlled by different organizations. Don't give or share your password, in particular to someone claiming to be from computer support or a vendor. Don't let anyone watch you enter your password. Don't enter your password to a computer you don't trust or if things "look funny"; someone may be trying to hijack your password. Use the password for a limited time and change it periodically.

Choose a hard-to-guess password.

passwd, through the calls to the pam_cracklib PAM module, will try to prevent you from choosing a really bad password, but it isn't foolproof; create your password wisely. Don't use something you'd find in a dictionary (in any language or jargon). Don't use a name (including that of a spouse, parent, child, pet, fantasy character, famous person, and location) or any variation of your personal or account name. Don't use accessible information about you (such as your phone number, license plate, or social security number) or your environment. Don't use a birthday or a simple pattern (such as "qwerty", "abc", or "aaa"). Don't use any of those backwards, followed by a digit, or preceded by a digit. Instead, use a mixture of upper and lower case letters, as well as digits or punctuation. When choosing a new password, make sure it's unrelated to any previous password. Use long passwords (say at least 8 characters long). You might use a word pair with punctuation inserted, a passphrase (an understandable sequence of words), or the first letter of each word in a passphrase.

We explored setting passwords and generating good ones in Chapter 40 of Volume 2, along with locking accounts to prevent any login access at all.

Checking Logins

Another tool we have is the list of user logins. This is made easy with the last and lastb commands, which prevent us from having to scan the /var/log/secure log files. The last command displays all successful logins.

The lastb command displays a list of failed logins. These can be your own or other users' failed logins due to fumble-fingers as I sometimes have, or it could be the result of an attack on your system.

EXPERIMENT 46-1: EXAMINING USER LOGINS

Perform this experiment as the root user on StudentVM1. The last command can be run by a non-root user, but lastb cannot.

Let's start with a view of successful logins. I have piped the result through the less command because this list can be very long and head truncates the data stream for me. You can do this both with and without piping it through less. The specifics of your data will be different from mine, but it should look very similar to this:

```
[root@studentvm1 ~]# last | less
student  tty1         :0                  Thu May 11 16:11    still logged in
student  :0                               Thu May 11 16:11    still logged in
student1 pts/7        192.168.0.1         Thu May 11 16:07 - 16:07  (00:00)
student1 tty1         :0                  Thu May 11 16:07 - 16:11  (00:04)
```

```
student1 :0                          Thu May 11 16:07 - 16:11  (00:04)
student1 pts/6       192.168.0.1     Thu May 11 16:06    still logged in
student1 pts/5       192.168.0.1     Thu May 11 16:06    still logged in
student1 tty2                        Thu May 11 15:39 - 15:39  (00:00)
student1 pts/5       192.168.0.1     Thu May 11 15:34 - 15:39  (00:04)
tuser5   pts/5       192.168.0.1     Thu May 11 08:41 - 08:41  (00:00)
student  pts/4       192.168.0.1     Wed May 10 10:23    still logged in
student  pts/5       192.168.0.1     Mon May  8 15:00 - 09:13 (1+18:12)
root     pts/5       192.168.0.1     Mon May  8 14:56 - 15:00  (00:04)
student  tty1        :0              Mon May  8 14:53 - 16:06 (3+01:13)
student  :0                          Mon May  8 14:53 - 16:06 (3+01:13)
root     pts/0       192.168.0.1     Mon May  8 08:11    still logged in
reboot   system boot 6.1.18-200.fc37. Mon May  8 04:10    still running
<snip>
[root@studentvm1 ~]#
```

Using journalctl we can see a number of reboots, the student and root logins, and whether they are still logged in or not. The login times and durations are also recorded here. We also looked previously at ways to list all of the system boots using journalctl:

```
[root@studentvm1 etc]# journalctl --list-boots
```

This information can be useful in a forensic investigation into who was logged in at the time a specific file was changed or accessed or some specific event took place. Experienced crackers can cover their tracks, but this information could still have some value, especially if you are looking for someone who is not an experienced cracker.

So now let's look at failed logins. You may not have had any, so this result will be empty as it is for my instance of StudentVM1:

```
[root@studentvm1 ~]# lastb

btmp begins Tue Jun  4 08:27:54 2019
```

So create a few bad logins. Using virtual console 2, try to log in as the users root, jhgd, !@#$%^, news, chrony, rpcuser, student, james, henry, and alice. Be sure to use completely random and bogus passwords. Look again at the list of failed logins:

```
[root@studentvm1 ~]# lastb
alice    tty2                        Fri May 12 09:14 - 09:14  (00:00)
henry    tty2                        Fri May 12 09:14 - 09:14  (00:00)
```

```
james     tty2                        Fri May 12 09:14 - 09:14  (00:00)
student   tty2                        Fri May 12 09:13 - 09:13  (00:00)
rpcuser   tty2                        Fri May 12 09:13 - 09:13  (00:00)
chrony    tty2                        Fri May 12 09:13 - 09:13  (00:00)
news      tty2                        Fri May 12 09:13 - 09:13  (00:00)
!@#$%^    tty2                        Fri May 12 09:13 - 09:13  (00:00)
jhgd      tty2                        Fri May 12 09:13 - 09:13  (00:00)
*[[2~*[[2~ tty2                       Fri May 12 09:12 - 09:12  (00:00)
root      tty2                        Fri May 12 09:12 - 09:12  (00:00)
root      tty2                        Fri May 12 09:12 - 09:12  (00:00)
tuser5    pts/4                       Thu May 11 08:38 - 08:38  (00:00)
tuser3    pts/4                       Wed May 10 10:23 - 10:23  (00:00)

btmp begins Wed May 10 10:23:22 2023
```

The list of failed logins shows the user account that the attempt was targeted at, if it exists. In the past, if the account did not exist, the account name would be shown as (Unknown). So it appears that this has been updated to show the actual user ID that was used for the attempted login. This is more helpful.

Now let's look at a small bit of the `lastb` data stream from my firewall system. I use a Linux host as a firewall and router. These login attempts are via the Internet over SSH. I use SSH to remotely log into my network through this firewall, so I have the SSHD server running and accepting connections.

The leftmost column of this output shows the user account name that the attack targeted. The second column shows the attack against SSH, and "notty" means the no tty was assigned. Column 3 is the IP address from which the attack generated, although that can be spoofed. The rest of the columns list the date and time the attack occurred. The "(00:00)" (MM:SS) column just means that the connection did not get made:

```
karika    ssh:notty   91.134.241.32     Tue Jun  4 08:12 - 08:12  (00:00)
karika    ssh:notty   91.134.241.32     Tue Jun  4 08:12 - 08:12  (00:00)
gfa       ssh:notty   79.6.34.129       Tue Jun  4 08:11 - 08:11  (00:00)
gfa       ssh:notty   79.6.34.129       Tue Jun  4 08:11 - 08:11  (00:00)
mjestel   ssh:notty   91.134.241.32     Tue Jun  4 08:09 - 08:09  (00:00)
mjestel   ssh:notty   91.134.241.32     Tue Jun  4 08:09 - 08:09  (00:00)
redmine   ssh:notty   128.199.170.177   Tue Jun  4 08:09 - 08:09  (00:00)
redmine   ssh:notty   128.199.170.177   Tue Jun  4 08:09 - 08:09  (00:00)
cow       ssh:notty   79.6.34.129       Tue Jun  4 08:08 - 08:08  (00:00)
```

```
cow       ssh:notty    79.6.34.129      Tue Jun  4 08:08 - 08:08  (00:00)
alberta   ssh:notty    51.75.124.76     Tue Jun  4 08:08 - 08:08  (00:00)
alberta   ssh:notty    51.75.124.76     Tue Jun  4 08:08 - 08:08  (00:00)
<snip>
ec2-user  ssh:notty    181.114.209.13   Sat Jun  1 00:23 - 00:23  (00:00)
ec2-user  ssh:notty    181.114.209.13   Sat Jun  1 00:23 - 00:23  (00:00)
!@#$%^    ssh:notty    180.76.108.110   Sat Jun  1 00:22 - 00:22  (00:00)
!@#$%^    ssh:notty    180.76.108.110   Sat Jun  1 00:22 - 00:22  (00:00)
performe  ssh:notty    180.76.108.110   Sat Jun  1 00:19 - 00:19  (00:00)
performe  ssh:notty    180.76.108.110   Sat Jun  1 00:19 - 00:19  (00:00)
zhuang    ssh:notty    129.204.46.170   Sat Jun  1 00:18 - 00:18  (00:00)
zhuang    ssh:notty    129.204.46.170   Sat Jun  1 00:18 - 00:18  (00:00)
usp       ssh:notty    181.114.209.13   Sat Jun  1 00:16 - 00:16  (00:00)
usp       ssh:notty    181.114.209.13   Sat Jun  1 00:16 - 00:16  (00:00)
geminroo  ssh:notty    140.143.93.31    Sat Jun  1 00:16 - 00:16  (00:00)
geminroo  ssh:notty    140.143.93.31    Sat Jun  1 00:16 - 00:16  (00:00)
trinity   ssh:notty    218.75.102.110   Sat Jun  1 00:12 - 00:12  (00:00)
trinity   ssh:notty    218.75.102.110   Sat Jun  1 00:12 - 00:12  (00:00)
fv        ssh:notty    140.143.93.31    Sat Jun  1 00:12 - 00:12  (00:00)
fv        ssh:notty    140.143.93.31    Sat Jun  1 00:12 - 00:12  (00:00)
script    ssh:notty    129.204.46.170   Sat Jun  1 00:12 - 00:12  (00:00)
script    ssh:notty    129.204.46.170   Sat Jun  1 00:12 - 00:12  (00:00)
mongo     ssh:notty    5.39.88.4        Sat Jun  1 00:11 - 00:11  (00:00)
mongo     ssh:notty    5.39.88.4        Sat Jun  1 00:11 - 00:11  (00:00)
zi        ssh:notty    5.39.88.4        Sat Jun  1 00:08 - 00:08  (00:00)
zi        ssh:notty    5.39.88.4        Sat Jun  1 00:08 - 00:08  (00:00)

btmp begins Sat Jun  1 00:08:40 2019
```

This output had 4600 lines in it and the last two do not count. There are 4598 lines of failed login attempts. Look at the dates. These data run from midnight on June 1 of 2019 through 08:12 a.m. of June 4. So we have almost 4600 failed login attempts in three days and a bit over eight hours.

Note the different and sometimes strange user account names used in the attacks. Some are those belonging to Linux system services, some are apparently legitimate user account names, but others are clearly random and concocted. I particularly like !@#$%^, which consists of the special characters above the 1, 2, 3, 4, 5, and 6 keys on the US keyboard. "Cow" is also kind of strange.

The full results from my firewall host in Experiment 46-1 show only some of the many failed login attempts against my firewall. That is only partially because I snipped most of them out of what you see here. It is also because after four failed attempts logged from any single IP address within a period of 24 minutes (1440 seconds), I block any further attempts from that IP for 24 minutes. Any connection attempts from blocked IP addresses do not even get logged; they just get dropped. I use an open source tool called Fail2Ban for this, and we will explore SSH and firewalls and Fail2Ban in the next sections.

The point here is that there are constant and large numbers of attacks against every host connected to the Internet.

Before we go further, however, we need a tool that will let us explore TCP packets and their contents. The tcpdump utility allows us to do that and it is already installed.

EXPERIMENT 46-2: GETTING STARTED WITH TCPDUMP

Perform this experiment as the root user on StudentVM1. Let's start with a bit of preparation. Previous experiments may have launched some network connections that have not been dropped, and we want to start this experiment with as few connections as possible. So reboot StudentVM1.

The nmcli command displays the IP address of the default gateway router. Do this in a terminal session as root. Your default route should be the same as mine, 10.0.2.1, but there is a possibility that it might be different. Regardless, the IP address of the router is given on the "route4 default via" line of the results:

```
[root@studentvm1 ~]# nmcli
enp0s3: connected to enp0s3
        "Intel 82540EM"
        ethernet (e1000), 08:00:27:01:7D:AD, hw, mtu 1500
        ip4 default
        inet4 10.0.2.25/24
        route4 10.0.2.0/24 metric 100
        route4 default via 10.0.2.1 metric 100
        inet6 fe80::a00:27ff:fe01:7dad/64
        route6 fe80::/64 metric 256
<SNIP>
```

Now dump off the headers of all the packets on the enp0s3 interface. The headers tell us what kind of packet it is and a bit of other information about the packet. The source and destination IP addresses that are contained in the packet are also displayed.

In another terminal session as root, start `tcpdump`. The -i option specifies the interface we want to view. Without the -i option, tcpdump will display packets from all interfaces including lo; specifying an interface makes it easier for us to see the packets we want:

```
[root@studentvm1 ~]# tcpdump -i enp0s3
dropped privs to tcpdump
tcpdump: verbose output suppressed, use -v[v]... for full protocol decode
listening on enp0s3, link-type EN10MB (Ethernet), snapshot length
262144 bytes
```

At this point you should see only those couple lines to indicate that `tcpdump` is listening on enp0s3. Be sure to have the terminal session with `tcpdump` running in a location where you can see it. Now let's generate a bit of traffic in a different terminal session as root:

```
[root@studentvm1 ~]# ping example.com
10:28:12.769418 IP 65-100-46-166.dia.static.qwest.net.hostmon >
studentvm1.41180: Flags [R.], seq 50723, ack 1007603219, win 32768, length 0
10:28:12.808906 IP _gateway.domain > studentvm1.38712: 18353 1/0/1 PTR
65-100-46-166.dia.static.qwest.net. (103)
10:28:17.487485 ARP, Request who-has _gateway tell studentvm1, length 28
10:28:17.488036 ARP, Reply _gateway is-at 52:54:00:12:35:00 (oui Unknown),
length 46
10:28:19.072789 IP studentvm1.50844 > _gateway.domain: 49976+ [1au] AAAA?
example.com. (40)
10:28:19.072932 IP studentvm1.33662 > _gateway.domain: 12950+ [1au] A?
example.com. (40)
10:28:19.074117 IP _gateway.domain > studentvm1.50844: 49976 1/0/1 AAAA 260
6:2800:220:1:248:1893:25c8:1946 (68)
10:28:19.074118 IP _gateway.domain > studentvm1.33662: 12950 1/0/1 A
93.184.216.34 (56)
10:28:19.074275 IP studentvm1 > 93.184.216.34: ICMP echo request, id 2, seq
1, length 64
10:28:19.088307 IP 93.184.216.34 > studentvm1: ICMP echo reply, id 2, seq 1,
length 64
```

```
10:28:19.412052 IP studentvm1.38152 > 93.184.216.34.hostmon: Flags [S],
seq 2365494104, win 64240, options [mss 1460,sackOK,TS val 3862231212 ecr
0,nop,wscale 7,tfo  cookiereq,nop,nop], length 0
10:28:19.412202 IP studentvm1.38158 > 93.184.216.34.hostmon: Flags [S],
seq 2120284674, win 64240, options [mss 1460,sackOK,TS val 3862231212 ecr
0,nop,wscale 7,tfo  cookiereq,nop,nop], length 0
10:28:20.431504 IP studentvm1.38158 > 93.184.216.34.hostmon: Flags [S],
seq 2120284674, win 64240, options [mss 1460,sackOK,TS val 3862232231 ecr
0,nop,wscale 7], length 0
10:28:20.431568 IP studentvm1.38152 > 93.184.216.34.hostmon: Flags [S],
seq 2365494104, win 64240, options [mss 1460,sackOK,TS val 3862232231 ecr
0,nop,wscale 7], length 0
10:28:20.686353 IP studentvm1 > 93.184.216.34: ICMP echo request, id 2, seq
2, length 64
10:28:20.700589 IP 93.184.216.34 > studentvm1: ICMP echo reply, id 2, seq 2,
length 64
<snip>
```

First, the network client looks for the name server for the domain; in this case, that's the virtual router. Then we see an ARP[4] request that indicates that our host is looking for the MAC address of the router and the corresponding response. This is those two devices making their layer 1 physical connection. It is a request to the router, using the router's known IP address, that seeks the MAC address of the router, and it also sends the MAC address for the enp0s3 NIC. The router then responds with a message targeted to the MAC address of enp0s3 on the studentvm1 host. This is the layer at which hosts actually communicate with each other when they are on the same physical (or virtual) network segment.

After that, there are several ping (ICMP[5]) requests from StudentVM1 and the corresponding responses from the router.

---

[4] ARP, Address Resolution Protocol, is a protocol that enables discovery of the MAC (hardware) address of a network interface on a remote host using the host's IP address.

[5] ICMP, according to the Free On-line Dictionary of Computing (FOLDOC), is an extension to the Internet Protocol (IP) that allows for the generation of error messages, test packets, and informational messages related to IP. It is defined in STD 5, RFC 792.

Terminate the ping events with Ctrl+C and continue to watch the data stream for several minutes. You will eventually see some additional traffic, which should mostly be NTP traffic and related ARP traffic. You may also see some DHCP traffic when the IP address given to the studentvm1 host expires and it requests a new lease from the DHCP server.

This is a very basic introduction to a powerful and complex tool. All we have seen so far are the packet headers – information about the packets – not the contents of the packets. Exit `tcpdump` with Ctrl+C.

Opensource.com has an excellent introductory article[6] about `tcpdump` on their website. There are any number of tools, both CLI and GUI, as well as free open source and for a fee commercial, that provide many or all of these functions. The `tcpdump` tool is free and open source and has been around for a long time.

Now we'll install Telnet and the Telnet server.

Tip   The xinetd package was used to manage a number of older server types, including Telnet. It is not required on most modern Linux hosts. It was configured with a main file, /etc/xinetd.conf, and with individual service files in the /etc/xinetd.d directory. xinetd is no longer even available to install, and the Telnet client is no longer installed by default on the Fedora spins I use including Xfce.

Telnet

Telnet is an old and well-known terminal emulator that provides an easy way to connect to remote hosts. Telnet was developed in a time before the advent of the Internet for everyone, when the only Internet was the Arpanet connecting large universities with each other and the Department of Defense (DOD). There were few connections and everyone was collaborative. There was no malware and it was a safe place.

---

[6] Ricardo Gerardi, "An introduction to using tcpdump at the Linux command line," `https://opensource.com/article/18/10/introduction-tcpdump`

As a result, Telnet was not developed with security as a prime consideration. All communications between hosts were in plain ASCII text with no encryption – including the user ID and password. As the Internet grew and the cast of players on the dark side also grew, this lack of security became a problem.

However, a short exploration of Telnet can provide some interesting insight into how easily anyone with just a bit of knowledge can eavesdrop on an unencrypted connection, such as the typical wireless connections in public places that do not require passwords.

EXPERIMENT 46-3: INSTALL THE TELNET CLIENT AND SERVER

Perform this experiment as root on StudentVM1. We will install telnet and the telnet-server packages:

```
[root@studentvm1 etc]# dnf -y install telnet telnet-server
```

Since xinetd is no longer in use, Telnet and many other services that used xinetd now open sockets to listen on their appropriate ports for incoming connections. You can think of a socket as an automated switchboard waiting for a call to come in on its special number. In the case of Telnet, that number is 23. The socket then activates the Telnet service so that the conversation can begin.[7]

Activate the Telnet socket:

```
[root@studentvm1 ~]# systemctl enable --now telnet.socket
```

How do we know the port number? The /etc/services file contains a listing of all assigned and commonly recognized ports and the services assigned to them:

```
[root@studentvm1 ~]# grep -i telnet /etc/services
telnet          23/tcp
telnet          23/udp
rtelnet         107/tcp                    # Remote Telnet
rtelnet         107/udp
telnets         992/tcp
```

---

[7] Note that this sequence of events is very similar to that of the old xinetd server function.

```
telnets           992/udp
su-mit-tg         89/tcp                    # SU/MIT Telnet Gateway
su-mit-tg         89/udp                    # SU/MIT Telnet Gateway
<SNIP>
```

The data stream from this command shows many Telnet variants, many dating from early days of computer communications. We want the first one, plain Telnet, which is port 23.

We need to allow Telnet through our firewall. This command adds Telnet to the firewall permanently. We don't really need the port number, although it is a good idea to know what services use which ports.[8] firewalld allows us to simply specify the service name:

```
[root@studentvm1 ~]# firewall-cmd --permanent --add-service=telnet
success
```

Check the firewall status:

```
[root@studentvm1 ~]# firewall-cmd --list-services --zone=public
dhcpv6-client mdns ssh telnet
[root@studentvm1 ~]#
```

StudentVM1 is now ready for testing tcpdump using Telnet.

We are now ready to explore Telnet.

EXPERIMENT 46-4: USING TCPDUMP

Perform this experiment as root. In one root terminal session that should remain visible on the desktop for the rest of this experiment, start tcpdump and monitor the lo (local) interface for Telnet communications on port 23. Start a Telnet session with the localhost:

```
[root@studentvm1 ~]# telnet localhost
Trying ::1...
Connected to localhost.
Escape character is '^]'.
```

---

[8] Wikipedia, List of TCP and UDP port numbers, https://en.wikipedia.org/wiki/
List_of_TCP_and_UDP_port_numbers

```
Kernel 5.0.7-200.fc29.x86_64 on an x86_64 (7)
studentvm1 login: root
Password: <enter the root password>
Last login: Mon Jun 10 21:33:49 from 192.168.0.1
[root@studentvm1 ~]#
```

The tcpdump terminal session should now contain a data stream that looks similar to this. I have only reproduced a few lines here to save space:

```
tcpdump: verbose output suppressed, use -v or -vv for full protocol decode
listening on lo, link-type EN10MB (Ethernet), capture size 262144 bytes
14:02:59.472466 IP6 localhost.39640 > localhost.telnet: Flags [S], seq
612902319, win 65476, options [mss 65476,sackOK,TS val 1287054799 ecr
0,nop,wscale 7], length 0
14:02:59.472496 IP6 localhost.telnet > localhost.39640: Flags [S.], seq
3258934320, ack 612902320, win 65464, options [mss 65476,sackOK,TS val
1287054799 ecr 1287054799,nop,wscale 7], length 0
14:02:59.472512 IP6 localhost.39640 > localhost.telnet: Flags [.], ack 1, win
512, options [nop,nop,TS val 1287054799 ecr 1287054799], length 0
14:02:59.473651 IP6 localhost.39640 > localhost.telnet: Flags [P.], seq 1:25,
ack 1, win 512, options [nop,nop,TS val 1287054800 ecr 1287054799], length
24 [telnet DO SUPPRESS GO AHEAD, WILL TERMINAL TYPE, WILL NAWS, WILL TSPEED,
WILL LFLOW, WILL LINEMODE, WILL NEW-ENVIRON, DO STATUS [|telnet]
14:02:59.473674 IP6 localhost.telnet > localhost.39640: Flags [.], ack 25,
win 512, options [nop,nop,TS val 1287054800 ecr 1287054800], length 0
14:02:59.478708 IP6 localhost.telnet > localhost.39640: Flags [P.], seq 1:13,
ack 25, win 512, options [nop,nop,TS val 1287054805 ecr 1287054800], length
12 [telnet DO TERMINAL TYPE, DO TSPEED, DO XDISPLOC, DO NEW-ENVIRON [|telnet]
14:02:59.478736 IP6 localhost.39640 > localhost.telnet: Flags [.], ack 13,
win 512, options [nop,nop,TS val 1287054805 ecr 1287054805], length 0
```

Now run the **ll** command while watching the tcpdump data stream.

So far, we have only looked at the packet headers for this Telnet session. Terminate the tcpdump command and restart it using the -A option, which dumps the data contents of the packets in ASCII format:

```
[root@studentvm1 ~]# tcpdump -i lo port 23 -A
tcpdump: verbose output suppressed, use -v or -vv for full protocol decode
listening on lo, link-type EN10MB (Ethernet), capture size 262144 bytes
```

One packet you should find will look something like this one from my StudentVM1 host. You can see the data contained in the packet. This is quite insecure and could result in the exposure of private data to anyone on the Internet who cares enough to listen in:

```
14:26:09.919600 IP6 localhost.telnet > localhost.39642: Flags [P.], seq
623:1175, ack 8, win 512, options [nop,nop,TS val 1288445246 ecr 1288445246],
length 552
`....H.@....................................J..c\e.......P.....
L..>L..>-rw-------. 1 root root 2118 Dec 22 11:07 anaconda-ks.cfg
drwxr-xr-x  2 root root 4096 Apr 16 17:24 .[0m.[01;34mbin.[0m
-rwxrwx---  1 root root 3318 Apr 16 08:17 .[01;32mdoUpdates.[0m
-rw-r--r--. 1 root root  308 Dec 22 11:06 ifcfg-enpOs3
-rw-r--r--. 1 root root 2196 Dec 22 12:47 initial-setup-ks.cfg
-rw-r--r--. 1 root root  308 Dec 22 11:06 original.ifcfg-enpOs8w
-rw-r--r--  1 root root    0 May 14 15:17 .[01;35msystemd.svg.[0m
-rw-r--r--  1 root root  101 May 14 08:57 TestFS.automount
-rw-r--r--  1 root root  284 Apr 18 14:59 test.log
```

Use Ctrl+C to terminate the tcpdump session. Close the Telnet session using the **exit** command. Stop the Telnet socket:

```
[root@studentvm1 ~]# systemctl disable --now telnet.socket
```

Despite its lack of security, Telnet is an excellent tool for learning about network communications. The **tcpdump** command has an extensive man page that provides an excellent reference.

It is worth noting at this point that Telnet, the venerable but totally insecure remote terminal utility, can still have its uses as we have just seen. There is more to come.

Some Basic Steps

There are some steps that can be taken for any Linux host to harden it against attacks of many different types. These steps range from easy to difficult and, as mentioned previously, the ones you choose to put in place depend upon the amount of pain you would experience should the defenses of your systems be breached. The cost trade-off is a judgment that must be made by those at each installation, but I recommend taking as many of these steps as possible.

Some of these steps are included here for the sake of completeness but will not be covered here. We will cover some:

1. Limit physical access to prevent unauthorized passers-by from inserting malware via a USB thumb drive or just pocketing one that is already sitting there. It can also prevent curious fingers from pushing power or reset buttons.

2. Strong passwords are a simple security measure and easily enforced as we have seen. This makes brute-force cracking of passwords much more difficult.

3. Change passwords frequently to ensure that any that are cracked are not usable for more than a short period of time. Password aging can be used to enforce this.

4. Do not share user accounts. When multiple users have access to a common account, it becomes more difficult to determine the user responsible for security problems. It's also a breach of users' individual privacy and security. If users must collaborate on shared documents, create a shared directory separate from their own home directories and use a separate group to allow access to only the people who need it. We covered shared directories and files in Chapter 18.

5. Deleting old user accounts is important in keeping a system secure. Old, supposedly unused accounts can be used to gain access to a system. Cleaning out the cruft is a good security practice.

6. Strong firewalls are always an important part of any security regimen.

7. Use public/private key pairs (PPKPs) with SSH. These are stronger than passwords and cannot be memorized so cannot be divulged under duress. (Yes, that happens!)

8. Don't store sensitive data on computers that are firewalls or routers that are directly accessible to the Internet.

9. In larger organizations data should not be stored on any host in the DMZ.[9]

10. Intrusion detection can be used to detect when an intrusion has occurred, hopefully before any damage has been done.

11. Verify open ports with tools like nmap. There should be no open ports that you are not expecting and that are not consistent with the services that you want exposed to the outside world.

12. Use a BIOS password to prevent changes to the hardware boot sequence.

13. Use a GRUB password to prevent changes to Linux initialization and startup.

14. Turn off or remove unused services to prevent attacks against any possible known vulnerabilities in those services.

15. Use firewalls to limit in- and outbound traffic to only what would be expected on a given host.

16. Use SELinux to prevent crackers from making changes even if they do gain access to a host. This is an advanced tool when used to do more than warn of potential problems and can be a bit of a nuisance to work around when doing updates or adding new software. It does provide very strong protection by preventing potential system alteration rather than just reporting the changes after the fact.

17. Use intrusion detection software like Tripwire to report altered files and other signs of a successful or attempted intrusion.

18. Disable ZEROCONF (Zero Configuration), a network self-configuration program when static configuration has not been performed and DHCP is not available. It is on by default in Fedora. This service is sometimes known as Avahi and is a part of mDNS. I always remove the avahi package and its dependencies.

---

[9] DMZ is a network segment that contains servers that respond to external requests for web pages and so on but in which no data is stored. All data is stored in a more secure network with another set of firewalls between it and the DMZ.

19.   Sync all system times using NTP to make it easier to compare log files.

20.   Only allow root to run cron jobs.

21.   Enable only the ssh2 protocol, which is the default in Fedora and other Red Hat–based distros.

22.   Do not allow root logins, especially remote ones. Log in as a non-root user and then su to root.

23.   Real SysAdmins don't use sudo. Don't use sudo yourself as the SysAdmin. I discuss this in Chapter 11 in my book *The Linux Philosophy for SysAdmins*[10] and in an excerpt[11] from that book on my website.

24.   If a non-root user really does need access to a command that requires root privilege, configure sudo for that one user to use that one command.

25.   Back up everything – frequently. This is so important that it has a chapter of its own and we explore it in Chapter 47.

PAM

PAM stands for Pluggable Authentication Modules. It is a key component of security on Linux hosts and provides a dynamic and flexible means to manage user access to their accounts and resources.

PAM divides the function of authentication into four parts:

1.   Account management determines things like whether the user's password is expired or locked and whether the user is authorized to access a particular service.

2.   Authentication management is the task of authenticating the user, as in verifying that the password and user ID are correct. This can be extended to include biometric authentication and smart-card hardware and methods.

---

[10] Both, David, *The Linux Philosophy for SysAdmins*, Apress, 2018, 375
[11] Both, David, "Real SysAdmins don't sudo – book excerpt," `www.both.org/?p=960`

3. Password management is used in the process of performing password updates.

4. Session management is used to enable user access to services such as their home directory or resource allocation and deals with logging for audit trails.

The PAM man page has a good explanation of PAM and contains references to other resources. The man page indicates that it is not necessary for a SysAdmin to understand the internal workings of the PAM libraries that implement this tool. The reason for this is that the configuration file /etc/pam.conf (if it exists, which it does not in Fedora 29 and later) and the files located in the /etc/pam.d directory are the tools used to configure PAM.

The PAM configuration items most likely to be used are mostly related to resource management such as specifying limits on the CPU time, memory, and number of processes that specific users or groups may consume. This capability can be used to aid in the allocation of limited resources to those who have more need or are authorized such access.

Of course many of today's Linux hosts have huge amounts of all of the resources required on a modern computer system. Even then certain environments such as development, test, large database systems, high-performance computing (HPC), high-traffic websites, and others may have contention among users and their running tasks for one or more system resources. And, of course, users in many organizations don't have access to the huge systems that some of us do, which again leads to contention for scarce resource.

There are also the individual users who manage to suck up as much of any resources as they are allowed. This seems to be especially true on systems with resources already strained to the limit. We have already explored setting resource limits and password quality restrictions in Chapters 37 and 40, but we didn't link the /etc/security/limits.conf file to PAM. It is, in fact, PAM that deals with enforcing any limits or other configurations we set with the files in the /etc/security directory.

Advanced DNS Security

The BIND DNS service is not especially secure and, with certain vulnerabilities, can allow a malicious user to gain access to the root filesystem and possible privilege escalation. This issue is easily resolvable with the use of the BIND chroot package.

We have already had a brief brush with the chroot command in Chapter 43, but did not cover it in any detail. Tightening security on BIND DNS requires that we use chroot, so let's take a closer look.

About chroot

The chroot tool is used to create a secure copy of parts of the Linux filesystem. In this way, if a cracker does force a vulnerability in BIND to access the filesystem, this chroot'ed copy of the filesystem is the only thing at risk. A simple restart of BIND is sufficient to revert to a clean and unhacked version of the filesystem. The chroot utility can be used for more than adding security to BIND, but this is one of the best illustrations for its use.

Enabling bind-chroot

It takes only a little work to enable the chroot'ed BIND environment. We installed the bind-chroot package in Chapter 43 of this volume, and we will now put it to use.

EXPERIMENT 46-5: ENABLING BIND-CHROOT

Perform this task as the root user on StudentVM2. Because the bind-chroot package was previously installed, we need only to stop and disable the named service and then enable and start the named-chroot service.

First, explore the /var/named directory. It already contains the chroot subdirectory because we installed the bind-chroot package. Explore the contents of the /var/named/chroot directory for a few moments. Note that there are directories for /dev, /etc, /run, /usr, and /var. Each of those directories contains copies of only the files required to run a chroot'ed version of BIND. This is so that if a cracker gains access to the host via BIND, these copies are all that they will have access to.

Notice also that there are no zone or other configuration files in the /var/named/chroot/var/named/ directory structure.

Make /var/named the PWD. Stop and disable named:

```
[root@studentvm2 ~]# systemctl disable --now named
Removed /etc/systemd/system/multi-user.target.wants/named.service.
[root@studentvm2 ~]#
```

Now start and enable the named-chroot service:

```
[root@studentvm2 ~]# systemctl enable --now named-chroot
Created symlink /etc/systemd/system/multi-user.target.wants/named-chroot.
service → /usr/lib/systemd/system/named-chroot.service.
[root@studentvm2 ~]#
```

Now examine the /var/named/chroot/var/named/ directory and see that the required configuration files are present. Verify the status of the named-chroot service:

```
[root@studentvm2 ~]#  systemctl status named-chroot
● named-chroot.service - Berkeley Internet Name Domain (DNS)
   Loaded: loaded (/usr/lib/systemd/system/named-chroot.service; enabled;
   vendor preset: disabled)
   Active: active (running) since Mon 2019-08-26 13:46:51 EDT; 2min 43s ago
  Process: 20092 ExecStart=/usr/sbin/named -u named -c ${NAMEDCONF} -t /var/
named/chroot $OPTIONS (code=>
  Process: 20089 ExecStartPre=/bin/bash -c if [ ! "$DISABLE_ZONE_CHECKING" ==
"yes" ]; then /usr/sbin/na>
 Main PID: 20093 (named)
    Tasks: 5 (limit: 4696)
   Memory: 54.7M
   CGroup: /system.slice/named-chroot.service
           └─20093 /usr/sbin/named -u named -c /etc/named.conf -t /var/
              named/chroot

Aug 26 13:46:51 studentvm2.example.com named[20093]: network unreachable
resolving './DNSKEY/IN': 2001:5>
<SNIP>
Aug 26 13:46:51 studentvm2.example.com named[20093]: resolver priming query
complete
lines 1-21/21 (END)
```

Now do a lookup to further verify that it is working as it should. Check that the server that responds to this query has the correct IP address for StudentVM2:

```
[root@studentvm2 ~]# dig studentvm1.example.com

; <<>> DiG 9.18.15 <<>> studentvm1.example.com
;; global options: +cmd
;; Got answer:
;; ->>HEADER<<- opcode: QUERY, status: NOERROR, id: 51875
;; flags: qr aa rd ra; QUERY: 1, ANSWER: 1, AUTHORITY: 0, ADDITIONAL: 1

;; OPT PSEUDOSECTION:
; EDNS: version: 0, flags:; udp: 1232
; COOKIE: 130debcd5f5056b601000000648c4cddca4d9d199e924e26 (good)
;; QUESTION SECTION:
;studentvm1.example.com.                IN      A

;; ANSWER SECTION:
studentvm1.example.com. 86400   IN      A       192.168.56.21

;; Query time: 1 msec
;; SERVER: 192.168.56.11#53(192.168.56.11) (UDP)
;; WHEN: Fri Jun 16 07:51:57 EDT 2023
;; MSG SIZE  rcvd: 95

[root@studentvm2 ~]#
```

You should also check to see if the correct results are returned for external domains such as www.example.org, opensource.com, and apress.com.

Note   When using the chroot'ed version of named, changes to the zone files must be made in /var/named/chroot/var/named.

It's also possible to add ACL (Access Control List) to specify which hosts are allowed to access the name server. These ACL definitions and host lists are added to the /etc/named.conf file. Hosts can be explicitly allowed or denied. Figure 46-1 shows how this can be configured. These statements would be added to the options section of /etc/named.conf.

```
acl block-these {
  10.0.2.0/24;
};
acl allow-these {
  192.168.56.0/24;

};
options {
  blackhole { block-these; };
  allow-query { allow-these; };
};
```

Figure 46-1. *Sample ACL entries for named.conf*

In the simple example shown in Figure 46-1, we allow queries from the local network and block queries from the network that leads to the outside world.

Hardening the Network in the Kernel

There are some additional steps we can take to harden our network interfaces. Several lines can be added to the /etc/sysctl.d/98-network.conf file, which will make our network interfaces more secure. This is advisable on all hosts but especially so on the firewall/router. These changes make it more difficult for crackers to obtain information about a host and harder to exploit.

This is not a firewall function; rather, it is a Linux kernel function.

EXPERIMENT 46-6: HARDENING THE NETWORK

Begin this experiment as the root user on StudentVM2.

Add the entries shown to the /etc/sysctl.d/50-network.conf file so that the file looks like Figure 46-2. We created this file in Chapter 44 of this volume when we made our StudentVM2 host into a router.

The comments provide a brief description of the functions of each entry. Internet searches can find more information if you want it:

```
# Controls IP packet forwarding
net.ipv4.ip_forward = 1


# Since we *DO* want to act as a router, we need to comment these out
# If the host is not a router, then uncomment these.
# net.ipv4.conf.all.send_redirects = 0
# net.ipv4.conf.default.send_redirects = 0

# Don't reply to broadcasts. Prevents joining a smurf attack
net.ipv4.icmp_echo_ignore_broadcasts = 1

# Enable protection bad icmp error messages
net.ipv4.icmp_ignore_bogus_error_responses = 1

# Enable syncookies SYN flood attack protection
net.ipv4.tcp_syncookies = 1

# Log spoofed, source routed, and redirects packets.
net.ipv4.conf.all.log_martians = 1
net.ipv4.conf.default.log_martians = 1

# Don't allow source routed packets
net.ipv4.conf.all.accept_source_route = 0
net.ipv4.conf.default.accept_source_route = 0

# Turn on reverse path filtering
net.ipv4.conf.all.rp_filter = 1
net.ipv4.conf.default.rp_filter = 1

# Disallow outsiders alter the routing tables
net.ipv4.conf.all.accept_redirects = 0
net.ipv4.conf.default.accept_redirects = 0
net.ipv4.conf.all.secure_redirects = 0
net.ipv4.conf.default.secure_redirects = 0
```

Figure 46-2. *Add these entries to the /etc/sysctl.d/50-network.conf file to provide additional network security*

These changes will take effect at the next boot. Of course you can also enable them immediately without a reboot by making the appropriate changes to the associated files in the /proc filesystem, but that can take a while.

After making the preceding additions to the /etc/ sysctl.d/50-network.conf file, reboot the computer. We don't really need to reboot, but it is faster for the purposes of this experiment – unless you want to make these changes directly to the specified files in the /proc filesystem. In my opinion, testing these changes with a reboot is the correct way to test this because the file is intended to set these variable values during the Linux startup.

After the reboot, verify in the /proc filesystem that the variables have their values set as defined in the sysctl.conf file.

It is difficult to test how the changes themselves work without a way in which to generate offending packets. What we can test is that things still work as they should. Ping each host from the other and log into each from the other using SSH. From StudentVM1, ping a host outside the local network, use SSH to log into an external host, send email, and use a browser to view an external website. If these tests work, then everything should be in good shape.

I found an error of my own during this testing so you might also. In my case I had not set ip_forward to 1 in order to configure StudentVM2 as a router. As a result I could not ping hosts outside the local network.

These changes can be added to all Linux hosts in a network but should always be added to a system acting as a router with an outside connection to the Internet. Be sure to change the statements related to routing as required for a non-routing host.

Restrict SSH Root Login

Sometimes it's necessary to allow SSH connections from external sources, and it may not be possible to specify which IP addresses might be the source. In this situation we can prevent root logins via SSH entirely. It would be necessary to log into the host as a non-root user and then su or sudo to root.

Early in the course, we set the SSHD configuration on both VMs to allow direct root login with a password from a virtual console or an SSH login. If we reconfigure SSHD to disallow root login using a password, we can improve security. Let's try this on StudentVM1 first.

EXPERIMENT 46-7: RESTRICTING SSH ACCESS

As the root user on StudentVM1, log into StudentVM2 via SSH. You should be able to do this. After confirming that you have logged into StudentVM2, log out again.

On StudentVM2, edit the etc/ssh/sshd_config file and change the following line

```
PermitRootLogin yes
```

to

```
PermitRootLogin no
```

And restart SSHD to enable the change:

```
[root@studentvm2 ~]# systemctl restart sshd.service
```

As the root user on StudentVM1, try to log into StudentVM2 as root.

You should receive a "Permission denied" error. Also be sure to verify that you can log into StudentVM2 as the student user.

You can also use the PermitRootLogin option of "prohibit-password" to disable root login using a password only. This still allows root to log in using public/private key pairs.

Change this back to "yes" and revert to allowing remote root login on SSH and test to ensure that you can log into StudentVM1 as root from StudentVM2 or StudentVM3.

This configuration only affects root logins remotely using SSH. It does not affect local logins using virtual consoles or the use of su or sudo to escalate a regular user's privilege to root.

More firewalld

Our firewall is already quite good, but there are some additional things we can do to improve the efficacy of our firewall. We can also use it to deal with a massive and persistent cyberattack.

Disabling All Traffic in Case of Emergency Using CLI

In an emergency situation, such as a determined cyberattack like the ones that seem to be launched every few weeks, it is possible to quickly disable all network traffic and cut off the attacker. Although I have seen an administrator just yank the network cable out of the wall, I don't recommend that unless there is no other option. It does take time, however short, to log in and execute the command to enter panic mode.

EXPERIMENT 46-8: FIREWALLD PANIC MODE

To see whether panic mode is switched on or off, use

```
[root@studentvm2 ~]# firewall-cmd --query-panic
no
```

To immediately disable networking traffic, switch panic mode on:

```
~]# firewall-cmd --panic-on
```

Now attempt to log into StudentVM2 from StudentVM1 and observe the result.

Switching off panic mode reverts the firewall to its permanent settings. Here's how to switch panic mode off:

```
~]# firewall-cmd --panic-off
```

Turning panic mode off requires direct access to physical hosts.

Warning   Be careful about entering panic mode on remote hosts. Panic mode disables all remote access. You may need to drive a long distance to get back out of panic mode.

Access from Specific IP Addresses or Networks

Suppose we want StudentVM2 to be less open to the outside world on interface enp0s3 so that it can accept SSH access to StudentVM2 from StudentVM3, which is located in the external 10.0.2.0/24 network, but to reject everything else.

The problem with using the external or public zones is that they allow access for SSH and other services from any IP address. So that's a bit of a conundrum. We want to block all external connections except for SSH from StudentVM3. Our primary strategy for that is to specify the IP address of StudentVM3 from which the firewall will accept SSH packets requesting a connection to StudentVM2 while rejecting all others.

To accomplish this we will switch to the block zone and then modify the firewall to allow SSH from the IP address of StudentVM3. The block zone sends rejection notices back to the source, which is better for our experiments and more friendly in a real-world environment. firewalld has a tool called "rich rules" that allow us to create a rule to allow SSH from only our StudentVM3.

EXPERIMENT 46-9: ALLOW ACCESS BY IP ADDRESS

Testing the firewall from the outside network is a bit complicated, but we can do it since we have some control over the 10.0.2.0/24 network and that network is on the "outside" network interface of our server. Remember the StudentVM3 virtual machine? We can use that VM for this purpose. It should already be configured to use the NAT network "StudentNetwork," 10.0.2.0/24, and it should still be configured to boot from the live USB image.

First, let's change the enp0s3 interface to assign it to the block zone:

```
[root@studentvm2 ~]# firewall-cmd --change-interface=enp0s3 --zone=block
success
```

Boot StudentVM3 to the Fedora live image. When the StudentVM3 startup has completed, open a terminal session and su to root. Ping StudentVM2 from the live image on StudentVM3. You must use its external IP address of 10.0.2.11 because there is no name server for the 10.0.2.0/24 network:

```
[root@localhost-live ~]# ping -c2 10.0.2.11
PING 10.0.2.11 (10.0.2.11) 56(84) bytes of data.
From 10.0.2.11 icmp_seq=1 Packet filtered
From 10.0.2.11 icmp_seq=2 Packet filtered
```

```
--- 10.0.2.11 ping statistics ---
2 packets transmitted, 0 received, +2 errors, 100% packet loss, time 1012ms
```

Now SSH as root from StudentVM3 to StudentVM2. This tests the login using SSH from the external interface of StudentVM2. You should get a "No route to host" error message:

```
[root@localhost-live ~]# ssh 10.0.2.11
ssh: connect to host 10.0.2.11 port 22: No route to host
```

Determine the IP address of StudentVM3 because you will need it to create the rule on StudentVM2. If you ever want to repeat this experiment, be sure to check the IP address of StudentVM2 when booted from the live USB image because it is likely to change. The IP address for StudentVM3 in my lab is 10.0.2.24/24. Be sure to use the correct IP address for StudentVM3 in your virtual lab setup.

Execute this command on StudentVM2:

```
[root@studentvm2 ~]# firewall-cmd --list-rich-rules
[root@studentvm2 ~]#
```

This result tells us that there are no rich rules currently configured. Now enter the following commands to add the rule to both runtime and permanent rules and verify that the rule has been added:

```
[root@studentvm2 ~]# firewall-cmd --zone=block --add-rich-rule='rule
family=ipv4 source address=10.0.2.24/24 service name=ssh accept'
success
[root@studentvm2 ~]# firewall-cmd --permanent --zone=block --add-rich-
rule='rule family=ipv4 source address=10.0.2.24/24 service name=ssh accept'
success
[root@studentvm2 ~]# firewall-cmd --permanent --zone=block --list-rich-rules
rule family="ipv4" source address="10.0.2.24/24" service name="ssh" accept
[root@studentvm2 ~]# firewall-cmd --zone=block --list-rich-rules
rule family="ipv4" source address="10.0.2.24/24" service name="ssh" accept
[root@studentvm2 ~]#
```

As root on StudentVM3, ping StudentVM2 just to verify the connection blocks all packets with a message:

```
[root@localhost-live ~]# ping -c2 10.0.2.11
PING 10.0.2.11 (10.0.2.11) 56(84) bytes of data.
```

```
From 10.0.2.11 icmp_seq=1 Packet filtered
From 10.0.2.11 icmp_seq=2 Packet filtered

--- 10.0.2.11 ping statistics ---
2 packets transmitted, 0 received, +2 errors, 100% packet loss, time 1021ms

[root@localhost-live ~]#
```

Now test an SSH connection from StudentVM3 to StudentVM2. You should be able to log in successfully.

We can also test to ensure that connection attempts from an IP address other than 10.0.2.24 get rejected. Leave StudentVM3 running while you create a new VM, StudentVM4. Use the same virtual hardware configuration similar to StudentVM3 with a dynamically allocated 120GB hard drive, one or two CPUs, and 4GB of RAM. Be sure the VM uses the NAT network StudentNetwork.

Boot to the most recent Fedora live USB image ISO file that you have. After the live image boots, open a terminal session and verify that the network configuration is correct and that the IP address falls within the "guest" host range specified in the declaration. On my StudentVM4 the IP address is 10.0.2.25.

Start with a ping to StudentVM2 (10.0.2.11), which should give "Packet filtered" messages. Then try an SSH connection:

```
[liveuser@localhost-live ~]$ ssh 10.0.2.11
The authenticity of host '10.0.2.11 (10.0.2.11)' can't be established.
ED25519 key fingerprint is SHA256:KPPOqz8eIne7ztEP9hFIRb5Trtg2d7DsBY
ZcMeBAZGU.
This key is not known by any other names
Are you sure you want to continue connecting (yes/no/[fingerprint])? yes
Warning: Permanently added '10.0.2.11' (ED25519) to the list of known hosts.
liveuser@10.0.2.11's password: <Enter password>
Permission denied, please try again.
liveuser@10.0.2.11's password: <Enter password>
Permission denied, please try again.
liveuser@10.0.2.11's password: <Enter password>
liveuser@10.0.2.11: Permission denied (publickey,gssapi-with-mic,password).
[liveuser@localhost-live ~]$
```

It is also possible to reject SSH from StudentVM3 and allow other connections. Don't do this, but this is what that firewalld command would look like:

```
# firewall-cmd --add-rich-rule='rule family=ipv4 source
address=172.92.10.90/32 service name="ssh" reject'
```

This is just a small part of the interesting things that can be done using firewalld. It would take a book of its own to cover its full capabilities. In fact there are some books about firewalld that I found on Amazon. A couple are free ebooks if you have a reader and Kindle unlimited.

Malware

Protecting our systems against malware like viruses, root kits, and Trojan horses is a big part of security. We have several tools we can use to do this, four of which we will cover here. Viruses and Trojan horses are usually delivery agents and can be used to deliver malware such as root kits.

Root Kits

A root kit is malware that replaces or modifies legitimate GNU utilities to both perform its own activities and hide the existence of its own files. For example, a root kit can replace tools like **ls** so that it won't display any of the files installed by the root kit. Other tools can scan log files and remove any entries that might betray the existence of files belonging to the root kit.

Most root kits are intended to allow a remote attacker to take over a computer and use it for their own purposes. With this type of malware, the objective of the attacker is to remain undetected. They are not usually after ransom or to damage your files.

There are two good programs that can be used to scan your system for root kits. The chkrootkit[12] and Rootkit Hunter[13] tools are both used to locate files that may have been infected, replaced, or compromised by root kits.

---

[12] chkrootkit, www.chkrootkit.org
[13] Rootkit Hunter, http://rkhunter.sourceforge.net/

Rootkit Hunter also checks for network breaches such as backdoor ports that have been opened or normal services that are listening on various ports such as HTTP and IMAPS. If those services are listening, a warning is printed.

EXPERIMENT 46-10: CHECKING FOR ROOT KITS

Perform this experiment as root on StudentVM2. Install the chkrootkit and rkhunter RPMs:

```
[root@studentvm2 ~]# dnf -y install chkrootkit rkhunter
```

Run the **chkrootkit** command. You should get a long list of tests as they are run:

```
[root@studentvm2 ~]# chkrootkit
ROOTDIR is `/'
Checking `amd'... not found
Checking `basename'... not infected
Checking `biff'... not found
Checking `chfn'... not infected
Checking `chsh'... not infected
Checking `cron'... not infected
Checking `crontab'... not infected
Checking `date'... not infected
Checking `du'... not infected
Checking `dirname'... not infected
Checking `echo'... not infected
Checking `egrep'... not infected
<snip>
Searching for Hidden Cobra ... nothing found
Searching for Rocke Miner ... nothing found
Searching for suspect PHP files... nothing found
Searching for anomalies in shell history files... nothing found
<SNIP>
Checking `chkutmp'...  The tty of the following user process(es) were
not found
 in /var/run/utmp !
! RUID        PID TTY    CMD
! student    2310 pts/0  bash
! student    2339 pts/0  su -
```

```
! root          2344 pts/0  -bash
! root          2367 pts/0  screen
! -oPubkeyAcceptedKeyTypes=rsa-sha256,rsa-sha2-256-cert-v01@openssh.
com,ecdsa-sha2-nistp256,ecdsa-sha2-nistp256-cert-v01@openssh.com,ecdsa-sha2-
nistp384,ecdsa-sha2-nistp384-cert-v01@openssh.com,rsa-sha2-512,rsa-sha2-512-
cert-v01@openssh.com,ecdsa-sha2-nistp521,ecdsa-sha2-nistp521-cert-v01@
op    28783 sh-ed25519-cert-v01@openssh.com,-oPubkeyAcceptedKeyTypes=rsa-
sha256,rsa-sha2-256-cert-v01@openssh.com,ecdsa-sha2-nistp256,ecdsa-
sha2-nistp256-cert-v01@openssh.com,ecdsa-sha2-nistp384,ecdsa-sha2-
nistp384-cert-v01@openssh.com,rsa-sha2-512,rsa-sha2-512-cert-v01@openssh.
com,ecdsa-sha2-nistp521,ecdsa-sha2-nistp521-cert-v01@op 256,rsa-sha2-256-
cert-v01@openssh.com,ecdsa-sha2-nistp256,ecdsa-sha2-nistp256-cert-v01@
openssh.com,ecdsa-sha2-nistp384,ecdsa-sha2-nistp384-cert-v01@openssh.com,rsa-
sha2-512,rsa-sha2-512-cert-v01@openssh.com,ecdsa-sha2-nistp521,ecdsa-sha2-
nistp521-cert-v01@opchkutmp: nothing deleted
Checking `OSX_RSPLUG'... not tested
```

You can see all of the checks performed by this tool. Any anomalies would be noted. There is no man page for **chkrootkit**, but there is some documentation in /usr/share/doc/chkrootkit. Be sure to read that for additional information.

I think that the Rootkit Hunter program is a better and more complete program. It is more flexible because it can update the signature files without upgrading the entire program. Like chkrootkit, it also checks for changes to certain system executable files that are frequently targeted by crackers.

Before running Rootkit Hunter the first time, update the signature files:

```
[root@testvm3 sbin]# rkhunter --update
Checking rkhunter data files...
  Checking file mirrors.dat                              [ Updated ]
  Checking file programs_bad.dat                         [ Updated ]
  Checking file backdoorports.dat                        [ No update ]
  Checking file suspscan.dat                             [ Updated ]
  Checking file i18n/cn                                  [ No update ]
  Checking file i18n/de                                  [ Updated ]
  Checking file i18n/en                                  [ No update ]
  Checking file i18n/tr                                  [ Updated ]
  Checking file i18n/tr.utf8                             [ Updated ]
```

```
  Checking file i18n/zh                                       [ Updated ]
  Checking file i18n/zh.utf8                                  [ Updated ]
  Checking file i18n/ja                                       [ Updated ]
[root@studentvm2 ~]#
```

Now create the initial database of critical files:

```
[root@studentvm2 ~]# rkhunter --propupd
[ Rootkit Hunter version 1.4.6 ]
File created: searched for 177 files, found 138
[root@studentvm2 ~]#
```

Note   The rkhunter --propupd command should be run after updates are installed and after upgrades to new releases such as from Fedoras 38 to Fedora 39.

Now run the command to check for root kits. The --sk option skips the normal pause between the different tests, which requires a keypress to continue to the next test. The -c option tells rkhunter to check for root kits:

```
[root@studentvm2 ~]# rkhunter -c --sk
[ Rootkit Hunter version 1.4.6 ]

Checking system commands...

  Performing 'strings' command checks
    Checking 'strings' command                                [ OK ]

  Performing 'shared libraries' checks
    Checking for preloading variables                         [ None found ]
    Checking for preloaded libraries                          [ None found ]
    Checking LD_LIBRARY_PATH variable                         [ Not found ]

  Performing file properties checks
    Checking for prerequisites                                [ OK ]
    /usr/sbin/adduser                                         [ OK ]
    /usr/sbin/chkconfig                                       [ OK ]
<snip>
    Knark Rootkit                                             [ Not found ]
    ld-linuxv.so Rootkit                                      [ Not found ]
    LiOn Worm                                                 [ Not found ]
```

```
    Lockit / LJK2 Rootkit                          [ Not found ]
    Mokes backdoor                                 [ Not found ]
    Mood-NT Rootkit                                [ Not found ]
    MRK Rootkit                                    [ Not found ]
    NiO Rootkit                                    [ Not found ]
    Ohhara Rootkit                                 [ Not found ]
    Optic Kit (Tux) Worm                           [ Not found ]
    Oz Rootkit                                     [ Not found ]
    Phalanx Rootkit                                [ Not found ]
    Phalanx2 Rootkit                               [ Not found ]
    Phalanx2 Rootkit (extended tests)              [ Not found ]
    Portacelo Rootkit                              [ Not found ]
    R3dstorm Toolkit                               [ Not found ]
<snip>
System checks summary
======================

File properties checks...
    Files checked: 136
    Suspect files: 0

Rootkit checks...
    Rootkits checked : 497
    Possible rootkits: 0

Applications checks...
    All checks skipped

The system checks took: 3 minutes and 34 seconds

All results have been written to the log file: /var/log/rkhunter/rkhunter.log

One or more warnings have been found while checking the system.
Please check the log file (/var/log/rkhunter/rkhunter.log)
```

This program also displays a long list of tests and their results as it runs, along with a nice summary at the end. You can find a complete log with even more detailed information at /var/log/rkhunter/rkhunter.log.

The installation RPM for Rootkit Hunter sets up a daily cron job with a script in /etc/cron.daily. The script performs this check every morning at about 03:00 a.m. If a problem is detected, an email message is sent to root. If no problems are detected, no email or any other indication that the rkhunter program was even run is provided.

ClamAV

Viruses are much less a problem for Linux than for Windows, but there are some out there. So we do need an anti-virus tool, and ClamAV is a good open source anti-virus program. There are others, and there are some that are not open source with versions for Linux.

ClamAV is not installed by default. When we install it, the empty database file will fail when run if a valid database is not installed. We will install the ClamAV update utility, which will also install all dependencies. Installing the clamav-update package allows easy update of the ClamAV database using the freshclam command.

EXPERIMENT 46-11: CLAMAV

Perform this experiment as the root user on StudentVM2. First, install clamav and clamav-update:

[root@studentvm2 ~]# **dnf -y install clamav clamav-update**

Now edit the /etc/freshclam.conf file and delete or comment out the "Example" line. Update the ClamAV database:

```
[root@studentvm2 ~]# freshclam
ClamAV update process started at Thu Aug 29 12:17:31 2019
WARNING: Your ClamAV installation is OUTDATED!
WARNING: Local version: 0.101.3 Recommended version: 0.101.4
DON'T PANIC! Read https://www.clamav.net/documents/upgrading-clamav
Downloading main.cvd [100%]
main.cvd updated (version: 58, sigs: 4566249, f-level: 60, builder: sigmgr)
Downloading daily.cvd [100%]
daily.cvd updated (version: 25556, sigs: 1740591, f-level: 63, builder:
raynman)
Downloading bytecode.cvd [100%]
```

```
bytecode.cvd updated (version: 330, sigs: 94, f-level: 63, builder: neo)
Database updated (6306934 signatures) from database.clamav.net (IP:
104.16.219.84)
[root@studentvm2 ~]#
```

You will notice that there are a couple warnings in that output data. ClamAV needs to be updated, but the latest version has not yet been uploaded to the Fedora repository.

Now you can run the clamscan command on arbitrary specified directories. Using the -r option scans directories recursively. The output data stream is a list of files. Those that are not infected have OK at the end of the line:

```
[root@studentvm2 ~]# clamscan -r /root /var/spool /home
/root/.viminfo: OK
/root/.local/share/mc/history: OK
/root/.razor/server.c303.cloudmark.com.conf: OK
/root/.razor/server.c302.cloudmark.com.conf: OK
/root/.razor/server.c301.cloudmark.com.conf: OK
/root/.razor/servers.nomination.lst: OK
/root/.razor/servers.discovery.lst: OK
/root/.razor/servers.catalogue.lst: OK
/root/.config/htop/htoprc: OK
/root/.config/mc/panels.ini: Empty file
<snip>
/home/student/.thunderbird/w453leb8.default/AlternateServices.txt: Empty file
/home/student/.thunderbird/w453leb8.default/SecurityPreloadState.txt:
Empty file
/home/student2/.bash_logout: OK
/home/student2/.bashrc: OK
/home/student2/.bash_profile: OK
/home/student2/.bash_history: OK
/home/email1/.bash_logout: OK
/home/email1/.bashrc: OK
/home/email1/.esd_auth: OK
/home/email1/.bash_profile: OK
/home/email1/.config/pulse/b62e5e58cdf74e0e967b39bc94328d81-default-
source: OK
/home/email1/.config/pulse/b62e5e58cdf74e0e967b39bc94328d81-device-
volumes.tdb: OK
```

```
/home/email1/.config/pulse/b62e5e58cdf74e0e967b39bc94328d81-card-
database.tdb: OK
/home/email1/.config/pulse/b62e5e58cdf74e0e967b39bc94328d81-stream-
volumes.tdb: OK
/home/email1/.config/pulse/cookie: OK
/home/email1/.config/pulse/b62e5e58cdf74e0e967b39bc94328d81-default-sink: OK
/home/smauth/.bash_logout: OK
/home/smauth/.bashrc: OK
/home/smauth/.bash_profile: OK

----------- SCAN SUMMARY -----------
Known viruses: 8669437
Engine version: 1.0.1
Scanned directories: 95
Scanned files: 191
Infected files: 0
Data scanned: 9.97 MB
Data read: 34.88 MB (ratio 0.29:1)
Time: 52.070 sec (0 m 52 s)
Start Date: 2023:06:20 10:18:48
End Date:   2023:06:20 10:19:40
[root@studentvm2 ~]#
```

This command emits a very long data stream, so I reproduced only a bit of it here. Using the **tee** command records the data stream in the specified file while also sending it on to STDOUT. This makes it easy to use different tools and searches on the file.

View the content of the clamscan.txt file. See if you can find files that do not have "OK" appended to the end of the line.

ClamAV currently has about 8.7 million virus signatures. That's up from the 6.3 million at the time I wrote the first edition of this chapter.

The **clamscan** utility should be run on a regular basis to ensure that no viruses have penetrated your defenses.

Tripwire

Tripwire is intrusion detection software. It can report on system files that have been altered in some way, possibly by malware installed as part of a root kit or Trojan horse. Like many tools of this type, Tripwire cannot prevent an intrusion; it can only report on one after it has occurred and left behind some evidence that can be detected and identified.

Tripwire[14] is also a commercial company that sells a version of Tripwire and other cybersecurity products. We will install an open source version of Tripwire and configure it for use on our server.

EXPERIMENT 46-12: TRIPWIRE

Perform this experiment as the root user on StudentVM2. First, install Tripwire:

```
[root@studentvm2 ~]# dnf -y install tripwire
```

The Tripwire RPM for Fedora does not create a complete and working configuration. The documentation in the /usr/share/doc/tripwire/README.Fedora file contains instructions for performing that configuration. I strongly suggest you read that file, but we will proceed here with the bare minimum required to get Tripwire working.

Next, we need to create the Tripwire key files that will be used to encrypt and sign the database files:

```
[root@studentvm2 tripwire]# tripwire-setup-keyfiles

-----------------------------------------------
The Tripwire site and local passphrases are used to sign a  variety  of
files, such as the configuration, policy, and database files.

Passphrases should be at least 8 characters in length and contain  both
letters and numbers.
```

---

[14] Tripwire, https://www.tripwire.com

See the Tripwire manual for more information.

Creating key files...

(When selecting a passphrase, keep in mind that good passphrases typically have upper and lower case letters, digits and punctuation marks, and are at least 8 characters in length.)

Enter the site keyfile passphrase:**<Enter passphrase>**
Verify the site keyfile passphrase:**<Enter passphrase>**
Generating key (this may take several minutes)...Key generation complete.

(When selecting a passphrase, keep in mind that good passphrases typically have upper and lower case letters, digits and punctuation marks, and are at least 8 characters in length.)

Enter the local keyfile passphrase:**<Enter passphrase>**
Verify the local keyfile passphrase:**<Enter passphrase>**
Generating key (this may take several minutes)...Key generation complete.

Signing configuration file...
Please enter your site passphrase: **<Enter passphrase>**
Wrote configuration file: /etc/tripwire/tw.cfg

A clear-text version of the Tripwire configuration file:
/etc/tripwire/twcfg.txt
has been preserved for your inspection. It is recommended that you move this file to a secure location and/or encrypt it in place (using a tool such as GPG, for example) after you have examined it.

Signing policy file...
Please enter your site passphrase: **<Enter passphrase>**
Wrote policy file: /etc/tripwire/tw.pol

A clear-text version of the Tripwire policy file:
/etc/tripwire/twpol.txt
has been preserved for your inspection. This implements a minimal policy, intended only to test essential Tripwire functionality. You

should edit the policy file to describe your system, and then use twadmin to generate a new signed copy of the Tripwire policy.

Once you have a satisfactory Tripwire policy file, you should move the clear-text version to a secure location and/or encrypt it in place (using a tool such as GPG, for example).

Now run "tripwire --init" to enter Database Initialization Mode. This reads the policy file, generates a database based on its contents, and then cryptographically signs the resulting database. Options can be entered on the command line to specify which policy, configuration, and key files are used to create the database. The filename for the database can be specified as well. If no options are specified, the default values from the current configuration file are used.

```
[root@studentvm2 tripwire]#
```

Now we need to initialize the Tripwire database. This command scans the files and creates a signature for each file. It encrypts and signs the database to ensure that it cannot be altered without alerting us to that fact. This command can take several minutes to complete. We can use the --init option or its synonym, -m i:

```
[root@studentvm2 ~]# tripwire --init
```

You will see some warnings about files that the default policy expects to see. You can ignore those for this experiment, but for a production environment, you would want to create a policy file that reflects the files you actually have and the actions to be taken if one changes.

We can now run an integrity check of our system:

```
[root@studentvm2 tripwire]# tripwire --check | tee /root/tripwire.txt
```

Once again Tripwire generates the same warnings. Explore the Tripwire report file we created, which contains a nice summary near the beginning.

Note that the file created by Tripwire, /var/lib/tripwire/report/studentvm2.example.com-<DATE>-<RANDOM NUMBER>.twr, is an encrypted file. It can only be viewed using the twprint utility:

```
[root@studentvm2 ~]# ll /var/lib/tripwire/report/
total 32
-rw-r--r--. 1 root root 12350 Jun 20 12:28 studentvm2-20230620-122611.twr
```

```
-rw-r--r--. 1 root root 12350 Jun 20 12:33 studentvm2-20230620-123102.twr
[root@studentvm2 ~]# twprint --print-report --twrfile /var/lib/tripwire/
report/studentvm2-20230620-122611.twr | less
```

I find the output from Tripwire to be a bit ambiguous about problems. Even though I initialized the database, I still get a lot of errors indicating that files or directories don't exist. It's still a good tool; it just requires a bit of research and patience to view the reports and determine whether a break-in has occurred.

SELinux

We configured SELinux to simply report problems early in this course so we would not need to deal with side effects in other experiments caused by this important security tool. SELinux was developed by the NSA to provide a highly secure computing environment. True to the GPL, they have made this code available to the rest of the Linux community, and it is included as a part of nearly every mainstream distribution.

I have no idea how much we should trust the NSA itself, but because the code is open source and can be and has been examined by many programmers around the world, the likelihood of it containing malicious code is quite low. With that said, SELinux is an excellent security tool.

SELinux provides Mandatory Access Control (MAC), which ensures that users must be provided explicit access rights to each object in the host system. The objective of SELinux[15] is to prevent a security breach – an intrusion – and to limit the damage that crackers may wreak if they do manage to access a protected host. It accomplishes this by labeling every filesystem object and processes. It uses policy rules to define the possible interactions between labeled objects, and the kernel enforces these rules.

Red Hat has a well-done document that covers SELinux.[16] Although written for RHEL 7, it will also apply to all current versions of RHEL, CentOS, Fedora, and other Red Hat–derived distributions.

---

[15] Opensource.com, "A sysadmin's guide to SELinux: 42 answers to the big questions," https://opensource.com/article/18/7/sysadmin-guide-selinux

[16] Red Hat, "Selinux User's And Administrator's Guide," https://access.redhat.com/documentation/en-us/red_hat_enterprise_linux/7/html/selinux_users_and_administrators_guide/index

Under Fedora, SELinux has provided three sets of policy files although you can create your own and other distros may have other pre-configured policies. By default, only the Targeted policy files are installed by Fedora. Figure 46-3 shows the pre-configured policies along with a short description of each.

SELinux Policy Name	Description
Minimum	A very limited policy that protects very little. A good starting place for testing and learning in a real-world environment.
Targeted	This is the default policy that targets only specific processes and files. Daemons for dhcpd, httpd, named, nscd, ntpd, portmap, snmpd, squid, and syslogd may be protected – the specific ones depend upon the distribution and release. Anything unprotected runs in the unconfined_t domain which allows subjects and objects with that security context to operate using standard Linux security.
Multi-level Security (MLS)	This policy gives full SELInux protection to all objects. This is what you want if you are really paranoid.

Figure 46-3. *These are the three default SELinux policies provided by Fedora*

SELinux also has three modes of operation, disabled, enforcing, and permissive, as described in Figure 46-4.

SELinux Mode	Description
Disabled	SELinux is disabled.
Permissive	Behaves as if it were enforcing the active policy, including labeling objects and adding entries to log files. It does not actually enforce the policy. This mode could be used to test SELinux policies while not interfering with any aspect of the system.
Enforcing	Enforces the current policy. This is the default SELinux policy.

Figure 46-4. *SELinux operational modes*

In this section we will explore some basic SELinux tasks.

EXPERIMENT 46-13: SELINUX

Perform this experiment as the root user on StudentVM2.

Go to the /etc/selinux directory and view the directories there. You should see that, by default, only the Targeted policy files are installed by Fedora. Install the MLS and Minimal SELinux policy files and look at the contents of this directory again:

```
[root@studentvm2 selinux]# dnf install -y selinux-policy-minimum selinux-policy-mls
```

Each policy is installed in a subdirectory of /etc/selinux. Look at the contents of the /etc/selinux directory again and notice the new minimum and mls subdirectories for their respective policy files.

Install the SELinux policy man pages and documentation:

```
[root@myworkstation ~]# dnf -y install selinux-policy-doc
```

Rebuild the man page database if you installed the SELinux man pages:

```
[root@myworkstation ~]# mandb
```

You should find over 900 relevant man pages.

The default mode for SELinux is "Targeted – Permissive." An early experiment had you disable SELinux. Edit the /etc/selinux/config file and set the following options to their defaults upon installation:

```
SELINUX=permissive
SELINUXTYPE=targeted
```

Reboot the system. It will take several minutes during the first reboot while SELinux relabels the targeted files and directories. This can be seen in Figure 46-5. Labeling is the process of assigning a security context to a process or a file. The system will reboot again at the end of the relabel process.

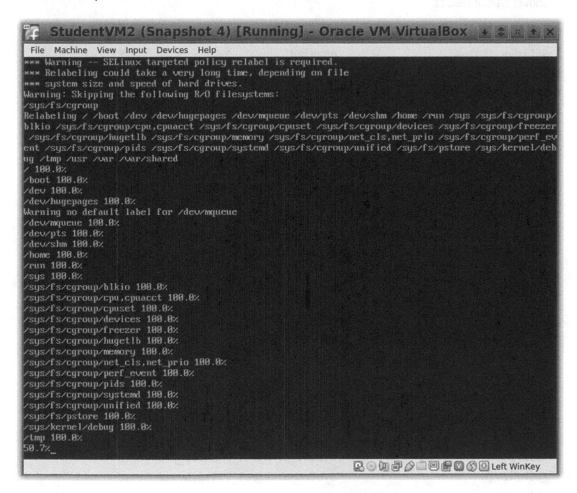

Figure 46-5. *SELinux relabels system objects during a reboot*

Log into the desktop as student. Open a terminal session as student and another as root. Run the command id -Z in both terminals. The results should be the same, with both IDs being completely unconfined:

```
[root@studentvm2 ~]# id -Z
unconfined_u:unconfined_r:unconfined_t:s0-s0:c0.c1023
```

As root, use the getenforce command to verify the current state of enforcement:

```
[root@studentvm2 ~]# getenforce
Enforcing
```

Run the **sestatus** command to view an overall status for SELinux. The following sample output shows typical results:

```
[root@studentvm2 etc]# sestatus -v
SELinux status:                 enabled
SELinuxfs mount:                /sys/fs/selinux
SELinux root directory:         /etc/selinux
Loaded policy name:             targeted
Current mode:                   permissive
Mode from config file:          permissive
Policy MLS status:              enabled
Policy deny_unknown status:     allowed
Memory protection checking:     actual (secure)
Max kernel policy version:      31

Process contexts:
Current context:                unconfined_u:unconfined_r:unconfined_t:s0-
s0:c0.c1023
Init context:                   system_u:system_r:init_t:s0
/usr/sbin/sshd                  system_u:system_r:sshd_t:s0-s0:c0.c1023

File contexts:
Controlling terminal:           unconfined_u:object_r:user_devpts_t:s0
/etc/passwd                     system_u:object_r:passwd_file_t:s0
/etc/shadow                     system_u:object_r:shadow_t:s0
/bin/bash                       system_u:object_r:shell_exec_t:s0
/bin/login                      system_u:object_r:login_exec_t:s0
/bin/sh                         system_u:object_r:bin_t:s0 ->
system_u:object_r:shell_exec_t:s0
```

```
/sbin/agetty                        system_u:object_r:getty_exec_t:s0
/sbin/init                          system_u:object_r:bin_t:s0 ->
system_u:object_r:init_exec_t:s0
/usr/sbin/sshd                      system_u:object_r:sshd_exec_t:s0
[root@studentvm2 ~]#
```

Run the following command to set the mode to enforcing. Run the sestatus -v command to verify that the SELinux mode is set to "enforcing." Run the id command to determine the user's context. The user should still be unconfined:

```
[root@studentvm2 ~]# setenforce enforcing
```

Install the HTTPD service if it is not already. We're going to need this soon anyway so that we can create a website, but it is handy for this experiment:

```
[root@studentvm2 ~]# dnf -y install httpd
```

Start the HTTPD service, but it is not necessary to enable it to start at every boot:

```
[root@studentvm2 ~]# systemctl start httpd.service
```

Run the following command:

```
[root@studentvm2 ~]# ps -efZ
```

This displays the context of the running processes. Note that many processes are unconfined but that some processes, such as various kernel and HTTPD ones, are running in the system_u:system_r context. Some services run in the kernel_t domain, while the HTTPD service tasks run in a special httpd_t domain.

Users who do not have authority for those contexts via SELinux are unable to manipulate those processes, even when they su to root. This is part of the additional security provided by SELinux.

However, the "Targeted – Enforcing" mode allows all users to have all privileges, so it would be necessary to restrict some or all users in the seusers file.

To see this, as root, stop the HTTPD service and verify that it has stopped.

Log out of the user student session. As root, add the following line to the /etc/selinux/targeted/ seusers file. Note that each policy has its own seusers file:

```
student:user_u:s0-s0:c0.c1023
```

It is not necessary to reboot or restart SELinux. Now log in as the user student. What happens?

This is a rather blunt approach, but SELinux does allow you to get much more granular. Creating and compiling those more granular policies is beyond the scope of this course.

Ensure that SELinux is now set to Targeted – Enforcing on all of your student VMs to ensure maximum security.

Additional SELinux Considerations

Making changes to the filesystem while SELinux is disabled may result in improperly labeled objects and possible vulnerabilities. The best way to ensure that everything is properly labeled is to add an empty file named /.autorelabel in the root directory and reboot the system.

SELinux is intolerant of extra whitespace. Be sure to eliminate extra whitespace in SELinux configuration files in order to ensure that there are no errors.

Social Engineering

There is not room or time to delve into all the ways that crackers can use social engineering to convince users to click a URL that will take them to a website that will infect their computer with some form of malware. The human factor is well beyond the scope of this book, but there are some excellent websites that can be used as references to help users understand the online threats and how to protect themselves. Figure 46-6 lists some of these websites.

Name	URL	Notes
Organization for Social Media Safety	https://ofsms.org	Aimed at youth and parents especially and provides information about how to be safe when using social media.
Safe Connects	https://www.netliteracy.org/safe-connects/	More on-line safety aimed at teens.
Kaspersky	https://usa.kaspersky.com/resource-center/preemptive-safety/top-10-internet-safety-rules-and-what-not-to-do-online	General tips for protecting your financial and identity information as well as general safety information.
Web MD	https://www.webmd.com/parenting/guide/internet-safety#1	Again, generally aimed at parents but really applies to all.
Center for Cyber Safety and Education	https://www.iamcybersafe.org/	A good site for anyone with sections for children, parents and senior citizens.

Figure 46-6. *A few of the many websites that provide Internet safety materials*

A search on "internet safety" will result in a huge number (well, over a billion) of hits, but the best results will be in the first few pages. Many are aimed at youth, teens, and parents, but they have good information for everyone.

Chapter Summary

This chapter has explored some additional security precautions that we can take to further harden our Fedora systems against various types of attacks. It also explored some advanced backup techniques because, failing all else, good, usable backups can allow us to recover from almost any disaster including crackers.

None of the tools discussed in this chapter provide a single solution for Linux system security – because there is no such thing. Taken together in combinations that make sense for your environment, as well as along with all of the other security we have previously implemented in this course, these tools can significantly improve the security of any Linux host. Although our virtual network and the virtual machines contained in it are now safer, there is always more that can be done. The question we need to ask is whether the cost of the effort required to lock down our systems and networks even more is worth the benefits accrued by doing so.

Remember, like most of the subjects we have covered in this course, we have just touched the surface. You should now be aware of a few of the dangers and some of the tools we have to counter those threats. This is only the beginning, and you should explore these tools and others not covered here in more depth in order to ensure that Linux hosts for which you have responsibility are secured to the greatest extent possible.

You should also now have a little idea of how a live USB device can be used to boot to a host with or without an installed operating system. The good side of that is that I and many others have used a live Linux thumb drive to recover many systems from crashes regardless of their installed operating system. The flip side is that anyone with a live USB drive can boot into any host for any reason. Act accordingly.

Exercises

Perform the following exercises to complete this chapter:

1. On StudentVM2, identify the network ports that we have open with iptables rules and which should be open only on the internal network and not the external network. Modify those rules to accept connections only from the internal network. Test the results.

2. If you have not already, download the rsbu.tar.gz file from the Apress website `https://github.com/Apress/using-and-administering-linux-volume-3/blob/master/rsbu.tar.gz` and install it. Using the enclosed script and configuration file, set up a simple backup configuration that runs once per day and backs up the entire home directories of both StudentVM1 and StudentVM2.

3. With SELinux enabled determine the student user's context.

4. Why should clamscan be run on the /home directory of a mail server?

5. Configure Tripwire to the files that do not exist on StudentVM2. Initialize the database and run the integrity check.

6. Why are the Tripwire report files encrypted?

7. What other services, besides HTTPD, have their own SELinux domains?

8. What is the best way to protect against any type of login attacks such as dictionary-based attacks?

9. What is the second best way to protect against any type of login attacks such as dictionary-based attacks?

10. In Experiment 46-2, the ping and tcpdump commands both display the hostname "router" as part of their output, instead of or in addition to the IP address of the router, 10.0.2.1. Why does this happen?

11. Use tcpdump to monitor the network traffic your studentvm1 host generates when you use a browser to connect to a remote web page such as www.example.com. Look at the content as well as the headers.

12. What is the result of setting the default policy of the INPUT chain of the filter table to REJECT?

13. What is the function of Avahi?

14. Is the Avahi daemon running on your StudentVM1 host? If so disable it.

15. Use the logwatch program to view report on Fail2Ban activity.

16. Are there any easy steps left that you can take to improve security on your StudentVM1 instance? If so take them.

CHAPTER 47

Back Up Everything – Frequently

In this chapter you will learn

- Why backups are important

- How to use Self-Monitoring, Analysis, and Reporting Technology (SMART) to predict hard drive failures before they occur

- How to create simple backups using the `tar` command

- How to devise an effective yet simple backup strategy

Introduction

Nothing can ever go wrong with my computer, and I will never lose my data. *Riiiiight*.

I have experienced data loss for a myriad of reasons, many of them my own fault. Keeping excellent backups has always enabled me to continue with minimal interruption. There are many ways in which data can be lost, compromised, or corrupted. This chapter discusses the use of backups for preventing catastrophic data loss and facilitating easy recovery. Performing regular backups and ensuring that data can be restored from them is a critical part of any security plan.

There are many scenarios that can result in the loss of data. These are just three of many:

Disgruntled employees can maliciously destroy data. Proper security procedures can mitigate this type of threat, but backups are still handy.

Common theft is also a way to lose data. Soon after we moved to Raleigh, NC, in 1993, there was a series of articles in the local paper and TV that covered the tribulations of a scientist at one of our better-known universities. This scientist kept all of his data on

© David Both 2023

D. Both, *Using and Administering Linux: Volume 3*, https://doi.org/10.1007/978-1-4842-9786-5_47

a single computer. He did have a backup – to another hard drive on that same computer. When the computer was stolen from his office, all of his experimental data went missing as well, and it was never recovered.

Natural disasters occur. Fire, flood, hurricanes, tornadoes, mud slides, tsunamis, and so many more kinds of disasters can destroy computers and locally stored backups as well. I can guarantee that, even if I have a good backup, I will never take the time during a fire, tornado or disaster that places me in imminent danger to save the backups.

Back up everything – frequently. And keep the most recent backups someplace off-site. I store my backups in a safe deposit box. If my home office is devastated by a disaster, I can rebuild from my backups.

Backups to the Rescue

While working on the first edition of this book, I encountered a problem in the form of a hard drive crash that destroyed the data in my home directory. I had been expecting this for some time, so it came as no surprise.

Of course in real life, I would have replaced that defective hard drive long before it actually failed. However, being the weird, strange, nerdy, and curious SysAdmin that I am, I thought I would like to see just how this drive failed so I could use it in my articles and books. So I let it degrade until it finally failed.

The Problem

The first indication I had that something was wrong was a series of emails from the SMART (Self-Monitoring, Analysis and Reporting Technology)-enabled hard drive on which my home directory resided.[1] Each of these emails indicated that one or more sectors had become defective and that the defective sectors had been taken offline and reserved sectors allocated in their place. This is normal operation; storage devices are designed intentionally with a lot of reserved sectors for just this reason.

I used the `smartctl` command to view the internal statistics for the hard drive in question. The original, defective hard drive has been replaced, but, yes, I keep some old, defective devices for teachable moments like this. I installed this damaged hard drive

---

[1] Your host must have a mail transfer agent (MTA) such as Sendmail installed and running. The /etc/aliases file must have an entry to send root's email to your email address.

in my docking station to demonstrate what the results of a defective hard drive look like. You can perform this experiment along with me, but your results will be different – hopefully healthier than my defective drive.

The SMART reports used in Experiment 47-1 can be a bit confusing. The web page "Understanding SMART Reports,"[2] can help somewhat with that. Wikipedia also has an interesting page on this technology.[3] I recommend reading those documents before attempting to interpret the SMART results; they can be very confusing.

EXPERIMENT 47-1: VIEWING HDD SMART DATA

This experiment must be performed as root. It will work better on a physical Linux host, but you can follow along just the same. You can use any physical hard drive installed in your host, even if it is in use.

After installing my failed hard drive in the docking station and turning it on, the dmesg command showed the drive to be assigned as device special file /dev/sdg. Be sure to use the correct device special file for your hard drive.

I have divided the results of the command into sections for easier reference during the discussion, and I have removed a large amount of irrelevant data. You should use /dev/sda for the hard drive on your VM:

```
[root@myworkstation ~]# smartctl -x /dev/sd1 | less
smartctl 6.5 2016-05-07 r4318 [x86_64-linux-4.15.6-300.fc27.x86_64]
(local build)
Copyright (C) 2002-16, Bruce Allen, Christian Franke, www.smartmontools.org

=== START OF INFORMATION SECTION ===
Model Family:     Seagate Barracuda 7200.11
Device Model:     ST31500341AS
Serial Number:    9VS2F303
LU WWN Device Id: 5 000c50 01572aacc
Firmware Version: CC1H
User Capacity:    1,500,301,910,016 bytes [1.50 TB]
Sector Size:      512 bytes logical/physical
```

---

[2] Understanding SMART Reports, https://wiki.unraid.net/Understanding_SMART_Reports
[3] Wikipedia, SMART, https://en.wikipedia.org/wiki/SMART

```
Rotation Rate:      7200 rpm
Device is:          In smartctl database [for details use: -P show]
ATA Version is:     ATA8-ACS T13/1699-D revision 4
SATA Version is:    SATA 2.6, 3.0 Gb/s
Local Time is:      Wed Mar 14 14:19:03 2018 EDT
SMART support is: Available - device has SMART capability.
SMART support is: Enabled
AAM level is:       0 (vendor specific), recommended: 254
APM feature is:     Unavailable
Rd look-ahead is: Enabled
Write cache is:     Enabled
ATA Security is:  Disabled, NOT FROZEN [SEC1]
Wt Cache Reorder: Unknown
=== START OF READ SMART DATA SECTION ===
SMART Status not supported: Incomplete response, ATA output registers missing
SMART overall-health self-assessment test result: PASSED
Warning: This result is based on an Attribute check.
```

The first section of results, shown just here, provides basic information about the hard drive capabilities and attributes such as brand, model, and serial number. This is interesting and good information to have, but it is all you will see on your VM.

This section shows that this SMART data report must be taken with a bit of skepticism. Notice that my known defective drive has passed the self-assessment test. That appears to mean that the drive is not about to fail catastrophically even though it already has.

The data we are most interested in at present is in the next two sections. Notice that I have trimmed out a great deal of the information not essential to this experiment:

```
=== START OF READ SMART DATA SECTION ===
<snip - removed list of SMART capabilities.>

SMART Attributes Data Structure revision number: 10
Vendor Specific SMART Attributes with Thresholds:
ID# ATTRIBUTE_NAME          FLAGS    VALUE WORST THRESH FAIL RAW_VALUE
  1 Raw_Read_Error_Rate     POSR--   116   086   006    -    107067871
  3 Spin_Up_Time            PO----   099   099   000    -    0
  4 Start_Stop_Count        -O--CK   100   100   020    -    279
  5 Reallocated_Sector_Ct   PO--CK   048   048   036    -    2143
  7 Seek_Error_Rate         POSR--   085   060   030    -    365075805
```

```
  9 Power_On_Hours          -O--CK   019   019   000    -    71783
 10 Spin_Retry_Count        PO--C-   100   100   097    -    0
 12 Power_Cycle_Count       -O--CK   100   100   020    -    279
184 End-to-End_Error        -O--CK   100   100   099    -    0
187 Reported_Uncorrect      -O--CK   001   001   000    -    1358
188 Command_Timeout         -O--CK   100   098   000    -    12885622796
189 High_Fly_Writes         -O-RCK   001   001   000    -    154
190 Airflow_Temperature_Cel -O---K   071   052   045    -    29 (Min/
Max 22/29)
194 Temperature_Celsius     -O---K   029   048   000    -    29 (0 22 0 0 0)
195 Hardware_ECC_Recovered  -O-RC-   039   014   000    -    107067871
197 Current_Pending_Sector  -O--C-   100   100   000    -    0
198 Offline_Uncorrectable   ----C-   100   100   000    -    0
199 UDMA_CRC_Error_Count    -OSRCK   200   200   000    -    20
240 Head_Flying_Hours       ------   100   253   000    -    71781 (50 96 0)
241 Total_LBAs_Written      ------   100   253   000    -    2059064490
242 Total_LBAs_Read         ------   100   253   000    -    260980229
                            ||||||_ K auto-keep
                            |||||__ C event count
                            ||||___ R error rate
                            |||____ S speed/performance
                            ||_____ O updated online
                            |_____ P prefailure warning
```

The preceding section of results from the smartctl command displays raw data accumulated in the hardware registers on the drive. The raw values are not particularly helpful for some of the error rates; as you can see, some of the numbers are clearly bogus. The "VALUE" column is usually more helpful. Read the referenced web pages to understand a bit about why. In general, numbers like 100 in the VALUE column mean 100% good, and low numbers like 001 mean close to failure – sort of 99% of the useful life is used up. It is really very strange.

In this case, 048 in the VALUE column for Reallocated_Sector_Ct – Reallocated Sector Count – sort of might mean that about half of the sectors allocated for reallocation have been used up.

The number 001 for Reported_Uncorrect – reported defective sectors that are not correctable – and High_Fly_Writes, writes in which the heads were flying further off the recording surface of the hard drive than is optimal, means that the life of this hard drive is effectively over. This has been shown to be the case with empirical evidence.

This next section actually lists errors and information about them when they occur. This is the most helpful part of the output. I do not try to analyze every error; I simply look to see if there are multiple errors. The number 1350, on the first line in the following, is the total number of errors detected on this hard drive:

```
<Snip>

Error 1350 [9] occurred at disk power-on lifetime: 2257 hours (94 days +
1 hours)
 When the command that caused the error occurred, the device was active
or idle.

 After command completion occurred, registers were:
 ER -- ST COUNT  LBA_48  LH LM LL DV DC
 -- -- -- == -- == == == -- -- -- -- --
 40 -- 51 00 00 00 04 ed 00 14 59 00 00  Error: UNC at LBA = 0x4ed001459 =
21156074585

 Commands leading to the command that caused the error were:
 CR FEATR COUNT  LBA_48   LH LM LL DV DC  Powered_Up_Time  Command/
Feature_Name
 -- == -- == -- == == == -- -- -- -- --  ---------------  -----------------
 60 00 00 00 08 00 04 ed 00 14 58 40 00 11d+10:44:56.878  READ FPDMA QUEUED
 27 00 00 00 00 00 00 00 00 00 00 e0 00 11d+10:44:56.851  READ NATIVE MAX
ADDRESS EXT [OBS-ACS-3]
 ec 00 00 00 00 00 00 00 00 00 00 a0 00 11d+10:44:56.849  IDENTIFY DEVICE
 ef 00 03 00 46 00 00 00 00 00 00 a0 00 11d+10:44:56.836  SET FEATURES [Set
transfer mode]
 27 00 00 00 00 00 00 00 00 00 00 e0 00 11d+10:44:56.809  READ NATIVE MAX
ADDRESS EXT [OBS-ACS-3]

Error 1349 [8] occurred at disk power-on lifetime: 2257 hours (94 days +
1 hours)
 When the command that caused the error occurred, the device was active
or idle.

 After command completion occurred, registers were:
 ER -- ST COUNT  LBA_48  LH LM LL DV DC
 -- -- -- == -- == == == -- -- -- -- --
```

```
40 -- 51 00 00 00 04 ed 00 14 59 00 00  Error: UNC at LBA = 0x4ed001459 =
21156074585
```

Commands leading to the command that caused the error were:

```
CR FEATR COUNT  LBA_48  LH LM LL DV DC  Powered_Up_Time  Command/
Feature_Name
-- == -- == -- == == == -- -- -- -- --  ---------------  --------------------
60 00 00 00 08 00 04 ed 00 14 58 40 00  11d+10:44:53.953  READ FPDMA QUEUED
60 00 00 00 08 00 04 f4 00 14 10 40 00  11d+10:44:53.890  READ FPDMA QUEUED
60 00 00 00 10 00 04 f4 00 14 00 40 00  11d+10:44:53.887  READ FPDMA QUEUED
60 00 00 00 10 00 04 f3 00 14 f0 40 00  11d+10:44:53.886  READ FPDMA QUEUED
60 00 00 00 10 00 04 f3 00 14 e0 40 00  11d+10:44:53.886  READ FPDMA QUEUED
```

Error 1348 [7] occurred at disk power-on lifetime: 2257 hours (94 days +
1 hours)
When the command that caused the error occurred, the device was active
or idle.

After command completion occurred, registers were:

```
ER -- ST COUNT  LBA_48  LH LM LL DV DC
-- -- -- == -- == == == -- -- -- -- --
40 -- 51 00 00 00 04 ed 00 14 59 00 00  Error: UNC at LBA = 0x4ed001459 =
21156074585
```

Commands leading to the command that caused the error were:

```
CR FEATR COUNT  LBA_48  LH LM LL DV DC  Powered_Up_Time  Command/
Feature_Name
-- == -- == -- == == == -- -- -- -- --  ---------------  --------------------
60 00 00 00 08 00 04 ed 00 14 58 40 00  11d+10:44:50.892  READ FPDMA QUEUED
27 00 00 00 00 00 00 00 00 00 00 e0 00  11d+10:44:50.865  READ NATIVE MAX
ADDRESS EXT [OBS-ACS-3]
ec 00 00 00 00 00 00 00 00 00 00 a0 00  11d+10:44:50.863  IDENTIFY DEVICE
ef 00 03 00 46 00 00 00 00 00 00 a0 00  11d+10:44:50.850  SET FEATURES [Set
transfer mode]
27 00 00 00 00 00 00 00 00 00 00 e0 00  11d+10:44:50.823  READ NATIVE MAX
ADDRESS EXT [OBS-ACS-3]
```

Error 1347 [6] occurred at disk power-on lifetime: 2257 hours (94 days +
1 hours)

```
When the command that caused the error occurred, the device was active
or idle.

<Snip - removed many redundant error listings>
```

These errors are indicative that something really is wrong with the disk. Hopefully you won't have any errors on your virtual disk.

Because I am naturally very curious, I decided I would wait to see what else occurred before I replaced the hard drive. The failure numbers were not as bad in the beginning. The error count rose to 1350 at the time of the catastrophic failure.

Some testing of over 67,800 SMART drives[4] by a cloud company named Backblaze provides some statistically based insight into failure rates of storage devices that experienced various numbers of reported errors. This web page is the first I have found that demonstrates a statistically relevant correlation between reported SMART errors and actual failure rates. Their web page also helped improve my understanding of the five SMART attributes that they found should be closely monitored.

In my opinion, the bottom line of the Backblaze analysis is that storage devices should be replaced as soon as possible after they begin to experience error reports in any of the five statistics they recommend monitoring. My experience seems to confirm that although it was not even close to being statistically significant. My drive failed within a couple months of the first indications that there was a problem. The number of errors my drive experienced before failing beyond recovery is very high, and I had been very lucky to have been able to recover from several errors that caused the /home filesystem to switch to read-only (ro) mode. This occurs when the Linux EXT4 filesystem determines that the drive is unstable and cannot be trusted.

Backup Options

There are many options for performing backups. In addition to old favorites like `tar`, most Linux distributions are provided with one or more additional open source programs especially designed to perform backups. There are many commercial options available as well. However, fancy and expensive backup programs are not really necessary to design and implement a viable backup program.

---

[4] Backblaze, "What SMART Stats Tell Us About Storage Devices," `www.backblaze.com/blog/what-SMART-stats-indicate-hard-drive-failures/`

tar

The tar command is used to make archives, more commonly referred to today as backups. The name "tar" stands for Tape ARchive, but it can be used with any type of recording media such as tape, storage devices, thumb drives, and more. We saw this when we learned about SSH, but we'll explore it more here.

The tar command is simple and easy, but there are a few things to watch for. It can be used quite effectively by non-root users to create their own personal backups.

EXPERIMENT 47-2: BACKUPS WITH TAR

Perform this experiment as the student user. Make the student user's home directory the PWD.

We will use tar to create a backup of the student home directory on the local host to the student.tar file – tar files and their compressed versions are also called tarballs – in the /tmp directory.

The -c option creates a new tarball; the -v option indicates verbose mode, which prints the name and path of every file placed in the tarball. The -f option specifies the file name and path for the tarball being created. The final dot is the directory being archived, and the dot (.) is the shortcut for specifying the current directory. The tar command archives all subdirectories of the specified directory:

```
[student@studentvm1 ~]$ tar -cvf /tmp/student.tar .
```

This command created a tar file named student.tar in the /tmp directory. That file is a backup of everything in the student user's home directory and is about 1.4GB on my VM. That's nice and it works, but also not very interesting.

Let's look in the tarball we just created. There are a couple ways to do this. First, we can use tar to list the table of contents (TOC) of the tarball. This just lists the file names and their attributes, not their contents. The contents of your directory will be different.

The -t option displays the table of contents for the tarball, and -f is the input file name. The -v option again specifies verbose:

```
[student@studentvm1 ~]$ tar -tvf /tmp/student.tar
drwx------ student/student     0 2023-06-18 13:58 ./
drwxr-xr-x student/student     0 2023-02-18 14:19 ./Documents/
```

```
-rw-r--r-- student/student   19 2023-02-09 16:17 ./Documents/testfile19
-rw-r--r-- student/student   19 2023-02-09 16:17 ./Documents/testfile04
-rw-r--r-- student/student   19 2023-02-09 16:17 ./Documents/testfile13
-rw-r--r-- student/student    0 2023-02-09 16:17 ./Documents/test03
<SNIP>
```

Now we have a simple backup of the student user's home directory and have verified its contents. Let's delete a single file and restore it from the tarball we just created. Let's just do a simple restore. We will delete and restore the ~./cpuHog file.

Now let's verify that the cpuHog file is present in the tarball and in the home directory:

```
[student@studentvm1 ~]$ tar -tvf /tmp/student.tar | grep cpuHog
-rwxr-xr-x student/student          91 2023-02-20 15:02 ./cpuHog
-rw------- student/student       11989 2023-02-28 21:46 ./chapter26/cpuHog-
job_6.pdf
-rw------- student/student       11989 2023-03-01 16:28 ./chapter26/cpuHog-
job_10.pdf
<SNIP>
[student@studentvm1 ~]$ ll
total 160024
drwxr-xr-x  2 student student     4096 Feb 27 08:05 chapter25
drwxr-xr-x  2 student student     4096 Mar  1 16:28 chapter26
drwxr-xr-x  9 student student   143360 Mar  5 08:40 chapter28
-rwxr-xr-x  1 student student       91 Feb 20 15:02 cpuHog
drwxr-xr-x. 2 student student     4096 Jan 17 09:46 Desktop
```

Now delete the file that is in the student user's home directory:

```
[student@studentvm1 ~]$ rm ~/cpuHog
```

Verify that the file is no longer present before continuing.

We see all of the cpuHog files that match the pattern. Note that we must specify the path, in this case the path relative to the directory in which the file was located.

Now let's restore the file. The -x option extracts the desired file or files from the tarball:

```
[student@studentvm1 ~]$ tar -xvf /tmp/student.tar ./cpuHog
./cpuHog.Linux
```

List the contents of the home directory to ensure that the file has been restored. Create a new ~/tmp directory and make it the PWD. Then extract the file again using the same command to illustrate a problem to consider when restoring files:

```
[student@studentvm1 ~]$ mkdir ~/tmp ; cd ~/tmp ; tar -xvf /tmp/student.tar
./cpuHog ; ll
./cpuHog
total 4
-rwxr-xr-x 1 student student 91 Feb 20 15:02 cpuHog
```

Notice that the file is extracted to the current directory. Let's restore a file in a subdirectory of the student's home directory, ./Documents/file09, but let's keep ~/tmp as the PWD:

```
[student@studentvm1 tmp]$ tar -tvf /tmp/student.tar | grep file09
-rw-rw-r-- student/student        13 2018-12-30 16:33 ./Documents/file09
-rw-rw-r-- student/student     41876 2018-12-30 16:32 ./Documents/testfile09
[student@studentvm1 tmp]$ tar -xvf /tmp/student.tar file09
tar: file09: Not found in archive
tar: Exiting with failure status due to previous errors
```

Note that we must specify the exact file we want including the path as it appears in the tarball:

```
[student@studentvm1 tmp]$ tar -xvf /tmp/student.tar ./Documents/file09
./Documents/file09
[student@studentvm1 tmp]$ ll
total 16
-rwxr-xr-x 1 student student    92 Mar 21 08:34 cpuHog.Linux
drwxrwxr-x 2 student student 4096 Jun 17 13:40 Documents
```

The Documents directory has been created here along with file09 contained in it. One of the important things to learn about using the `tar` command is that the files specified to be restored are extracted into the PWD. In order to restore any file to its proper location, the PWD during extraction must be the same directory specified in the original command that created the tarball.

If the target output file is not specified using the -f option, the output of the tar command is sent directly to STDOUT, so we can redirect it to a file:

```
[student@studentvm1 ~]$ cd ; tar -cv . > /tmp/tarball2.tar
```

This command performs the same function as the first tar command in this section, just in a somewhat different and more interesting manner.

Clean up a bit by deleting the two tarballs in the /tmp directory.

So far we have done this as the student user. There are files such as configuration files that need to be backed up too. Non-root users do not have the access required to archive most system configuration files such as many of those in /tmp.

Part of our job as SysAdmins is to ensure that we back up – archive – everything that needs to be preserved in case of disaster. That includes the entire /home filesystem and configuration files in /etc/. Although we could just target specific files to archive from /etc and other configuration files, I think it is best to archive the entire /etc directory structure, and then I have all possible files I might ever need to restore. I can just restore the ones I want if they are all there, and there is no danger of not having selected the file I need.

Let's now do a backup as the root user and back up a bit more.

EXPERIMENT 47-3: USING TAR AS ROOT

Perform this experiment as root. We will back up the /home and /etc directories to a tarball in /tmp. Be sure to use the -p option to preserve file permissions and ownership. This should be done for both creating the archive and extracting the files from it. Archiving multiple directories just requires listing each one as part of the final arguments of the **tar** command. Also use the time utility to get a feel for how long these backups take on our VMs:

```
[root@studentvm1 ~]# time tar -cvpf /tmp/backup.tar /etc /home /root
```

The resulting tarball took about seven seconds to create on my VM and was about 1.4GB in size. One of the things we can do is to compress the data to save space. So let's do that and compare the results:

```
[root@studentvm1 ~]# time tar -czvpf /tmp/backup.tgz /etc /home /root
```

Using compression took about 1 minute 55 seconds on my VM, but it reduced the file size to a little over 1GB, a reduction of about 30% of the original.

Let's see how we can recover a single file from the backup.tgz file in a little different manner. This will also work for standard tar and zip files and for any user who has access rights to the archive files.

Delete the cpuHog program from /root.

Start Midnight Commander (MC) in a root terminal and use one pane to view the contents of the backup.tgz tarball. Just highlight the tarball with the Midnight Commander cursor and press **Enter** just like you would for any directory. It will take some time to load and uncompress the tarball – 30 seconds or so depending upon your physical host. You can then navigate around the contents of the tarball just as if it were a filesystem on your VM – and in one sense it is because it is just contained inside a single archive file. Locate the /root directory in the tarball.

In the other pane of MC, navigate to the actual /root directory if it is not already the PWD for that pane. Locate the archive file /root/backup.tgz, highlight it, and copy it to /root using the **F5** key. When you see the Copy dialog box, just press **Enter** to do the copy.

It is very easy to navigate through archive files using MC and many other file managers, in order to find and extract a single file.

Exit from MC using **F10** and make root's home directory the PWD.

Off-Site Backups

Creating good backups is an important first step in a backup strategy. Keeping the resulting backup media in the same physical location as your original data is a mistake although we have done that in the previous experiments for experimental purposes.

We have seen that theft of a computer that has all its backups on an internal drive can result in the complete and irrecoverable loss of important data. Fire and other disasters can also result in the loss of original data and the backup data if it is stored in the same location. Fireproof safes are one option that can reduce the threat from both theft and a disaster like fire. Such safes are usually rated in minutes at specified temperatures for which they are supposed to protect their contents. I guess my personal concern here is that I have no idea how long or hot a fire will burn. Perhaps the safe will hold out long enough, but what if it doesn't?

I prefer to do for my own backups what the large companies do. I keep current off-site backups. For me this is in the safe deposit box at my credit union. For others this might be "in the cloud" somewhere. I like the end-to-end control I have with my safe deposit box solution. I know it is well protected. If my little home office is destroyed, the credit union is likely far enough away that it will not be affected by whatever disaster occurred. If a disaster affects both my house and the credit union, I won't be worrying about my computers any time soon.

For large companies there are services that store your backups in a remote, high-security location with climate-controlled vaults. Most of these services will even send armored trucks to your facilities to pick up and transport your backup media. Some provide high-speed network connections so that backups can be made directly onto their own storage media at their remote locations.

Many people and organizations are making backups to the cloud these days. I have serious reservations about the so-called "cloud." First, "cloud" is just another word for someone else's computer. Second, considering the number of hacks into allegedly secure computing facilities that I have been reading about, I am not likely to trust my data to any external organization that maintains online backups accessible from the Internet. I would much prefer my remote backup data to be offline until I need it.

1. The concern I have with the cloud is that, aside from the marketing information the providers put on their websites, there is no way for me to actually know whether their security measures are better than I can do for myself. Perhaps they are, but as a SysAdmin I would like some proof of this. I have no doubt that a good portion of the cloud providers can do a better job of managing the security of the data entrusted to them than many businesses and individuals do. How do I know which ones those are? Remember that we are talking about cloud-based backup solutions, not application or web presence solutions.

2. What I think I can say with some level of confidence is that the established and recognized cloud providers, such as Amazon, Azure, Google, and others, are certainly more trustworthy when it comes to security than are many small or medium organizations. I am thinking about the ones that don't have a full-time SysAdmin or outsource IT to small, local companies that are not especially reputable. I also think that many less experienced SysAdmins are not ready to deal with the high level of security required on the Internet in today's world of constant cyberattack.

3. So for many organizations, the cloud may be a viable option. For others, an experienced and knowledgeable SysAdmin may be the best choice. As with many IT decisions, it is a matter of weighing the risk factors and determining how much you are willing to accept.

Disaster Recovery Services

Taking backups a step further, some of the places I have worked at maintained a contract with one or more disaster recovery services. This type of service is paid to maintain a complete computer and network environment that can replace your own on a moment's notice. That usually includes everything from mainframes down to Intel-based servers and workstations. Of course, this is in addition to keeping massive amounts of data in off-site backup storage.

At one of the places I worked, we had quarterly assessments of our disaster recovery plan. We shut down all of the computers from the mainframes down to the Intel servers. We notified the disaster recovery company that we were conducting a test, and they prepared their site with the various computers we would require to get back up and operational. We had the backup storage service transport the latest backup media from their secure facility in Raleigh, NC, to the recovery site in Philadelphia.

A group of folks from our offices traveled up to the recovery site and restored all of the data from our backup media, brought everything online, and tested to ensure that everything was working properly.

There were always problems. Always. But that was the whole point of the exercise – to find the problems with our strategies and procedures and then to fix them.

Options

Not everyone needs a disaster recovery service or huge amounts of backup data storage. For some individuals and very small businesses with only one or a few computers, a couple USB thumb drives and a manual backup to one of those drives is more than sufficient. For others, a relatively small external USB hard drive works well.

For my own needs, I use several 4TB external USB 3.0 storage devices and rotate them each week. The most current backup goes to my safe deposit box, and the one in the box comes home and goes back into the rotation. I also have a 4TB SATA hard drive in my main workstation that I also back up to every night. This means I always have the most recent backup right online where and when I need it most. Two complete sets of backups every day work best for me. Of course I have seen so many ways to lose data that I am quite paranoid about it.

It is all in what you need for your circumstances.

What About the "Frequently" Part?

What does this really mean? Because it actually opens up a wide range of questions:

- What does "frequently" really mean?

- What does "full" mean?

- If I have 24TB of movies on my NAS,[5] do I make a full backup of those every day or just a diff?[6]

- What should I think about in terms of setting up a cron job for a full backup?

- What if my system is off when the backup is supposed to run?

How Frequent Is "Frequently?"

Let's start with this question because it is part of the chapter title, after all. Always make a backup at least once every day. No matter what.

We are talking about the absolute minimum requirement for any system administered by a Linux SysAdmin. This means that the most work that could be lost is 24 hours or less. This frequency will be sufficient for many office and even development environments.

In many other cases, a once-daily frequency will not be nearly enough. Think about banks, stock markets, high-intensity agile development environments, and scientific data collection and processing such as weather prediction. All of these environments require almost near-instantaneous duplication of huge amounts of data in case of hardware failures and, even more, minute-to-minute backups of the already duplicated data.

---

[5] Network Attached Storage.

[6] Changes to files between one backup and the next – the difference.

These high-performance requirements can be met, at least partially, using various forms and combinations of RAID arrays, high-availability network storage devices, cloud storage, and remote storage. Those solutions are outside the scope of this course.

What Does "Full" Really Mean?

This should include all of the files you would need to rapidly recover from a major disaster. A full backup will obviously cover all data files but that should not be all. A complete and quick recovery also means making backups of system configuration files and other system-level data.

So where are your data files? I back up the entire /home directory, thus ensuring I can restore everything including the user application data as well as user-level configuration files. I also make backups of /root, which is root's home directory.

For the system, I also make backups of the entire /etc directory, which contains configuration files for almost every system-level tool. I have used this backup data many times to recover from various self-inflicted forms of data loss. I do the entire /etc directory because one never knows what data will need to be restored after a disaster.

When creating a backup strategy for servers, we also want to make sure we include the appropriate configuration and user data. For example, the MariaDB database stores some configuration data in etc and user data such as WordPress content in /var.

The specific directories to be backed up will differ between organizations and even hosts within an organization. It will be necessary to determine what needs to be backed up for each host.

I never back up the operating system itself, such as /boot, /usr, /bin, /sbin, and /lib. A re-installation can easily and quickly recover the operating system. And snapshots can make recovery of VMs particularly easy – so long as you are making them.

Some organizations use what is called bare-metal restores, which mean take an empty hard drive and restore everything as a complete disk image. This takes "full" to the ultimate level. Such a bare-metal restoration is beyond the scope of this course, but I bet you are already thinking about how to do it with dd.

All vs. Diff

When using the `tar` utility as we have here in this chapter, we simply made a complete backup of everything specified. The `tar` utility can also add a diff – a complete replacement of an altered file – to the end of a tarball, but the diff consists the entirety of the files that are altered and not just the individual portions that have changed.

Advanced tools like `rsync` can be used to alter the changed portions of a file in the target backup, thus making recovery faster and easier. The structure of an rsync backup is significantly different and more accessible for the average user as we will see momentarily.

Considerations for Automation of Backups

Backups are one of those tasks best automated to ensure consistency in the timing of their runs. It also prevents someone forgetting to start it off.

Consideration needs to be given to things such as which automation tools to use, for example, cron vs. systemd timers or something else. Also, do we want to consider commercial backup systems, advanced open source backup tools, or locally created tools such as scripts?

Timing of the backups also needs some consideration. For example, do we start the backups in the evening or the early morning? If they are too close together, will they overlap and create problems?

I had one instance where a backup took so long that the next iteration started before the first was finished. This caused those two instances to lock each other out as well as the next several ones. Once discovered, it was simple to terminate all instances of the backup programs, reset the timing of backups, and start over. A situation like this highlights the need for warning messages in case of problems as well as the need to check the backups on a regular basis.

Dealing with Offline Hosts

This can be a problem and I have encountered it myself. Most backup systems, including locally written scripts, will simply time out and proceed to the next remote host. This is usually due to the attempted SSH connection timing out.

A simple system will ignore the missing backup on the next iteration and make a new one. It could also take the more sophisticated approach in which the backup software determines the latest successful backup, creates a new instance, and proceeds with the current backup while transferring only altered portions of files. This latter is the approach taken by the script I wrote for my own backups.

Advanced Backups

The tarball backups we experimented with earlier in the chapter are fine for some organizations, but they are not as elegant as they might be. For example, a complete backup is made every day with a complete new tarball. This takes a lot of time every day, as well as consuming a massive amount of storage space for the backups.

Let's look at the **rsync** utility as an advanced tool for backups. Because of the way it works, we can save much of the time required to make daily backups as well as a significant amount of storage space.

rsync

None of the commercial or more complex open source backup solutions fully met my needs, and restoring from a tarball can be time-consuming and sometimes a bit frustrating. I also really wanted to try another tool I had heard about, rsync. [7]

I had been experimenting with the rsync command, which has some very interesting features that I have been able to use to good advantage. My primary objectives were to create backups from which users could locate and restore files quickly without having to extract data from a backup tarball and to reduce the amount of time taken to create the backups.

This section is intended only to describe my own use of rsync in a backup scenario. It is not a look at all of the capabilities of rsync or the many other interesting ways in which it can be used.

The rsync command was written by Andrew Tridgell and Paul Mackerras and first released in 1996. The primary intention for rsync is to remotely synchronize the files on one computer with those on another. Did you notice what they did to create the name there? rsync is open source software and is provided with all of the distros with which I am familiar.

---

[7] Wikipedia, rsync, https://en.wikipedia.org/wiki/Rsync

The `rsync` command can be used to synchronize two directories or directory trees whether they are on the same computer or on different computers, but it can do so much more than that. `rsync` creates or updates the target directory to be identical to the source directory. The target directory is freely accessible by all the usual Linux tools because it is not stored in a tarball or zip file or any other archival file type; it is just a regular directory with regular Linux files that can be navigated by regular users using basic Linux tools. This meets one of my primary objectives.

One of the most important features of `rsync` is the method it uses to synchronize preexisting files that have changed in the source directory. Rather than copying the entire file from the source, it uses checksums to compare blocks of the source and target files. If all of the blocks in the two files are the same, no data is transferred. If the data differs, only the blocks that have changed on the source are transferred to the target. This saves an immense amount of time and network bandwidth for remote sync. For example, when I first used my `rsync` Bash script to back up all of my hosts to a large external USB hard drive, it took about three hours. That is because all of the data had to be transferred because none of it had been previously backed up. Subsequent backups took between three and eight minutes of real time, depending upon how many files had been changed or created since the previous backup. I used the `time` command to determine this so it is empirical data. Last night, for example, it took 3 minutes and 12 seconds to complete a backup of approximately 750GB of data from six remote systems and the local workstation. Of course, only a few hundred megabytes of data were actually altered during the day and needed to be backed up.

The simple `rsync` command shown in Figure 47-1 can be used to synchronize the contents of two directories and any of their subdirectories. That is, the contents of the target directory are synchronized with the contents of the source directory so that at the end of the sync, the target directory is identical to the source directory.

```
rsync -aH sourcedir targetdir
```
The -a option is for archive mode which preserves permissions, ownerships and symbolic (soft) links. The -H is used to preserve hard links rather than creating a new file for each hard link. Note that either the source or target directories can be on a remote host.

Figure 47-1. *The minimum command necessary to synchronize two directories using rsync*

The -a option is for archive mode, which preserves permissions, ownerships, and symbolic (soft) links. The -H is used to preserve hard links rather than creating a new file for each hard link. Note that either the source or target directory can be on a remote host.

Let's see how this works.

EXPERIMENT 47-4: BASIC RSYNC USAGE

Start this experiment as the student user on StudentVM2. Use the tree command to view the current contents of the student user's home directory:

```
[student@studentvm2 ~]$ tree
.
├── Desktop
├── Documents
├── Downloads
├── Music
├── Pictures
├── Public
├── random.txt
├── Templates
├── textfile.txt
└── Videos

9 directories, 2 files
[student@studentvm2 ~]$
```

Do the same on StudentVM1. They should be quite different:

```
[student@studentvm1 ~]$ tree
[student@studentvm1 ~]$ tree | head
.
├── chapter25
│   ├── Experiment_6-1.txt
│   └── Experiment_6-3.txt
├── chapter26
│   ├── bashrc-2.pdf
│   ├── bashrc-job_8.pdf
│   ├── bashrc.ps
├── testfile
```

```
<SNIP>
├── tmp
│   ├── cpuHog
│   └── Documents
│       └── file09
├── umask.test
├── Videos
└── zoom_x86_64.rpm
```

Now we want to sync the student user's home directory on StudentVM1 to that on StudentVM2. As the student user on StudentVM1, use the following command to do that. You may not need to enter a password if you have set up a PPKP for SSH:

```
[student@studentvm1 ~]$ time rsync -aH . studentvm2:/home/student
Password: <Enter password>

real    0m19.675s
user    0m2.205s
sys     0m3.363s
[student@studentvm1 ~]$
```

That was easy! Now check the home directory for the student user on StudentVM2. All of the student user's files that were present on StudentVM1 are now on StudentVM2.

Now let's change a file and see what happens when we run the same command. Pick an existing file and append some more data to it. I did this:

```
[student@studentvm1 ~]$ dmesg >> random.txt
```

Verify the file sizes on both VMs. They should be different. Now run the previous command again:

```
[student@studentvm1 ~]$ time rsync -aH . studentvm2:/home/student
Password: <Enter password>

real    0m6.243s
user    0m0.029s
sys     0m0.060s
[student@studentvm1 ~]$
```

Verify that random.txt (or whichever file you chose to use) is now the same larger size on both hosts. Compare the times for both instances of the command. The real time is not important because that includes the time we took to type in the password. The important times are the amount of user and system time used by the commands, which is significantly less during the second invocation. Although some of that savings may be due to caching, on a system where the command is run once a day to synchronize huge amounts of data, the time savings is very noticeable.

Now let's assume that yesterday we used rsync to synchronize two directories. Today we want to resynchronize them, but we have deleted some files from the source directory. The normal way in which rsync would work using the syntax we used in Experiment 47-4 is to simply copy all the new or changed files to the target location and leave the deleted files in place on the target. This may be the behavior you want, but if you would prefer that files deleted from the source also be deleted from the target, that is, the backup, you can add the --delete option to make that happen.

Another interesting option, and my personal favorite because it increases the power and flexibility of rsync immensely, is the --link-dest option. The --link-dest option uses hard links[8,9] to create a series of daily backups that take up very little additional space for each day and also take very little time to create.

Specify the previous day's target directory with this option and a new directory for today. The rsync command then creates today's new directory, and a hard link for each file in yesterday's directory is created in today's directory. So we now have a bunch of hard links to yesterday's files in today's directory. No new files have been created or duplicated. After creating the target directory for today with this set of hard links to yesterday's target directory, rsync performs its sync as usual, but when a change is detected in a file, the target hard link is replaced by a copy of the file from yesterday and the changes to the file are then copied from the source to the target.

So now our command looks like that in Figure 47-2. This version of our rsync command first creates hard links in today's backup directory for each file in yesterday's backup directory. The files in the source directory – the one being backed up – are then compared to the hard links that were just created. If there are no changes to the files in the source directory, no further action is taken.

---

[8] Wikipedia, Hard Links, https://en.wikipedia.org/wiki/Hard_link
[9] Both, David, "Using hard and soft links in the Linux filesystem," www.linux-databook. info/?page_id=5087, DataBook for Linux

```
rsync -aH --delete --link-dest=yesterdaystargetdir sourcedir todaystargetdir
```

Figure 47-2. *This command uses hard links to link unchanged files from yesterday's directory to today's. This saves a lot of time*

If there are changes to files in the source directory, rsync deletes the hard link to the file in yesterday's backup directory and makes an exact copy of the file from yesterday's backup. It then copies the changes made to the file from the source directory to today's target backup directory. It also deletes files on the target drive or directory that have been deleted from the source directory.

There are also times when it is desirable to exclude certain directories or files from being synchronized. We usually do not care about backing up cache directories and, because of the large amount of data they can contain, the amount of time required to back them up can be huge compared to other data directories. For this there is the --exclude option. Use this option and the pattern for the files or directories you want to exclude. You might want to exclude browser cache files, so your new command will look like Figure 47-3.

```
rsync -aH --delete --exclude Cache --link-dest=yesterdaystargetdir
sourcedir todaystargetdir
```

Figure 47-3. *This syntax can be used to exclude specified directories or files based on a pattern*

Note that each file pattern you want to exclude must have a separate exclude option.

The **rsync** command has a very large number of options that you can use to customize the synchronization process. For the most part, the relatively simple commands that I have described here are perfect for making backups for my personal needs. Be sure to read the extensive man page for rsync to learn about more of its capabilities as well as details of the options discussed here.

Performing Backups

I automated my backups because "automate everything." I wrote a Bash script, **rsbu**, that handles the details of creating a series of daily backups using **rsync**. This includes ensuring that the backup medium is mounted, generating the names for yesterday's and today's backup directories, creating appropriate directory structures on the backup medium if they are not already there, performing the actual backups, and unmounting the medium.

The end result of the method in which I employ the rsync command in my script is that I end up with a date-sequence of backups for each host in my network. The backup drives end up with a structure similar to the one shown in Figure 47-4. This makes it easy to locate specific files that might need to be restored.

So, starting with an empty disk on January 1, the rsbu script makes a complete backup for each host of all the files and directories that I have specified in the configuration file. This first backup can take several hours if you have a lot of data like I do.

On January 2, the rsync command uses the –link-dest= option to create a complete new directory structure identical to that of January 1; then it looks for files that have changed in the source directories. If any have changed, a copy of the original file from January 1 is made in the January 2 directory, and then the parts of the file that have been altered are updated from the original.

After the first backup onto an empty drive, the backups take very little time because the hard links are created first and then only the files that have been changed since the previous backup need any further work. The resulting backups will look similar to that in Figure 47-4.

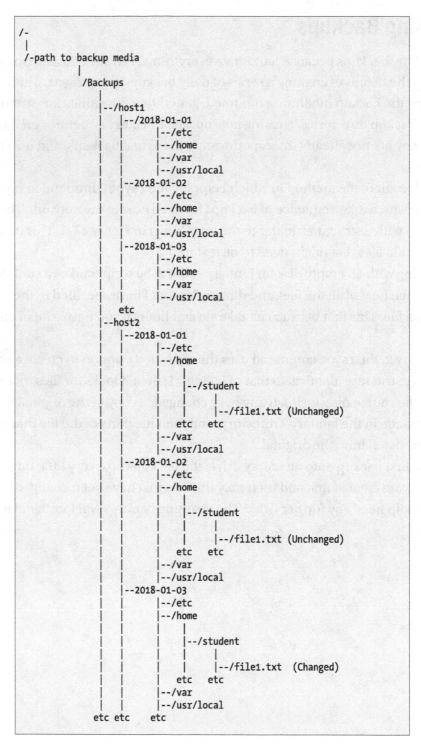

Figure 47-4. *The directory structure for my backup data disks*

Figure 47-4 also shows a bit more detail for the host2 series of backups for one file, /home/student/file1.txt, on the dates January 1, 2, and 3. On January 2 the file has not changed since January 1. In this case, the rsync backup does not copy the original data from January 1. It simply creates a directory entry with a hard link in the January 2 directory to the January 1 directory, which is a very fast procedure. We now have two directory entries pointing to the same data on the hard drive. On January 3, the file has been changed. In this case, the data for ../2018-01-02/home/student/file1.txt is copied to the new directory, ../2018-01-03/home/student/file1.txt, and any data blocks that have changed are then copied to the backup file for January 3. These strategies, which are implemented using features of the `rsync` program, allow backing up huge amounts of data while saving disk space and much of the time that would otherwise be required to copy data files that are identical.

One of my procedures is to run the backup script twice each day from a single systemd timer. The first iteration performs a backup to an internal 4TB hard drive. This is the backup that is always available and always at the most recent version of all my data. If something happens and I need to recover one file or all of them, the most I could possibly lose is a few hours worth of work.

The second backup is made to one of a rotating series of 4TB external USB hard drives. I take the most recent drive to my safe deposit box at the bank at least once per week. If my home office is destroyed and the backups I maintain there are destroyed along with it, I just have to get the external hard drive from the bank, and I have lost at most a single week of data. That type of loss is easily recovered.

The drives I am using for backups, not just the internal hard drive but also the external USB storage devices that I rotate weekly, never fill up. This is because the `rsbu` script I wrote checks the ages in days of the backups on each drive before a new backup is made. If there are any backups on the drive that are older than the specified number of days, they are deleted. The script uses the `find` command to locate these backups. The number of days is specified in the rsbu.conf configuration file.

Of course after a complete disaster, I would first have to find a new place to live with office space for my wife, and I would purchase parts and build new computers, restore from the remaining backup, and then recreate any lost data.

My script, rsbu, is available along with its configuration file, rsbu.conf, and a READ.ME file as a tarball, rsbu.tar.gz, from `https://github.com/Apress/using-and-administering-linux-volume-3/blob/master/rsbu.tar.gz`.

You can use that script as the basis for your own backup procedures. Be sure to make any modifications you need and test thoroughly.

Tip   I have looked at a number of expensive commercial backup programs over the years. None of them are as easy to use as my script using rsync, and some of them are actually just commercial front ends for an rsync back end.

Recovery Testing

No backup regimen would be complete without testing. You should regularly test recovery of random files or entire directory structures to ensure not only that the backups are working but that the data in the backups can be recovered for use after a disaster. I have seen too many instances where a backup could not be restored for one reason or another and valuable data was lost because the lack of testing prevented discovery of the problem.

Just select a file or directory to test and restore it to a test location such as /tmp so that you won't overwrite a file that may have been updated since the backup was performed. Verify that the files' contents are as you expect them to be. Restoring files from a backup made using the preceding rsync commands is simply a matter of finding the file you want to restore from the backup and then copying it to the location to which you want to restore it.

I have had a few circumstances where I have had to restore individual files and, occasionally, a complete directory structure. I have had to restore the entire contents of a hard drive on a couple occasions. Most of the time this has been self-inflicted when I accidentally deleted a file or directory. At least a few times, it has been due to a crashed hard drive. So those backups do come in handy.

Chapter Summary

Backups are an incredibly important part of our jobs as SysAdmins. I have experienced many instances where backups have enabled rapid operational recovery for places I have worked as well as for my own business and personal data.

We experimented with using the tar command for performing backups. This is a great tool for relatively simple setups, but it can be very effective. We did some backups and then tested methods for restoring single files and entire directory structures.

We also used the rsync command as the basis for making backups that save both time and storage space. These backups can also be directly accessible to regular users. The script I have provided for download can get you started using this advanced and powerful backup method.

Like everything else, backups are all about what you need. Whatever you do, do something! Figure out how much pain you would have if you lost everything – data, computers, hard copy records, everything. The pain includes the cost of replacing the hardware and the cost of the time required to restore data that was backed up and to recover data that was not backed up. Then plan and implement your backup systems and procedures accordingly.

There are many options for performing and maintaining data backups. I do what works for me and have never had a situation where I lost more than a few hours worth of data.

Exercises

Perform the following exercises to complete this chapter:

1. If you are running your VM on a Linux host, you will of necessity have access to root. As root, run **smartctl -x /dev/sda** on that physical host. Explore the output for signs of disk failure.

2. If you are running your VM on a Windows host, create a live USB thumb drive from the downloaded ISO image used to install Fedora on your VM. Then boot that host using the live USB device. As root, run **smartctl -x /dev/sda** on that physical host. Explore the output for signs of disk failure.

3. List three advantages of using the **tar** command for backups.

4. Determine how much space you need to back up the /home, /root, and /etc directories. Locate a USB drive large enough to contain that much data and make it available to your VM. Make a backup of those three directories on the USB drive.

5.   What advantages might there be to use "the cloud" for backups?

6.   Write a simple script to automate backups of /home, /root, and /etc, and configure a systemd timer to run the script every morning at 02:00 a.m. Create a new filesystem from the existing space in your volume group, fedora_studentvm1, for storage of the backup; use this as a substitute for an external device. Test it to verify that it works.

7.   Wipe out the /home/student home directory by deleting the directory and all the files in it. Restore /home/student from the backup you made in the previous exercise.

8.   Can the Thunar GUI file manager be used to access the archive tarballs and extract files from them?

CHAPTER 48

Introducing Email

Objectives

In this chapter you will learn

- How email clients and servers function to transmit email from one user to another

- How to install and configure Sendmail to act as a mail transfer agent (MTA)

- To configure the firewall for email

- To configure name services to accommodate email with an MX record

- How to test email using a command-line email client

- To use email headers to trace the origin and route of an email

- To configure a host to use the email server as a smart host

- To configure the aliases file to forward system-level email intended for root to another email address like the student user

Introduction

Email is a ubiquitous messaging service and is available on devices ranging from work and home desktop computers to various mobile devices such as smart phones and tablets. There are two sides to email. The protocols IMAP and POP are used to receive email on your device, and the protocol SMTP is used to send email from your device to and between email servers.

© David Both 2023
D. Both, *Using and Administering Linux: Volume 3*, https://doi.org/10.1007/978-1-4842-9786-5_48

Email is an asynchronous messaging protocol at the macro level. That is, if I send you an email message, you do not have to be at the receiving computer at that moment in order to receive the message. The computer does not even need to be turned on. The message is stored at the server until the computer is turned on and you retrieve it.

A typical synchronous messaging system is a face-to-face conversation or a telephone call, which requires both parties to the conversation to be on the line or in the same place at the same time. Voicemail is just a corrupted version of a telephone call in which we leave messages for each other – another form of asynchronous messaging.

Email services were originally limited to users on a local Unix computer. All users of an email system had to be connected via a hardware terminal to the Unix computer. Because computers were not normally connected in any way, email systems were very localized. As slow dial-up connections became available, remote computers could be connected but only for specified and relatively short periods of time. Email messages could be stored on the sending server until the connection was made, and all messages intended for the remote email server would be sent using that temporary connection. Email bound for other remote servers was held on the local server until a connection to the destination remote server was made. It is these ancient requirements that helped define many of today's email protocols such as the ability to store messages for a period of time until the remote server is available.

Today we can send email to almost anyone on the planet, but spam is a major issue. With so many people connected to the same Internet that allows us to communicate with email, there are also those who use email for scamming the rest of us. We will discuss dealing with spam in Chapter 50.

Definitions

Let's define a few terms before going any further:

> **Protocol**: A set of formal rules describing how to transmit data, especially across a network.

> **SMTP**: Simple Mail Transfer Protocol, a protocol used to transfer electronic mail between computers.

> **POP**: Post Office Protocol, a simple protocol designed to allow single-user computers to retrieve electronic mail from a POP server. Once retrieved by the client, the email is deleted from the server.

IMAP: Internet Message Access Protocol, a protocol allowing a client to access and manipulate electronic mail messages on a server. Emails are retained on the server until explicitly deleted by the user.

MTA: Mail transfer agent – an agent such as Sendmail that transfers email from one host to another. These transfers may not only be between email servers but also from a sending email client to an email server.

Sendmail: A very common MTA that has been around for many years.

Email Data Flow

Figure 48-1 is a simplified diagram of the flow of an email message from the sending client to the receiving client. Note that the sending client uses SMTP as the protocol to send the outbound email to the local email server. Let's track the progress of an email through this diagram.

1. The client adds an initial set of headers to the email to be sent. This includes the subject line, a date stamp, and the From: and To: lines.

2. The sending client uses SMTP to send the email to the local email (SMTP) server, SMTP Server1, as defined in the client configuration. So, for clients in the domain example.com, their email would typically go to an email server for example.com. One common method is to identify that server as mail.example.com in the internal name service (DNS) database.

3. SMTP Server1 receives the email and adds a Received: line to the headers that lists where the email came from with IP address and hostname if possible, along with a timestamp. The header entry also indicates the addressee.

4. SMTP Server1 parses the address(es) to which the email is destined.

5. SMTP Server1 uses DNS to specifically request the MX (Mail eXchanger) record for the target domain.

6. SMTP Server1 then sends the email to the receiving server, SMTP Server2, through the Internet.

7. SMTP Server2 adds another Received: line to the headers.

8. SMTP Server2 holds the email in the user's inbox until the client connects to the server to retrieve the email. Using the relatively more common and newer protocol IMAP on the receiving client, the user can view the email on SMTP Server2.

Emails remain in the inbox, which is located in /var/spool/email/<username>, until they are moved to another email folder or deleted. The email remains on the server until it is deleted regardless of which folder it is in.

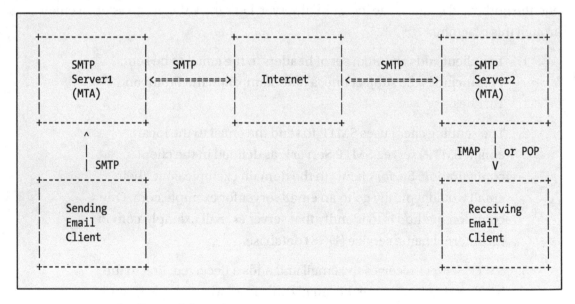

Figure 48-1. *The flow of data for email messages*

Structure of an Email

The primary structure of an email message has two parts as defined in RFC 822, the headers and the message body. The headers are separated from the message body by a single blank line.

The message body can contain ASCII plain text or MIME[1] components consisting of HTML messages, images, or other types. The text body content of an email message is limited to 7-bit ASCII, which is why MIME is used to attach data types based on 8-bit data.

Email Headers

The email headers provide a record of the email's travels and can help us identify its true source. Each MTA adds one or more lines to the headers to record the email's passage. The email headers are normally hidden from users by the email clients, but a SysAdmin can access them to use in the task of problem determination for email delivery issues. I refer to email headers frequently for various types of problems including spam source identification, to determine where an email may have been delayed in its transit across the Internet from sender to receiver, and to use as the basis for blocking spam.

Figure 48-2 shows the headers from a test email I sent to myself from a network for which I am the SysAdmin. This email was sent from the remote host, host1, using the following command. We will use `mailx` commands like this to test our own email server later in this chapter:

```
echo "This is a test email" | mailx -s "Test email" linuxgeek46@both.org
```

I have hacked some of the hostnames and external IP addresses in Figure 48-2 to obscure their true identities.

---

[1] MIME, Multipurpose Internet Mail Extensions, is used in email messages to contain data types other than text messages. Images, HTML, and audio data are commonly embedded in email as MIME types.

```
Received: from mailserver.example.net (rrcs-96-10-0-10.se.biz.rr.com [96.10.0.10])
        by yorktown.both.org (8.15.2/8.15.2) with ESMTP id x5Q7sZwg006558
        for <linuxgeek46@both.org>; Wed, 26 Jun 2019 03:54:38 -0400
Received: from host1.example.net (host1.example.net [192.168.0.1])
        by mailserver.example.net (8.14.7/8.14.4) with ESMTP id x5Q7sZgN028979
        for <linuxgeek46@both.org>; Wed, 26 Jun 2019 03:54:35 -0400
Received: from host1.example.net (localhost [127.0.0.1])
        by host1.example.net (8.14.7/8.14.7) with ESMTP id x5Q7sZx0032630
        for <linuxgeek46@both.org>; Wed, 26 Jun 2019 03:54:35 -0400
Received: (from root@localhost)
        by host1.example.net (8.14.7/8.14.7/Submit) id x5Q7sZZ3032629
        for linuxgeek46@both.org; Wed, 26 Jun 2019 03:54:35 -0400
From: root <root@host1.example.net>
Message-Id: <201906260754.x5Q7sZZ3032629@host1.example.net>
Date: Wed, 26 Jun 2019 03:54:35 -0400
To: linuxgeek46@both.org
Subject: Test email
User-Agent: Heirloom mailx 12.5 7/5/10
MIME-Version: 1.0
Content-Type: text/plain; charset=us-ascii
Content-Transfer-Encoding: 7bit
X-Spam-Score: -40.5 () ALL_TRUSTED,USER_IN_WHITELIST
X-Spam-Status: No, score=-28.2 required=10.6
tests=BAYES_50,RDNS_DYNAMIC,USER_IN_WHITELIST
X-Spam-Status: No, score=-40.5 required=10.9 tests=ALL_TRUSTED,USER_IN_WHITELIST
X-Scanned-By: MIMEDefang 2.84 on 192.168.0.52
X-Scanned-By: MIMEDefang 2.84 on 192.168.0.75

This is a test email
```

Figure 48-2. *Typical email headers*

Let's examine these headers from bottom to top as that is the order in which they will make the most sense.

```
X-Spam-Score: -40.5 () ALL_TRUSTED,USER_IN_WHITELIST
X-Spam-Status: No, score=-28.2 required=10.6 tests=BAYES_50,RDNS_
DYNAMIC,USER_IN_WHITELIST
X-Spam-Status: No, score=-40.5 required=10.9 tests=ALL_TRUSTED,USER_IN_
WHITELIST
X-Scanned-By: MIMEDefang 2.84 on 192.168.0.52
X-Scanned-By: MIMEDefang 2.84 on 192.168.0.75
```

This series of headers were all added by MIMEDefang and SpamAssassin, the anti-spam software we will explore in Chapter 50. There are two sets of entries because the email was scanned by the outbound server and the inbound server. Email should be scanned before it is sent in order to ensure that we are not spamming others from our mail server or via an internal email client that uses our outbound mail server.

```
Content-Type: text/plain; charset=us-ascii
Content-Transfer-Encoding: 7bit
```

These two lines define the basic content type in our message. In this case it is simple plain text, 7-bit ASCII, which was the original encoding for email when it was first developed. This is the simplest form of encoding for email messages and requires no special processing like that needed for special forms like various MIME types.

```
Content-Type: multipart/mixed; boundary="-----------=_1560989912-23914-8"
```

Although this line does not appear in our headers, you will see a header like this if there are multiple MIME parts in the body. The long number at the end is a boundary identifier to specify the beginning and ending of a MIME part.

```
MIME-Version: 1.0
```

This line is an indicator that the body of the email is ASCII plain text or that there is a non-text attachment. It can also mean that the message body has multiple parts, that is, more than one type such as text and image.

This header can also mean that some other header information might be in a non-ASCII text character set. This can occur when spammers try to obfuscate the subject line in order to circumvent anti-spam filters. A typical sample of this is shown here:

```
Subject: =?utf-8?B?V2hpdGXCoEtpZG5lecKgQmVhbnPCoEJsb2NrwqBDYXJicw==?=
```

By specifying the character set utf-8 at the beginning of the subject line, the client can use that set to generate the ASCII text version of the subject so that you can read whatever nastiness they are peddling.

```
User-Agent: Heirloom mailx 12.5 7/5/10
```

The user agent is the sending email client. In this case it is the mailx command I used to send the email. You might also see something like this that is for Thunderbird or the Mozilla-based email clients.

```
User-Agent: Mozilla/5.0 (X11; Linux x86_64; rv:52.0) Gecko/20100101
```

```
Subject: Test email
```

This is the subject line. It can contain almost anything. I have seen some users that are new to email manage to place their entire message in the subject line. I have also seen this field to be blank. This is normally a few words describing the subject of the email.

```
To: linuxgeek46@both.org
```

This is, quite obviously, the email account to which this email is addressed.

```
Date: Wed, 26 Jun 2019 03:54:35 -0400
```

This header specifies the date and time the email was sent as well as the time zone offset. In this case -0400 means GMT -4 hours or EDT.

```
Message-Id: <201906260754.x5Q7sZZ3032629@host1.example.net>
```

Every message has an ID, and this is the ID for the message from which our headers were extracted. This message ID was generated after the sending software, Fail2Ban, sent it to the local email MTA on the local host.

Each message has a different ID on every server through which it travels. This is to prevent the possibility of having a message sent from one server having the same ID as a message sent from another server. These message IDs are stored in the headers as a permanent record, which enables us to locate log entries pertaining to the message in each server.

The first part of the message ID is a date and time in YYYYMMDDNNNN where NNNN is a sequence number. Many email servers are so busy that many emails can arrive at exactly the same time. The second part of the ID is the assigned ID. Message ID formats may vary between email servers that use different operating systems, but that is okay so long as we have the IDs in the headers to work with.

```
From: root <root@host1.example.net>
```

This line identifies the sending host of the email. This, like many of the other headers, can be spoofed so that it looks like it came from another email account entirely. We will explore that later in this chapter. But for this example, we can be sure that none of the headers have been tampered with.

This line is added by the mailx email client, which now sends the email to the MTA on the local host.

```
Received: (from root@localhost)
     by host1.example.net (8.14.7/8.14.7/Submit) id x5Q7sZZ3032629
     for linuxgeek46@both.org; Wed, 26 Jun 2019 03:54:35 -0400
```

This header tells us that the email MTA on host1 received the email from the localhost. It might sound confusing, but so far we are still working on host1, which originated the email message. Each MTA that the email passes through always adds its own received header.

The fact that this was received from root@localhost indicates that the mailx email program sent this email to the MTA.

```
Received: from host1.example.net (localhost [127.0.0.1])
     by host1.example.net (8.14.7/8.14.7) with ESMTP id x5Q7sZx0032630
     for <linuxgeek46@both.org>; Wed, 26 Jun 2019 03:54:35 -0400
```

This received header was also added by host1. It indicates that the email has passed into the mail queue and that it has a new ID. At this point, host1 sends the email to the mail server in its own domain, example.net.

```
Received: from host1.example.net (host1.example.net [192.168.0.1])
     by mailserver.example.net (8.14.7/8.14.4) with ESMTP id
     x5Q7sZgN028979
     for <linuxgeek46@both.org>; Wed, 26 Jun 2019 03:54:35 -0400
```

This, the third received header, shows that the email was received by the email server for the example.net domain.

Note that there is no time difference within the one-second granularity of these headers between the original date stamp placed on the email and this header. All of these timestamps so far place the date and time at Wed, 26 Jun 2019 03:54:35 -0400. So far the email has been processed on two computers.

Now the mail server for the example.net domain sends the email to the destination domain, my own both.org.

```
Received: from mailserver.example.net (rrcs-96-10-0-10.se.biz.rr.com
[96.10.0.10])
     by yorktown.both.org (8.15.2/8.15.2) with ESMTP id x5Q7sZwg006558
     for <linuxgeek46@both.org>; Wed, 26 Jun 2019 03:54:38 -0400
```

The email has now been received by my email server, yorktown.both.org. We now notice a three-second time difference since the previous header. This is due to two factors, the time required to process the email through the spam detection software on the mailserver.example.net system and the time needed to connect with my server and to perform the handshaking and data transfer. Almost all of this time is due to the spam filtering.

Different email servers use somewhat different formats for some of the headers, and they also may insert headers in different places in the stream. As we proceed through this chapter and the next chapters that also relate closely to email, I suggest that you take time to view the headers of the emails we send as part of the experiments.

Sendmail on the Server

Sendmail is a common email transfer agent. It has been around since 1983 and is still widely used on many email servers. There are a number of other good MTAs available, many of which are open source. Understanding Sendmail – at least what we will be able to do here in this course – will provide a good basis for understanding email and mail transfer agents in general.

Although I use Sendmail for my domain email server, it is also useful on a host that is not being used as the primary email server for a domain. Sendmail can be used on any host to provide an MTA to deal with emails sent to root by various system-level applications and servers. If not sent on to an email server, the local emails will be sent to the root user on the local host. Thus, they may never be read and acted upon. Sendmail is required for each host that is intended to send its system management emails to a central mail server for further relay and distribution. When a network of hosts is configured to send all emails to the email server for the domain, that central email server is called a smart host.

In the experiments below, we will install and configure Sendmail as the primary mail server for our domain on StudentVM2, and we will install Sendmail on StudentVM1 to act as a transfer agent, which can forward emails to the domain smart server on StudentVM2. From there these emails can be sent to any email client account.

Sendmail Installation

Let's start by installing Sendmail on both of our virtual machines.

EXPERIMENT 48-1: INSTALLING SENDMAIL

Perform this experiment as the root user on both StudentVM1 and StudentVM2 VMs. We will install the sendmail and sendmail-cf packages on both of our virtual machines in this experiment.

StudentVM1 may already have Sendmail installed. Even so, the sendmail-cf RPM must also be installed. The sendmail-cf package provides the makefiles[2] and configuration files that allow configuration and recompilation of sendmail.mc and other Sendmail configuration files and databases.

We also install mailx, an email client that can be used as a text-mode email client and as a command in a pipeline to send a data stream from its STDIN to the local mail transfer agent. This is a good tool for use to send emails in scripts. We can also use it from the command line to easily send test email.

The make tool is used with makefiles to create completed projects, performing configuration, compiling source code if necessary, and installing files in the correct locations.

Do this on both VMs:

```
# dnf -y install sendmail sendmail-cf mailx make
```

This installation does not require a reboot.

---

[2] A makefile is a series of shell commands and variable statements that are used to create a finished project from a group of input files. Although we use it here with Sendmail to create very complex configuration files and databases from various ASCII text input files, makefiles can also be used to compile programs using languages such as C. The makefile is the recipe that combines all of the input ingredients into the final product.

Sendmail Configuration

Sendmail is already well configured by Red Hat in its distributions including Fedora. Sendmail does still need a bit of additional configuration, and it needs to be configured just a bit differently for the domain email server than for a system that will only send emails to the smart host.

It is only necessary to make some minor changes to the Sendmail configuration itself.

EXPERIMENT 48-2: INITIAL SENDMAIL CONFIGURATION ON STUDENTVM2

Perform this experiment as root on StudentVM2. Later we will make StudentVM2 into the domain mail server. For the moment we will concentrate on sending email from our server although this first change is for inbound email.

Use a text editor to make the changes to the configuration files.

To receive email from any remote computer in your virtual network, you will need to comment out the following line (approximately line number 121) in /etc/mail/sendmail.mc. This line forces Sendmail to listen for email only on the internal lo localhost interface. We want Sendmail to listen on the external interface, enp0s8, as well:

```
DAEMON_OPTIONS(`Port=smtp,Addr=127.0.0.1, Name=MTA')dnl
```

Prepend "dnl " to the preceding line in order to "comment it out." Sendmail will now listen for inbound emails on all network interfaces:

```
dnl DAEMON_OPTIONS(`Port=smtp,Addr=127.0.0.1, Name=MTA')dnl
```

In the M4 language used in sendmail.mc, dnl means "delete through newline," which further translates into something meaningful as "ignore the rest of this line." It is an instruction for the specialized compiler used by Sendmail.

Add the following lines to the /etc/mail/local-host-names file. This will tell Sendmail to accept email addressed to this domain as well as the specified hostnames, which are all aliases for the mail server:

```
example.com
studentvm2.example.com
mail.example.com
```

Add the following lines to the access database file, /etc/mail/access. This allows hosts in the 192.168.56.0/24 network to relay email through this mail server. By limiting the IP addresses to those of our network, spammers are unable to use our mail server to relay spam for them. Without this limitation we would be running an "open relay," and the IP address of our server would be blocked by many legitimate email systems:

```
# Relay for our virtual network
192.168.56                RELAY
```

Now, with /etc/mail as the PWD, run the make command. The make command runs the instructions required to convert the various text configuration files we have modified into the database files in the proper formats needed by Sendmail. This takes only a second or two:

```
# make
```

Verify that the timestamps for the *.db files that correspond to the altered files have been changed.

In a separate terminal session as the root user, tail the /var/log/maillog file. This will inform us of any Sendmail activity including startup information and any errors that might occur. This terminal session should be placed somewhere it can be seen on the desktop while you work in the other session to make changes and start and stop Sendmail:

```
[root@studentvm2 ~]# cd /var/log/ ; tail -f maillog
```

Start Sendmail, enable it to restart on boot, and verify the results:

```
# systemctl start sendmail
Job for sendmail.service failed because a timeout was exceeded.
See "systemctl status sendmail.service" and "journalctl -xeu sendmail.
service" for details.
```

That took a long time, too long in fact. Figuring this one out was pretty easy because you should find some error messages in the maillog file like I did:

```
Jun 27 11:56:36 studentvm2 sendmail[6078]: My unqualified host name
(studentvm2) unknown; sleeping for retry
```

You can also run the journalctl command suggested by the output of the preceding systemctl command.

This error occurs because we set the virtual machine's hostname without using the fully qualified domain name (FQDN).

What?! You did not think I would divulge all of my secrets at once, did you? I learned a lot about configuring Sendmail from the many mistakes I made while doing so the first several times I did it. It took me hours to work my way through some of these problems even using search engines. So my intent here is to give you a feel for Sendmail, not just *what* we need to do, but also the *why* of it.

So let's set the system's hostname and this time we will include the FQDN:

```
[root@studentvm2 mail]# hostnamectl
   Static hostname: studentvm2
         Icon name: computer-vm
           Chassis: vm
        Machine ID: b62e5e58cdf74e0e967b39bc94328d81
           Boot ID: 7ae8d2bbbfaf44a6b1dd8082321d2f81
    Virtualization: oracle
  Operating System: Fedora 29 (Twenty Nine)
       CPE OS Name: cpe:/o:fedoraproject:fedora:29
            Kernel: Linux 5.1.9-200.fc29.x86_64
      Architecture: x86-64
[root@studentvm2 mail]# hostnamectl set-hostname studentvm2.example.com
[root@studentvm2 mail]# hostnamectl
   Static hostname: studentvm2.example.com
<snip>
```

Also check the /etc/hostname file, which is where the hostname is stored. We could have changed the hostname in that file, but activating it would require a reboot. Using the **hostnamectl** command does all of that for us.

Now restart Sendmail:

```
# systemctl restart sendmail
```

Okay, even though I know that's been a problem and blocks the start of Sendmail, there is another problem here that I did not encounter when writing the first edition of this course. I used the following error message to search the Internet:

```
sendmail[1587]: unable to write pid to /var/run/sendmail.pid:
Permission denied
```

I found this bug report on the Red Hat Bugzilla website.

Bug 1253840 - `sendmail startup complains "sendmail.pid not readable (yet?)` `after start"`[3]

This bug has been closed without being fixed. However, the text of the bug contains the simple fix that is impossible to solve without an Internet search. I find that using a copy of the message starting at the service name is the best way to get the optimum results.

Edit the /usr/lib/systemd/system/sendmail.service file and comment out the PIDFile entry:

```
#PIDFile=/run/sendmail.pid
```

Now restart Sendmail – again:

```
# systemctl restart sendmail
```

You should notice immediately that the command only took a very short time. You should also see an informational message on the screen following the maillog and the same error as before. However, you can check the status of Sendmail to verify that it is running:

```
[root@studentvm2 ~]# systemctl status sendmail.service
● sendmail.service - Sendmail Mail Transport Agent
     Loaded: loaded (/usr/lib/systemd/system/sendmail.service; disabled;
     preset: disabled)
    Drop-In: /usr/lib/systemd/system/service.d
             └─10-timeout-abort.conf
     Active: active (running) since Thu 2023-06-22 08:45:51 EDT; 16min ago
    Process: 1706 ExecStartPre=/etc/mail/make (code=exited, status=0/SUCCESS)
    Process: 1708 ExecStartPre=/etc/mail/make aliases (code=exited, status=0/
    SUCCESS)
    Process: 1712 ExecStart=/usr/sbin/sendmail -bd $SENDMAIL_OPTS $SENDMAIL_
    OPTARG (code=exited, status=0/SUCCESS)
   Main PID: 1713 (sendmail)
      Tasks: 1 (limit: 4634)
     Memory: 3.5M
        CPU: 238ms
     CGroup: /system.slice/sendmail.service
             └─1713 "sendmail: accepting connections"
```

---

[3] Red Hat Bugzilla, https://bugzilla.redhat.com/show_bug.cgi?id=1253840

```
Jun 22 08:45:51 studentvm2.example.com systemd[1]: Starting sendmail.
service - Sendmail Mail Transport Agent...
Jun 22 08:45:51 studentvm2.example.com sendmail[1713]: starting daemon
(8.17.1): SMTP+queueing@01:00:00
Jun 22 08:45:51 studentvm2.example.com systemd[1]: Started sendmail.service -
Sendmail Mail Transport Agent.
Jun 22 08:45:51 studentvm2.example.com sendmail[1713]: unable to write pid to
/var/run/sendmail.pid: Permission denied
[root@studentvm2 ~]#
```

It is time to test our server. Let's first test from StudentVM2 in order to verify that it is working because we have not yet configured the firewall to let other hosts send email through this server. We will use the `mailx` command to test for us. As the student user on StudentVM2, enter the following command. The -s option of the mailx command sets the subject text – in double quotes – of the email:

[student@studentvm2 ~]$ **echo "Hello world" | mailx -s "Test mail 1 from StudentVM2" student@example.com**

You should also see four log entries added to the maillog file. The last one should have a status of Sent.

Let's use the `mailx` command in its role as an interactive email client to view our email. In another session as the student user on StudentVM2, start `mailx`. You may have some emails in this student account but probably not:

```
[student@studentvm2 ~]$ mailx
Heirloom Mail version 12.5 7/5/10.  Type ? for help.
"/var/spool/mail/student": 1 message 1 new
>N  1 Student User        Thu Jun 27 12:34  21/895    "Test mail 1 from
StudentVM2"
&
```

The ampersand (&) is the command prompt for the **mailx** email client interface. Just hit the Enter key to start looking at the email messages starting with the first one:

```
& <Enter>
Message  1:
From student@studentvm2.example.com  Thu Jun 27 12:34:50 2019
Return-Path: <student@studentvm2.example.com>
```

```
From: Student User <student@studentvm2.example.com>
Date: Thu, 27 Jun 2019 12:34:48 -0400
To: student@example.com
Subject: Test mail 1 from StudentVM2
User-Agent: Heirloom mailx 12.5 7/5/10
Content-Type: text/plain; charset=us-ascii
Status: RO

Hello world

&
```

Do not delete this email. That worked and you could use **q<Enter>** to quit from **mailx**, but let's just leave it open because we will be using it a bit more.

Notice that there are very few headers because the message was delivered by the email server on the local host, StudentVM2.

It's time to send an email message to the outside world. For this, you will need an external email account that you can access from wherever you are taking this course. A computer, mobile phone, or tablet that you have configured to access your real-world email account would work. If you do not have one of these, you will be able to determine the success of sending these emails from the maillog. This is what SysAdmins and especially email administrators need to do in real life anyway.

As the student user on StudentVM2, do the following. Remember, these commands are all on a single line unless otherwise noted:

```
[student@studentvm2 ~]$ echo "Hello world" | mailx -s "Test mail 2 from
StudentVM2" linuxgeek46@both.org
```

But don't be fooled by the last line of the latest set of log entries. It does say "Sent" but check the To: address. Read through this list of log entries and see if you can figure out what happened before continuing below my sample log entries. I have separated the outbound log entries from the inbound ones with an empty line to make it a bit easier:

```
Jun 27 13:02:17 studentvm2 sendmail[6565]: x5RH2HBh006565: from=student,
size=245, class=0, nrcpts=1, msgid=<201906271702.x5RH2HBh006565@studentvm2.
example.com>, relay=student@localhost
```

```
Jun 27 13:02:18 studentvm2 sendmail[6565]: STARTTLS=client,
relay=[127.0.0.1], version=TLSv1.3, verify=FAIL, cipher=TLS_AES_256_GCM_
SHA384, bits=256/256
Jun 27 13:02:18 studentvm2 sendmail[6572]: STARTTLS=server, relay=localhost
[127.0.0.1], version=TLSv1.3, verify=NOT, cipher=TLS_AES_256_GCM_SHA384,
bits=256/256
Jun 27 13:02:18 studentvm2 sendmail[6572]: x5RH2IT4006572: from=<student@
studentvm2.example.com>, size=524, class=0, nrcpts=1, msgid=<201906271702.
x5RH2HBh006565@studentvm2.example.com>, proto=ESMTPS, daemon=MTA,
relay=localhost [127.0.0.1]
Jun 27 13:02:19 studentvm2 sendmail[6565]: x5RH2HBh006565: to=linuxgeek46@
both.org, ctladdr=student (1000/1000), delay=00:00:02, xdelay=00:00:01,
mailer=relay, pri=30245, relay=[127.0.0.1] [127.0.0.1], dsn=2.0.0, stat=Sent
(x5RH2IT4006572 Message accepted for delivery)

Jun 27 13:02:19 studentvm2 sendmail[6574]: x5RH2IT4006572: to=<linuxgeek46@
both.org>, ctladdr=<student@studentvm2.example.com> (1000/1000),
delay=00:00:01, xdelay=00:00:00, mailer=esmtp, pri=120524, relay=mail.both.
org. [24.199.159.59], dsn=5.1.8, stat=User unknown
Jun 27 13:02:19 studentvm2 sendmail[6574]: x5RH2IT4006572: x5RH2JT3006574:
DSN: User unknown
Jun 27 13:02:20 studentvm2 sendmail[6574]: x5RH2JT3006574: to=<student@
studentvm2.example.com>, delay=00:00:01, xdelay=00:00:00, mailer=local,
pri=31843, dsn=2.0.0, stat=Sent
```

So did you figure it out? It took me a long time at first, so let me explain it. The first set of five log entries from Jun 27 13:02:17 through Jun 27 13:02:19 are from the outbound interaction with the remote email server. In my case this was the email server for the both.org domain. The last log entry for this series shows that the message was accepted by the remote server.

However, starting almost immediately, the next set of log entries shows that the mail server for both.org has sent us a notification, via the connection that we initiated to send the mail in the first place, that the user is unknown. The final line is the indication that our email server sent an email to the sender indicating that this was the case.

As the student user in the already open mailx session, press **h** to refresh and view the headers of any new emails. You should see a new entry, message number 2. Type 2 and view the new message:

& **h**
    1 Student User   Thu Jun 27 12:34   22/906   "Test mail 1 from
StudentVM2"
>   2 Mail Delivery Subsys Thu Jun 27 13:11   73/2862   "Returned mail: see
transcript fo"
& **2**
Message 2:
From MAILER-DAEMON@studentvm2.example.com Thu Jun 27 13:11:29 2019
Return-Path: <MAILER-DAEMON@studentvm2.example.com>
Date: Thu, 27 Jun 2019 13:11:28 -0400
From: Mail Delivery Subsystem <MAILER-DAEMON@studentvm2.example.com>
To: <student@studentvm2.example.com>
Content-Type: multipart/report; report-type=delivery-status;
    boundary="x5RHBSk3006610.1561655488/studentvm2.example.com"
Subject: Returned mail: see transcript for details
Auto-Submitted: auto-generated (failure)
Status: RO

Part 1:

The original message was received at Thu, 27 Jun 2019 13:11:27 -0400
from localhost [127.0.0.1]

    ----- The following addresses had permanent fatal errors -----
<linuxgeek46@both.org>
    (reason: 553 5.1.8 <linuxgeek46@both.org>... Domain of sender address
student@studentvm
2.example.com does not exist)

   ----- Transcript of session follows -----
... while talking to mail.both.org.:
>>> DATA
<<< 553 5.1.8 <linuxgeek46@both.org>... Domain of sender address student@
studentvm2.example
.com does not exist
550 5.1.1 <linuxgeek46@both.org>... User unknown
<<< 503 5.0.0 Need RCPT (recipient)

Part 2:
Content-Type: message/delivery-status

```
Part 3:
Content-Type: message/rfc822

From student@studentvm2.example.com Thu Jun 27 13:11:27 2019
Return-Path: <student@studentvm2.example.com>
From: Student User <student@studentvm2.example.com>
Date: Thu, 27 Jun 2019 13:11:25 -0400
To: linuxgeek46@both.org
Subject: Test mail 2 from StudentVM2
User-Agent: Heirloom mailx 12.5 7/5/10
Content-Type: text/plain; charset=us-ascii

Hello world
&
```

Note the 553 message that says, "Domain of sender address student@studentvm2.example.
com does not exist)." Do you see the problem now? The domain for this email is not really a
domain; it is a hostname, studentvm2.example.com. It includes the domain name. I ran into
this problem, too, the first couple times I set up an email server. It is an unintended side effect
of specifying the hostname of our server with the FQDN.

The reason for this failure is that the Internet name servers, not the ones in our own network,
do not have any domains named <hostname>.example.com. They do have example.com. The
remote mail server, in my case mail.both.org, checks to see that DNS has an IP address for the
domain name in the From: header of the email message. If studentvm2.example.com does not
exist, the mail server rejects the email.

However, we do have some good news. Our server is definitely talking to the remote server, or
we would not be getting this type of error message. The other good news is that this, too, is
easily correctable. Down near the bottom of the sendmail.mc file there are three lines we need
to change so that Sendmail will change the domain from host.example.com to just example.
com. Change the highlighted lines

```
dnl # The following example makes mail from this host and any additional
dnl # specified domains appear to be sent from mydomain.com
dnl #
dnl MASQUERADE_AS(`mydomain.com')dnl
dnl #
dnl # masquerade not just the headers, but the envelope as well
dnl #
```

```
dnl FEATURE(masquerade_envelope)dnl
dnl #
dnl # masquerade not just @mydomainalias.com, but @*.mydomainalias.
com as well
dnl #
dnl FEATURE(masquerade_entire_domain)dnl
```

to this:

```
dnl # The following example makes mail from this host and any additional
dnl # specified domains appear to be sent from mydomain.com
dnl #
MASQUERADE_AS(`example.com')dnl
dnl #
dnl # masquerade not just the headers, but the envelope as well
dnl #
FEATURE(masquerade_envelope)dnl
dnl #
dnl # masquerade not just @mydomainalias.com, but @*.mydomainalias.
com as well
dnl #
FEATURE(masquerade_entire_domain)dnl
```

These lines now masquerade hostnames like studentvm1.example.com and studentvm2.example.com to a true, two-part domain name, example.com.

With /etc/mail as the PWD, make and restart Sendmail:

```
# make ; systemctl restart sendmail
```

Now send the email to your real-world email account. The log should show a successful delivery with no entries to indicate a return error message. Check your external email account to verify the successful receipt of the test email.

This is the source of the email as viewed on my real mail client:

```
Received: from studentvm2.example.com (wally1.both.org [192.168.0.254])
    by yorktown.both.org (8.15.2/8.15.2) with ESMTP id x5RKTGa1030600
    for <linuxgeek46@both.org>; Thu, 27 Jun 2019 16:29:16 -0400
Received: from studentvm2.example.com (localhost [127.0.0.1])
    by studentvm2.example.com (8.15.2/8.15.2) with ESMTPS id x5RKTFBw007324
```

```
        (version=TLSv1.3 cipher=TLS_AES_256_GCM_SHA384 bits=256 verify=NOT)
    for <linuxgeek46@both.org>; Thu, 27 Jun 2019 16:29:15 -0400
Received: (from student@localhost)
    by studentvm2.example.com (8.15.2/8.15.2/Submit) id x5RKTE1h007323
    for linuxgeek46@both.org; Thu, 27 Jun 2019 16:29:14 -0400
From: Student User <student@example.com>
Message-Id: <201906272029.x5RKTE1h007323@studentvm2.example.com>
Date: Thu, 27 Jun 2019 16:29:14 -0400
To: linuxgeek46@both.org
Subject: Test mail 3 from StudentVM2
User-Agent: Heirloom mailx 12.5 7/5/10
MIME-Version: 1.0
Content-Type: text/plain; charset=us-ascii
Content-Transfer-Encoding: 7bit
X-Spam-Status: No, score=-0.5 required=10.6 tests=ALL_TRUSTED,BAYES_50
X-Scanned-By: MIMEDefang 2.84 on 192.168.0.52

Hello world
```

Now enable Sendmail to restart on boot, and verify the results:

```
# systemctl enable --now sendmail ; systemctl status sendmail
```

In Chapter 49 we'll use TLS to provide encryption to outbound emails. Sendmail is already configured for that, and there are appropriate but "untrusted" self-signed certificates installed. The following lines enable TLS in sendmail.mc. You don't need to do anything to Sendmail to enable this:

```
dnl # Basic sendmail TLS configuration with self-signed certificate for
dnl # inbound SMTP (and also opportunistic TLS for outbound SMTP).
dnl #
define(`confCACERT_PATH', `/etc/pki/tls/certs')dnl
define(`confCACERT', `/etc/pki/tls/certs/ca-bundle.crt')dnl
define(`confSERVER_CERT', `/etc/pki/tls/certs/sendmail.pem')dnl
define(`confSERVER_KEY', `/etc/pki/tls/private/sendmail.key')dnl
define(`confTLS_SRV_OPTIONS', `V')dnl
```

Our email server is now capable of sending emails to external, real-world mail servers so long as the email originates from a local account.

DNS Configuration

Now that our email server can send emails, we need it to also receive emails. We need to configure DNS, but our firewall is already configured to receive email from internal sources because we used the trusted zone on that interface. We'll need to add rules to the firewall for the external interface to allow incoming email from other servers and for email clients. But that is for a little later.

Let us start with using it as a "smart host" so that it accepts email from other hosts in our network and can pass them on to the external world. We also want to set up a CNAME record for mail.example.com and a Mail eXchanger (MX) record that explicitly defines the mail server for a domain no matter its given hostname.

The MX record contains a number, 10 in this case, which is a priority in the event that an organization has more than one mail server to handle large email loads. This can be used to define which server gets all the mail and which ones take over if the primary server is unavailable. Or it can be used to configure what's called "round-robin" selection of the email server where DNS is used to perform a crude form of load balancing among all the available email servers.

EXPERIMENT 48-3: DNS CONFIGURATION

Perform this experiment as root on StudentVM2.

Let's start with DNS. Edit the DNS forward lookup database file, /var/named/example.com. zone. Edit this file and add the following lines to it. You can add them at the bottom of the file or wherever your own organizational desires decide, so long as they are placed after the Origin line. Be sure to change the serial number to the current date and time using the format YYYYMMDDHHMMSS, where SS is a sequence number and not seconds:

```
mail                   IN     CNAME   studentvm2
example.org.           IN     MX      10       mail.example.org.
```

My file looks like this after making these changes as shown highlighted in bold:

```
; Authoritative data for example.com zone
;
$TTL 1D
@   IN SOA  studentvm2.example.com   root.studentvm2.example.com. (
                                 2019062701      ; serial
```

```
                                  1D              ; refresh
                                  1H              ; retry
                                  1W              ; expire
                                  3H )            ; minimum

$ORIGIN          example.com.
example.com.         IN     NS      studentvm2.example.com.
router               IN     A       192.168.56.1
studentvm2           IN     A       192.168.56.1
server               IN     CNAME   studentvm2
mail                 IN     CNAME   studentvm2
studentvm1           IN     A       192.168.56.21
workstation1         IN     CNAME   studentvm1
ws1                  IN     CNAME   studentvm1
wkst1                IN     CNAME   ws1
studentvm3           IN     A       192.168.56.22
studentvm4           IN     A       192.168.56.23
testvm1              IN     A       192.168.56.50

; Mail server MX record
example.com.         IN     MX      10      mail.example.com.
```

Restart name services:

```
# systemctl restart named
```

The email server is now ready to accept emails from hosts inside our virtual network.

Sendmail on the Client

Now we can configure Sendmail on the StudentVM1 client host. We already installed it in Experiment 48-1.

EXPERIMENT 48-4: CONFIGURING SENDMAIL ON THE CLIENT

Perform this experiment starting as root on StudentVM1. We will configure this host to use StudentVM2, the domain mail server, as the smart host. Start by using the FQDN for the hostname:

```
# hostnamectl set-hostname studentvm1.example.com
```

Edit /etc/mail/sendmail.mc and change the following line

dnl define(`SMART_HOST', `smtp.your.provider')dnl

to

define(`SMART_HOST', `mail.example.com')dnl

We also need to set up email domain masquerading on StudentVM1 as we did on StudentVM2. Near the bottom of the sendmail.cf file there are the three lines we need to change so that Sendmail will change the domain from host.example.com to just example.com. Change the highlighted lines

```
dnl # The following example makes mail from this host and any additional
dnl # specified domains appear to be sent from mydomain.com
dnl #
dnl MASQUERADE_AS(`mydomain.com')dnl
dnl #
dnl # masquerade not just the headers, but the envelope as well
dnl #
dnl FEATURE(masquerade_envelope)dnl
dnl #
dnl # masquerade not just @mydomainalias.com, but dnl # @*.mydomainalias.com
dnl # as well
dnl #
dnl FEATURE(masquerade_entire_domain)dnl
```

to this:

```
dnl # The following example makes mail from this host and any additional
dnl # specified domains appear to be sent from mydomain.com
dnl #
MASQUERADE_AS(`example.com')dnl
dnl #
dnl # masquerade not just the headers, but the envelope as well
dnl #
FEATURE(masquerade_envelope)dnl
dnl #
```

dnl # masquerade not just @mydomainalias.com, but @*.mydomainalias.
com as well
dnl #
FEATURE(masquerade_entire_domain)dnl

With /etc/mail as the PWD, make and restart Sendmail:

make ; systemctl restart sendmail

Enable Sendmail for it to start on boot, and check its status to ensure that it started correctly:

systemctl enable sendmail ; systemctl status sendmail

Now let's test our configuration. On StudentVM1, open a terminal window as root and use it to **tail -f /var/log/maillog**. Do the same thing on StudentVM2. On StudentVM1, enter the following command and watch the log files. You may see some log entries indicating deliveries of logwatch notifications to root@studentvm1.example.com. This is normal and I had about 30 days worth.

As root on StudentVM1, enter the following to send an email:

echo "Hello world from StudentVM1" | mailx -s "Test email 1" student@example.com

You should first see some log messages on StudentVM1 indicating that its own instance of Sendmail has received the message and various steps in processing it. A moment or so later, you should also see some messages in the log for StudentVM2 indicating it has received the email and is processing it.

Now, as the student user on StudentVM2, use **mailx** to view the email. It should look something like this:

```
From student@studentvm1.example.com  Sat Jun 29 09:06:35 2019
Return-Path: <student@studentvm1.example.com>
From: Student User <student@studentvm1.example.com>
Date: Sat, 29 Jun 2019 09:06:30 -0400
To: student@example.com
Subject: Test email 1
User-Agent: Heirloom mailx 12.5 7/5/10
Content-Type: text/plain; charset=us-ascii
Status: RO

Hello world from StudentVM1
```

We now know that our email server is working and that it is being used as the smart host by StudentVM1. Let's send our message a bit further afield. This time we send the email to an external email account.

Keep following the log files on both hosts. On StudentVM1, send the following message. Please use your own external email account rather than mine, which I use for illustrative purposes:

echo "Hello world from StudentVM1" | mailx -s "Test email 3 from StudentVM1" linuxgeek46@both.org

Here is the source of the message I received on my own email system:

```
Received: from studentvm2.example.com (wally1.both.org [192.168.0.254])
    by yorktown.both.org (8.15.2/8.15.2) with ESMTP id x5TDaORu011406
    for <linuxgeek46@both.org>; Sat, 29 Jun 2019 09:36:00 -0400
Received: from studentvm1.example.com ([192.168.56.21])
    by studentvm2.example.com (8.15.2/8.15.2) with ESMTPS id x5TDaOB9004335
     (version=TLSv1.3 cipher=TLS_AES_256_GCM_SHA384 bits=256 verify=NOT)
    for <linuxgeek46@both.org>; Sat, 29 Jun 2019 09:36:00 -0400
Received: from studentvm1.example.com (localhost [127.0.0.1])
    by studentvm1.example.com (8.15.2/8.15.2) with ESMTPS id x5TDZxp8011175
     (version=TLSv1.3 cipher=TLS_AES_256_GCM_SHA384 bits=256 verify=NOT)
    for <linuxgeek46@both.org>; Sat, 29 Jun 2019 09:35:59 -0400
Received: (from root@localhost)
    by studentvm1.example.com (8.15.2/8.15.2/Submit) id x5TDZw6c011174
    for linuxgeek46@both.org; Sat, 29 Jun 2019 09:35:58 -0400
From: Student User <student@example.com>
Message-Id: <201906291335.x5TDZw6c011174@studentvm1.example.com>
Date: Sat, 29 Jun 2019 09:35:58 -0400
To: linuxgeek46@both.org
Subject: Test email 3 from StudentVM1
User-Agent: Heirloom mailx 12.5 7/5/10
MIME-Version: 1.0
Content-Type: text/plain; charset=us-ascii
Content-Transfer-Encoding: 7bit
```

```
X-Spam-Status: No, score=-26.2 required=10.6 tests=BAYES_50,RDNS_NONE,USER_
IN_WHITELIST
X-Scanned-By: MIMEDefang 2.84 on 192.168.0.52

Hello world from StudentVM1
```

Trace the route of the email through the various hosts using the headers and the mail logs on the virtual hosts.

We now have a working email system with a server and a simple client. Note that with the setup we currently have, the student user needs to log into the StudentVM2 host to retrieve email using `mailx`. We will discuss email clients and the server requirements to support them in more detail in Chapter 49 of this volume.

SMTP: The Protocol

SMTP – Simple Mail Transfer Protocol – is an ASCII plain text conversation used to transfer email between servers and from a sending email client to a server and is defined in RFC 821. SMTP uses TCP port 25. SMTP is well defined in the Internet RFCs, so it is an open standard. SMTP servers are known as mail transfer agents (MTAs) because their function is to transfer email messages between one another.

Let's watch this conversation.

```
EXPERIMENT 48-5: EXPLORING SMTP
```

As the student user on StudentVM1, send an email using the -v option of the `mailx` command. SMTP commands are shown with preceding **>>>** characters. These lines are highlighted to enhance their visibility. The responses from the mail server are not highlighted and begin with message ID numbers.

We send the email from the terminal session:

[student@studentvm1 ~]$ **echo "This is a test email." | mailx -v -s "Test email from StudentVM1" student@example.com**

The `mailx` session connects to the MTA on the local host, which responds with the 220 message:

```
student@example.com... Connecting to [127.0.0.1] via relay...
220 studentvm1.example.com ESMTP Sendmail 8.15.2/8.15.2; Sat, 29 Jun 2019
12:38:30 -0400
```

The MTA on StudentVM1 sends this line, which is "hello – I am studentvm1.example.com." The mail server on StudentVM2 responds with its side of the greeting and a list of features it supports:

```
>>> EHLO studentvm1.example.com
250-studentvm1.example.com Hello localhost [127.0.0.1], pleased to meet you
250-ENHANCEDSTATUSCODES
250-PIPELINING
250-8BITMIME
250-SIZE
250-DSN
250-ETRN
250-AUTH GSSAPI DIGEST-MD5 CRAM-MD5
250-STARTTLS
250-DELIVERBY
250 HELP
```

The local MTA has determined that TLS is supported and tells the remote MTA to start the TLS handshaking. TLS is an encryption protocol that is configured and enabled by default in current releases of Fedora and other Linux distributions. TLS ensures that the connection between the two MTAs is encrypted and that the data can be sent between them without being read by a casual observer to the conversation:

```
>>> STARTTLS
220 2.0.0 Ready to start TLS
```

We restart the conversation now that TLS is active:

```
>>> EHLO studentvm1.example.com
250-studentvm1.example.com Hello localhost [127.0.0.1], pleased to meet you
250-ENHANCEDSTATUSCODES
250-PIPELINING
250-8BITMIME
250-SIZE
250-DSN
250-ETRN
```

```
250-AUTH GSSAPI DIGEST-MD5 CRAM-MD5
250-DELIVERBY
250 HELP
```

The local MTA tells the remote MTA whom the mail is from and a bit about it. The remote MTA responds by saying that the sender is okay. That means the sending domain has not been blocked by the remote MTA:

>>> MAIL From:<student@studentvm1.example.com> SIZE=253 AUTH=student@ studentvm1.example.com
```
250 2.1.0 <student@studentvm1.example.com>... Sender ok
```

The local MTA tells the remote MTA whom the email is addressed to:

>>> RCPT To:<student@example.com>

We tell the remote MTA that we are ready to send the data, which consists of the body of the email. The remote MTA returns a message that implies the recipient of the email has a valid mailbox on the server and that it is not full or otherwise blocked. It also sends a response of 354, which indicates that the local MTA can begin sending the body of the email:

>>> DATA
```
250 2.1.5 <student@example.com>... Recipient ok
354 Enter mail, end with "." on a line by itself
```

Sending the dot (.) on a line by itself to the remote MTA indicates that this is the end of the email. The remote MTA returns the message ID that it has assigned to the email and that the message was accepted by the remote MTA. It also indicates it is ready to close the connection from its end:

>>> .
```
250 2.0.0 x5TGcUtk013404 Message accepted for delivery
student@example.com... Sent (x5TGcUtk013404 Message accepted for delivery)
Closing connection to [127.0.0.1]
```

The local MTA sends QUIT to close the connection. The local MTA responds with a message to indicate that it is closing the connection:

>>> QUIT
```
221 2.0.0 studentvm1.example.com closing connection
```

SMTP return messages[4] fall into the following categories shown in Figure 48-3.

Code	Class	Description
1xx	Informational	The request was received by the server and the process that sent the message is continuing.
2xx	Successful	The server understood and accepted the request sent from the client or other server.
3xx	Redirection	Some additional action needs to be taken by the server to complete the client's request.
4xx	Client Error	The request from the client cannot be completed due to an error such as incorrect syntax.
5xx	Server Error	The SMTP server is unable to complete the client's request despite the fact that it appears to be a valid request with correct syntax.

Figure 48-3. *The SMTP return code classifications*

Sometimes these messages, especially when they are error codes, are embedded in a returned email rejection. Other times the only way to see them is to use a tool like mailx to observe the conversation for yourself.

---

[4]Wikipedia, List of SMTP Server Return Codes, https://en.wikipedia.org/wiki/
List_of_SMTP_server_return_codes

Email-Only Accounts

Although the student user is a valid user in our experimental environment, it is a login account. Email servers need to be secure so that the owners of email accounts are unable to actually log into the server. This is accomplished by creating nologin accounts for email-only users.

EXPERIMENT 48-6: EMAIL-ONLY ACCOUNTS

As the root user on the server, StudentVM2, add an account with the username of email1 that can only be used as an email account. The -s option is used to specify the special nologin shell:

```
[root@studentvm2 ~]# useradd -c "Email only account" -s /sbin/nologin email1
```

Create a password for this account. The password is used when an email client attempts to retrieve email from this account while the nologin shell prevents a login as a Linux user:

```
[root@studentvm2 ~]# passwd email1
Changing password for user email1.
New password: <Enter the password>
BAD PASSWORD: The password is shorter than 8 characters
Retype new password: <Enter the password again>
passwd: all authentication tokens updated successfully.
```

Test to verify that you cannot log in with this new account by attempting to do so as the user email1 using a virtual console.

As the user student, on StudentVM1, send an email to the user email1:

```
[student@studentvm1 ~]$ echo "Test email to email1 email only account." |
mailx -v -s "Test email" email1@example.com
```

You cannot log in as user email1, so you must retrieve this email with mailx a bit differently. Because root can do anything, you will have to issue the following command as root on StudentVM2. You would get an error if you tried to do it as a non-root user:

```
[root@studentvm2 ~]# mailx -u email1
Heirloom Mail version 12.5 7/5/10.  Type ? for help.
"/var/mail/email1": 1 message 1 new
```

```
>N  1 Student User          Sat Jun 29 21:10  25/1128  "Test email"
& 1
Message  1:
From student@example.com  Sat Jun 29 21:10:57 2019
Return-Path: <student@example.com>
From: Student User <student@example.com>
Date: Sat, 29 Jun 2019 21:10:51 -0400
To: email1@example.com
Subject: Test email
User-Agent: Heirloom mailx 12.5 7/5/10
Content-Type: text/plain; charset=us-ascii
Status: R

Test email to email1 email only account.

&
```

Who Gets Email for Root?

Many system-level services can send email to root@localhost to notify the root user of the completion of an at job, for example, the daily logwatch report, and more, depending upon the specific tools and their configuration. These emails can get missed and ignored on many hosts that the SysAdmin does not log into frequently. Even with only a few hosts to log into each day, I found it a chore to do so just to check root's emails.

I found an easy way to fix that now that our internal StudentVM1 host can use StudentVM2 as a smart host. I use the /etc/aliases file to send the email to my personal email address.

The /etc/aliases file contains aliases for the system users that define who gets email sent to them. Many system services have user accounts associated, and some of those services send email notifications to root or to another user. Websites also have nonspecific email accounts such as abuse@example.com or webmaster@example.com. So if someone sends email to abuse@example.com, the aliases file tells Sendmail to route that email to root. This email ends up in root's local mailbox on the local host. If that is not what you want, and it usually is not, we need to change the /etc/aliases file.

I like to get email that is addressed to root sent to me at one of my regular email accounts so that I will be sure to get it. This allows me to keep track of notifications that might indicate a problem of some sort.

EXPERIMENT 48-7: EMAIL FOR ROOT

Start this experiment as the root user on StudentVM1. We will change a few things to send notifications intended for root to the student user instead.

First, copy the current version of the /etc/aliases file to /tmp for a short-term backup. Then open /etc/aliases with a text editor. Study the entries and notice that some, like the ftp entry, send emails to root, while further down, four other entries, ftpadm, ftpadmin, ftp-adm, and ftp-admin, all redirect email to ftp.

Down at the bottom of the file is a line that is commented out. It is an example of how to forward root's email to another user:

```
#root:          marc
```

Below that, place the following line and save the file:

```
root:           student@example.com
```

Now run the **newaliases** command without any options or arguments to activate your changes:

```
[root@studentvm1 etc]# newaliases
/etc/aliases: 77 aliases, longest 19 bytes, 794 bytes total
```

As root on StudentVM1, send a test email to ftp without the FQDN:

```
[root@studentvm1 etc]# echo "Test of /etc/aliases" | mailx -v -s "Test email for aliases" ftp
```

Verify that the email has been delivered to the user student on StudentVM2. Remember that StudentVM2 is our mail server, so that's where this should end up.

Now make the same change to the aliases file on StudentVM2 and test it with emails sent to root or one of the other aliases like ftp.

By making this one change in the aliases file, I don't need to change the default email address in many different services.

Things to Remember

There are some things to remember about email.

It Is Not Instant

One of the most common misconceptions that most end users have about email is that it is instant. It is not. Email may get held up at one of the MTAs for various reasons. Heavy traffic can delay emails, and anything marked as bulk in one of the headers will be placed at the bottom of the queue and only sent when all emails with higher precedence have been sent. Any email without a precedence header is considered to be normal. Bulk email is sent from listservs and may have many addressees at any one domain.

I had one situation when working in a government organization where a PHB tried to ream me out and threatened me with some sort of disciplinary action because an email he sent did not get to the people in his building immediately upon being sent. The email he sent was to warn of an imminent tornado, which was, in fact, bearing down on that part of the city at the time. But the email was sent to a list, and between being bulk mail and having hundreds of recipients in an email system that received more than 20,000,000 (yes, 20 million) emails per day, it took some time to process and deliver of all those emails.

And, as we have mentioned before, one must be sitting at their computer with the email client up and running and watching for new emails to come in for this asynchronous communication system to be effective. Email is just not an appropriate communication method for that type of imminent danger.

There Is No Delivery Guarantee

Another popular misconception is that email will always get delivered. It won't. Many email systems drop emails that don't conform to their anti-spam or bulk mail policies. They may reject emails for many reasons, and there is nothing that we on the sending end can do about it. Sure, we can call or email the designated contact for the domain, but in most cases they ignore this type of complaint.

Emails also get dropped when routers become overburdened and start dropping packets. In this case the sending server may try to send the email again, but there is still no guarantee of its ultimate delivery.

Chapter Summary

In this chapter we have learned to use Sendmail as an SMTP mail transfer agent. We have configured Sendmail to be our mail server as well as to forward internal emails from our own network hosts to the mail server as a smart host. We have used the `mailx` email client on both hosts to retrieve and send emails. We have also added an MX record and a supporting record to our DNS server and added a rule to the firewall on the server to allow incoming SMTP packets on port 25.

Although we cannot yet receive email from the outside world on our email server, be assured that it would work. Once it can receive email from internal network hosts, and with configuration of Sendmail to listen on the appropriate external network interface, we would also be able to receive emails from outside domains.

There is more to be done to make this into a fully functioning email system, but we are well on the way.

Exercises

Perform these exercises to complete this chapter:

1. Where are emails located in your inbox stored? Be specific with the host and the complete directory path.

2. Why do we need to masquerade the email sending addresses?

3. What TCP port does SMTP use?

4. Why does email on our virtual network get sent to our own instance of example.com and not to the outside world instance?

5. When sending email to an alias like www on StudentVM1, what is the To: address when the email arrives in the student email account on StudentVM2?

6. How does an email-only account differ from a regular Linux user account?

7. What other things can you think of that we need to do to make our email server more functional and more secure?

CHAPTER 49

Advanced Email Topics

Objectives

In this chapter you will learn

- To use email clients to test email server configuration

- More about using the `mailx` email client

- To install and configure the IMAP server, which allows remote email clients to access email on the server

- To install and configure the Alpine text-mode email client

- To install and configure Thunderbird for a graphical email client

- To use the STARTTLS protocol to encrypt the email data stream transmissions between clients and servers that are configured to support it

- To enable SMTP AUTH as a means to prevent our server being an open relay for spammers

Introduction

In the previous chapter of this volume, we created an email server for our virtual domain, example.com. We installed Sendmail and the tools needed to modify and recompile the Sendmail configuration. We also installed and learned some basic usage for the `mailx` email client. mailx is a powerful ASCII plain text email client that has two interfaces. It can be used with Standard I/O (STDIO) as part of a command pipeline

© David Both 2023
D. Both, *Using and Administering Linux: Volume 3*, https://doi.org/10.1007/978-1-4842-9786-5_49

to send email from shell scripts or command-line programs. It can also be used as an interactive text-mode user interface that uses keyboard commands to perform tasks like reading and deleting email, composing and sending new emails, and much more.

In this chapter we will explore email in more detail and the use of Telnet and email clients as tools for testing advanced email configurations. We will install and configure the IMAP email access protocol on the server, which will enable access to emails on the server from remote clients. We will also look at the popular open source GUI email client, Thunderbird, along with Alpine, a full-featured text-mode email client. We will use TLS[1] to provide encryption between our email clients and our own email server.

We will be making modifications to the server configuration and then use different email clients to test those changes. It's important to understand the server configurations in order to properly configure the email clients.

Of course, in addition to being useful tools for testing, the email clients we explore in this chapter can also be used to send and receive email.

The Real Problem with Email

Email is not secure. Ever. Many politicians and executives have discovered that in embarrassing ways with career-ending consequences.

Although we will add encryption and authentication to our email server in this chapter, we have no control whatsoever over the email servers through which email passes after it leaves our server. We can only control what happens within our own network. We can also offer encryption to those email servers that exchange email with us but can't force them to use it. Besides, the email is decrypted when it enters any email server.

Weldon Whipple states in his tutorial "Configuring Sendmail for STARTTLS,"[2] "[STARTTLS] does not guarantee that e-mail opened by the recipient has been encrypted at every step of its transmission from its origin." He goes on to say, "In fact, since only a miniscule[sic] number of public mail servers implement STARTTLS, it is highly unlikely that any given e-mail will remain encrypted during its journey from sender to recipient."

---

[1] Wikipedia, Transport Layer Security, `https://en.wikipedia.org/wiki/Transport_Layer_Security`

[2] Whipple, Weldon, "Configuring Sendmail for STARTTLS," `https://weldon.whipple.org/sendmail/starttlstut.html`

So why bother with this chapter in which we mostly explore email encryption and authentication? What use is it anyway? We do it mostly because "it's there." Some organizations do use it, so you may need to at least know the basics of how it works.

Preparation

Before getting started with this chapter, be sure to install updates on both VMs and take snapshots of both after doing so.

I have found email setup and configuration to be less than straightforward, and I have had to start over from a snapshot taken at the beginning of this chapter more than once. We also explore two different IMAP servers in this chapter. There are two distinct IMAP servers, and each requires a different path through parts of this chapter. You may wish to try both, but because they may interfere with each other, you should restart from the snapshot to get a truly clean system.

More mailx

Although the `mailx` client and its predecessor, `mail`, have been around since the early days of Unix, it still has an important place in today's Linux environment. We have already seen how useful the `mailx` utility can be in testing email servers and mail transfer agents (MTAs).

Much of the utility of the `mailx` program comes from its flexible interface. We have already used it as part of a pipeline to send output from one utility to an email address. This makes it a powerful tool for the SysAdmin when installing or repairing email systems. Now we want to explore the use of mailx as an ASCII text email client from which we can send and retrieve emails.

As an email client, `mailx` has some limitations that make it less suitable for the average user – it is typically run as a text-mode tool on the email server itself. It is not intended to run on a local host to access email on a remote server although it can do that. The user must use SSH to log into the email server in order to access their email so that the email users must have a login account on the server and not the safer nologin account. This can be a security issue although using SSH to log into the server is very secure.

That said, `mailx` does have extensions that will allow it to connect to an IMAP server. We will get to IMAP later in this chapter but will not use `mailx` with IMAP. Experiment 49-1 uses `mailx` to further explore its capabilities and usefulness as a tool for testing email.

EXPERIMENT 49-1: MORE TESTING WITH MAILX

Start this experiment as the student user on StudentVM1. This experiment is an exploration of mailx as a basic email client and using it as a tool for testing that email is getting into the inbox. In our case that's var/spool/mail/student.

As the student user on StudentVM1, SSH to StudentVM2. Start the interactive user interface (UI) of `mailx`, and then enter a question mark to get help. Note that the ampersand (&) is the command prompt for `mailx`:

```
[student@studentvm2 ~]$ mailx
Heirloom Mail version 12.5 7/5/10.  Type ? for help.
"/var/spool/mail/student": 6 messages 3 unread
     1 Student User         Sat Jun 29 12:38  26/1140  "Test email from StudentVM1"
     2 Student User         Sun Jun 30 08:59  26/1130  "Test email for aliases"
     3 Student User         Sun Jun 30 09:06  26/1130  "Test email for aliases"
>U   4 Student User         Sun Jun 30 09:10  26/1132  "Test email for aliases"
 U   5 Student User         Sun Jun 30 12:45  26/1147  "Test email for aliases"
 U   6 logwatch@example.com Mon Jul  1 03:44  62/2610  "Logwatch for studentvm1.
                                                        example.com (Lin"
& ?
                   mailx commands
type <message list>            type messages
next                           goto and type next message
from <message list>            give head lines of messages
headers                        print out active message headers
delete <message list>          delete messages
undelete <message list>        undelete messages
save <message list> folder     append messages to folder and mark as saved
copy <message list> folder     append messages to folder without
                               marking them
write <message list> file      append message texts to file, save
                               attachments
```

preserve \<message list\>	keep incoming messages in mailbox even if saved
Reply \<message list\>	reply to message senders
reply \<message list\>	reply to message senders and all recipients
mail addresses	mail to specific recipients
file folder	change to another folder
quit	quit and apply changes to folder
xit	quit and discard changes made to folder
!	shell escape
cd \<directory\>	chdir to directory or home if none given
list	list names of all available commands

A \<message list\> consists of integers, ranges of same, or other criteria
separated by spaces. If omitted, mailx uses the last message typed.
&

We can also send emails using the mail command from within the mailx interface. Use your own external email address instead of mine. Thanks!

& **mail linuxgeek46@both.org student@example.com**
Subject: **Test email**
This is a test.

•

EOT
&

If you were not already familiar with the structure of an email message, would it ever occur to you to finish the message with a period on a line by itself? You could also use Ctrl+D to accomplish the same thing.

Verify that those emails were received. Here's what that email looks like when I view it using mailx as the student user on StudentVM2. I used the **P** command to view the headers:

```
Message 22:
From root@studentvm1.example.com  Thu Jul  6 09:43:22 2023
Return-Path: <root@studentvm1.example.com>
Received: from studentvm1.example.com ([192.168.56.56])
        by studentvm2.example.com (8.17.1/8.17.1) with ESMTPS id
        366DhJpw370791
        (version=TLSv1.3 cipher=TLS_AES_256_GCM_SHA384 bits=256 verify=NOT);
        Thu, 6 Jul 2023 09:43:19 -0400
```

```
Received: from studentvm1.example.com (localhost [127.0.0.1])
        by studentvm1.example.com (8.17.1/8.17.1) with ESMTPS id
        366DhISWO15581
        (version=TLSv1.3 cipher=TLS_AES_256_GCM_SHA384 bits=256 verify=NOT);
        Thu, 6 Jul 2023 09:43:18 -0400
Received: (from root@localhost)
        by studentvm1.example.com (8.17.1/8.17.1/Submit) id 366DhGlO015580;
        Thu, 6 Jul 2023 09:43:16 -0400
From: root <root@studentvm1.example.com>
Message-Id: <202307061343.366DhGlO015580@studentvm1.example.com>
Date: Thu, 06 Jul 2023 09:43:16 -0400
To: student@example.com, linuxgeek46@both.org
Subject: ####NOT SPAM#### (-1) Test email
User-Agent: Heirloom mailx 12.5 7/5/10
MIME-Version: 1.0
Content-Type: multipart/mixed; boundary="-----------=_1688650999-3318-14"
X-Spam-Status: Spam, score=-1 required=5 tests=ALL_TRUSTED
X-Scanned-By: MIMEDefang 3.4.1
Status: R

Part 1:
Content-Type: text/plain; charset=us-ascii
Content-Transfer-Encoding: 7bit

This is a test.

Part 2:
Content-Type: text/plain; name="SpamAssassinReport.txt"
Content-Disposition: inline; filename="SpamAssassinReport.txt"
Content-Transfer-Encoding: 7bit

Spam detection software, running on the system "studentvm2.example.com",
has NOT identified this incoming email as spam.  The original
message has been attached to this so you can view it or label
similar future email.  If you have any questions, see
@@CONTACT_ADDRESS@@ for details.

Content preview:  This is a test.

Content analysis details:   (-1.0 points, 5.0 required)
```

```
pts rule name               description
---- --------------------    --------------------------------------------
-1.0 ALL_TRUSTED             Passed through trusted hosts only via SMTP
```

As we have already discovered, many commands can be invoked with just their first letter. Note that "R" and "r" are different commands. Now enter **l** (lowercase l – el) to list all of the available commands. You can always view the help and list of commands if you get stuck.

You may find that the email doesn't arrive at your external address. It didn't for me. If you ran your own email server, you would see some messages in the maillog file that look something like this:

```
Jul  6 07:59:48 mymailserver sendmail[759738]: 366Bxl3R759738: ruleset=check_
rcpt, arg1=<linuxgeek46@both.org>, relay=_gateway [192.168.0.254],
reject=553 5.
1.8 <linuxgeek46@both.org>... Domain of sender address root@studentvm1.
example.com does not exist

Jul  6 07:59:48 mymailserver sendmail[759738]: 366Bxl3R759738: from=<root@
studentvm1.example.com>, size=2025, class=0, nrcpts=0, proto=ESMTPS,
daemon=MTA, relay=_gateway [192.168.0.254]
```

Why does this happen? In my case it was because I had not yet configured StudentVM1 to use StudentVM2 as the smart host. That happened for me because I had reverted to a VM snapshot in which I hadn't yet configured that.

This problem illustrates two things. One is that any Linux host that has Sendmail running will try to send email to the destination but using the FQDN, studentvm1.example.com, as a return path. That hostname is not defined in any public name service, so it generates an error. Then the second thing is that my email server did a DNS lookup for that FQDN as an anti-spam test. Since it didn't exist, my Sendmail server discarded the email.

After fixing that problem and restarting MIMEDefang and Sendmail in that order, I sent another email that looks like this in Alpine on my main workstation:

```
Received: from studentvm2.example.com (_gateway [192.168.0.254])
    by mymailserver.both.org (8.17.1/8.17.1) with ESMTPS id 366FmxSY771163
    (version=TLSv1.3 cipher=TLS_AES_256_GCM_SHA384 bits=256 verify=NOT)
    for <linuxgeek46@both.org>; Thu, 6 Jul 2023 11:48:59 -0400
Received: from studentvm1.example.com ([192.168.56.56])
    by studentvm2.example.com (8.17.1/8.17.1) with ESMTPS id 366FmvMn371237
```

```
    (version=TLSv1.3 cipher=TLS_AES_256_GCM_SHA384 bits=256 verify=NOT);
    Thu, 6 Jul 2023 11:48:57 -0400
Received: from studentvm1.example.com (localhost [127.0.0.1])
    by studentvm1.example.com (8.17.1/8.17.1) with ESMTPS id 366FmvR5001826
    (version=TLSv1.3 cipher=TLS_AES_256_GCM_SHA384 bits=256 verify=NOT);
    Thu, 6 Jul 2023 11:48:57 -0400
Received: (from student@localhost)
    by studentvm1.example.com (8.17.1/8.17.1/Submit) id 366FmtLI001825;
    Thu, 6 Jul 2023 11:48:55 -0400
From: Student User <student@example.com>
Message-Id: <202307061548.366FmtLI001825@studentvm1.example.com>
Date: Thu, 06 Jul 2023 11:48:55 -0400
To: student@example.com, linuxgeek46@both.org
Subject: ####NOT SPAM#### (-1) Test email 20230706
User-Agent: Heirloom mailx 12.5 7/5/10
MIME-Version: 1.0
Content-Type: multipart/mixed; boundary="-----------=_1688658537-3318-19"
X-Spam-Status: No, score=-75.7 required=10.6 tests=BAYES_20,RDNS_NONE,SPF_
HELO_NONE,USER_IN_WELCOMELIST,USER_IN_WHITELIST
X-Spam-Status: Spam, score=-1 required=5 tests=ALL_TRUSTED
X-Scanned-By: MIMEDefang 3.4.1 on 192.168.0.52
X-Scanned-By: MIMEDefang 3.4.1
Parts/Attachments:
   1 Shown     2 lines  Text
   2 Shown    16 lines  Text
----------------------------------------
```

This is a test.

    [Part 2: "Attached Text"]

Spam detection software, running on the system "studentvm2.example.com",
has NOT identified this incoming email as spam. The original
message has been attached to this so you can view it or label
similar future email. If you have any questions, see
@@CONTACT_ADDRESS@@ for details.

Content preview: This is a test.

Content analysis details: (-1.0 points, 5.0 required)

```
pts rule name                description
---- -------------------- --------------------------------------------
-1.0 ALL_TRUSTED          Passed through trusted hosts only via SMTP
```

In addition to using `mailx` to send a STDIN data stream as an email, we can also invoke it from the command line. This gives us a more interactive means of using it for testing. Let's exit from the `mailx` user interface and then send an email to ourselves:

```
[student@studentvm2 ~]$ mailx student@example.com
Subject: Testing mailx
This email is a test of using mailx to send email.
EOT
[student@studentvm2 ~]$
```

After entering the `mailx` command, it prompts you for the subject. After entering that you get an empty line and you can simply start typing your message. When you have finished entering the message, use Ctrl+D (EOT or End Of Text) to tell `mailx` to send the message.

Now view the message in the interactive interface on StudentVM1. Be sure to examine the headers.

Although mailx is a powerful and flexible tool for the SysAdmin, it leaves much to be desired with respect to the normal email experience that users expect today. We will look at other email clients in this chapter, but first we need to install a mail access server – IMAP.

Setup

We are going to use the Telnet communications program to test our IMAP server, whichever one we install. Telnet can be used to test many of the services we use because many use plain ASCII text protocols. We can use this bit of historical fortune to our good advantage. So we'll install Telnet on both student VMs to allow us to perform some interesting command-line testing.

```
┌─────────────────────────────────────────────────────────────┐
│                  EXPERIMENT 49-2: SETUP                       │
└─────────────────────────────────────────────────────────────┘
```

Install the following Telnet packages on StudentVM2, which we'll use for testing:

```
[root@studentvm2 ~]# dnf -y install telnet telnet-server
```

Also install Telnet on StudentVM1:

```
[root@studentvm1 ~]# dnf -y install telnet telnet-server
```

Installing IMAP on the Server

Once email has been delivered to the server, you must retrieve it from the mail spool file in order to read it. Email can be retrieved from remote servers using the protocol IMAP.[3] IMAP was designed explicitly to allow users to access all of their emails from multiple devices running an email client. This was originally conceived as multiple computers, but in this Internet age, it encompasses all types of connected devices.

IMAP is a much better tool to use for multiple devices than the old and much simpler Post Office Protocol (POP). Clients connecting to an email server using POP download all of the messages to the local host and delete them from the server. Thus, those messages that have already been downloaded cannot be viewed by any of the other devices. We will cover only IMAP in this course.

There are three good IMAP servers. The one I have used for years, the University of Washington IMAP[4] package, is no longer maintained or supported. Despite that, uw-imap remains the reference implementation of IMAP, so we will use that because it is also easy and still performs its singular task very well. I find uw-imap much simpler to install and configure than either Cyrus or Dovecot. I believe in the KISS tenet of the Linux Philosophy for SysAdmins – Keep It Simple S* – so we will start by using uw-imap for this chapter despite the need to use RPMs from Fedora 33.

---

[3] IMAP, Internet Message Access Protocol (RFC 2060).

[4] Wikipedia, UW IMAP, https://en.wikipedia.org/wiki/UW_IMAP

The two other IMAP servers, Dovecot[5] and Cyrus IMAP,[6] are significantly different from each other. Cyrus provides IMAP support but also calendar and contacts functions. It also uses a somewhat different approach to user accounts than the historical uw-imap. Dovecot only provides IMAP functions and is more compatible with the uw-imap functional strategies. It is, however, much more complex.

I had a significant amount of time and research to get the Dovecot IMAP server installed and properly configured. However, with some help from Peter Boy, who translated his German version of a step-by-step installation procedure for Dovecot into English, I was able to make that work too. So I will include the instructions for that in this chapter as well. Then, when – not if – the uw-imap hack that I have used here fails to work, you can move on to Dovecot.

Tip   I have included two experiments that install IMAP servers. UW IMAP will probably no longer work at some point in the future, even with the hack I use in Experiment 49-3. If that experiment fails, remove the UW IMAP packages and perform Experiment 49-4 to install the Dovecot IMAP server.

Installing UW IMAP

Experiment 49-3 has us install UW IMAP and some IMAP utilities. The xinetd daemon is also needed to launch the IMAP server when an IMAP connection comes in.

---

[5] Wikipedia, Dovecot IMAP, `https://en.wikipedia.org/wiki/Dovecot_(software)`
[6] Wikipedia, Cyrus IMAP, `https://en.wikipedia.org/wiki/Cyrus_IMAP_server`

EXPERIMENT 49-3: INSTALL UW IMAP ON THE SERVER

As I mentioned previously, uw-imap is no longer included in the Fedora 37 or 38 repository nor probably any later ones. The most recent packages are located in the Fedora 33 archival repository, so we can download them from there. We want both the IMAP and utilities RPMs.

It took me a few minutes to work through the dependencies that are needed by the uw-imap packages and to determine the correct sequence in which to install them. I won't make you work through that yourself, but it does remind me of the days in which we had to work our way through "dependency hell" to install almost any new package.

Make root's home directory /root the PWD on StudentVM2. Use wget to download the uw-imap packages and the other required packages:

```
[root@studentvm2 ~]# wget https://mirror.math.princeton.edu/pub/fedora-
archive/fedora/linux/releases/33/Everything/x86_64/os/Packages/u/uw-imap-
utils-2007f-26.fc33.x86_64.rpm
[root@studentvm2 ~]# wget https://mirror.math.princeton.edu/pub/fedora-
archive/fedora/linux/releases/33/Everything/x86_64/os/Packages/u/uw-
imap-2007f-26.fc33.x86_64.rpm
[root@studentvm2 ~]# wget https://mirror.math.princeton.edu/pub/fedora-
archive/fedora/linux/releases/33/Everything/x86_64/os/Packages/x/
xinetd-2.3.15-34.fc33.x86_64.rpm
[root@studentvm2 ~]# wget https://mirror.math.princeton.edu/pub/fedora-
archive/fedora/linux/releases/33/Everything/x86_64/os/Packages/l/libc-
client-2007f-26.fc33.x86_64.rpm
```

Install these RPMs in the correct sequence. If we install them in the wrong sequence, we'll get errors indicating that the needed dependencies are not available. My personal experiments revealed that we can install the two dependencies first and together:

```
[root@studentvm2 ~]# dnf -y install ./xinetd-2.3.15-34.fc33.x86_64.rpm ./
libc-client-2007f-26.fc33.x86_64.rpm
```

And now the uw-imap packages can be installed in a single command:

```
[root@studentvm2 ~]# dnf -y install ./uw-imap-*
```

Warning   If either of the previous two commands fails, do not continue with this experiment. Delete any packages that did install and then proceed to Experiment 49-4 to install Dovecot IMAP.

There is only a bit of configuration to do. You must enable IMAP and start xinetd. Edit the /etc/xinetd.d/imap file and change the line that says "**disable = yes**" to "**disable = no**" to enable IMAP. Then start the xinetd service and configure it to start upon reboot:

[root@studentvm2 ~]# **systemctl enable --now xinetd.service**
Verify that IMAP is configured and running with the following two commands:

[root@studentvm2 xinetd.d]# **systemctl status xinetd**

If you finished this experiment without encountering any errors, you can skip the next section, "Installing Dovecot IMAP," and Experiment 49-4. Jump instead to the "Testing IMAP" section and Experiment 49-5.

Installing Dovecot IMAP

If you did not encounter errors in Experiment 49-3 and UW IMAP installed correctly, you can skip this section and go directly to section "Testing IMAP" and Experiment 49-5. Otherwise, you are here to install Dovecot IMAP because UW IMAP did not install.

Dovecot IMAP requires more configuration than does UW IMAP. There are at least ten files that need to be modified. One reason for this is that Dovecot has its own passwd file because it doesn't use the Linux passwd file. That means that IMAP users don't have a Linux account on the email server, which provides better overall security for the host than UW IMAP.

Installing Dovecot and making it work with Sendmail has been a long and currently unsuccessful project. I will continue to work on this and post details on my website when I know it can be done reliably.

EXPERIMENT 49-4: INSTALLING DOVECOT IMAP

Refer to my personal website for details of installing Dovecot IMAP with Sendmail:

www.both.org

I will post those details when I have them worked out reliably.

Testing IMAP

Regardless of which IMAP server you installed, testing it remains the same. We will use the Telnet client to perform our initial testing so that any failures will be obvious and we can directly read the failure messages.

This will also provide you with a sense of how IMAP works. Because the protocol is in plain ASCII text, we can easily send commands to the IMAP server and see the responses, good or bad. This is an excellent example of standardized, open protocols that anyone can access using simple tools.

EXPERIMENT 49-5: TESTING THE IMAP SERVER

Do a quick test. I did mine from StudentVM1, but you can do this from either StudentVM1 or StudentVM2. Be sure to add the "a01" at the beginning of the login line; it's intended as a sequence indicator. You'll get an error if you don't use it. I usually use a01, a02, …, etc., but you can use a, b, c, etc. or just numeric sequences. Just use something with an increasing value for the sequence:

```
[student@studentvm1 ~]$ telnet studentvm2 143
Trying 192.168.56.11...
Connected to studentvm2.
Escape character is '^]'.
* OK [CAPABILITY IMAP4REV1 I18NLEVEL=1 LITERAL+ SASL-IR LOGIN-REFERRALS
STARTTLS] studentvm2.example.com IMAP4rev1 2007f.404 at Wed, 28 Jun 2023
11:15:18 -0400 (EDT)
```

a01 login student <password>

a01 OK [CAPABILITY IMAP4REV1 I18NLEVEL=1 LITERAL+ IDLE UIDPLUS NAMESPACE
CHILDREN MAILBOX-REFERRALS BINARY UNSELECT ESEARCH WITHIN SCAN SORT
THREAD=REFERENCES THREAD=ORDEREDSUBJECT MULTIAPPEND] User student
authenticated

Now tell IMAP that you want to use the inbox:

a02 select inbox

* 11 EXISTS
* 2 RECENT
* OK [UIDVALIDITY 1687965682] UID validity status
* OK [UIDNEXT 12] Predicted next UID
* FLAGS (\Answered \Flagged \Deleted \Draft \Seen)
* OK [PERMANENTFLAGS (* \Answered \Flagged \Deleted \Draft \Seen)]
Permanent flags
* OK [UNSEEN 2] first unseen message in /var/spool/mail/student
a02 OK [READ-WRITE] SELECT completed

We can see that there are eleven (11) messages and that two (2) are recent. Let's look at
the headers for message 11. The number of messages in your email queue will probably be
different, and it doesn't really matter which message you look at. Just pick any message
number in the queue you have:

a03 fetch 11 body[header]

* 11 FETCH (BODY[HEADER] {1086}
Return-Path: <root@studentvm1.example.com>
Received: from studentvm1.example.com ([192.168.56.56])
        by studentvm2.example.com (8.17.1/8.17.1) with ESMTPS id
        35S7AB6k003362
        (version=TLSv1.3 cipher=TLS_AES_256_GCM_SHA384 bits=256 verify=NOT)
        for <student@example.com>; Wed, 28 Jun 2023 03:10:11 -0400
Received: from studentvm1.example.com (localhost [127.0.0.1])
        by studentvm1.example.com (8.17.1/8.17.1) with ESMTPS id
        35S7AADZ003701
        (version=TLSv1.3 cipher=TLS_AES_256_GCM_SHA384 bits=256 verify=NOT)
        for <root@studentvm1.example.com>; Wed, 28 Jun 2023 03:10:10 -0400
Received: (from root@localhost)
        by studentvm1.example.com (8.17.1/8.17.1/Submit) id 35S7A7d8003454;
        Wed, 28 Jun 2023 03:10:07 -0400

```
Date: Wed, 28 Jun 2023 03:10:07 -0400
Message-Id: <202306280710.35S7A7d8003454@studentvm1.example.com>
To: root@studentvm1.example.com
From: logwatch@example.com
Subject: Logwatch for studentvm1.example.com (Linux)
Auto-Submitted: auto-generated
Precedence: bulk
MIME-Version: 1.0
Content-Transfer-Encoding: 8bit
Content-Type: text/plain; charset="UTF-8"

)
* 11 FETCH (FLAGS (\Recent \Seen))
a03 OK FETCH completed
```

Now logout.

a04 logout
```
* BYE studentvm2.example.com IMAP4rev1 server terminating connection
a04 OK LOGOUT completed
Connection closed by foreign host.
[root@studentvm1 ~]#
```

This tells us that the basic functions of uw-imap are working. We are not yet using authentication or encryption.

Notice our use of Telnet to connect with the IMAP server for testing. This is only possible because the standard Internet protocols such as SMTP, IMAP, and others use ASCII plain text commands and responses. That makes it easy for us to simulate a connection from a client.

We could have done the same thing with SMTP to actually send an email because it, too, uses ASCII plain text protocols. However, mailx was a better tool to use for that.

Email Clients

So far we have used Telnet and mailx to test our email, and we have been limited to using mailx to look at our email only on the email server, StudentVM2. The mailx client can use IMAP from remote servers, but it's not as easy as other clients. We really need to use an email client that is more user-friendly to use and is easier to configure.

There are many email clients available, both in text mode and for a graphical desktop. Thunderbird is a very popular open source email client, and Alpine is an excellent text-mode email client. I like Thunderbird but I like Alpine even more, so I prefer it as my client. I like Alpine because it can be used as a powerful tool for testing our email server, so let's start with a long look at Alpine.

Alpine

Alpine is a text-mode email client that provides a more advanced user interface than mailx. It's fast and has all of the features I need and want in an email client. I have been using it as my preferred email client for a few years.

I frankly got tired of the relatively slow speed of Thunderbird as it downloads all of the graphics attached to emails from almost everywhere. Many users include pictures and background images in their emails to make them prettier, but that all takes time, even with a fast Internet connection. I also don't want to see many of the images that spam emails deliver to my computer. Just no.

I found Pine, the predecessor to Alpine, over 20 years ago and returned to it via Alpine about 5 years ago. If you want to take a link or see an image, you can still do that. But the best part is the control I have over what I see.

I'm not saying that Thunderbird is a horrible email client. It's just not what I usually want. This desire to go retro with my email client originally surfaced back in 2017 when I wrote an article[7] about Alpine for Opensource.com. At the time I used Alpine for circumventing problems with sending emails from some ISP networks other than my home email system, and that article describes my solution.

I recently decided that I wanted to use Alpine exclusively for email. The attraction for me is the ease of use that keeping my hands on the keyboard offers by reducing the number of times I need to reach for the mouse. It is also about scratching my SysAdmin itch to just do something different sometimes and to use an excellent text-mode interface in the process.

However, the reason we will spend so much time with it in this chapter is that it is one of the best full-featured tools I know for both learning and testing email.

---

[7] Both, David, "Using the Alpine Linux email client to access messages from any network,"
https://opensource.com/article/17/10/alpine-email-client

Installation

For Fedora, the installation of Alpine is simple because it is available from the Fedora repository.

EXPERIMENT 49-6: INSTALLING ALPINE

As root on StudentVM1, install Alpine:

```
[root@studentvm1 ~]# dnf -y install alpine
```

This command installs Alpine and any necessary prerequisite packages that are not already installed. In my case Alpine itself was the only package installed. Alpine's primary dependencies are sendmail, hunspell, openldap, openssl, krb5-libs, ncurses, and a couple others.

Exploring Alpine

Although we need to configure Alpine, let's first take a few minutes to explore its text-mode interface.

EXPERIMENT 49-7: EXPLORING ALPINE

To launch Alpine, open a terminal session, type **alpine** on the command line, and press **Enter**.

The first time you start Alpine, it displays a message that it is creating the user directory structure on the local host. It then displays a "Welcome" message, and if you press **Enter**, you are treated to a copy of the Apache license under which Alpine is distributed. That is good, and you should read the license at some point so that you know its terms, but the most important thing right now is to configure Alpine so that we can get our email.

Tip   The first time you start Alpine, it does not ask you to log in. After you complete the configuration, it will ask you to log in with the username and password of your email account on StudentVM2.

For now, just press lowercase **e** to exit from the greeting message. You should now see the
Alpine Main Menu as in Figure 49-1

```
ALPINE 2.26    MAIN MENU        Folder: INBOX                   1 Message

            ?      HELP             -  Get help using Alpine
            C      COMPOSE MESSAGE  -  Compose and send a message
            I      MESSAGE INDEX    -  View messages in current folder
            L      FOLDER LIST      -  Select a folder to view
            A      ADDRESS BOOK     -  Update address book
            S      SETUP            -  Configure Alpine Options
            Q      QUIT             -  Leave the Alpine program


                   For Copyright information press "?"

? Help                          P PrevCmd              R RelNotes
O OTHER CMDS       > [ListFldrs] N NextCmd             K KBLock
```

Figure 49-1. *The Alpine Main Menu. I have deleted several blank lines of this
output to save space*

Note that Alpine creates the ~mail directory on the local host during this initial use. When
you configure the IMAP server, the default ~/mail and ~/mail/sent-mail and saved-messages
folders are created in your home directory on the IMAP server. Those defaults can be
changed, but I recommend against it. When using IMAP emails are not stored locally unless
you copy them to local folders. All emails are stored in the inbox on the SMTP server until
saved to a folder on the IMAP server. The SMTP and IMAP servers might be the same host or
different hosts.

The fact that Alpine creates the ~/mail directory on the local host is due to its intended use
as the mail client on the email server. You would log into the mail server using SSH and start
Alpine there. That SSH tunnel is encrypted end-to-end from the local host to the remote host
for all your interactions with Alpine, although it does nothing for the mail transport from one
email server to another.

Alpine also assumes that the inbox is located at /var/spool/mail/<user_id> on the email SMTP server. We will configure both IMAP and SMTP servers. You will add your account to the IMAP server and create the initial password.

The Alpine user interface is a text-mode, menu-driven user interface (UI), which is known as a text-mode user interface (TUI). This type of interface is also sometimes known as a captive user interface – a CUI – that does not provide a command-line interface that can be used in scripts, for example. You must exit from the program in order to perform other tasks in the same terminal session. Of course we can always launch new terminal sessions in any of multiple ways. So this is really not a limitation to our ability to do our jobs.

By contrast, we've already seen that the mailx program (man mailx) is an email program that can be used with either a text-mode menu-driven interface or from the command line or in scripts.

Notice in Figure 49-1 that all of the possible options in the main menu in the center of the interface as well as the menu items along the bottom of the Alpine UI are shown as uppercase letters. But you can use either uppercase or lowercase when issuing commands; Alpine recognizes and responds to both. The use of uppercase in the interface is for better visibility and recognition, but the use of lowercase to enter commands and make menu selections is easier than using uppercase. I will use uppercase letters in bold throughout this experiment to indicate menu selections as is used in the Alpine UI.

You can also use the up/down arrow keys to move the highlight bar to a different choice in the main menu and then press **Enter**. The menu items along the bottom of the Alpine screen – which I call the secondary menu for lack of a better term – are only accessible using the designated letter for each. There are two sets of these secondary menu items. You can press **O** (the letter, not the number) to switch to the next set of commands and press **O** again to return to the original set. This only changes the secondary menu items.

Use the **Page Down** and **Page Up** keys to scroll through the commands if you can't see them all. The secondary menu at the bottom of the page usually lists all of the commands available from the current menu.

Should you find yourself at a place you don't want to be, such as creating a new email, responding to one, or making changes to settings, and you decide you don't want to do that, **Ctrl+C** allows you to cancel the current task. In most cases you will be asked to confirm that you really do want to cancel by a press of the **C** key. Note that **^C** in the secondary menu represents **Ctrl+C**. There are many commands that use the **Ctrl** key, so you will see **^** quite frequently in some menus.

Finally, to quit Alpine, you can press **Q**, and when asked, "Really quit Alpine?" respond with **Y** to exit Alpine. Like many commands, **Q** is not available from all menus.

Help

Help is available from all of the menus I have tried. Detailed help for each menu item is available. Just highlight the item you need information for and press the **?** key to obtain contextual help.

Configuration

Configuration for using Alpine on the same host as the email server is relatively simple. Using it on a remote computer requires a good bit more. When I started using Alpine on a regular basis, I just made the minimum amount of changes to the configuration that were necessary to send and receive email. As I gained more experience using Alpine, I found other configuration items that I changed to make things work easier or in ways more to my personal liking. In this section we will start with the basic configuration requirements to make Alpine work and then move on to those that make it work better.

If you have been exploring a bit on your own – which is a good thing – you should now return to the main menu. To get to the Alpine configuration menu from the main menu, type **S** for Setup. At this point you will see the menu in Figure 49-2

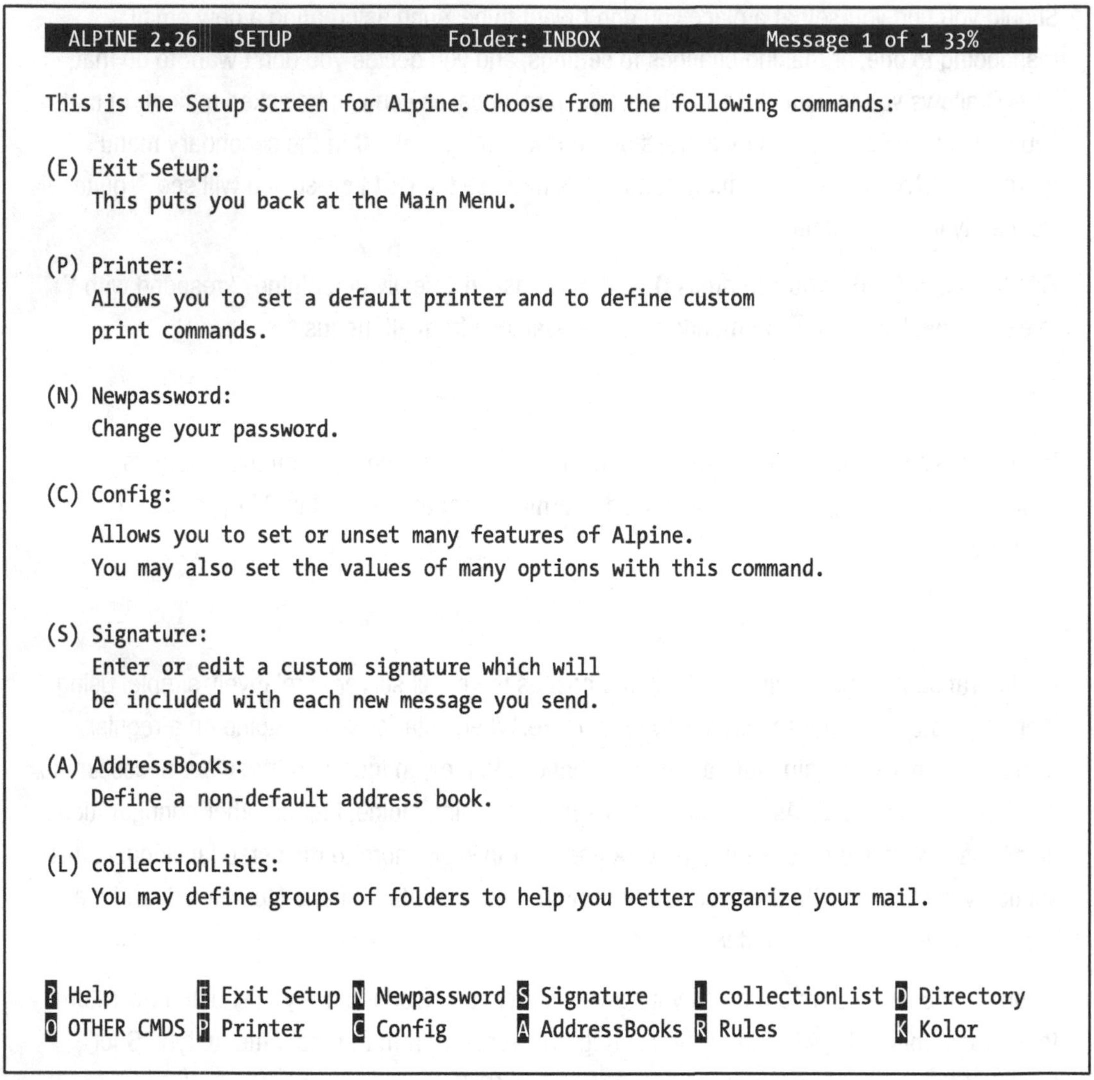

```
ALPINE 2.26   SETUP              Folder: INBOX           Message 1 of 1 33%

This is the Setup screen for Alpine. Choose from the following commands:

(E) Exit Setup:
    This puts you back at the Main Menu.

(P) Printer:
    Allows you to set a default printer and to define custom
    print commands.

(N) Newpassword:
    Change your password.

(C) Config:

    Allows you to set or unset many features of Alpine.
    You may also set the values of many options with this command.

(S) Signature:
    Enter or edit a custom signature which will
    be included with each new message you send.

(A) AddressBooks:
    Define a non-default address book.

(L) collectionLists:
    You may define groups of folders to help you better organize your mail.


? Help        E Exit Setup N Newpassword S Signature    L collectionList D Directory
O OTHER CMDS P Printer     C Config      A AddressBooks R Rules          K Kolor
```

Figure 49-2. *The Setup menu groups many setup options together so they can be easily found. Use Page Down and Page Up to scroll through the commands if you can't see them all*

This Setup menu has grouped the very large number of setup items into categories of related ones that, hopefully, make the ones you want easier to locate.

Basic Configuration

The Configuration section of Setup contains 15 pages (on my large screen) of option and feature configuration items. These settings can be used to set up your SMTP and IMAP connections to the email server as well define how many aspects of Alpine work. This might seem overwhelming, but the few we really need to get Alpine working are all on the first page – or two if your terminal is small. Let's start with only those necessary to get email – the entire purpose of Alpine – up and running.

I will use the example.com domain name, which is the virtual network I use for testing and experimenting. The configuration for Alpine is stored in the ~/.pinerc file, which is created the first time you start Alpine.

The first page of this extensive menu looks like Figure 49-3

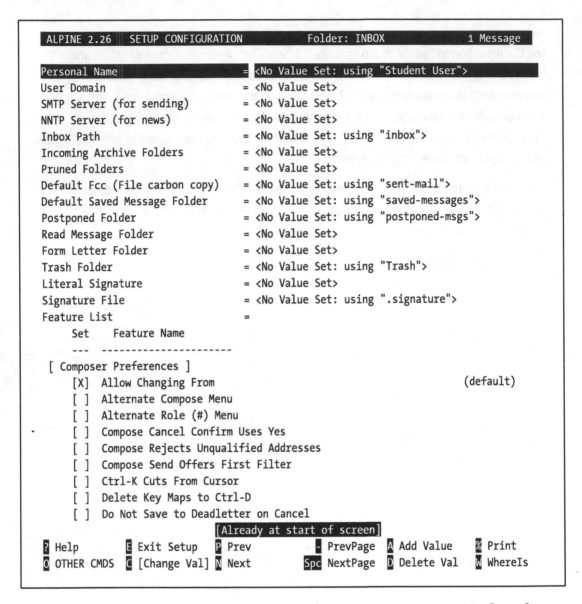

```
ALPINE 2.26 ∥ SETUP CONFIGURATION          Folder: INBOX          1 Message

Personal Name                      = <No Value Set: using "Student User">
User Domain                        = <No Value Set>
SMTP Server (for sending)          = <No Value Set>
NNTP Server (for news)             = <No Value Set>
Inbox Path                         = <No Value Set: using "inbox">
Incoming Archive Folders           = <No Value Set>
Pruned Folders                     = <No Value Set>
Default Fcc (File carbon copy)     = <No Value Set: using "sent-mail">
Default Saved Message Folder       = <No Value Set: using "saved-messages">
Postponed Folder                   = <No Value Set: using "postponed-msgs">
Read Message Folder                = <No Value Set>
Form Letter Folder                 = <No Value Set>
Trash Folder                       = <No Value Set: using "Trash">
Literal Signature                  = <No Value Set>
Signature File                     = <No Value Set: using ".signature">
Feature List                       =
        Set     Feature Name
        ---     ----------------------
   [ Composer Preferences ]
      [X]  Allow Changing From                              (default)
      [ ]  Alternate Compose Menu
      [ ]  Alternate Role (#) Menu
      [ ]  Compose Cancel Confirm Uses Yes
      [ ]  Compose Rejects Unqualified Addresses
      [ ]  Compose Send Offers First Filter
      [ ]  Ctrl-K Cuts From Cursor
      [ ]  Delete Key Maps to Ctrl-D
      [ ]  Do Not Save to Deadletter on Cancel
                        [Already at start of screen]
 ? Help          E Exit Setup   P Prev        - PrevPage   A Add Value   % Print
 O OTHER CMDS    C [Change Val] N Next        Spc NextPage D Delete Val  W WhereIs
```

Figure 49-3. *The first page of the Setup Configuration menu contains those few settings required to configure Alpine to send and receive email*

Figure 49-3 shows the first page of the Setup Configuration menu, which is where you define the parameters required to communicate with the email server. To change a setting, use the arrow keys to move the selection bar (reverse video) to the desired configuration item and press **Enter**. You can see in Figure 49-3 that all of the basic configuration items have no value set.

The Personal Name item uses the GECOS field of the Unix /etc/passwd entry for the logged-in user to obtain the default name. This is just a name Alpine uses for display and has no role in actually receiving or sending email. I usually call this the "pretty name." In this case the default name is fine, so we will leave it as it is.

There are some configuration items that must be set, so let's start with the User Domain, which is the domain name of this computer. In my case this is a virtual machine I use for testing and for examples in my books. We can get the fully qualified domain name (FQDN) along with the hostname using the command line. In Figure 49-4 we see that the domain name is example.com.

```
[student@testvm1 ~]$ hostnamectl
   Static hostname: testvm1.example.com
         Icon name: computer-vm
           Chassis: vm
        Machine ID: 616ed83d97594a53814c35bc6c078d43
           Boot ID: fd721c46a9c44c9ab8ea392cef77b661
    Virtualization: oracle
  Operating System: Fedora 33 (Xfce)
       CPE OS Name: cpe:/o:fedoraproject:fedora:33
            Kernel: Linux 5.10.23-200.fc33.x86_64
      Architecture: x86-64
[student@testvm1 ~]$
```

Figure 49-4. *Obtaining the hostname and domain name*

Now that we have the FQDN, we can set the User Domain entry in the Alpine configuration. Select the User Domain entry and press **Enter** to see the entry field at the bottom of the Alpine screen as shown in Figure 49-5. Type the domain name as shown and press **Enter**.

```
┌────────────────────────────────────────────────────────────────────────┐
│ ▐ALPINE 2.24▌ SETUP CONFIGURATION       Folder: INBOX         1 Message  │
│                                                                          │
│ Personal Name                = <No Value Set: using "Student User">      │
│ ▐User Domain                 = <No Value Set>                         ▌  │
│ SMTP Server (for sending)     = <No Value Set>                           │
│ NNTP Server (for news)        = <No Value Set>                           │
│ Inbox Path                    = <No Value Set: using "inbox">            │
│                                                                          │
│ Incoming Archive Folders      = <No Value Set>                           │
│ Pruned Folders                = <No Value Set>                           │
│ Default Fcc (File carbon copy) = <No Value Set: using "sent-mail">       │
│ Default Saved Message Folder  = <No Value Set: using "saved-messages">   │
│ Postponed Folder              = <No Value Set: using "postponed-msgs">   │
│ Read Message Folder           = <No Value Set>                           │
│ Form Letter Folder            = <No Value Set>                           │
│ Trash Folder                  = <No Value Set: using "Trash">            │
│ Literal Signature             = <No Value Set>                           │
│ Signature File                = <No Value Set: using ".signature">       │
│ Feature List                  =                                          │
│     Set     Feature Name                                                 │
│     ---   ----------------------                                         │
│  [ Composer Preferences ]                                                │
│     [X]   Allow Changing From                              (default)     │
│     [ ]   Alternate Compose Menu                                         │
│     [ ]       Alternate Role (#) Menu                                    │
│     [ ]   Compose Cancel Confirm Uses Yes                                │
│     [ ]   Compose Rejects Unqualified Addresses                          │
│     [ ]   Compose Send Offers First Filter                               │
│     [ ]   Ctrl-K Cuts From Cursor                                        │
│     [ ]   Delete Key Maps to Ctrl-D                                      │
│     [ ]   Do Not Save to Deadletter on Cancel                            │
│                                                                          │
│ ▐Enter the text to be added : example.com:25                         ▌  │
│                                                                          │
│ ▐?▌ Help       ▐E▌ Exit Setup  ▐P▌ Prev    ▐-▌ PrevPage  ▐A▌ Add Value  ▐%▌ Print  │
│ ▐O▌ OTHER CMDS ▐C▌ [Change Val] ▐N▌ Next  ▐Spc▌ NextPage ▐D▌ Delete Val ▐W▌ WhereIs │
└────────────────────────────────────────────────────────────────────────┘
```

Figure 49-5. *Type the domain name into the text entry field and press Enter*

In Figure 49-6 the table of configuration items contains the settings you should use and a description of each. This table covers only the basic configuration items needed to send and receive email. There are a couple that should not yet be changed, but I have noted that.

Item	Value	Description
Personal Name	Your name	This is the pretty name Alpine uses for the From and Return fields in emails.
User Domain	example.com	The email domain for your SMTP server. This might be different from the User Domain name. This line may also contain the user name for SMTP authentication. We aren't using that yet but we will. Just enter what's shown in the Value column for this item.
SMTP server	mail:25	The name and port number for the outbound SMTP email server. This combines with the User Domain name to create the FQDN for the email server.
Inbox Path	{mail}Inbox	The name of the IMAP server enclosed in curly braces {} and the name of the Inbox. Note that this directory location is different from the usual location for the inbox on the server is /var/spool/mail/user_name. When you press Enter on this field it prompts you for the server name and then the inbox name.
Default Fcc (File carbon copy)	{mail}mail/sent	The mailbox (folder) in which sent mail is stored. On the server the default mail directory is usually ~/mail but "mail/" must be specified in this and the next two entries or the folders will be placed in the home directory instead.
Default Saved Message Folder	{mail}mail/saved-messages	When saving a message to a folder, this is the default folder if you don't use ^t to specify a different one.
Postponed Folder	{mail}mail/	
Trash Folder	{mail}mail/Trash	The trash folder.
Literal Signature	Student User	A literal signature. Press Enter to open a simple editor. Type the string from the Value column and Use Ctrl-X then S to save your signature. You can create multi-line signatures in this editor.

Figure 49-6. *A table of the basic configuration items I modified for my use of Alpine. This table covers only those items needed to send and receive email*

Figure 49-7 shows all those settings necessary for Alpine to send and receive email using the current server configuration. The ones we explicitly set are highlighted in bold. The rest of the configuration settings are about personal preferences and setting up news feeds, chat, and other non-email communications.

```
Personal Name                  = <No Value Set: using "Student User">
User Domain                    = example.com
SMTP Server (for sending)      = mail:25
NNTP Server (for news)         = <No Value Set>
Inbox Path                     = {mail}inbox
Incoming Archive Folders       = <No Value Set>
Pruned Folders                 = <No Value Set>
Default Fcc (File carbon copy) = {mail}mail/Sent
Default Saved Message Folder   = {mail}/saved-messages
Postponed Folder               = {mail}/postponed-msgs
Read Message Folder            = <No Value Set>
Form Letter Folder             = <No Value Set>
Trash Folder                   = {mail}mail/Trash
Literal Signature              = Student User\n
Signature File                 = <Ignored: using Literal-Signature instead>
Feature List                   =
```

Figure 49-7. *These are the minimum setting values needed for Alpine to send and receive email*

After making these changes, press **E** and then **S** to save them and then **E** again to completely exit Setup. Alpine will request your username and password. The username will already be displayed, so all you need to do is press the **Enter** key to proceed to enter the password.

Now let's test Alpine. Select Folder List, and you'll see the list of four folders that you set up in the configuration. INBOX is highlighted, so just press **Enter** to continue. Alpine displays the list of files in the inbox. My StudentVM1 inbox looks like Figure 49-8.

```
ALPINE 2.26   MESSAGE INDEX               Folder: INBOX              Message 26 of 27 NEW

+    1 Jun 22     Student User           (851) Test mail 1 from StudentVM2
     2 Jun 22     Mail Delivery Subsystem (3K) Returned mail: see transcript for details
     3 Jun 22     Mail Delivery Subsystem (3K) Returned mail: see transcript for details
     4 Jun 22     Student User           (884) Test mail 2 from StudentVM2
+    5 Jun 22     To: student@example.com (1K) Test email 1
  N  6 Jun 22     To: ftp@studentvm1.exam (1K) Test email for aliases
+    7 Jun 22     To: student@example.com (854) Testing mailx
     8 Jun 23     logwatch@example.com   (16M) Logwatch for studentvm1.example.com (Linux)
  N  9 Jun 24     logwatch@example.com    (4K) Logwatch for studentvm1.example.com (Linux)
  N 10 Jun 25     logwatch@example.com    (5K) Logwatch for studentvm1.example.com (Linux)
    11 Jun 28     logwatch@example.com    (5K) Logwatch for studentvm1.example.com (Linux)
    12 Jun 29     logwatch@example.com    (3K) Logwatch for studentvm1.example.com (Linux)
  . 13 Monday     To: student@example.com (1K) Test from StudentVM1
  . 14 Monday     To: student@example.com (1K) Test from StudentVM1
  . 15 Monday     To: student@example.com (2K) ####NOT SPAM#### (-1) Test 9 from StudentVM1
+ N 16 Monday     Super User             (3K) ####SPAM#### (999) Test spam
  N 17 Tuesday    logwatch@example.com    (6K) ####NOT SPAM#### (-1) Logwatch for studentvm1.
  N 18 Yesterday  logwatch@example.com    (4K) ####NOT SPAM#### (-1) Logwatch for studentvm1.
. N 19 Yesterday  To: student@example.com (2K) ####NOT SPAM#### (-1) Test email 20230705
  N 20  3:33      logwatch@example.com    (5K) ####NOT SPAM#### (-1) Logwatch for studentvm1.
  . 21  7:59      root                   (2K) ####NOT SPAM#### (-1) Test email
  . 22  9:43      root                   (2K) ####NOT SPAM#### (-1) Test email
  . 23 10:23      root                   (2K) ####NOT SPAM#### (-1) Test 20230706
. N 24 11:39      To: student@example.com (2K) ####NOT SPAM#### (-1) Test from StudentVM1
+ N 25 11:45      To: student@example.com (2K) ####NOT SPAM#### (1.344) ^X
. N 26 11:46      To: student@example.com (2K) ####NOT SPAM#### (-1) Test from StudentVM1
  . 27 11:48      To: student@example.com (2K) ####NOT SPAM#### (-1) Test email 20230706

? Help        < FldrList    P PrevMsg       - PrevPage    D Delete     R Reply
O OTHER CMDS  > [ViewMsg]   N NextMsg     Spc NextPage    U Undelete   F Forward
```

Figure 49-8. *The Alpine inbox lists the emails we've sent for the testing we've done so far*

This tells us definitively that IMAP is working as expected and that we have configured Alpine properly to receive email. Be sure to remember how easy this was.

Let's test sending an email. Press **C**, which stands for Compose. This opens a simple form that you fill in. Not all fields need to be completed. For example, the Cc: and Attchmnt: fields are optional. You will need a To: address though. Send this email to yourself as student and also to your external email address. Separate multiple addresses with a comma. My email looks like this before sending:

```
From    : Student User <student@example.com>
To      : student@example.com,
```

```
                     linuxgeek46@both.org
Cc       :
Attchmnt:
Subject : Test Email from Alpine
----- Message Text -----
Hello World.

Student User
```

Press Ctrl+X to send the email. Alpine asks for a confirmation so press Y to send. Verify that the emails were received.

Configuring User Preferences

Figure 49-9 is a list of the features I changed to make Alpine work more to my liking. These features are not about getting Alpine to send and receive email but about making Alpine work the way we, the users, want it to. Unless otherwise noted, I have turned all of these features on. Features that are turned on by default have the string "(default)" next to them in the Alpine configuration menu. Because they are already turned on, I do not cover them in this table.

You do not need to make any changes to these settings, but at least look at them to see what can be done. If any of them look interesting, go ahead and change them.

Feature	Description
Alternate Role (#) Menu	Allows multiple identities using different email addresses on the same client and server. The server must be configured to allow multiple addresses to be delivered to your primary email account.
Compose Rejects Unqualified Addresses	Alpine will not accept an address that is not fully qualified. That is, it must be in the form username@example.com.
Enable Sigdashes	Enables Alpine to automatically add dashes (--) in the row just above the signature. This is a common way of delineating the start of the signature.
Prevent User Lookup in Password File	This prevents lookup of the full user name from the GECOS field of the passwd file.
Spell Check Before Sending	Although you can invoke the spell checker at any time while composing an email, this forces a spell check when you use ^X keystroke to send the email.
Include Header in Reply	Include the headers of a message when replying to it.
Include Text in Reply Signature at Bottom	Includes the text of the original message in a reply. Many people prefer to have their signature placed at the very bottom of the email instead of the default at the end of their reply and before the attached message being replied to.
Preserve Original Fields	Preserves the original addresses in the To: and CC: fields of a message in the reply. Otherwise if you reply to such message, and this feature is disabled, then the original sender of the message is added to the To: field, and all other recipients are added to the Cc: field, while your address is added to the From: field.
Enable Background Sending	Speeds up the Alpine user interface response when sending an email which is performed in the background when this feature is set on.
Enable Verbose SMTP Posting	Produces more verbose information during SMTP conversations with the server. This is a problem determination aid for the Sysadmin.
Warn if Blank Subject	Prevents sending emails with no subject.

Figure 49-9. *The features in this list can (mostly) be turned on with an X or off when blank. They are listed in the Configuration page alphabetically by related groups*

Combined Folder Display	Combines all folder collections into a single main display. Otherwise collections are in separate views.
Combined Subdirectory Display	Combines all subdirectories collections into a single main display. Otherwise subdirectories are in separate views. Useful when searching for a subdirectory to attach or save files.
Enable Incoming Folders Collection	This feature lists all incoming folders in the same collection as the Inbox. Incoming folders can be used with a tool like procmail to presort email into folders other than the Inbox. This makes it easier to see the folders into which new emails have been sorted.
Enable Incoming Folders Checking	Enables Alpine to check for new emails in the incoming folders collection.
Incoming Checking Includes Total	Displays the number of old/new emails in the incoming folders.
Expanded View of Folders	Displays all folders in each collection when you view the Folder List screen. Otherwise only the collections are shown and the folders are not until selected.
Separate Folder and Directory Entries	If your mail directory has both email folders and regular directories that use the same name, this causes Alpine to list them separately.
Use Vertical Folder List	Sorts mail folders vertically first and then horizontally. The default is horizontal first then vertically.
Convert Dates To Localtime	By default all dates and times are displayed as in their originating time zones. This converts the dates to display in local time.
Show Sort in Titlebar	Alpine can sort emails in a mail folder using multiple criteria. This causes the sort criteria to be displayed in the title bar.
Enable Message View Address Links	Highlights email addresses in the body of the email.
Enable Message View Attachment Links	Highlights URL links in the body of the email.

Figure 49-9. *(continued)*

Prefer Plain Text	Many emails today contain two versions of the text, plain text and HTML. When this feature is turned on Alpine always displays the plain text version. You can use the **A** key to toggle to the "preferred" version which is usually the HTML one. I find the plain text to be easier to visualize the structure of the email and to read. This can depend upon the sending client and so I do use the **A** key sometimes.
Enable Print Via Y Command	Print a message using the previous default, **Y**. The new default is **%** which can prevent inadvertently printing a message since **Y** is also used for confirmation of many commands. I do like the ease of this but it has caused me some extra print jobs so I am thinking about turning this feature off.
Print Formfeed Between Messages	Prints each message starting on a new sheet of paper.
Customized Headers	Customized headers enables overriding of the default From: and Reply-To: headers. I set mine to: From: "David Both" <david@example.com> Reply-To: "David Both" <david@example.com>
Sort key	The default sort key for messages in a folder is by arrival time. I found this to be a bit confusing so I changed it to Date which can be significantly different from arrival time. Many spammers use dates and times in the past or future so this can sort all the future ones to the top of the list (or bottom depending on your preferences for forward or reverse sorts).
Image Viewer	This feature allows us to specify the image viewer we want to use when displaying graphics attached to or embedded in an email. This only works when using Alpine in a terminal window on the graphical desktop. It will not work in a text-only virtual console. I always set this to `= okular` because that is my preferred viewer.
URL-Viewer	This defines to Alpine the web browser you want to use. I set this for `= /bin/firefox` but you could use Chrome or some other browser. Be sure to verify the location of the Firefox executable.

Figure 49-9. *(continued)*

293

This is a long list of what I consider to be my critical features. They are the ones that make Alpine work the way I like. Your preferences will be different, so I suggest you spend some time experimenting with them to determine what works best for you.

Printing

It is quite easy to set up Alpine for printing. Select the (P) Printer: menu from the Setup menu page. This allows you to set a default printer and to define custom print commands. The default is probably set to "attached-to-ansi". Move the cursor down to the "Standard UNIX print command" section and highlight the printer list as shown:

```
Standard UNIX print command
     Using this option may require setting your "PRINTER" or "LPDEST"
     environment variable using the standard UNIX utilities.
       Printer List: ""                          lpr
```

Then press the Enter key to set the standard Unix **lpr** command as the default.

Your VM is probably not connected to a printer, but if you can do so easily, try it and print an email message or two. Exit from Alpine when you have finished your own experimentation.

Alpine is easy to configure and use. It has a huge number of features that can be configured to give the best email client experience possible. You should use the Help feature to get more information about the fields I have explored previously as well as the ones that I have not covered here. You will undoubtedly find some ways to configure Alpine that works better for you than the defaults or what I have changed for myself. Hopefully this will at least give you a start for some of the more common settings you might want.

Thunderbird

Thunderbird is available for all platforms including Linux and Windows and is very popular. It is my current GUI email client of choice. The Xfce version of Fedora that we installed contains the Claws GUI email client, but we will install and configure Thunderbird because it is so widely used.

I personally find configuring GUI email clients to be difficult. Remember how easy it was to configure Alpine and no configuration was required for mailx? Thunderbird requires a more detailed and exacting configuration while possessing an interesting and sometimes frustrating set of quirks. In order to do this, I organized some details of the IMAP server and other information we will need to configure Thunderbird in Figure 49-10.

No.	Item	Value	Comments
		Existing Email Address	
1	Account user name	Student User	The pretty name. It has no effect on sending or receiving email.
2	Email address	student@example.com	
3	Password	<User Password>	This is the login password for the student user on StudentVM2.
4	Remember Password	Checked	
		Server Settings (IMAP)	
5	IMAP Server Name	mail.example.com	The FQDN
6	Port	143	The IMAP server port
7	User ID	student	The user login ID
8	Connection Security	None	The connection is not encrypted.
9	Authentication method	Password transmitted insecurely	We do need a password but it is not encrypted.
10	IMAP server directory	mail	The ~/mail directory that contains the email folders.
		SMTP Server Settings	
11	SMTP server name	studentvm2.example.com	Thunderbird requires that this be different from the IMAP server name
12	SMTP port number	25	Required for STARTTLS
13	Connection Security	STARTTLS	Encrypts outbound the email connection to the server. Doesn't do anything for transmitting the email from our server to the destination server.
14	Authentication Method	No authentication	Does not require a login to authenticate with our SMTP server. We will change this.

Figure 49-10. *The most basic things we need to know to configure Thunderbird*

Now we can begin to configure Thunderbird.

EXPERIMENT 49-8: CONFIGURING THUNDERBIRD EMAIL CLIENT

Perform this experiment as the root user on StudentVM1. Install Thunderbird:

[root@studentvm1 ~]# **dnf -y install thunderbird**
That's the easy part.

Configuring IMAP

Launch Thunderbird from the **Applications ➤ Internet** menu. The first time you start Thunderbird, it will take a relatively long time – about 45 seconds on my VM. This is so that it can create its configuration directory and default configuration files.

The first thing you will see is a dialog window, "Help Keep Thunderbird Alive," in which you are asked to donate money to help keep the project going. I donate to various projects, and this is a good thing to do. Few open source projects are funded by large companies, and many are run on very little money and a few volunteers. I discuss ways to give back in Chapter 57, and donating money to projects that are important to you is one very good way. Close this window to continue.

Firefox then displays the "Account Setup" dialog tab as seen in Figure 49-11. Enter the information shown in Figure 49-11. Figure 49-12 has the same information but in a tabular form that may be easier to read.

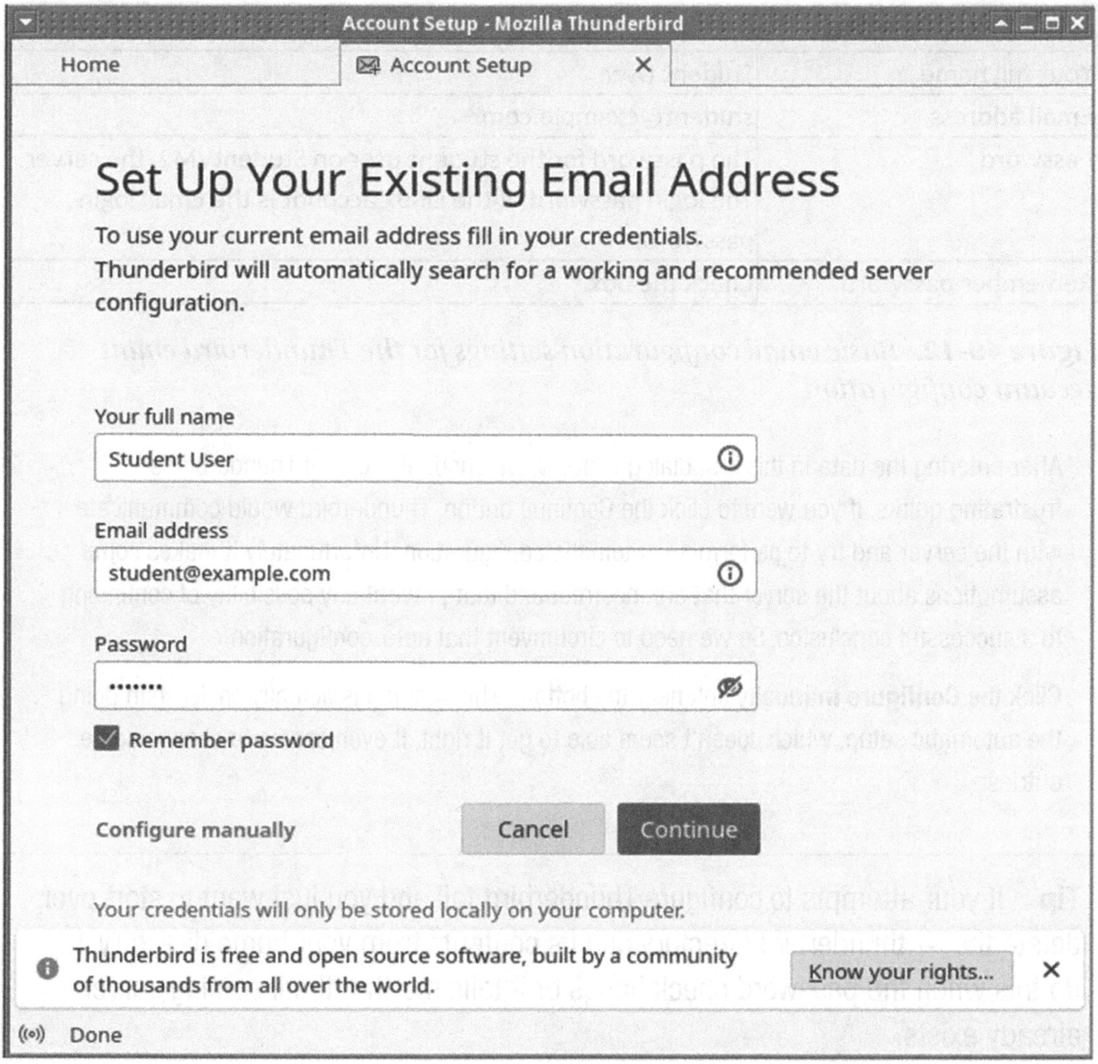

Figure 49-11. *This dialog starts the email account setup the first time Thunderbird is launched. Enter the data as shown and then click the Configure manually link*

Use the information in Figure 49-12 to start the setup for an IMAP email account using the Thunderbird email client.

Field name	Value
Your full name	Student User
Email address	student@example.com
Password	The password for the student user on StudentVM2, the server. The login password of the Linux account is the Email login password.
Remember password	Check the box.

Figure 49-12. *Basic email configuration settings for the Thunderbird email account configuration*

After entering the data in this first dialog window, we encounter one of Thunderbird's frustrating quirks. If you were to click the Continue button, Thunderbird would communicate with the server and try to perform an automatic configuration. Unfortunately it makes some assumptions about the server that are incorrect and that prevent any possibility of continuing to a successful conclusion. So we need to circumvent that auto-configuration.

Click the **Configure manually** link near the bottom. This method is actually easier than doing the automatic setup, which doesn't seem able to get it right. It even seems to change some entries.

Tip   If your attempts to configure Thunderbird fail and you just want to start over, delete the ~/.thunderbird directory and its contents from your home directory. I do this when the password check hangs or it tells me that the incoming server already exists.

Don't change anything in the next dialog. Just click the **Advanced Config** link to bypass the rest of the configuration dialogs that don't seem to work. You'll see the dialog shown in Figure 49-13. Click the **OK** button to access the Advanced Configuration dialogs so we can do it in the way that results in a proper configuration.

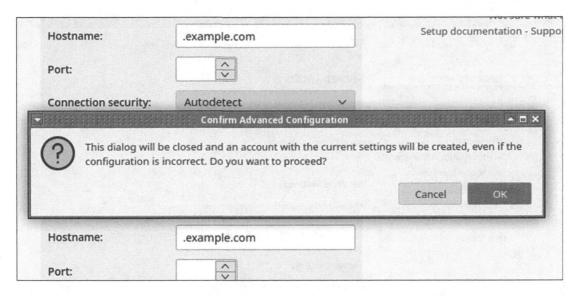

Figure 49-13. *Accessing the Thunderbird Advanced Config menu*

I have discovered during my experimentation that Thunderbird requires that the IMAP and SMTP servers have different names. If I use mail.example.com for both servers, I get an error message indicating the server already exists. I guess the developers assumed – incorrectly – that we won't use the same server for both inbound and outbound emails. We already have a circumvention in place for this because we have both mail.example.com and studentvm2. example.com in our name server. This will work for us because they both point to the same server.

We use the Server Settings dialog to configure the IMAP server settings shown in Figure 49-14. Refer to items 5–10 in Figure 49-10 if you can't read them in Figure 49-14.

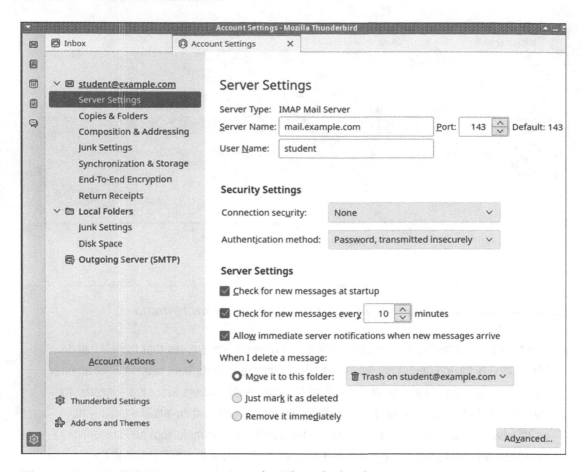

Figure 49-14. *IMAP server settings for Thunderbird*

Click the **Advanced** button.

Then enter "mail" in the "IMAP server directory" field shown in Figure 49-15. Remember when we set up that mail directory previously? That's all you need to change here. Don't add leading or trailing slashes (/). We only do this for the student login account on StudentVM2 in order to keep email separate from the directories and the Bash configuration files in the home directory. For non-login email accounts, this would not be required. It's a good idea to do this anyway for the sake of consistency. This way you can use login accounts for system administrators and non-login accounts for email-only accounts.

You should uncheck the "Server supports folders that contain sub-folders and messages" box if it is checked.

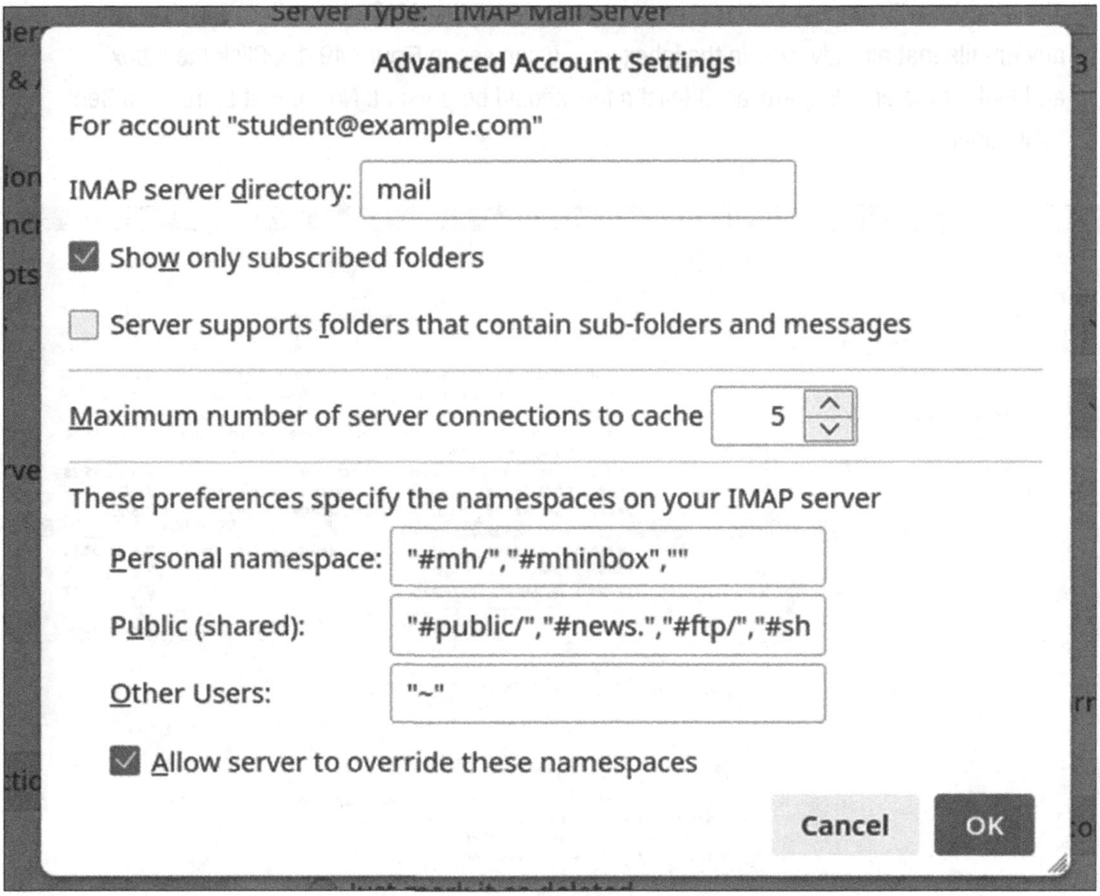

Figure 49-15. *Be sure to enter "mail" in the IMAP server directory field*

Click OK to complete this dialog. Be sure to check the IMAP server name in Figure 49-14 because I find it sometimes changes after setting the mail directory. I also found that the username in Figure 49-14 had been altered. This is one of those quirks I mentioned.

When you do that, you will be presented with a dialog that says you must restart Thunderbird to make those changes effective. Click **OK**.

When Thunderbird restarts you'll be asked for the password again. Enter it and ensure that there is a check in the box that you want to have the password manager store this password. You might need to do this twice as I did. Another quirk.

Thunderbird will connect to the server, authenticate for the IMAP connection, and download any emails that already exist in the inbox as you can see in Figure 49-16. Click the inbox and look at the emails there, as at least a few should be present. Notice that there is no Sent mail folder.

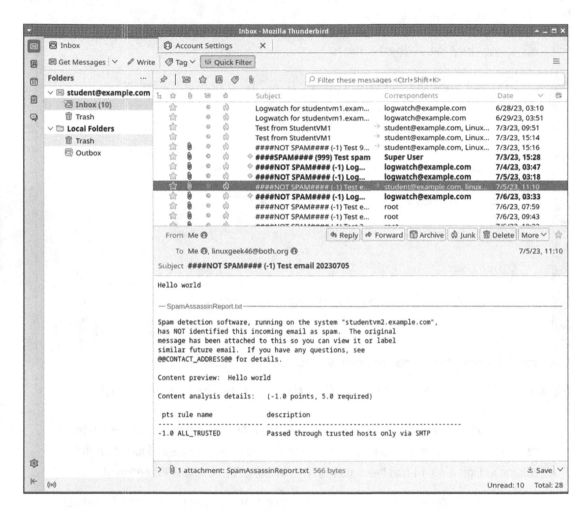

Figure 49-16. Thunderbird after initial IMAP configuration with downloaded email

When you see your emails listed in the Thunderbird window, you know that IMAP is properly configured.

Configuring SMTP

There is still a little Thunderbird configuration left to do before we can send email. Fortunately this is much easier than it was for Thunderbird IMAP configuration.

Go back to the **Account Settings** tab of Thunderbird and click **Outgoing Server**. Select the only server in the list[8] and then **Edit**.

Enter the SMTP settings shown in Figure 49-17 with one exception. We are going to start with **None** for our first setting of Connection security. This way we can be assured that non-STARTTLS connections will work before we go on to STARTTLS.

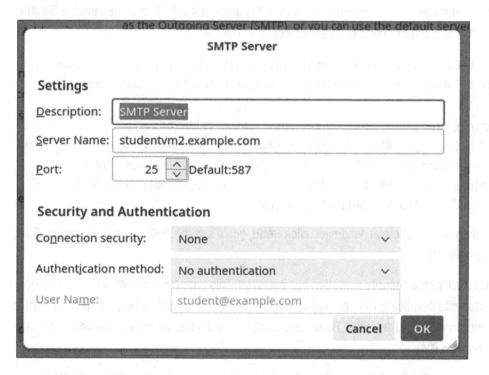

Figure 49-17. *Enter the SMTP settings in the SMTP Server dialog. Start with "None" for Connection security*

---

[8] Yes, this does correctly imply that multiple SMTP servers can be configured. Each account can use any of the servers, but the email clients will always use the SMTP server that's marked as the default unless the user chooses a different one.

After entering the required data, click OK.

Send a test email to student@example.com – yourself – and also to your external email address. Both email addresses can go on the same To: line. Just separate them with a space.

The Sent folder is created when the first email is sent.

STARTTLS for Outbound Email

If those emails go through without a problem, return to the SMTP Server dialog and change Connection security to STARTTLS as shown in Figure 49-17.

Remember these lines in sendmail.mc from Experiment 48-2? These lines enable Sendmail to use TLS so we don't need to create any certs of our own:

```
dnl # Basic sendmail TLS configuration with self-signed certificate for
dnl # inbound SMTP (and also opportunistic TLS for outbound SMTP).
dnl #
define(`confCACERT_PATH', `/etc/pki/tls/certs')dnl
define(`confCACERT', `/etc/pki/tls/certs/ca-bundle.crt')dnl
define(`confSERVER_CERT', `/etc/pki/tls/certs/sendmail.pem')dnl
define(`confSERVER_KEY', `/etc/pki/tls/private/sendmail.key')dnl
define(`confTLS_SRV_OPTIONS', `V')dnl
```

Send another test email. When you click **Send**, you'll see the Add Security Exception dialog in Figure 49-18

that indicates a security exception has occurred. This happens because we're not using a trusted site certificate from a certificate authority. Fedora installs a large number of certificates in subdirectories of /etc/pki/. Those certs simply identify the known and trusted certificate authorities (CA).

Do not click Get Certificate. Click Confirm Security Exception to accept the untrusted certificate.

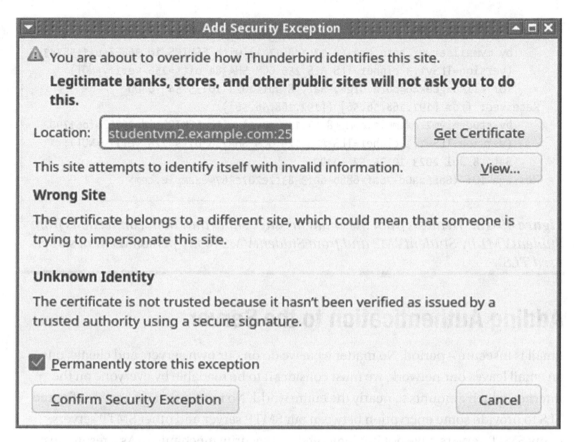

Figure 49-18. *Click Confirm Security Exception to accept the untrusted certificate*

In another fit of quirkiness, Thunderbird throws another error, but when you send a test email, it does work. Be sure to check the headers of the email when you receive it and verify that the received lines show that TLS was used for the connection. That should look similar to Figure 49-19.

```
Received: from studentvm2.example.com (_gateway [192.168.0.254])
    by mymailserver.both.org (8.17.1/8.17.1) with ESMTPS id 368EZsuI1158243
    (version=TLSv1.3 cipher=TLS_AES_256_GCM_SHA384 bits=256 verify=NOT)
    for <linuxgeek46@both.org>; Sat, 8 Jul 2023 10:35:54 -0400
Received: from [192.168.56.56] ([192.168.56.56])
    by studentvm2.example.com (8.17.1/8.17.1) with ESMTPS id 368EZqfo617902
    (version=TLSv1.3 cipher=TLS_AES_128_GCM_SHA256 bits=128 verify=NOT);
    Sat, 8 Jul 2023 10:35:52 -0400
Message-ID: <6a66aa0d-76af-688b-6af3-83c2e207c367@example.com>
```

Figure 49-19. Headers from the email message show that both connections from StudentVM1 by StudentVM2 and from StudentVM2 to my personal email server used TLS

Adding Authentication to the Server

Email is insecure – period. No matter what we do on our own servers and clients, once an email leaves our network, we must consider it to be readable by everyone on the Internet, which amounts to nearly the entire world. No matter that we have configured TLS to provide some encryption between our SMTP server and other SMTP servers, many SMTP servers have not implemented this security mechanism. As a result most SMTP servers talk to each other in unencrypted plain text.

One problem I have encountered when traveling is that I do not have an email account for the local ISPs for outbound SMTP. This is usually an attempt by the ISP to block spam sent directly from infected hosts in their networks. This means that I cannot send email from those networks without some sort of circumvention. I can use my own email server as the outbound SMTP server, but that means it is accessible to spammers as an open relay.

There are a couple things we can do to improve security and help prevent the use of our mail servers as open relays. For example, the use of authentication will allow a laptop to use our own email server as a relay while preventing others from using it the same way.

It is possible to use a number of different forms of authentication so that mobile users can authenticate with their own email server in order to allow relaying. Using authentication so that we can connect both SMTP and IMAP to our own email server allows us to send email from anywhere even if we don't have an email account on the local ISP.

SMTP Authentication

One remaining issue with our current email setup is that spammers can use our server (well, if it were exposed to the real world of the Internet) as a relay server through which they can send spam. This is a real problem but it has a pretty simple fix. We can force incoming SMTP connections to our email server to authenticate with an ID and password. Since only we will have that information, we can protect our server from use by bad actors.

Adding authentication to SMTP is relatively easy to set up. We can add a new user account and password to our server and require inbound SMTP connections to authenticate before they will be allowed to send email through our server. This is called SMTP AUTH. SMTP AUTH requires the saslauthd service and libraries for the various encryption methods that might be used. SASL is the Simple Authentication and Security Layer.

EXPERIMENT 49-9: ADDING SMTP AUTHENTICATION

Create a Nologin User Account

The first step is to create a nologin Linux account that can be used for our SMTP authentication. As root on StudentVM2, create an account for this purpose. For this experiment use the account name of myauth1:

```
[root@studentvm2 ~]# useradd -c "SMTP Authentication" -s /usr/sbin/nologin
myauth1
```

Then set a password for the account. Be sure to remember the password. Try to log into this account from one of the virtual consoles. You should not be able to do that.

Install Needed Packages

Verify that the packages needed by SMTP AUTH are all installed. They should be but it never hurts to be certain. All of these were previously installed on my VM, but if any are missing from your host, they will be installed by this command:

[root@studentvm2 ~]# **dnf install cyrus-sasl-gssapi cyrus-sasl-md5 cyrus-sasl cyrus-sasl-plain sendmail sendmail-cf**

Enable SASL.

[root@studentvm2 ~]# **systemctl enable --now saslauthd**

Configure Sendmail

The next step is to configure Sendmail to only accept incoming connections using authentication. Edit /etc/mail/sendmail,mc.

Add the following lines to your sendmail.mc file:

```
dnl #######################################################################dnl
dnl #######################################################################dnl
dnl # The following causes sendmail to additionally listen to port 587 dnl
dnl # for mail from MUAs that authenticate. Roaming users who can't    dnl
dnl # their preferred sendmail daemon due to port 25 being blocked or  dnl
dnl # redirected find this useful.                                     dnl
DAEMON_OPTIONS(`Port=submission, Name=MSA, M=Ea')dnl
dnl #######################################################################dnl
dnl # The following allows relaying if the user authenticates, and allows
dnl # plaintext authentication (PLAIN/LOGIN) on non-TLS links
define(`confAUTH_OPTIONS', `A')dnl
dnl #
dnl # By default, sendmail will ask e-mail clients for their SSL/TLS
dnl # certificates.
dnl # Since almost no clients have personal TLS certificates, you
dnl # can tell sendmail to skip the request with the line:
define(`confTLS_SRV_OPTIONS', `V')dnl
dnl #######################################################################dnl
dnl #######################################################################dnl
dnl # PLAIN is the preferred plaintext authentication method and used by
dnl # Mozilla Mail and Evolution, though Outlook Express and other MUAs do
```

```
dnl # use LOGIN. Other mechanisms should be used if the connection is not
dnl # guaranteed secure.
dnl # Please remember that saslauthd needs to be running for AUTH.
dnl #
TRUST_AUTH_MECH(`EXTERNAL DIGEST-MD5 CRAM-MD5 LOGIN PLAIN')dnl
define(`confAUTH_MECHANISMS', `EXTERNAL GSSAPI DIGEST-MD5 CRAM-MD5 LOGIN
PLAIN')dnl
```

The confAUTH_OPTIONS may already exist in some form. I have included it here to keep all of these in close proximity. Place them where the existing confAUTH_OPTIONS line is. The middle section contains three versions of confAUTH_OPTIONS. The one that worked for me is the uncommented one. If you want to try to enable encrypted passwords, those are other options you might want to experiment with.

Unfortunately configuring encryption for authentication is quite complex, and I have found no documentation that is successful at putting all the bits together in one place. So none of my own experiments along those lines have worked:

```
dnl TRUST_AUTH_MECH(`EXTERNAL DIGEST-MD5 CRAM-MD5 LOGIN PLAIN')dnl
dnl define(`confAUTH_MECHANISMS', `EXTERNAL GSSAPI DIGEST-MD5 CRAM-MD5 LOGIN
PLAIN')dnl
```
GSSAPI DIGEST-MD5 CRAM-MD5 were enabled by default when we installed the cyrus-sasl-md5 and cyrus-sasl-gssapi packages.

Restart saslauthd first and then Sendmail to activate these changes.

Testing

We could test this using Telnet, but OpenSSL can be used for this test as root on StudentVM2:

```
[root@studentvm2 ~]# openssl s_client -connect 127.0.0.1:25 -starttls
smtp | less
CONNECTED(00000003)
---
Certificate chain
 0 s:C = --, ST = SomeState, L = SomeCity, O = SomeOrganization, OU =
 SomeOrganizationalUnit, CN = studentvm2, emailAddress = root@studentvm2
   i:C = --, ST = SomeState, L = SomeCity, O = SomeOrganization, OU =
   SomeOrganizationalUnit, CN = studentvm2, emailAddress = root@studentvm2
   a:PKEY: rsaEncryption, 4096 (bit); sigalg: RSA-SHA256
```

```
     v:NotBefore: Jun 22 10:31:46 2023 GMT; NotAfter: Jun 21 10:31:46 2024 GMT
---
Server certificate
-----BEGIN CERTIFICATE-----
MIIGGzCCBAOgAwIBAgICTEwwDQYJKoZIhvcNAQELBQAwgaUxCzAJBgNVBAYTAiOt
<SNIP>
issuer=C = --, ST = SomeState, L = SomeCity, O = SomeOrganization, OU =
SomeOrganizationalUnit, CN = studentvm2, emailAddress = root@studentvm2
---
No client certificate CA names sent
Peer signing digest: SHA256
Peer signature type: RSA-PSS
Server Temp Key: ECDH, prime256v1, 256 bits
---
SSL handshake has read 2861 bytes and written 736 bytes
Verification error: self-signed certificate
---
New, TLSv1.3, Cipher is TLS_AES_256_GCM_SHA384
Server public key is 4096 bit
Secure Renegotiation IS NOT supported
Compression: NONE
Expansion: NONE
No ALPN negotiated
Early data was not sent
Verify return code: 18 (self-signed certificate)
---
<SNIP>
Post-Handshake New Session Ticket arrived:
SSL-Session:
    Protocol  : TLSv1.3
    Cipher    : TLS_AES_256_GCM_SHA384
    Session-ID: AA3E70749D50CAC223DEE70B275A58BAADDE8DAF2153E48FDA21D5
    CFD9073F71
    Session-ID-ctx:
    Resumption PSK: 8547C3616B36167DBE549C2A67DE440671E69C8DDF02829
    10CC891A9F96B9A46139AF1D4E9E66
    216880425873AC93D71
    PSK identity: None
```

```
    PSK identity hint: None
    SRP username: None
    TLS session ticket lifetime hint: 1 (seconds)
    TLS session ticket:
    0000 - 64 10 ef 25 a0 bf 12 f2-7a e6 25 f9 2f 5b da 92   d..%....z.%./[..
    0010 - d2 f0 a5 7e 4c 45 48 6e-5d 80 ec 4e e9 53 4b 49   ...~LEHn]..N.SKI
<SNIP>
    00b0 - 05 35 c8 4f 42 82 84 73-22 51 f2 97 82 2d 95 26   .5.OB..s"Q...-.&
    00c0 - 04 e3 03 a0 1e be 2e e2-34 67 fd af 3a ed 78 f2   ........4g..:.x.

    Start Time: 1688919784
    Timeout   : 7200 (sec)
    Verify return code: 18 (self-signed certificate)
    Extended master secret: no
    Max Early Data: 0
---
read R BLOCK
```

EHLO localhost   ←--------- **Enter this**

```
250-studentvm2.example.com Hello localhost [127.0.0.1], pleased to meet you
250-ENHANCEDSTATUSCODES
250-PIPELINING
250-8BITMIME
250-SIZE
250-DSN
250-ETRN
250-AUTH GSSAPI DIGEST-MD5 CRAM-MD5
250-DELIVERBY
250 HELP
```

There's a lot more that I pruned from this data stream, but you get the idea. This is an example of a working SMTP AUTH session.

Configure Thunderbird

Configure the SMTP server in Thunderbird as shown in Figure 49-20. Be sure to set the SMTP port to 587 because it won't work on port 25.

Figure 49-20.   SMTP AUTH configuration for Thunderbird

Functional Verification

We should always perform some level of functional verification. Send one or more emails from StudentVM1.

Run these commands yourself, but the data from my email server is more interesting than our VMs because it works in the real world. So the following is from my server so you can see what it will look like:

```
[root@mymailserver mail]# systemctl status saslauthd
● saslauthd.service - SASL authentication daemon.
    Loaded: loaded (/usr/lib/systemd/system/saslauthd.service; enabled;
    preset: disabled)
   Drop-In: /usr/lib/systemd/system/service.d
            └─10-timeout-abort.conf
    Active: active (running) since Sun 2023-07-02 12:20:02 EDT; 6 days ago
```

```
   Process: 1070 ExecStart=/usr/sbin/saslauthd -m $SOCKETDIR -a $MECH $FLAGS
   (code=exited, status=0/SUCCESS)
 Main PID: 1096 (saslauthd)
    Tasks: 5 (limit: 38300)
   Memory: 3.3M
      CPU: 222ms
   Cgroup: /system.slice/saslauthd.service
           ├─1096 /usr/sbin/saslauthd -m /run/saslauthd -a pam -r
           ├─1097 /usr/sbin/saslauthd -m /run/saslauthd -a pam -r
           ├─1098 /usr/sbin/saslauthd -m /run/saslauthd -a pam -r
           ├─1099 /usr/sbin/saslauthd -m /run/saslauthd -a pam -r
           └─1100 /usr/sbin/saslauthd -m /run/saslauthd -a pam -r

Jul 09 04:51:46 mymailserver.both.org saslauthd[1100]: DEBUG: auth_pam: pam_
authenticate failed: User not known to the underlying authentication module
Jul 09 04:51:46 mymailserver.both.org saslauthd[1100]:                        :
auth failure: [user=b.david@millennium-technology.com] [service=smtp]
[realm=millennium-technology.com] [mech=pam]>
Jul 09 04:51:51 mymailserver.both.org saslauthd[1097]: pam_unix(smtp:auth):
check pass; user unknown
Jul 09 04:51:51 mymailserver.both.org saslauthd[1097]: pam_unix(smtp:auth):
authentication failure; logname= uid=0 euid=0 tty= ruser= rhost=
Jul 09 04:51:53 mymailserver.both.org saslauthd[1097]: DEBUG: auth_pam: pam_
authenticate failed: User not known to the underlying authentication module
Jul 09 04:51:53 mymailserver.both.org saslauthd[1097]:                        :
auth failure: [user=b.david@millennium-technology.com] [service=smtp]
[realm=millennium-technology.com] [mech=pam]>
Jul 09 04:51:57 mymailserver.both.org saslauthd[1098]: pam_unix(smtp:auth):
check pass; user unknown
Jul 09 04:51:57 mymailserver.both.org saslauthd[1098]: pam_unix(smtp:auth):
authentication failure; logname= uid=0 euid=0 tty= ruser= rhost=
Jul 09 04:52:00 mymailserver.both.org saslauthd[1098]: DEBUG: auth_pam: pam_
authenticate failed: User not known to the underlying authentication module
Jul 09 04:52:00 mymailserver.both.org saslauthd[1098]:                        :
auth failure: [user=b.david] [service=smtp] [realm=] [mech=pam] [reason=PAM
auth error]
lines 1-27/27 (END)
```

313

Check the journal entries for the saslauthd unit. The messages will be the same as the ones seen here; however, this will show all of them, not just the last few:

```
[root@mymailserver log]# journalctl -u saslauthd
```

You can use -S today and other filters to narrow your search.

Remember that a summary of the journal data appears in your daily logwatch email – yes, the ones we saw earlier in this chapter. Where do those emails get sent? You can also run the logwatch command, and it will print a summary for yesterday.

Our implementation of email is not completely secure because the passwords are transmitted as ASCII plain text and are not encrypted. However, the data connections themselves are encrypted.

Certificates

Certificates are the key, if you will pardon the pun, to enabling secure authentication and encryption. These certificates provide a verifiable identity for the server and are also used to provide the encryption key for the connections.

For a real-world server, we would use the openssl tool to generate a certificate signing request and send it to a public certification authority (CA) and receive a signed certificate from them that verifies the identity of our server. A self-signed certificate like what we are using is fine for a closed environment like what we have in our virtual network, use inside an organization where no outsiders will be accessing the server, and other types of testing environments. Self-signed certificates should never be used on a server that allows public access.

A search on "certificate authorities list" will result in links to a good number of public CAs, many of which charge a fee for certificates. There are also some "open" and free CAs that you can find by searching "free certificate authority."

Let's Encrypt is a free certificate authority that is a collaborative project with the Linux Foundation. It is sponsored by Mozilla, Akamai, SiteGround, Cisco, Facebook, and many more organizations. It offers free SSL certificates.

We do need to create a certificate, but we don't need a certificate authority (CA) to create a certificate. We could use a free CA such as Let's Encrypt,[9] but instead we will use the already installed self-signed certificates for our experiments.

I do suggest using Let's Encrypt or some other (non-free) CA for production use. Certificates are sold by a number of recognized certificate authorities (CAs) such as Verisign, Symantec, DigiCert, GeoTrust, RapidSSL, and others. Let's Encrypt[10] provides a free and open certificate authority that is backed by many well-known and respected sponsors and donors. For our purposes, a self-signed certificate is perfect.

Other Considerations

Be aware that different email clients have some unique configuration requirements that will be different from Thunderbird. For example, some clients do not support certain types of encryption. If you have problems configuring those clients, refer to the web pages and other documentation for those clients and ensure that the server is configured to support their unique requirements.

Resources

I have found three books to be very helpful. These have been invaluable to me in writing about email in general and Sendmail in particular:

- Smith, Curtis, *Pro Open Source Mail*, Apress, 2006, ISBN-13 978-1-4302-1173-0

- Hunt, Craig, *Linux Sendmail Administration*, Sybex, 2001, ISBN 0-7821-2737-1

- Hunt, Craig, *Sendmail Cookbook*, O'Reilly, 2004, ISBN 0-596-00471-0

---

[9] Let's Encrypt, `https://letsencrypt.org/`
[10] Home page for Let's Encrypt, `https://letsencrypt.org/`

Chapter Summary

That was a lot of work. However, we do have a working email server that can send and receive email. Yet there is so much more. I spent five years working on the email system for one of my employers, and I learned a lot about email. I still feel like I've only scratched the surface.

This chapter explored the mailx client a bit more. Although it is a powerful tool for the SysAdmin, it leaves a lot to be desired for most users and even for us SysAdmins for daily email use. It does make an excellent tool for testing.

We installed Alpine and Thunderbird to use as email clients and used them to test various configurations of our email server. We've explored the use of encryption and authentication in a mostly futile attempt to improve the privacy of our emails. We have used SMTP AUTH to help secure our server and prevent its use as an open relay, which is probably the most useful part of this chapter.

There are other SMTP and IMAP servers and many email clients besides the ones we have explored in this chapter. They all have proponents, and all do a good job of dealing with email. That means that there are a large number of combinations of those tools that can be used to create an email server. We have only looked at one set of IMAP and SMTP servers, but we have explored three email clients.

In upcoming chapters we'll explore more aspects of email such as defending against spam and creating mailing lists.

Exercises

Perform the following exercises to complete this chapter:

1. What unique capability makes mailx an ideal tool for the SysAdmin who works with and supports email systems?

2. What limitations does mailx have that make it a poor choice for most of today's email users?

3. Where are the email inboxes for email users located?

4. From StudentVM1, use Telnet and SMTP to send an email from StudentVM2.

5. Where are email folders other than the inbox stored?

6. What other method could be used to create an encrypted TLS connection between the local email client such as Thunderbird on StudentVM1 and the remote email server on StudentVM2?

7. How does Alpine know your login ID?

8. Examine some of the logwatch emails. What do they tell you?

9. View the headers for any one or more of the emails in the Thunderbird inbox.

10. Does Alpine use STARTTLS when you send an email?

11. Create some saslauthd errors on your mail server and view them using the three methods you've seen in this chapter.

CHAPTER 50

Combating Spam

Objectives

In this chapter you will learn

- How to use SpamAssassin to identify spam email using a set of scoring rules

- How to create and modify SpamAssassin rules

- How to hack MIMEDefang to classify spam depending upon its spam score

- How to use Procmail to sort spam and other emails into mail folders

Introduction

Email is a powerful and useful tool and – despite other, newer types of communication such as texts and social media – retains a prime place in the communications strategies of most organizations and individuals. Email is not the oldest form of digital communication, having been preceded by tools such as the telegraph and teletype, but it has been around since the early years of Unix. Email is a well-defined tool and is available not just on computers but on nearly every connected device including mobile phones and tablets.

Email is also used as a tool by spammers and the distributors of malware. Spammers use email to defraud recipients of huge amounts of money each year, to steal IDs, and to peddle knock-off or nonexistent wares. Some crackers send emails with attached malware that they try to entice users into installing to their own detriment.

All of this criminal and disruptive spam requires some method for dealing with it. I use three open source programs to do this, and it has reduced my need to read or even to glance at offensive or undesirable material in order to identify and classify incoming email.

© David Both 2023
D. Both, *Using and Administering Linux: Volume 3*, https://doi.org/10.1007/978-1-4842-9786-5_50

The Problem

I like to sort incoming email into a couple folders besides the inbox. Spam is always filed into the spam folder, and I leave it there for a couple days so I can look at it later in case someone sends something that I want to receive but that got marked as spam because I have not welcome-listed them. Some of the incoming ham (good) email from a couple other sources is also sorted into other folders. The rest does get filed into the inbox by default.

So a quick word about terminology before going any further. Sorting is the process of classifying email and storing it in an appropriate folder. Filters like SpamAssassin classify the email. MIMEDefang uses that classification to mark it as spam by adding a text string to the subject line. That classification allows other software to file the email into the designated folders. It is this last bit of software that I was looking for – the one that does the filing.

I had several email filters set up in Thunderbird, my client of choice and the best GUI client I have found for my personal needs. I also had set up some email filters for my wife on her computer. When we travel or use our handheld devices, those filters would not always work because Thunderbird – or any other email client with filters – must be running in order to perform its filtering tasks. If I have my laptop with me, I can set that up to do the filtering, but that means I have to maintain multiple sets of identical filters – one set for each host I access my email with.

I also ran into a technical problem that I wanted to fix. Client-side email filtering relies on scanning messages after they are deposited in the inbox. For some unknown reason, this has resulted in situations where the client does not always delete (expunge) the moved messages from the inbox. This may be an issue with Thunderbird, or it may be a problem with my configuration of Thunderbird. I have worked on this problem for years with no success, even through multiple complete reinstallations of Fedora and Thunderbird.

I have my own email server and spam is a major problem for me. I have several email addresses I use, some of which I have had for a couple decades so they have become major spam magnets. In fact I get at a minimum 300 spam emails per day. The record was just over 2,500 spam emails in a single day. I currently get between 800 and 1,200 spam emails per day, and the numbers keep increasing.

So I needed a method for filing emails, that is, sorting them into appropriate folders that is server-based rather than client-based. This would solve a number of issues. I would no longer need to leave an email client running on my home workstation just to perform filtering. It would prevent the need to delete or expunge messages – especially the spam – from our inboxes. And it would require filter configuration in just one location, the server.

But Why?

By now, after two full chapters on email and just starting another one, you are probably asking yourself, "Why do I want to put myself through all of this aggravation just to have an email server? Why not just use Gmail or the email service provided by my ISP?" This is an excellent question because I ask it of myself on occasion.

When I decided that I wanted to become a Linux SysAdmin, I understood that I needed to learn about all aspects of system administration. I needed to deal with clients, but especially with servers of all types. Despite the fact that it takes a lot of work to set up, configure, and maintain a series of servers like the ones we cover in this volume of *Using and Administering Linux: Zero to SysAdmin,* I learn best with hands-on. Working with these servers and the clients that use them on a daily basis enabled me to learn so much more than I would have otherwise.

I believe that most of us who are truly well-suited for the role of SysAdmin are the same way – not everyone but many of us.

Even if we learn best in other ways, we always need a laboratory in which to perform our experiments and to learn to use and support hardware and software of all kinds. I have learned enough by doing this in my own home network that I have landed some amazing jobs, and I currently write prolifically about Linux.

Oh, and because it is fun![1]

My Email Server

Having grown up with Sendmail as the de facto email server in more than one of my jobs, I started using it for my own email server as soon as I switched permanently from OS/2 to Red Hat Linux 5 in about 1997. I have used it as my mail transfer agent (MTA) since then for both business and personal uses.

---

[1] Both, David, "The real reason we use Linux," `www.both.org/?page_id=844`

Note   I am not sure why Wikipedia refers to Sendmail as a "message" transfer agent. All my other references use "mail" transfer agent. The Talk tab of the Wikipedia page has a bit of discussion about this, which generated even more confusion for me.

I was already using SpamAssassin and MIMEDefang together to score and mark incoming emails as spam, placing a known string in the subject, "###SPAM###", so that I can identify and sort spam both as a human and with software. I use UW IMAP for client access to emails, but that is not a factor in server-side filtering and sorting.

Yes, I use a lot of old-school software for the server side of email, but it is well known and well documented, takes only minor configuration on the part of the SysAdmin, and works well and I understand how to make it do the things I need it to do. Understanding this old but still extensively used software is the key to understanding many of the more recent incarnations of email software. This software enables us to understand the protocols and requirements for any software that is used to perform these tasks. Current versions of Fedora provide all of these tools as packages in their standard repositories.

Project Requirements

Having a well-defined set of requirements before starting a project is imperative, so, based on the description of the problem, I created five simple requirements for this project:

1. Sort incoming spam emails into the spam folder on the server side using the identifying text that is already being added to the subject line by MIMEDefang.

2. Sort other incoming ham emails into designated folders.

3. Circumvent problems with moved messages not being deleted or expunged from the inbox.

4. Keep the SpamAssassin and MIMEDefang software that I was already using.

5. Any new software would have to be easy to install and configure.

This set of objectives meant that I would therefore need to be using a sorting program that would integrate well with the parts I already have. These requirements just happen to be the same as the ones we want for this chapter.

Procmail

After extensive research I settled on the venerable Procmail.[2] I know, more old stuff and *allegedly* unsupported these days too. But it does what we need it to do and is known to work well with the software we are already using. It is stable and has no known serious bugs. It can be configured for use at the system level as well as at the individual user level.

Red Hat and RH-related upstream distributions such as CentOS and Fedora use Procmail as the default mail delivery agent (MDA) for Sendmail, so it does not even need to be installed because it is already there. The MDA delivers email to users' mailboxes on the local host, so it can also be known as the LDA or local delivery agent.

Our email server runs Fedora, so this is a real no-brainer. I will use Procmail. Besides, Red Hat supports Procmail no matter what else you might read on the Internet, and several recent patches have been included in the most recent version. We can check the change log for Procmail to verify this.

EXPERIMENT 50-1: CHECKING PROCMAIL

Perform this experiment as the root user on StudentVM2:

```
[root@studentvm2 mail]# rpm -q --changelog procmail
* Thu Jan 12 2023 Jaroslav Škarvada <jskarvad@redhat.com> - 3.24-1
- Switched to the github fork
- New version
  Resolves: rhbz#2143702

* Fri Jul 22 2022 Fedora Release Engineering <releng@fedoraproject.
org> - 3.22-57
- Rebuilt for https://fedoraproject.org/wiki/Fedora_37_Mass_Rebuild
```

---

[2] RHEL 7 Deployment Guide, Procmail, https://access.redhat.com/documentation/en-us/red_hat_enterprise_linux/7/html/system_administrators_guide/s1-email-mda

```
* Fri Jan 21 2022 Fedora Release Engineering <releng@fedoraproject.
org> - 3.22-56
- Rebuilt for https://fedoraproject.org/wiki/Fedora_36_Mass_Rebuild
<snip>
```

I have shortened the output data stream here, but you can see that work continues.

The results of Experiment 50-1 also show that we should not always believe everything we read on the Internet, including Wikipedia. We should also explore the sources of statements we encounter online and look for ourselves at the original data – in this case the Procmail RPM package.

In addition to delivering email, Procmail can be used to filter and sort it. Procmail rules – known as recipes – can be used to identify spam and delete or sort it into a designated mail folder. Other recipes can identify and sort other mail as well such as sorting emails from specific email accounts or organizations into particular folders. Procmail can be used for many other things besides sorting email into designated folders, such as automated forwarding, duplication, and much more. In this chapter we will confine our use of it to identifying spam and sorting it into the spam folder.

How It Works

A complete discussion of the configuration of SpamAssassin, MIMEDefang, and Procmail is beyond the scope of this chapter, in part because there are so many options for implementing anti-spam solutions using these three programs. This chapter will be limited to the configuration I used to integrate these three packages to implement my own solution.

Processing of incoming email begins with Sendmail. Sendmail calls MIMEDefang as part of the normal email processing. MIMEDefang uses SpamAssassin as a subroutine. MIMEDefang sends email to SpamAssassin and receives the spam score as a return code.

SpamAssassin uses its default set of rules and scores, as well as any located in the local.cf file, to evaluate each email and generate a total score. We can modify the scores for existing rules, add our own rules, and create welcome- and blocklists that can assist you in adapting the rules and scoring to the needs of your own installation. The /etc/mail/spamassassin/local.cf file is used for all of this and it can grow quite large; mine is just over 70KB at this writing and still growing.

It is important to understand that when SpamAssassin scans an email, it checks every rule, both its default rules and local rule sets that are created and maintained by the SysAdmin or email administrator. For each rule that matches, the score defined for that rule is added to the total score for that email. This is not a "one and done" type of scan; the email is always checked against every rule.

SpamAssassin can be run as standalone software in some applications. However, in this environment, SpamAssassin is not run as a daemon; it is called by MIMEDefang. After the spam score for the email is returned to it, MIMEDefang calls the /etc/email/ mimedefang-filter program, which can perform any of several actions on the email. This program can add headers to the email, modify the subject, or just discard the email.

MIMEDefang is programmed in Perl, so it is easy to hack. I have hacked the last major portion of the code in /etc/mail/mimedefang-filter to provide a filtering breakdown with a little more granularity than it does by default. This code adds specified text to the subject line of the email as a means to identify how likely this particular email is to be spam.

Preparation

Although I had already installed MIMEDefang and SpamAssassin on my own email server prior to using Procmail for email sorting, our server, StudentVM2, does not have those tools, so we need to install them.

EXPERIMENT 50-2: INSTALL MIMEDEFANG AND SPAMASSASSIN

Perform this experiment as the root user on StudentVM2. We will install MIMEDefang and SpamAssassin:

```
[root@studentvm2 ~]# dnf -y install mimedefang spamassassin
```

Despite the fact that Perl is already installed on our VMs, this command results in the installation of many additional Perl packages that are required for MIMEDefang.

Verify that there are now some mimedefang* files and a spamassassin directory in /etc/mail.

Configuration

We need to configure MIMEDefang in order to have it add the text we need to the subject line, and we also need to set up some SpamAssassin rules that we can intentionally trigger with our test emails so that they will be marked as spam. We also need to configure Sendmail to call MIMEDefang as part of its normal mail processing tasks.

Configuring Sendmail

Sendmail must call MIMEDefang in order to start the spam filtering process. It does this by calling the MIMEDefang mail filter. The term "mail filter" is generally shortened to "milter."

We enable the MIMEDefang mail filter by inserting one line into our sendmail.cf configuration file.

EXPERIMENT 50-3: CONFIGURE SENDMAIL TO USE MIMEDEFANG

Perform this experiment as the root user on StudentVM2. Make /etc/mail the PWD. Edit the sendmail.mc file and insert the following lines. I placed them just after the EXPOSED_USER line:

```
dnl ####################################################################
####################dnl
dnl # The following line causes sendmail to use the MIMEdefang
milter.dnl
INPUT_MAIL_FILTER(`mimedefang', `S=unix:/var/spool/MIMEDefang/
mimedefang.sock, T=S:5m;R:5m')dnl
dnl ####################################################################
####################dnl
```

Tip   Be sure to not place a space between the last character of the INPUT_MAIL_FILTER command ")" and the trailing "dnl". Sendmail will not restart if there is a space preceding the trailing dnl.

Ensure that /etc/mail is the PWD and run the **make** command:

`[root@studentvm2 mail]# `**`make`**

Restart Sendmail.

Test to verify that we have not broken anything. Use tail -f to follow the maillog file on StudentVM2 and send an email from the student user on StudentVM1 to the student@ example.com account and your external email account:

`[student@studentvm1 ~]$ `**`echo "Hello World" | mailx -s "Test from`**
`StudentVM1" LinuxGeek46@both.org student@example.com`

Ensure that there are no errors in the maillog file and that the email is delivered to the addressees. Fix any problems and try again. I had a couple configuration errors the first time I tried this. The maillog file will give you some clues as will the `journalctl -xeu` `sendmail.service` command.

Open the email you sent to your external email account and display the headers. It should look similar to mine. My email server already has SpamAssassin and MimeDefang running, so you will see the entries pertaining to that. You should also be able to trace the path that your email took to arrive at your personal account:

```
Received: from studentvm2.example.com (_gateway [192.168.0.254])
    by yorktown.both.org (8.17.1/8.17.1) with ESMTPS id 363DpNXm186795
    (version=TLSv1.3 cipher=TLS_AES_256_GCM_SHA384 bits=256 verify=NOT)
    for <LinuxGeek46@both.org>; Mon, 3 Jul 2023 09:51:23 -0400
Received: from studentvm1.example.com ([192.168.56.56])
    by studentvm2.example.com (8.17.1/8.17.1) with ESMTPS id
    363DpL1o002745
    (version=TLSv1.3 cipher=TLS_AES_256_GCM_SHA384 bits=256 verify=NOT);
    Mon, 3 Jul 2023 09:51:21 -0400
Received: from studentvm1.example.com (localhost [127.0.0.1])
    by studentvm1.example.com (8.17.1/8.17.1) with ESMTPS id
    363DpLmRO01661
    (version=TLSv1.3 cipher=TLS_AES_256_GCM_SHA384 bits=256 verify=NOT);
    Mon, 3 Jul 2023 09:51:21 -0400
Received: (from student@localhost)
    by studentvm1.example.com (8.17.1/8.17.1/Submit) id 363DpJds001660;
    Mon, 3 Jul 2023 09:51:19 -0400
```

```
From: Student User <student@example.com>
Message-Id: <202307031351.363DpJds001660@studentvm1.example.com>
Date: Mon, 03 Jul 2023 09:51:19 -0400
To: student@example.com, LinuxGeek46@both.org
Subject: Test from StudentVM1
User-Agent: Heirloom mailx 12.5 7/5/10
MIME-Version: 1.0
Content-Type: text/plain; charset=us-ascii
Content-Transfer-Encoding: 7bit
X-Scanned-By: MIMEDefang 3.4.1 on 192.168.0.52
X-Scanned-By: MIMEDefang 3.4.1
X-Spam-Status: No, score=-78.7 required=10.6 tests=BAYES_00,RDNS_
NONE,SPF_HELO_NONE,USER_IN_WELCOMELIST

Hello World
```

We haven't yet configured an email client on StudentVM1 to retrieve email from StudentVM2. But we are getting there. Use the `mailx` client on StudentVM2 as the student user to retrieve and view that email. You can view all of the headers for the email using the **P** (yes, in uppercase) after selecting and viewing the test message. That looks like this:

```
U 10 logwatch@example.com  Sun Jun 25 03:38 128/4708   "Logwatch for
studentvm1.example.com (Linux)"
  11 logwatch@example.com  Wed Jun 28 03:10 136/5206   "Logwatch for
studentvm1.example.com (Linux)"
  12 logwatch@example.com  Thu Jun 29 03:51  73/2917   "Logwatch for
studentvm1.example.com (Linux)"
  13 Student User          Mon Jul  3 09:51  27/1098   "Test from
StudentVM1"
& 13
Message 13:
From student@example.com  Mon Jul  3 09:51:22 2023
Return-Path: <student@example.com>
From: Student User <student@example.com>
Date: Mon, 03 Jul 2023 09:51:19 -0400
To: student@example.com, LinuxGeek46@both.org
Subject: Test from StudentVM1
```

User-Agent: Heirloom mailx 12.5 7/5/10
Content-Type: text/plain; charset=us-ascii
X-Scanned-By: MIMEDefang 3.4.1
Status: RO

Hello World

& **P**
Message 13:
From student@example.com Mon Jul 3 09:51:22 2023
Return-Path: <student@example.com>
Received: from studentvm1.example.com ([192.168.56.56])
        by studentvm2.example.com (8.17.1/8.17.1) with ESMTPS id
        363DpL1o002745
        (version=TLSv1.3 cipher=TLS_AES_256_GCM_SHA384 bits=256
        verify=NOT);
        Mon, 3 Jul 2023 09:51:21 -0400
Received: from studentvm1.example.com (localhost [127.0.0.1])
        by studentvm1.example.com (8.17.1/8.17.1) with ESMTPS id
        363DpLmRO01661
        (version=TLSv1.3 cipher=TLS_AES_256_GCM_SHA384 bits=256
        verify=NOT);
        Mon, 3 Jul 2023 09:51:21 -0400
Received: (from student@localhost)
        by studentvm1.example.com (8.17.1/8.17.1/Submit) id
        363DpJds001660;
        Mon, 3 Jul 2023 09:51:19 -0400
From: Student User <student@example.com>
Message-Id: <202307031351.363DpJds001660@studentvm1.example.com>
Date: Mon, 03 Jul 2023 09:51:19 -0400
To: student@example.com, LinuxGeek46@both.org
Subject: Test from StudentVM1
User-Agent: Heirloom mailx 12.5 7/5/10
MIME-Version: 1.0

```
Content-Type: text/plain; charset=us-ascii
Content-Transfer-Encoding: 7bit
X-Scanned-By: MIMEDefang 3.4.1
Status: RO

Hello World

&
```

This is a bit less interesting as it doesn't have as many hops as the one to my external email. It does have one line indicating it was scanned by MIMEDefang, which means that our basic installation is working as expected.

Hacking mimedefang-filter

Let's hack mimedefang-filter and have it add the text "####SPAM####" to emails with high enough spam scores to be considered spam. This is easy even if you don't know Perl[3] because I will show you exactly what to do.

EXPERIMENT 50-4: HACKING THE MIMEDEFANG-FILTER

Perform this experiment as the root user on StudentVM2. The MIMEDefang files and the SpamAssassin configuration directory are located in /etc/mail. We are going to modify the mimedefang-filter Perl program, but make a backup copy first and then examine the code we want to change.

Ensure that /etc/mail is the PWD.

`[root@studentvm2 mail]# cp mimedefang-filter mimedefang-filter.bak`

After making a backup of the mimedefang-filter program, open it with the Vim editor. The following code is near the beginning of the file.

---

[3] I suggest that you learn at least some Perl basics because it is a very powerful string processing language. Many programmers today use Python, Ruby, and other languages, and that is fine, but I find Perl to still be relevant and quite useful for system administration. Perl uses a C-like syntax, so if you already program in C, Perl should seem familiar and be fairly easy to learn.

I have used many of the changes I made to the configuration file on my own email server as the example for this experiment.

You need to set the administrator's name and email address. I have highlighted the lines that need changed. You can see what I have changed them to.

```
#************************************************************************
# Set administrator's e-mail address here.  The administrator receives
# quarantine messages and is listed as the contact for site-wide
# MIMEDefang policy.  A good example would be 'defang-admin@
mydomain.com'
#************************************************************************
$AdminAddress = 'root@example.com';
$AdminName = "David Both";
```

This next section is the return address that will appear in emails sent by MIMEDefang:

```
#************************************************************************
# Set the e-mail address from which MIMEDefang quarantine warnings and
# user notifications appear to come.   A good example would be
# 'mimedefang@mydomain.com'.    Make sure to have an alias for this
# address if you want replies to it to work.
#************************************************************************
$DaemonAddress = 'mimedefang@example.com';
```

I added this section immediately after the preceding ones. It tells SpamAssassin to check Internet blocklist databases that list known spammers by DNS IP addresses:

```
# SpamAssassin should check DNSBL lookups and other non-local tests
# Added by David Both 04/23/2011
$SALocalTestsOnly = 0;
```

Now go to the section of the mimedefang-filter program that starts around line 271 when considering the lines I added earlier. We will replace all the following highlighted lines of code with some of our own:

```
    # Spam checks if SpamAssassin is installed
    if ($Features{"SpamAssassin"}) {
        if (-s "./INPUTMSG" < 100*1024) {
            # Only scan messages smaller than 100kB.  Larger messages
```

```
# are extremely unlikely to be spam, and SpamAssassin is
# dreadfully slow on very large messages.
my($hits, $req, $names, $report) = spam_assassin_check();
my($score);
if ($hits < 40) {
    $score = "*" x int($hits);
} else {
    $score = "*" x 40;
}
# We add a header which looks like this:
# X-Spam-Score: 6.8 (******) NAME_OF_TEST,NAME_OF_TEST
# The number of asterisks in parens is the integer part
# of the spam score clamped to a maximum of 40.
# MUA filters can easily be written to trigger on a
# minimum number of asterisks...
if ($hits >= $req) {
    action_change_header("X-Spam-Score", "$hits ($score)
    $names");
    md_graphdefang_log('spam', $hits, $RelayAddr);

    # If you find the SA report useful, add it, I guess...
    action_add_part($entity, "text/plain", "-suggest",
                    "$report\n",
                    "SpamAssassinReport.txt", "inline");
} else {
    # Delete any existing X-Spam-Score header?
    action_delete_header("X-Spam-Score");
}
}
}
```

The first two non-comment lines begin with "my" and are used to create local copies of certain variables that may be used in this code segment. The $hits variable is a numeric value that represents the spam score of the email.

The first if-else structure uses the Perl "x" operator to create a string that consists of a number of asterisks (*) equal to the integer number of the spam score. For example, a spam score of 7 would result in a string of seven asterisks "*******", which results in a bar graph of the spam score. The first part of this if statement does this so long as the value of the $hits variable is less than 40. The "else" part of the logic simply creates a string of 40 asterisks if the value of $hits is 40 or more.

The second if-else statement takes some defined actions. If $hits is larger than the $req (required) variable, a header named X-Spam-Score is added with the following structure:

```
numeric spam score ($hits), the string of asterisks, test names (hits)
that comprise the score
```

The line `md_graphdefang_log('spam', $hits, $RelayAddr);` adds an entry to a log file in the /var/log directory if we uncomment a line earlier in this file.

The final statement in this "if" section appends a SpamAssassin report to the email as an in-line attachment. I find this report makes it easy to do problem determination when issues arise with SpamAssassin and its scoring.

If the $hits variable is less than $req, any existing spam score headers are deleted. Since emails may be scanned by multiple mail servers, this prevents spam scores from other servers from looking like we think this is spam. The $req variable defines the score at or above which an email is considered to be spam. The default is 5. To change this value, you must change the following entry in the /etc/mail/sa-mimedefang.cf configuration file:

```
required_hits            5
```

Over years of working with MIMEDefang and SpamAssassin, I have decided that I do not like the default actions taken to mark this as spam. The bar graph is not visible to the end user, and although it could be used by Procmail to determine how to sort the spam, I wanted something in the subject line where the recipient could see it and decide what to do with the message. I created a set of actions that work better for me and enable me to see spam info more quickly.

In this experiment we change both sets of actions – the actions taken when an email is determined to be spam and those taken when it is not. That completely revised section of code is shown here. Replace the original section in your mimedefang-filter with the following code.

Be sure to note that the end of each line is a semicolon (;). The lines that don't end with a semicolon in the following listing are wrapped. Everything up to the next semicolon is part of the same line:

```
if ($hits >= $req) {
    action_add_header("X-Spam-Status", "Spam, score=$hits required=$req
    tests=$names");
    action_change_header("Subject", "####SPAM#### ($hits) $Subject");
    action_add_part($entity, "text/plain", "-suggest", "$report\n",
    "SpamAssassinReport.txt", "inline");
# action_discard();
} else {
    action_add_header("X-Spam-Status", "Spam, score=$hits required=$req
    tests=$names");
    action_change_header("Subject", "####NOT SPAM#### ($hits)
    $Subject");
    action_add_part($entity, "text/plain", "-suggest", "$report\n",
    "SpamAssassinReport.txt", "inline");
    # Delete any existing X-Spam-Score header?
    # action_delete_header("X-Spam-Score");
}
```

This revised code adds the X-Spam-Status header, prepends the "####SPAM####" string and the number of hits to the subject line, and attaches the SpamAssassin report to the end of the email message. It also does this for non-spam emails except that the message prepended to the subject is a bit different and says, "####NOT SPAM####". We do it this way in this experiment so that we can see that our spam detector is working even if the emails are not spam.

In a real-world environment, I add the X-Spam-Status line to the headers on non-spam messages (ham), but I do not normally add anything to the subject line or append the SpamAssassin report to the message.

Note that this revision of the code does not delete existing headers. That means you will see X-Spam headers from other email servers that the email has passed through.

Many users tend to freak out when they see that SpamAssassin report and the subject line with "####SPAM####" in it. As a result, I only add the report when I am trying to determine the source of a problem, such as a rule that is not working. The report allows me to easily see what is in the headers, but includes more information such as the exact score added by each rule. Also, if a user forwards an email to me, the report stays attached to the email, but the original headers are deleted so they would be useless at that point.

Now we can start and enable MIMEDefang and restart Sendmail. Note that Sendmail must always be restarted after starting or restarting MIMEDefang. I wrote a little shell script to stop both services and then restart them in the correct sequence because I automate everything. It does not matter in which order they are stopped, but they must be started MIMEDefang first and then Sendmail. This is because MIMEDefang opens a socket that Sendmail must find and also connect to. The socket is their communication channel:

```
[root@studentvm2 ~]# systemctl enable --now mimedefang
Created symlink /etc/systemd/system/multi-user.target.wants/mimedefang.
service → /usr/lib/systemd/system/mimedefang.service.
Created symlink /etc/systemd/system/multi-user.target.wants/mimedefang-
multiplexor.service → /usr/lib/systemd/system/mimedefang-multiplexor.
service.
[root@studentvm2 ~]#
```

MIMEDefang needs to start before Sendmail because it creates a socket for Sendmail to communicate with. That's the configuration we added to sendmail.cf. Restart Sendmail:

```
[root@studentvm2 ~]# systemctl restart sendmail
```

Test this as the student user on StudentVM1 and send an email to student@example.com. Use mailx as the student user on StudentVM2 to view the email and show the headers:

```
From student@example.com   Mon Jul  3 15:16:41 2023
Return-Path: <student@example.com>
Received: from studentvm1.example.com ([192.168.56.56])
        by studentvm2.example.com (8.17.1/8.17.1) with ESMTPS id
        363JGXOY003833
        (version=TLSv1.3 cipher=TLS_AES_256_GCM_SHA384 bits=256
        verify=NOT);
        Mon, 3 Jul 2023 15:16:34 -0400
Received: from studentvm1.example.com (localhost [127.0.0.1])
        by studentvm1.example.com (8.17.1/8.17.1) with ESMTPS id
        363JGXip002314
```

```
        (version=TLSv1.3 cipher=TLS_AES_256_GCM_SHA384 bits=256
        verify=NOT);
        Mon, 3 Jul 2023 15:16:33 -0400
Received: (from student@localhost)
        by studentvm1.example.com (8.17.1/8.17.1/Submit) id
        363JGWii002313;
        Mon, 3 Jul 2023 15:16:32 -0400
From: Student User <student@example.com>
Message-Id: <202307031916.363JGWii002313@studentvm1.example.com>
Date: Mon, 03 Jul 2023 15:16:32 -0400
To: student@example.com, LinuxGeek46@both.org
Subject: ####NOT SPAM#### (-1) Test 9 from StudentVM1
User-Agent: Heirloom mailx 12.5 7/5/10
MIME-Version: 1.0
Content-Type: multipart/mixed; boundary="-----------=_1688411794-3318-0"
X-Spam-Status: Spam, score=-1 required=5 tests=ALL_TRUSTED
X-Scanned-By: MIMEDefang 3.4.1
Status: R

Part 1:
Content-Type: text/plain; charset=us-ascii
Content-Transfer-Encoding: 7bit

Hello World

Part 2:
Content-Type: text/plain; name="SpamAssassinReport.txt"
Content-Disposition: inline; filename="SpamAssassinReport.txt"
Content-Transfer-Encoding: 7bit

Spam detection software, running on the system "studentvm2.example.com",
has NOT identified this incoming email as spam.  The original
message has been attached to this so you can view it or label
similar future email.  If you have any questions, see
@@CONTACT_ADDRESS@@ for details.

Content preview:  Hello World
```

```
Content analysis details:    (-1.0 points, 5.0 required)

 pts rule name                description
---- --------------------     ---------------------------------------------
-1.0 ALL_TRUSTED              Passed through trusted hosts only via SMTP
```

Now we need to find a way to test for true spam. SpamAssassin has provisions for this. In a terminal session as root on StudentVM2, make /usr/share/doc/spamassassin the PWD and list the contents. You will find, among other files, two text files that we can use to test with, sample-nonspam.txt and sample-spam.txt. Use the test mode of the spamassassin command to test this:

```
[root@studentvm2 spamassassin]# spamassassin --test-mode <
sample-spam.txt
X-Spam-Checker-Version: SpamAssassin 3.4.2 (2018-09-13) on
        studentvm2.example.com
X-Spam-Flag: YES
X-Spam-Level: **************************************************
X-Spam-Status: Yes, score=1000.0 required=5.0 tests=GTUBE,NO_RECEIVED,
        NO_RELAYS autolearn=no autolearn_force=no version=3.4.2
X-Spam-Report:
        * -0.0 NO_RELAYS Informational: message was not relayed via SMTP
        * 1000 GTUBE BODY: Generic Test for Unsolicited Bulk Email
        * -0.0 NO_RECEIVED Informational: message has no
Received headers
Subject: [SPAM] Test spam mail (GTUBE)
Message-ID: <GTUBE1.1010101@example.net>
Date: Wed, 23 Jul 2003 23:30:00 +0200
From: Sender <sender@example.net>
To: Recipient <recipient@example.net>
Precedence: junk
MIME-Version: 1.0
Content-Type: text/plain; charset=us-ascii
Content-Transfer-Encoding: 7bit
X-Spam-Prev-Subject: Test spam mail (GTUBE)
```

```
This is the GTUBE, the
        Generic
        Test for
        Unsolicited
        Bulk
        Email

<SNIP>
```

Note   This is a good example of using redirection of input from a file.

Be sure to read the entire message as I have trimmed quite a bit off to save space.

This method tests SpamAssassin and MIMEDefang but not the full path a real email would take through the MTAs, and the email never appears in our inbox. So we can also test using the mailx command so that the email goes to our inbox:

[root@studentvm2 spamassassin]# **cat sample-spam.txt | mailx -s "Test spam" student@example.com**

Open the email as the student user on StudentVM2 in the **mailx** client. Examine the email and view the added headers and the attached SpamAssassin report.

We can see that our anti-spam configuration is working as it should.

The subject line of the email now contains the string "####SPAM####" or "####NOT SPAM####" but without the quotes and the spam score, that is, the variable $hits. Having a known string in the subject line of spam makes further filtering and sorting easy.

The modified email is returned to Sendmail for further processing.

Configuring Procmail

The last thing that Sendmail does is call Procmail to act as the MDA. Procmail then checks the home directory of the user to which the email is addressed for the existence of a ~/.procmailrc file. If one does not exist, Procmail deposits the email into the user's inbox in /var/spool/mail. What happens when the ~/.procmailrc file does exist is the topic of this section.

What we need Procmail to do is to use the text now added to the subject line to look at the email before it gets placed in the inbox and to route it to a different folder, which we will call, naturally enough, "Spam."

Procmail uses global and user-level configuration files. The global /etc/procmailrc file and individual user ~/.procmailrc files must be created. The structure of the files is the same, but the global file operates on all incoming email, while the local files can be configured for each individual user. I do not use a global file, so all of the sorting is done on the user level.

Note that the ~/.procmailrc file must be located in the home directory of the email account on the email server. It does not go in the home directory on individual client workstations. Because most email accounts are not login accounts, they use the nologin program as the default shell. Therefore, the admin will need to create and maintain these files. The other option is to change to a login shell such as Bash and set passwords so that knowledgeable users can log into their email accounts on the server and maintain their ~/.procmailrc files.

Each recipe starts with :0 (yes, that is a zero) on the first line and contains a total of three lines. The second line starts with * and contains a conditional statement consisting of a regular expression (REGEX) that Procmail compares to each line in the incoming email. If there is a match, Procmail sorts the email into the folder specified by the third line. The use of the ^ symbol denotes the beginning of the line when making the comparison.

EXPERIMENT 50-5: USING PROCMAIL

Perform this part of the experiment as the student user on StudentVM2. Use a text editor to create a new /home/student/.procmailrc file and add the following content. This file should not be executable:

```
####################################################################
# .procmailrc file for student@example.com                        #
#  Rules are run sequentially - first match wins                  #
# It is not necessary to reboot or to restart email. Changes take place #
# as soon as the file is saved.                                   #
####################################################################
# Set the environment
PATH=/usr/sbin:/usr/bin
```

```
MAILDIR=$HOME/mail  #location of your mailboxes
DEFAULT=/var/spool/mail/student

# Send Spam to the spam mailbox
:0
* ^Subject:.*####SPAM####
$MAILDIR/Spam

# sorts all remaining messages into the default inbox
:0
* .*
$DEFAULT
###################################################################
```

The first recipe in my .procmailrc file sorts the spam identified in the subject line by MIMEDefang into my spam folder. Procmail ignores case, so there is no need to create recipes that look for various combinations of upper- and lowercase. The second and last recipe sorts all email that does not match another recipe into the default folder, usually the inbox.

Having the .procmailrc file in my home directory does not cause Procmail to filter my mail. I have to add one more file, the ~/.forward file, which tells Procmail to filter all of my incoming email. Create the /home/student/.forward file and add the following content:

```
# .forward file
# process all incoming mail through procmail - see .procmailrc for the
filter rules.
|/usr/bin/procmail
```

Ensure that both of these new files have ownership of student.student and they should not be executable. It is not necessary to restart either Sendmail or MIMEDefang when creating or modifying the Procmail configuration files.

Be sure that the /home/student/mail/Spam directory exists on StudentVM2. Create it if it doesn't with student:student ownership.

To test all of these changes, return to StudentVM2 as the root user and from a root terminal session send some test emails, both ham and spam. Make sure that /usr/share/doc/spamassassin is the PWD and then issue these commands:

```
[root@studentvm2 spamassassin]# cat sample-nonspam.txt | mailx -s "Test
nonspam" student@example.com
[root@studentvm2 spamassassin]# cat sample-spam.txt | mailx -s "Test
spam" student@example.com
```

The non-spam email should be sorted to the inbox and the spam email sorted to the spam folder – except that did not happen. So I looked in /var/log/maillog and found the following entries:

```
Jul 10 07:10:33 studentvm2 sendmail[3930]: x6ABAU7d003928:
x6ABAX7c003930: DSN: Service unavailable
Jul 10 07:10:33 studentvm2 smrsh[3932]: uid 1000: attempt to use
"procmail" (stat failed)
```

The problem here is that, as I did on my own mail server, I missed one step. It is easy to miss because I found the true answer in only one place.

We need to add a symbolic link in the /etc/smrsh directory. Smrsh stands for "Sendmail restricted shell," which is a reasonably secure shell in which Sendmail can run scripts and which will help prevent crackers from exploiting Sendmail for their own purposes.

Create the link, /etc/smrsh/procmail, using the following commands:

```
[root@studentvm2 ~]# cd /etc/smrsh ; ln -s /usr/bin/procmail
procmail ; ll
total 0
lrwxrwxrwx. 1 root root 17 Jul 10 07:15 procmail -> /usr/bin/procmail
```

Now perform the test again by sending the spam and non-spam email messages again. Now they should go into the correct folders.

We could have created both of these files as the student user on StudentVM2 but, in most environments, regular users will not have login access to the server.

Reports of Procmail's Demise

Having done many Internet searches while researching this chapter, I found a number of results dating from 2001 through about 2013 that declare Procmail to be dead. They point for evidence at the no longer working web pages, missing source code, and a short article on Wikipedia that does no more than declare Procmail to be dead and provides links to more recent replacements.

However, all Red Hat, Fedora, and CentOS distributions install Procmail as the MDA for Sendmail. The Red Hat, Fedora, and CentOS repositories all have the source RPMs for Procmail, and the source code is also on GitHub. Red Hat documentation for CentOS contains some decent documentation for Procmail.[4]

Considering the continued use of Procmail by Red Hat, I have no problem with using this mature software that does its job silently and without fanfare.

SpamAssassin Rules

Now that we have a working solution, what happens when we start getting spam that does not match any rules or for which the matched rules do not add up to a high enough score to make the cut as spam? We can adjust the default scores and write new rules using the /etc/mail/spamassassin/local.cf file.

The files located in /usr/share/spamassassin that begin with two-digit numbers are configuration files that define rules for specific types of spam. When SpamAssassin matches a rule in one of these files, it then searches for a score in the 72_scores.cf file. These files should not be altered because they will be overwritten when updates to SpamAssassin are installed.

There are also two files in /usr/share/spamassassin that we can use as templates or starting points for local configuration. These files make it easy for us to configure SpamAssassin by adding rules and changing scores so that we don't need to change the default configuration files. The default files can be replaced during an update and cause our changes to them to be overwritten.

The local.cf file, of which there is already a copy in /etc/mail/spamassassin, is used to create local rules, alter the scores of existing default rules, and set welcomelist and blocklist entries.

---

[4] Red Hat, "Red Hat Linux 8.0 The Official Red Hat Linux Reference," www-uxsup.csx.cam.ac.uk/pub/doc/redhat/redhat8/rhl-rg-en-80.pdf

The user_prefs.template can be used by individual users to override the default preferences. This file would need to be copied to the user's home directory and renamed to user_prefs. For example, a user might wish to specify a higher required_score to ensure that some emails with somewhat higher spam scores than the default of 5 be allowed through as ham. This would also be the file in which users would add welcomelist and blocklist entries, create their own rules, and change scores. In most modern installations, end users will not be knowledgeable enough, or not have login access to the email server, to perform these tasks, so it would fall to the SysAdmin to make those changes for them.

Before we make any changes, we need to look at the default rule set, which should never be changed in any way.

EXPERIMENT 50-6: CREATING SPAMASSASSIN RULES

Begin this experiment as the root user on StudentVM2. If you do not already have a root terminal session open on the desktop and following /var/log/maillog, do so now with this command:

```
[root@studentvm2 ~]# tail -f /var/log/maillog
```

In another root terminal session, make /usr/share/spamassassin the PWD. List the files in that directory. The files you see there are used for local configuration or, as in the case of the files that begin with "V", are version-specific configuration. We need only concern ourselves with the local.cf file to specify our local configuration changes.

We start by changing the score for a rule that we know the spam test email already matches. As the student user on StudentVM2, make /usr/share/doc/spamassassin the PWD and send this email:

```
[student@studentvm2 spamassassin]$ cat sample-spam.txt | mailx -s "Test email" student@example.com
```

As the student user on StudentVM1, open Thunderbird, if it is not already, and look in the spam folder for the new email. Select the spam email that was just received and scroll down to the SpamAssassin attachment. You will see that this email matched the GTUBE[5] rule, which gave the email a score of 1000, which is high enough that even the best non-spam rules, such as ALL_TRUSTED and many more, could not overcome to make it look like non-spam.

---

[5] The GTUBE rule is a special rule used for testing with the SpamAssassin test emails and should never be matched by a real email.

Let's change this number just to see how a score change works. As root on StudentVM2, edit /etc/mail/spamassassin/local.cf and add the following line:

```
score            GTUBE    600
```

Save the local.cf file but do not exit the editor because we will be making some additional changes to the local.cf file. Stop both Sendmail and MIMEDefang and then start them MIMEDefang first and then Sendmail:

```
[root@studentvm2 ~]# systemctl stop sendmail ; systemctl stop
mimedefang ; systemctl start mimedefang ; systemctl start sendmail
```

I wrote a little script to do this on my own mail server and you can, too, if you like. I experiment with this a lot and make changes to the local.cf, so a script with a short name can save a lot of typing. At any rate, these are the commands you need. It doesn't matter in which order you stop the services.

Now send the following email message as the student user on StudentVM2, where the number in the subject is in the form YYYYMMDDHHMM for easy identification:

```
[student@studentvm2 spamassassin]$ cat sample-spam.txt | mailx -s "Test
email 201907220828" student@example.com
```

Be sure to check the log file messages and then look at the email using Thunderbird on StudentVM1. If necessary, scroll down and look at the SpamAssassin report, which shows the scores. The score for GTUBE should be 600.

Now let's add a new rule to local.cf. It takes three lines to create a new rule. The first line defines the location of the search such as the header or body of the message and a Perl REGEX to define a specific line such as the subject and the pattern to be matched. Each line also contains an identifier, which is typically in uppercase.

The second line is a description of the rule that will be printed in the SpamAssassin report. And the third line contains the score that is applied to the message when the rule is matched. I also add a comment as a bit of explanation and a separator to make a long list of rules easier to read. And I have a very long list.

I get a lot of spam email that has something about "back taxes" in the body of the message. It can take a long time to scan the body of a message especially if the body is large, so I try to have as few rules that scan the body as possible, but I find this one necessary.

Add the following three lines below the score modification that we previously added to local.cf:

```
# Back Taxes
body            BACK_TAXES              /back taxes/i
describe        BACK_TAXES              Contains "back taxes" in the body
score           BACK_TAXES              6.0
```

The regular expression **/back taxes/i** looks for the text "back taxes", and the trailing "**i**" tells Perl to ignore the case so that any combination of upper- and lowercase will match.

Restart the MIMEDefang and Sendmail services in the correct order and send the following email as the student user on StudentVM2. Be careful because it is different and now has our trigger text in the body:

[student@studentvm2 spamassassin]$ **echo "Let us save your back taxes." | mailx -s "Test email 201907220910" student@example.com**

That test email still shows up as not spam because its score is 4.9 and a score of 5 points is needed to make it spam. Be sure to view the headers to see why the overall score for the email was 4.9.

So boost the score for our new rule to 10 and resend the test email. This time it should be classified as spam and sorted into the spam folder.

View the message and its source using Thunderbird. Notice the X-Spam-Status line and the SpamAssassin report.

Send an email that does not contain "back taxes" in the body to verify that this rule would not match. Also, send some emails with various upper- and lowercase combinations of "back taxes" to ensure that they do match.

Now add a rule that checks for the text string "XXX" in the subject line and adds 15 points to ensure that it gets counted as spam. The Perl regular expression uses =~ to specify that the subject "contains" the search pattern. So "I have XXX for you" would be a match:

```
# XXX
header          XXX                     Subject =~ /XXX/i
describe        XXX                     Contains "XXX" in the subject line
score           XXX                     15.0
```

Restart the Sendmail and MIMEDefang services in the proper sequence and test this new rule.

We want to ensure that emails from certain domains such as example.com, both.org, and opensource.com are allowed through regardless of their other spam scores. We can also block a domain like spammer.com.

Add the following lines to the local.cf file and restart the services. SpamAssassin now uses the terms blocklist and welcomelist:

```
welcomelist_from   *@example.com
welcomelist_from   linuxgeek46@both.org
welcomelist_from   *@opensource.com
blocklist_from     *@spammer.com              # Misc spammer
```

The * character is a metacharacter that matches all characters to the left of the @ sign in the email address. Entries using this metacharacter match all email accounts from the specified domain. I have specified a welcomelist for only my own email from my personal both.org domain. Other accounts from both.org will not be welcome-listed. That does not mean that they will be automatically considered spam because they would still need a score of at least +5.

We can only test this within the example.com domain by sending another email to ourselves. Send the following email as the student user on StudentVM1:

```
[student@studentvm1 ~]$ echo "This is a test email" | mailx -s "Test
email" student@example.com
```

Verify the email has arrived and check the spam score.

Additional Resources

There are few really good resources for someone who needs to create an email system from nothing. My intent in these chapters about and pertaining to email in this course was to at least partially fill that gap. This volume of the course provides enough information to get started with a reasonably well-constructed email server that can grow to absorb the workloads of a small- to medium-sized organization.

As part of my research for this course – these chapters dealing with email, spam, and malware in particular – I encountered the book *Pro Open Source Mail: Building an Enterprise Mail Solution*[6] by Curtis Smith. That book is the one I wish I had when I first started building my own email server. In many ways Smith takes the same path as I did and ends up with most of the same software. The only significant difference is his choice of Dovecot as his IMAP server, whereas we use UW-IMAP. The author of that book also goes into much more detail than I have in this course. I highly recommend *Pro Open Source Mail* despite the fact that it is somewhat older because it presents a complete, integrated solution rather than just one part as do most books. Despite the fact that the configuration for Dovecot has changed considerably since the book was written, it is still a good book overall.

You can also refer to Chapter 8 of the *SpamAssassin*[7] book for more information about using MIMEDefang with Sendmail and SpamAssassin.

Chapter Summary

Although we could have used Procmail by itself for spam filtering and sorting, I think SpamAssassin does a better job of scoring because it does not rely on a single rule to match, but rather the aggregate score from all of the rules, as well as scores from Bayesian filtering.

Procmail works very well when matches can be made very explicit with known strings such as the ones that I have configured MIMEDefang to place in the subject line. I think Procmail works better as a final sorting stage in the spam filtering process than as a complete solution all by itself. Of course, I know that many admins have made complete spam filtering solutions using nothing more than Procmail.

Now that I have server-side filtering, I am somewhat less limited in my choice of email clients because I no longer need a client that performs filtering and sorting. Nor do I have a need to leave an email client running all the time to perform that filtering and sorting.

---

[6] Smith, Curtis, *Pro Open Source Mail: Building an Enterprise Mail Solution*, Apress, 2006, ISBN 978-1-4302-1173-0

[7] Schwartz, Alan, *SpamAssassin: A Practical Guide to Configuration, Customization, and Integration*, [PACT] Publishing, ISBN 1-904811-12-4. This book also contains information about MIMEDefang and Procmail.

Exercises

Perform the following exercises to complete this chapter:

1. Add and test a SpamAssassin rule that adds two points when it matches the text "free money" in the subject line. Name the rule FREE_MONEY_1. Send an email to student@example.com from StudentVM1 that contains that phrase. View the SpamAssassin report to verify that the new rule is working.

2. Use the Thunderbird email client to add a new folder and name it FreeMoney. Then add a new rule to the Procmail file that matches any emails with the string FREE_MONEY_1 in the X-Spam-Status header and sorts them into the new folder. Then test.

3. Locate the file in which the default scores for welcomelists and blocklists are stored. What rule name is used when a user account is welcome-listed?

4. What is the score added to a user that is welcome-listed?

5. Why must MIMEDefang be started (or restarted) before Sendmail?

CHAPTER 51

Apache Web Server

Objectives

In this chapter you will learn

- How to install and configure the Apache web server
- How to create simple static web pages
- How to use multiple programming languages to generate dynamic CGI web content

Introduction

Apache is arguably the most common web server on the Internet. It is well understood, mature, and reliable. It is very configurable and flexible as you will see in this and later experiments. Apache is also free open source software that is provided under the Apache License 2.0.

Apache is an HTTP server that is available on Linux, other Unix-like operating systems, and Windows. HTTP stands for HyperText Transfer Protocol and is a text-based protocol that uses TCP for its transport layer. HTTPD is the HTTP daemon that runs on the server and responds to requests to serve a web page.

Although the name may seem strange, it is easily explained. Developed by Rob McCool – yes, really – at the National Center for Supercomputing Applications, it was the most common HTTP server on the Internet in 1995. As of 2023, it is still used by 31.3% of known web servers.[1]

---

[1] W3Techs, `https://w3techs.com/technologies/details/ws-apache`

© David Both 2023
D. Both, *Using and Administering Linux: Volume 3*, https://doi.org/10.1007/978-1-4842-9786-5_51

Some of the webmasters that were using it had created many of their own plug-in extensions and bug fixes because further development had stalled. Some of those people collaborated to add these extensions and fixes to the original code in the form of patches. There were many of these patches, so it was quite natural for the webmaster hackers to call it "a patchy web server."

You can find documentation, support, security information, mailing lists, downloads, and more at the Apache HTTP Server Project.[2]

In this chapter we will install Apache and explore its use as a simple web server. In following chapters we will explore its use as the basis for more complex tools such as the WordPress content management system (CMS) to produce complex yet easily manageable websites.

Installing Apache

Apache is very easy to install with a single command.

EXPERIMENT 51-1: INSTALLING APACHE

Perform this experiment as the root user on StudentVM2. Install the Apache web server with the following command:

```
[root@studentvm2 ~]# dnf -y install httpd
```

It takes only a few moments to install the HTTPD package and several dependencies.

You may also wish to install the httpd-tools and httpd-manual packages, but they are not necessary for these experiments.

Testing Apache

No initial configuration changes are required. The default configuration works just fine without modification.

---

[2] The Apache HTTP Server Project, https://httpd.apache.org/

EXPERIMENT 51-2: TESTING APACHE

Perform this experiment as the root user on StudentVM2. Start and enable Apache with the following command:

[root@studentvm2 ~]# **systemctl enable --now httpd**

Verify that the Apache web server is running with the following command:

```
[root@studentvm2 ~]# systemctl status httpd
● httpd.service - The Apache HTTP Server
   Loaded: loaded (/usr/lib/systemd/system/httpd.service; enabled; vendor
   preset: disabled)
   Active: active (running) since Wed 2019-07-24 15:52:42 EDT; 17s ago
     Docs: man:httpd.service(8)
 Main PID: 7147 (httpd)
   Status: "Running, listening on: port 80"
    Tasks: 213 (limit: 4696)
   Memory: 15.2M
   CGroup: /system.slice/httpd.service
           ├─7147 /usr/sbin/httpd -DFOREGROUND
           ├─7148 /usr/sbin/httpd -DFOREGROUND
           ├─7149 /usr/sbin/httpd -DFOREGROUND
           ├─7150 /usr/sbin/httpd -DFOREGROUND
           └─7151 /usr/sbin/httpd -DFOREGROUND
Jul 24 15:52:42 studentvm2.example.com systemd[1]: Starting The Apache HTTP
Server...
Jul 24 15:52:42 studentvm2.example.com httpd[7147]: Server configured,
listening on: port 80
Jul 24 15:52:42 studentvm2.example.com systemd[1]: Started The Apache
HTTP Server.
```

You can test Apache by starting a web browser and typing **localhost** in the URL field. Because no index.html or some other index file is located in /var/www/html, the test page shown in Figure 51-1 is displayed.

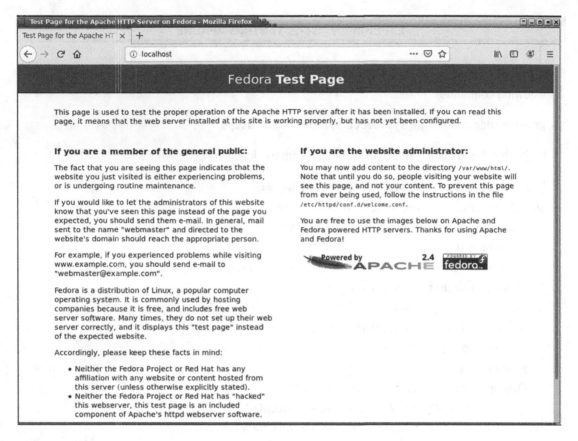

Figure 51-1. *The Fedora test page displayed in the browser shows that our Apache web server is working properly*

You can also install text-only browsers to use for testing from the CLI. The ones I use are Links and Lynx.

To test that external hosts can access our new website, open a browser on StudentVM1 and enter `http://studentvm2.example.com/` in the URL field. The test page should be displayed.

That was easy.

Creating a Simple Index File

Our web server is up and running, so now we need some content. An index file is the "home page" for any website. There are different types of index files, and we will explore a few in this section.

It is easy to create a very simple index file for your website. This can act as the starting point for a more complex site, or it can just be a placeholder until a more complex site can be built using tools such as Drupal or WordPress. We will use WordPress in Chapter 52 of this volume to create a professional-looking website. For now, we will look at creating some simple static and dynamic web pages.

EXPERIMENT 51-3: CREATE AN INDEX FILE

Perform this experiment as the root user on StudentVM2. In this experiment we will create a simple index file and then embellish it just a bit.

First, make /var/ the PWD. Then change the ownership of all files and directories to student:student:

```
[root@studentvm2 var]# chown -R student:student www
```

Make /var/www/html the PWD. Create the index.html file and add the content "Hello World" to it – without the quotes. Ensure that the ownership of the new file is apache.apache and change it if it is not.

On either StudentVM1 or StudentVM2 – or both – refresh the web browser. The result of using an index file is shown in Figure 51-2.

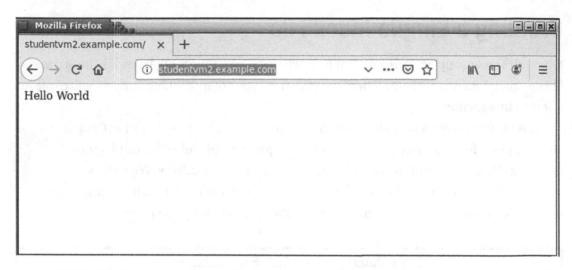

Figure 51-2. *Using a simple index file for our website*

Note that our index.html file has no HTML (HyperText Markup Language) in it at all. It is just ASCII plain text. Because the formatting performed by the browser is based upon the HTML markup, a long document would be run together with no regard for paragraphs or spacing of any kind. So let's add a bit of HTML to pretty it up.

Edit the index.html file and add HTML tags so that it looks like the following. The <h1> tag starts a first-level header and </h1> tag ends it. Many tags start a format such as headers, strong (usually bold), emphasis (usually italics), and more, and they end with a tag:

```
<h1>Hello World!</h1>
```

Save the file and refresh the browser. You should see a result identical to Figure 51-3.

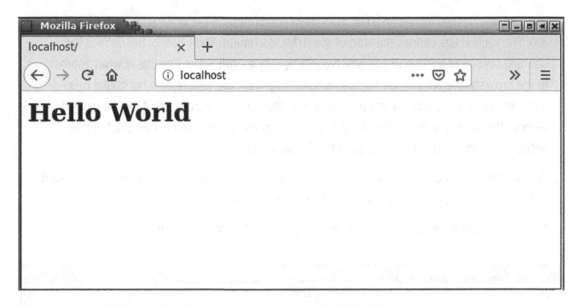

Figure 51-3. *The result of using some minimal HTML tags*

Some browsers will not know how to handle this minimal HTML, so we would need more to make a complete and universally compatible web page. Edit your index.html file to have the following content:

```
<!DOCTYPE HTML PUBLIC "-//w3c//DD HTML 4.0//EN">
<html>
<head>
<title>Student Web Page</title>
</head>
<body>
<h1>Hello World!</h1>
<hr>
Welcome to my world.<p>
Student
</body>
</html>
```

This is pretty much the minimum requirements for an HTML document that conforms to W3C HTML standards.

The first line defines this as an HTML document conforming to the W3C[3] standards for HTML 4.0. The second line defines the start of the HTML document. The <head> tag defines the heading section of the document, which contains only a <title> tag. The title is what appears in the browser title bar and tab for this website. The <hr> tag generates a horizontal rule – bar – to use as a separator. The <p> tag defines the start of a paragraph. It can be used without the corresponding </p> tag as I have here in this simple web document, but it is better if you do use it to mark the end of each paragraph.

You can create this document without the enclosing <html>, <body>, and <head> tags, but it will work best with all browsers if you use all of those tags.

Now refresh the browser and see that your page looks like that in Figure 51-4.

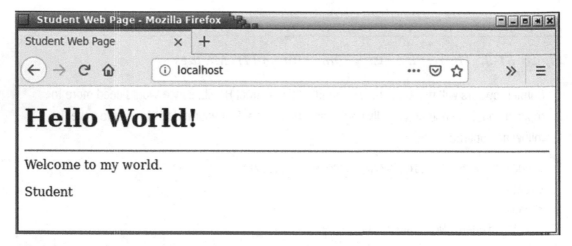

Figure 51-4. *We have now generated a complete static web page*

As you can see, creating a simple web page is quite easy.

Adding DNS

Most websites are accessed using the form "www.domain.com", so let's do that for our domain.

---

[3] World Wide Web Consortium.

EXPERIMENT 51-4: DNS SETTINGS

Perform this experiment as the root user on StudentVM2. Add the following entry to your DNS zone file for `www.example.com`:

`www              IN      A       192.168.56.1`

Restart the named service.

Type `www.example.com` in the URL field of your browser and press **Enter** to verify that this new DNS entry for our web server works.

Good Practice Configuration

There is one bit of configuration that is always good practice to follow. By default, the "Listen" directive tells Apache to listen for incoming HTTP requests on port 80. In the event your host is multi-homed, that is, it has more than one active NIC or multiple IP addresses bound to a single NIC, Apache would bind to all IP addresses by default. This is probably not the desired behavior. It is good practice to use the Listen directive to specify the IP address on which Apache should listen.

For our server we will limit access to the internal network. In a real-world environment, we would allow access to the outside world via the Internet as well.

EXPERIMENT 51-5: SET THE IP ADDRESS FOR APACHE TO LISTEN ON

Perform this experiment as the root user on StudentVM2.

Edit the /etc/httpd/conf/httpd.conf file and change the "Listen" line to the internal IP address of the server:

`Listen 192.168.56.11:80`

Restart httpd and refresh the browser on StudentVM1 to test your website. It shouldn't change, and you shouldn't see any errors.

Virtual Hosts

Apache provides the capability to host multiple websites on a single Linux host by using its Name Virtual Hosts feature. I host multiple websites on my own personal web server; it's easy and only requires a few changes to the httpd.conf configuration file.

Part of the HTTP protocol can be used to differentiate between different virtual servers hosted on a single Linux computer. It means that we can set up our second website using a different virtual hostname and use that name to request web pages.

The experiments in this section will take you through the process of creating a second website.

Configuring the Primary Virtual Host

Before adding a second website, we need to convert the existing one to a Name Virtual Host and test it. The httpd.conf file contains the global configuration for any and all websites that we might configure on this server. We will add new Name Virtual Host stanzas for each website that we create and comment out the equivalent global stanzas.

We do this because people sometimes type in example.com instead of `www.example.com`. In that event the global stanza that identifies the website would point to an incorrect directory. The changes we make will prevent that and, in the event that someone does use just example.com, it will result in the correct web page being served.

EXPERIMENT 51-6: CREATING A NAME VIRTUAL HOST

Perform this experiment as the root user on StudentVM2.

Start by commenting out all stanzas in /etc/httpd/conf/httpd.conf that contain a reference to /var/www. All of these stanzas will be recreated in the Name Virtual Host stanzas. This includes the single DocumentRoot statement at about line number 124. Be sure to comment out all lines in the <Directory "/var/www"> stanza at about line 129. It is not necessary to comment out the lines that are already comments.

Change the name of the directory that contains the primary website to positively identify it from /var/www to /var/www1. Create the following virtual host stanza at the end of the current httpd.conf file:

```
###############################################################
# Configure for name based virtual hosting. The individual web
# site stanzas are located below.
###############################################################
# The primary website
<VirtualHost 192.168.56.11:80>
    ServerName www1.example.com
    ServerAlias www1.example.com
    DocumentRoot "/var/www1/html"
    ErrorLog "logs/error_log"
    ServerAdmin student@example.com
    <Directory "/var/www1/html">
        Options Indexes FollowSymLinks
        AllowOverride None
        Require all granted
    </Directory>
</VirtualHost>
```

Change the DNS record for www to www1:

```
www1            IN      A       192.168.56.11
```

Reload the configuration files for HTTPD and named, and verify that there are no errors. It's not necessary to restart these services; we can make them reload their configuration files:

```
[root@studentvm2 html]# systemctl reload httpd ; systemctl reload named
[root@studentvm2 named]# systemctl status httpd ; systemctl status named
```

Test the website with your browser. Now edit the /var/www1/html/index.html file and make the changes indicated in bold:

```
<!DOCTYPE HTML PUBLIC "-//w3c//DD HTML 4.0//EN">
<html>
<head>
<title>Primary Web Page</title>
</head>
<body>
```

```
<h1>Hello World!</h1>
<hr>
Welcome to my world.<p>
Primary website
</body>
</html>
```

It is not necessary to restart the HTTPD server service when web page content is changed. Test the website by refreshing the browser, and the changed line should now be displayed.

Configuring the Second Virtual Host

Adding the second virtual host is easy. We will copy the data for the new host from the existing one and then make any necessary changes.

EXPERIMENT 51-7: ADD A SECOND VIRTUAL HOST

Perform this experiment as the root user on StudentVM2.

First, change the PWD to /var. Copy the original website data to a new directory to form the basis of the second website. The -r option copies the directory structure and data recursively. The -p option preserves ownership and permissions:

```
[root@studentvm2 var]# cp -rp www1/ www2
```

Verify the ownership of the copied files and directories is apache.apache. Edit the file /var/www2/http/index.html as shown in the following to differentiate it from the original website:

```
<!DOCTYPE HTML PUBLIC "-//w3c//DD HTML 4.0//EN">
<html>
<head>
<title>Second Web Page</title>
</head>
<body>
<h1>Hello World!</h1>
<hr>
Welcome to my world.<p>
```

```
This is the second website
</body>
</html>
```

Add a new DNS entry for this second website. We could also do this with a CNAME record instead of an A record:

```
www1                IN      A       192.168.56.11
www2                IN      A       192.168.56.11
```

Reload the configuration for named.

Create a new virtual host stanza. Change the data to look like that in the following for the second website. Because the data is so similar, you can copy the stanza for the first and make any required alterations:

```
# The secondary website
<VirtualHost 192.168.56.11:80>
    ServerName www2.example.com
    ServerAlias www2.example.com
    DocumentRoot "/var/www2/html"
    ErrorLog "logs/error_log"
    ServerAdmin student@example.com
    <Directory "/var/www2/html">
        Options Indexes FollowSymLinks
        AllowOverride None
        Require all granted
    </Directory>
</VirtualHost>
```

Test both websites to be sure that they are both working correctly. The second website should fail.

Using Telnet to Test the Website

Another way to test your Apache web server is with Telnet. Telnet is a terribly insecure tool to use for a remote terminal session, but it is a great way to test many services. The only reason this is so is that these services, such as IMAP, SMTP, HTTPD, and many more, use plain text data protocols, which are easy to read and interact with directly.

I use this to view the actual data stream that's returned from the server instead of just seeing the results in the browser. It is much more helpful when doing problem determination than just getting a page that says "Error 500" or something equally unhelpful.

EXPERIMENT 51-8: TESTING THE WEBSITE WITH TELNET

Perform this experiment as the student user on StudentVM1:

```
[student@studentvm1 ~]$ telnet www.example.com 80
Trying 192.168.56.1...
Connected to www.example.com.
Escape character is '^]'.
GET /index.html HTTP/1.1<Enter>
Host: www.example.com<Enter>
<Enter>
HTTP/1.1 200 OK
Date: Thu, 13 Jul 2023 17:46:17 GMT
Server: Apache/2.4.57 (Fedora Linux)
Last-Modified: Thu, 13 Jul 2023 17:39:05 GMT
ETag: "b9-58e819452ee58"
Accept-Ranges: bytes
Content-Length: 185
Content-Type: text/html; charset=UTF-8

<!DOCTYPE HTML PUBLIC "-//w3c//DD HTML 4.0//EN">
<html>
<head>
<title>Student Web Page</title>
</head>
<body>
<h1>Hello World!</h1>
<hr>
Welcome to my world.<p>
Student
</body>
</html>
Connection closed by foreign host.
[student@studentvm1 ~]$
```

The data sent as a result of your GET request should be the exact contents of the index.html file. It is the function of the web browser to interpret the HTML data protocols and generate a nicely formatted web page.

Now do this on the second website:

```
[root@studentvm1 ~]# telnet www2.example.com 80
Trying 192.168.56.11...
Connected to www2.example.com.
Escape character is '^]'.
GET /index.html HTTP/1.1
Host: www2.example.com<Enter>
<Enter>

HTTP/1.1 403 Forbidden
Date: Fri, 14 Jul 2023 15:40:46 GMT
Server: Apache/2.4.57 (Fedora Linux)
Content-Length: 199
Content-Type: text/html; charset=iso-8859-1

<!DOCTYPE HTML PUBLIC "-//IETF//DTD HTML 2.0//EN">
<html><head>
<title>403 Forbidden</title>
</head><body>
<h1>Forbidden</h1>
<p>You don't have permission to access this resource.</p>
</body></html>
```

When this happened to me while writing this chapter, I checked the journal and found errors indicating that SELinux, which is set to Enforcing, caused this. As a temporary test, you can do this:

```
# setenforce Permissive
```

Test again. I had successful results as the second web page was displayed. The section "SELinux" in Chapter 46 provides an explanation of this.

This occurrence is a good example of how SELinux provides an extra layer of protection for your system. For now, and because the task of resolving SELinux permission issues is outside the scope of this book, set SELinux to Permissive in the /etc/selinux/conf file so that it is persistent in the event of a reboot.

Using CGI Scripts

CGI scripts allow creation of simple or complex interactive programs that can be run to provide a dynamic web page. A dynamic web page can change based on input, calculations, current conditions in the server, and so on.

CGI stands for Common Gateway Interface.[4] CGI is a protocol specification that defines how a web server should pass a request to an application program and then receive the data from the program so that it may be passed back to the requesting web browser. There are many languages that can be used for CGI scripts. The language you choose for any project should be based upon the needs of the project. We will look at two languages, Perl and Bash. Other popular CGI languages are PHP and Python.

Using Perl

Perl is a very popular language for CGI scripts. Its primary strength is that it is a very powerful language for the manipulation of text. It also does math better than Bash. I used Perl as my CGI language of choice for several years. It was perfect for what we needed and easy to use.

EXPERIMENT 51-9: CGI WITH PERL

Perform this experiment as the root user on StudentVM2.

We need to add some lines to the first virtual host stanza in httpd.conf. We need to define the ScriptAlias, which specifies the location for CGI scripts. We also need to provide access for all to that directory, just like the access we specified for the html directory.

The Name Virtual Host stanza for the primary website should look like this. The new lines are highlighted in bold:

```
# The primary website
<VirtualHost 192.168.56.11:80>
    ServerName www1.example.com
    ServerAlias www1.example.com
```

---

[4]Wikipedia, Common Gateway Interface, https://en.wikipedia.org/wiki/
Common_Gateway_Interface

```
DocumentRoot "/var/www1/html"
ScriptAlias /cgi-bin/ "/var/www1/cgi-bin/"
ErrorLog "logs/error_log"
ServerAdmin student@example.com
<Directory "/var/www1/html">
    Options Indexes FollowSymLinks
    AllowOverride None
    Require all granted
</Directory>
<Directory "/var/www1/cgi-bin">
    Options Indexes FollowSymLinks
    AllowOverride None
    Require all granted
</Directory>
</VirtualHost>
```

Add the following Perl script to /var/www1/cgi-bin/index.cgi. Set the ownership to apache. apache and permissions to 755 because it must be executable:

```perl
#!/usr/bin/perl
print "Content-type: text/html\n\n";
print "<html><body>\n";
print "<h1>Hello World</h1>\n";
print "Using Perl<p>\n";
print "</body></html>\n";
```

Run this program from the CLI and view the results:

```
[root@studentvm2 cgi-bin]# ./index.cgi
Content-type: text/html

<html><body>
<h1>Hello World</h1>
Using Perl<p>
</body></html>
[root@studentvm2 cgi-bin]#
```

This is correct because we want the execution of this program to send the HTML code to the requesting browser. On StudentVM1, view the URL http://www1.example.com/cgi-bin/index.cgi in your browser. Your result should be identical to Figure 51-5.

Figure 51-5. Using a Perl CGI script to produce a web page

The preceding CGI program is still basically static because it always displays the same output. Add the following lines to your CGI program immediately after the "Hello World" line. The Perl "system" command executes the commands following it in a system shell and returns the result to the program. In this case we simply grep the current RAM usage out of the results from the free command:

```
system "free | grep Mem";
print "\n\n";
```

Now refresh the browser and view the results. You should see an additional line that displays the system memory statistics. Refresh the browser a few more times and notice that the memory usage should change occasionally.

Using Bash

Bash is probably the simplest language of all for use in CGI scripts. Its primary strengths for CGI programming are that all SysAdmins should know it and it has direct access to all of the standard GNU utilities and system programs.

EXPERIMENT 51-10: CGI USING BASH

Perform this experiment as the root user on StudentVM2.

Copy the existing index.cgi to Perl.index.cgi. Replace the content of the index.cgi with the following:

```bash
#!/bin/bash
echo "Content-type: text/html"
echo ""
echo '<html>'
echo '<head>'
echo '<meta http-equiv="Content-Type" content="text/html; charset=UTF-8">'
echo '<title>Hello World</title>'
echo '</head>'
echo '<body>'
echo '<h1>Hello World</h1><p>'
echo 'Using BASH<p>'
free | grep Mem
echo '</body>'
echo '</html>'
exit 0
```

Test this code by running it from the command line. It will produce HTML output. Refresh the browser on StudentVM1.

Redirecting the Web Page to CGI

All this CGI is very nice, but people don't usually type the full URL to your CGI page. They will type the domain name and hit the Enter key. We need to add one more line to the httpd.conf file in the virtual host stanza for the primary website.

EXPERIMENT 51-11: REDIRECTION

Perform this experiment as the root user on StudentVM2.

Add the highlighted line to the primary website Named Virtual Host stanza. The entire virtual host stanza now looks like this. The DirectoryIndex statement defines the possible names and locations of the index files:

```
# The primary website
<VirtualHost 192.168.56.1:80>
    ServerName www1.example.com
    ServerAlias www1.example.com
    DocumentRoot "/var/www1/html"
    DirectoryIndex index.html /cgi-bin/index.cgi
    ScriptAlias /cgi-bin/ "/var/www1/cgi-bin/"
    ErrorLog "logs/error_log"
    ServerAdmin student@example.com
    <Directory "/var/www1/html">
        Options Indexes FollowSymLinks
        AllowOverride None
        Require all granted
    </Directory>
    <Directory "/var/www1/cgi-bin">
        Options Indexes FollowSymLinks
        AllowOverride None
        Require all granted
    </Directory>
</VirtualHost>
```

Rename the /var/www1/html/index.html file to Old.index.html so that it will no longer match the definition of an index file. Note that the search in that statement is sequential, so rearranging that sequence so that the/cgi-bin/index.cgi is first would work also. However, there may be side effects of doing it that way that should be considered before doing so in a production environment.

Now type `http://www.example.com` in the URL line of your browser. The result should take you to the CGI script, which will display the current memory usage.

Refreshing the Page Automatically

Now that we have a page that gives us memory statistics, we do not want to manually refresh the page. We can do that with a statement in our CGI script.

EXPERIMENT 51-12: PAGE REFRESH

Perform this experiment as the root user on StudentVM2.

Replace the existing "meta" line with the following one, which points to the index.cgi file and contains a refresh instruction. The content=1 statement specifies a one-second refresh interval:

```
echo '<meta http-equiv="Refresh" content=1;URL=http://www1.example.com/cgi-
bin/index.cgi>'
```

Change the refresh rate to five seconds. Note that this change takes effect immediately.

Chapter Summary

In this chapter we created a simple static web page with minimal content and no HTML formatting. From there, we used HTML to create progressively more complex static content. We also created a second website hosted on the same VM. After a bit of testing with static content, we moved on to creating dynamic pages with Bash and Perl CGI scripts.

This is a very simple example of serving up two websites with a single instance of the Apache httpd server. Configuration of the virtual hosts becomes a bit more complex when other factors are considered.

For example, you may have some CGI scripts you want to use for one or both of these websites. You would create directories for the CGI programs in /var/www. One might be /var/www/cgi-bin and the other might be /var/www/cgi-bin2 to be consistent with the html directory naming. It would then be necessary to add configuration directives to the virtual host stanzas in order to specify the directory location for the CGI scripts. Each website could also have directories from which files could be downloaded, and that would also require entries in the appropriate virtual host stanza.

The Apache website has some very good documentation at `https://httpd.apache.org/docs/2.4/` that describes some other methods for managing multiple websites as well as configuration options ranging from performance tuning to security.

Exercises

Perform the following exercises to complete this chapter:

1. Describe the difference between a static web page and a dynamic one.

2. List at least five popular programming languages that are used to generate dynamic web pages.

3. What limitations might prevent a program language from being used with CGI?

4. What does CGI enable websites to do?

5. Why did we use grep to extract just the memory information from the free command?

6. Add some code to the CGI script that will display the current CPU usage on the web page in addition to the memory usage.

CHAPTER 52

WordPress

Objectives

In this chapter you will learn

- To install PHP and MariaDB – requirements for WordPress

- To create a MariaDB database for WordPress to use for a website

- To do the WordPress five-minute installation.

- To access the WordPress Dashboard to make administrative changes

- To change the WordPress theme for the website to alter its look and feel

Introduction

In the previous chapter, we installed the Apache HTTPD web server and configured it to serve two websites – one static and one dynamic. Dynamic websites are important for businesses and other organizations that have a need to constantly change the information on their websites.

The manual methods we used in Chapter 51 are slow. They force the user to be knowledgeable about the tools used to create and manage web pages in a way that detracts from fully engaging with the content. There is a better way. WordPress is one of a number of higher-level tools that allow users to create web pages and news feed posts using a GUI interface that works much like a word processor.

WordPress is a powerful, extensible combination of web publishing, blogging, and content management software (CMS). It takes only a few minutes to install and can get a good-looking, complex website up and running very quickly.

© David Both 2023
D. Both, *Using and Administering Linux: Volume 3*, https://doi.org/10.1007/978-1-4842-9786-5_52

There are many other open source options available for building a website. I use WordPress in this chapter because it is one of the easiest to install and configure and it is very popular. It is also the one I use to build and manage all of my own websites.

In this chapter we will convert the primary virtual host on StudentVM2 to WordPress and create a minimal website. This is not a chapter about using WordPress, so it only goes as far as getting a basic site up and running and then adding a blog post or two.

Install PHP and MariaDB

WordPress is written in PHP,[1] an open source hypertext preprocessing language specifically designed for use in web applications. PHP stands for yet another recursive algorithmic name, "PHP: Hypertext Preprocessor." PHP is a server-side language in which PHP code is embedded in HTML web pages. The PHP code is executed on the server, and the resultant HTML is sent to the client along with the surrounding HTML.

MariaDB is a fork of the MySQL project, which was subsumed by Oracle. It is an open source SQL database used by WordPress to store all of the data for a website. We also need to install the php-mysqlnd extension module.

These tools are not installed by default, so we need to install them.

EXPERIMENT 52-1: INSTALLING THE SOFTWARE DEPENDENCIES

Perform this experiment as the root user on StudentVM2. Install the required PHP and MariaDB tools:

[root@studentvm2 ~]# **dnf -y install php php-mysqlnd mariadb mariadb-server mariadb-server-utils**

Restart the HTTPD service to enable Apache to integrate with PHP and to enable the MySQL (MariaDB) plugin.

---

[1] PHP website, www.php.net/

Install WordPress

WordPress is usually available from the Fedora repository, but in the past it has been multiple releases behind that on the WordPress website. So, for this experiment, you will download and install WordPress from the WordPress website. This is also a good introduction to installing software that won't have a nicely prepackaged version.

The code for WordPress is located at `www.wordpress.org`. Documentation for installation is located at codex.wordpress.org/Installing_WordPress. You should view the WordPress installation documentation while doing this experiment, but everything you need is here.

EXPERIMENT 52-2: INSTALLING WORDPRESS

Perform this experiment as root on StudentVM2.

Delete or rename the index.html file in the /var/www1/html directory. It would be okay to delete it because it won't be needed again.

Download the latest tarball from the WordPress site into the /tmp directory:

```
[root@studentvm2 ~]# cd /tmp ; wget http://wordpress.org/latest.tar.gz
```

Extract the content of the tarball. The files are extracted to the ./wordpress directory, which is created during the process.

```
[root@studentvm2 tmp]# tar -xzvf latest.tar.gz
```

Make /tmp/wordpress the PWD. Copy the files from the wordpress directory to the /var/www1/ html directory. The -R option copies the files recursively so that all files in all subdirectories are copied:

```
[root@studentvm2 wordpress]# cp -R * /var/www1/html/
```

Make /var/www1/ the PWD and change the ownership of the files to apache.apache. Verify that the files are in the correct location and have the new ownership:

```
[root@studentvm2 wordpress]# cd /var/www1 ; chown -R apache:apache *
```

Enable MariaDB so it will start on boot, and then start it now. You also need to restart Apache to enable the MySQL plugin:

```
[root@studentvm2 ~]# systemctl enable --now mariadb ; systemctl restart httpd.service
```

Verify that MariaDB is up and running:

```
[root@studentvm2 ~]# systemctl status mariadb
● mariadb.service - MariaDB 10.3 database server
   Loaded: loaded (/usr/lib/systemd/system/mariadb.service; enabled; vendor
preset: disabled)
   Active: active (running) since Sat 2019-07-27 13:24:57 EDT; 1h 19min ago
     Docs: man:mysqld(8)
           https://mariadb.com/kb/en/library/systemd/
 Main PID: 27183 (mysqld)
   Status: "Taking your SQL requests now..."
    Tasks: 30 (limit: 4696)
   Memory: 73.2M
   CGroup: /system.slice/mariadb.service
           └─27183 /usr/libexec/mysqld --basedir=/usr

Jul 27 13:24:56 studentvm2.example.com mysql-prepare-db-dir[27082]: Please
report any problems at http://maria>
Jul 27 13:24:56 studentvm2.example.com mysql-prepare-db-dir[27082]: The
latest information about MariaDB is av>
Jul 27 13:24:56 studentvm2.example.com mysql-prepare-db-dir[27082]: You can
find additional information about >
<SNIP>
```

No password is required by default, so we will set a root password using the **mysqladmin** utility:

```
[root@studentvm2 ~]# mysqladmin -u root password <Your Password>
```

Now log into the MariaDB CLI to test the new password. Your results should look like this:

```
[root@studentvm2 ~]# mysql -u root -p
Enter password: <Enter your password>
Welcome to the MariaDB monitor.  Commands end with ; or \g.
Your MariaDB connection id is 10
```

```
Server version: 10.3.12-MariaDB MariaDB Server
Copyright (c) 2000, 2018, Oracle, MariaDB Corporation Ab and others.
Type 'help;' or '\h' for help. Type '\c' to clear the current input
statement.

MariaDB [(none)]>
```

This last line is the MariaDB command prompt. Don't exit from MariaDB yet.

HTTPD Configuration

Because Apache has not been configured for the index file used by WordPress, index. php, we need to add that to the virtual host stanza for the primary website. This ensures that Apache uses the correct index file for the WordPress website.

EXPERIMENT 52-3: SET THE INDEX FILE

Perform this experiment as root on StudentVM2. Use a different terminal session so you can remain logged into MariaDB. Edit the httpd.conf file. In the virtual host stanza for the www1 website, change the DirectoryIndex line from

```
DirectoryIndex index.html /cgi-bin/index.cgi
```

to

```
DirectoryIndex index.php
```

This ensures that the WordPress index file is the one that is used. Restart or reload Apache to activate the changes.

Creating the WordPress Database

At this stage, the basic databases required by MariaDB have been created, but we have created none for the WordPress website. In this experiment we will look at the existing databases and create the one required for WordPress.

EXPERIMENT 52-4: CREATE THE WORDPRESS DATABASE

Perform this experiment as root on StudentVM2 in the terminal session where you left the MariaDB interface running. Use the following command to view the basic databases required by MariaDB. Be sure to add the semicolon (;) to the end of each command:

```
MariaDB [(none)]> show databases;
+--------------------+
| Database           |
+--------------------+
| information_schema |
| mysql              |
| performance_schema |
+--------------------+
3 rows in set (0.001 sec)

MariaDB [(none)]>
```

Now we can create the database for the website we want to build and grant privileges to the root user (the MariaDB root user, not the Linux root user) to all tables in the new database:

```
MariaDB [(none)]> create database www1;
Query OK, 1 row affected (0.000 sec)

MariaDB [(none)]> grant all privileges on www1.* to "root"@"studentvm1"
identified by "<type the password here>";
Query OK, 0 rows affected (0.001 sec)

MariaDB [(none)]> flush privileges;
Query OK, 0 rows affected (0.000 sec)
```

Now check the new database. The MariaDB user interface has some command-line editing capabilities so you can just use the up arrow key to scroll back to the **show databases** command:

```
MariaDB [(none)]> show databases;
+--------------------+
| Database           |
+--------------------+
| information_schema |
| mysql              |
```

```
| performance_schema |
| www1               |
+--------------------+
4 rows in set (0.000 sec)
```

This completes all of the MariaDB configuration that is required to create a WordPress website. Remember your password or store it, along with all your others, in a secure password database such as KeePassXC.

These are all of the SQL commands that you will ever need to know when creating a MariaDB database for WordPress. However, I have taken some time to learn a bit more for myself, and we will do a little more a bit later in this chapter. So do not log out of MariaDB. We will explore it a little further later in this lab project.

Configuring WordPress

We are now ready to configure WordPress itself. We will set up a configuration file and then run an administrative program from the web browser to complete the website setup.

EXPERIMENT 52-5: CONFIGURING WORDPRESS

Perform this experiment as root on StudentVM2.

Change the PWD to /var/www1/html/. Copy the file wp-config-sample.php to wp-config. php. Copying the file leaves the original in case the copied file gets badly hosed. Change the ownership of wp-config.php to apache.apache.

Open wp-config.php in Vi for editing. Change some of the lines in the file so that they look like those in the portions of the file shown in the following. The specific lines to be changed are in bold:

```
// ** MySQL settings - You can get this info from your web host ** //
/** The name of the database for WordPress */
define('DB_NAME', 'www1');

/** MySQL database username */
define('DB_USER', 'root');
```

```
/** MySQL database password */
define('DB_PASSWORD', '<Your password goes here>');

. . .

/**
 * WordPress Database Table prefix.
 *
 * You can have multiple installations in one database if you give each
a unique
 * prefix. Only numbers, letters, and underscores please!
 */
$table_prefix  = 'www1_';

. . .

/** Absolute path to the WordPress directory. */
if ( !defined('ABSPATH') )
        define('ABSPATH', dirname(__FILE__) . '/var/www1/html/');
```

Save the file and exit from the editor.

Open a browser or a new tab in an existing browser instance on StudentVM2 and enter the following line in the URL field:

```
http://www1.example.com/wp-admin/install.php
```

This opens the initial WordPress website language configuration page. The default is usually correct for your location, but ensure that you select the correct locale. English (United States) was correct for me. Click the **Continue** button.

Fill in or choose the entries as shown in Figure 52-1.

Field	Value
Site Title	Student website
Username	student – This is the user ID that will be used to login to the administrative pages of the website.
Password	Enter a password for the WordPress Administration page.
Your E-mail	student@example.com - Your student email account.

Figure 52-1. *WordPress configuration settings*

Then click the **Install WordPress** button to complete the setup. This may take a few minutes depending upon the specs of your VM. There is no progress indicator, so be patient.

At the end of the process, you will be presented with a login page. Let's take a look at the website before we change anything. In a new tab of your browser, type in the website URL `http://www1.example.com` and press **Enter**.

You will see the WordPress website home page with the default theme. The default theme changes each year, so your website may look different from the one in Figure 52-2. It is a good thing that themes are easy to change because the default ones are pretty bland. This one seems to suck more than most – at least to me. We will change the theme as part of this chapter.

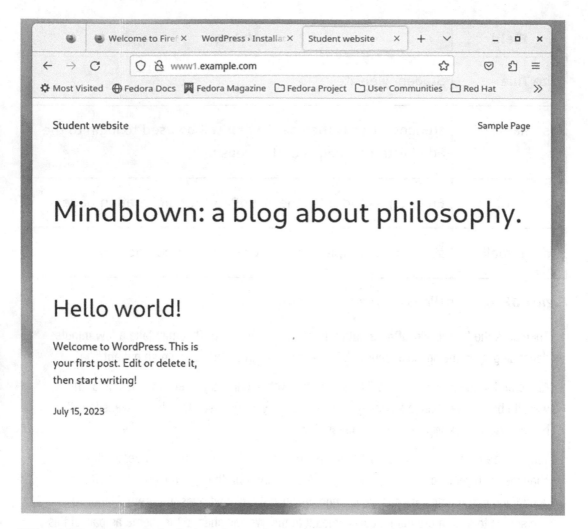

Figure 52-2. *The default WordPress home page. It may look different for you because the default theme changes each year*

Administering WordPress

WordPress is easy to administer, in terms of creation and maintenance of content, the management of the look and feel of the site, and the ability to obtain traffic metrics. In Experiment 52-6 we take a very brief look at administering WordPress.

EXPERIMENT 52-6: WORDPRESS ADMINISTRATION

Perform this experiment as the student user on StudentVM1. We are doing this from StudentVM1 to illustrate that administration of a WordPress website can be performed from any host that has local network or Internet access to the website. This is one good reason to use strong passwords and to not use the default admin account that we overwrote.

Open a browser on StudentVM1 if one is not already open and go to URL `http://www1.example.com`. Scroll down to the **Meta** section of the page and click **Log in**. Type in the username of student, enter the password, and click the **Log In** button. The WordPress Dashboard, from which all administrative activities can be performed, is shown in Figure 52-3.

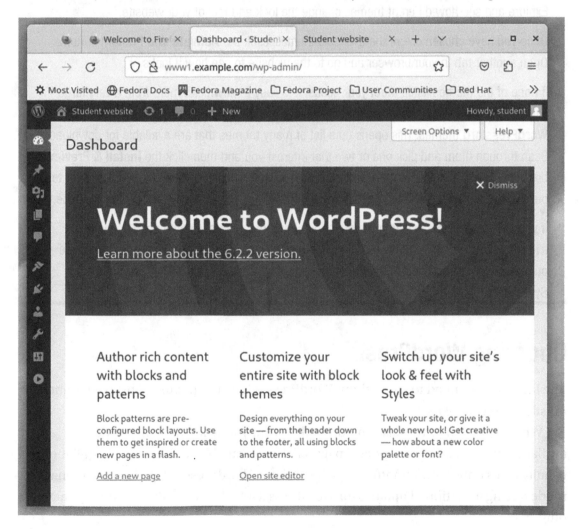

Figure 52-3. *The Welcome page of the WordPress Dashboard*

The WordPress Dashboard provides you with lists of things to do to get started customizing your website and next steps that will enable you to add pages and posts to the site. Skip all that, click **Dismiss** (upper right of the welcome screen), and look at the dashboard itself on the left side of the screen.

Hover over **Users** and then click **All Users**. Here you can manage users including adding and deleting them. Users can have roles. Since you are the admin, you might not want anyone else to have that role, so you would give them lesser roles.

Now hover over **Appearance** and click **Customize**. Here we can do things like change the theme, which is what provides your website with its personality. Click **Themes**, select one of the other themes, and click the **Live Preview** button to see what that theme would look like. Explore and see how different themes change the look and feel of your website.

Once you have chosen one of the available themes, click the **Activate and Publish** button. Open another tab in your browser and go to the website to see how it looks.

If none of the themes listed meet your needs, it is easy to download more from a very large selection of free ones. In the **Previewing themes** menu item, click **Change**, and then click **WordPress.org** themes. This opens up a list of many themes that are available for download. Scan through them and pick one or two that interest you and then click the **Install & Preview** button. This will install the theme and preview it so that you can decide whether you want to publish it. Experiment with themes for a few minutes just to get a feel for what can be done.

If you have an interest in learning more about WordPress, there is some good online help available at `https://wordpress.org/support/category/basic-usage/`. Because our objective here is to install it and get it running, we have mostly fulfilled our need as SysAdmins.

Updating WordPress

The last thing we need to know about WordPress is how to update it. This is easy and mostly takes care of itself.

When you log into the dashboard, it will inform you when there are updates available. You can go to the updates page, click the available updates, and install them. It usually takes only a few minutes to do the updates. WordPress will go into maintenance mode during a portion of updates for WordPress itself, the active theme, and any active plug-ins.

If you create an account at WordPress.org, you can choose for updates to be installed automatically.

Exploring MariaDB

The WordPress configuration procedure created the tables for the database, and there is now some content. So take a few minutes to explore the MySQL database.

EXPERIMENT 52-7: GETTING TO KNOW MARIADB

Perform this experiment as root on StudentVM2.

It is only possible to work with a given database when it is the "current" one, somewhat like the present working directory. This is called "connecting" with the database. Connect to the www1 database with the command **use www1;** and MariaDB will display a message that says "Database changed":

```
MariaDB [(none)]> use www1;
Reading table information for completion of table and column names
You can turn off this feature to get a quicker startup with -A

Database changed
MariaDB [www1]>
```

Now list the tables in the database. The results should look like these:

```
MariaDB [www1]> show tables;
+-------------------------+
| Tables_in_www1          |
+-------------------------+
| www1_commentmeta        |
| www1_comments           |
| www1_links              |
| www1_options            |
| www1_postmeta           |
| www1_posts              |
| www1_term_relationships |
| www1_term_taxonomy      |
```

```
| www1_termmeta           |
| www1_terms              |
| www1_usermeta           |
| www1_users              |
+-------------------------+
12 rows in set (0.001 sec)

MariaDB [www1]>
```

We can see that the WordPress installation procedure has created the tables in this database.

To explore the individual tables, you can use the **describe** command. This example shows the fields in the www1_posts table, along with their attributes:

```
MariaDB [www1]> describe www1_posts;
```

Use the following command to display the post_title rows of the database:

```
MariaDB [www1]> select post_title from www1_posts;
+-----------------+
| post_title      |
+-----------------+
| Hello world!    |
| Sample Page     |
| Privacy Policy  |
| Auto Draft      |
+-----------------+
4 rows in set (0.000 sec)

MariaDB [www1]>
```

Use the **exit** command to exit the MariaDB user interface.

This chapter is neither a course on web page design and creation nor one on MariaDB, so that is as far as we will go here. However, you now have at least a small bit of knowledge about using MariaDB and enough to get you started with WordPress.

Chapter Summary

WordPress is a powerful and reliable tool for creating content-based websites. It is one of the easiest ways to create and maintain a website I have ever used. Despite that, the WordPress five-minute installation is not really – at least not for me. I do it seldom and so need to look up the steps each time. Reading the directions every time I do the installation takes some time, and I always take more than five minutes – but not much more.

If you plan to work on websites using WordPress, spend some time learning to use it and to add posts and pages. My personal websites, `www.both.org` and `www.linux-databook.info/`, both use WordPress. I have also used it for some of my customers.

Exercises

Perform the following exercises to complete this chapter:

1. Why did we use the download from the WordPress website rather than the Fedora version of WordPress?

2. Add a new post to the WordPress site to see how easy that is.

3. WordPress users can be assigned to roles. What are those roles, and how would you use them to implement workflow?

CHAPTER 53

Mailing Lists

Objectives

In this chapter you will learn

- To install and configure the Sympa email listserv
- To integrate the existing services, Sendmail, MariaDB, and Apache, with Sympa to create a complete mailing list solution on a single host
- To create a simple mailing list
- To manage user subscriptions
- Why some listserv email gets rejected by large services such as AOL, EarthLink, and Gmail and a suggestion for further research to prevent those rejections

Introduction

Mailing lists are important in many environments. They provide a single administrative point for lists rather than depending upon everyone maintaining their own local copy of an email list. Sometimes the server is referred to as a listserv.

Sympa[1] is an excellent open source tool that is used for mailing lists. Of course there are others, but once again it is free, has many useful features, is quite configurable, and is fairly easy to install and use.

---

[1] Sympa home page, `www.sympa.community/`

© David Both 2023
D. Both, *Using and Administering Linux: Volume 3*, https://doi.org/10.1007/978-1-4842-9786-5_53

Sympa integrates with both your MTA for email services and the web server for administrative functions. All of the administrative tasks can be performed from the command line as well.

Sympa has excellent online documentation[2] that includes a section on how to integrate it with Sendmail. I also referred to the /usr/share/doc/sympa/README.RPM.md file, which provided a good map of the tasks that need doing to configure Sympa and integrate it with the MySQL (MariaDB) database and the Apache web server, both of which we have already installed. The "md" extension in the file name indicates that this file is written in markdown, which is really just plain ASCII text with a bit of special formatting so it can be easily converted to other readable formats. The reader in Midnight Commander, the `less` command, and Okular on the desktop can all display this file in the way it is intended.

The procedure I have created for the experiments in this chapter is derived from those documents. I've tried to streamline the process and have only included the tasks that are necessary to get it up and running.

Installing Sympa

Sympa installation is simple. Most Red Hat–based Linux distributions have recent versions, and Fedora usually has the most current in its repository.

Sympa is written in Perl, another powerful language. Because many of the Perl module packages required by Sympa are not installed by default, they will be installed as dependencies when we install Sympa.

EXPERIMENT 53-1: INSTALL SYMPA

Perform this experiment as the root user on StudentVM2. Install Sympa with the following command:

```
[root@studentvm2 ~]# dnf -y install sympa
```

This also installs a large number of packages as dependencies.

---

[2] Sympa Administration Manual, www.sympa.community/manual/

About Sympa Documentation

The Sympa website contains complete documentation for Sympa in the list administration manual.[3] There are also discussion lists that you can join for interaction with other Sympa users and administrators.

This is one of the best and most complete documentation I have encountered. It is thorough and complete. This documentation assumes little about my knowledge of Sympa and the other software I will be integrating with it. It took me a while to figure out some aspects of the documentation and its structure, but that was time well-spent.

Note that some of the work required to install and configure Sympa has already been performed by the Sympa RPMs we installed from the Fedora repository. Because of this the amount of work necessary was reduced considerably.

Now is a good time to take a little deeper look at the Sympa documentation so you will understand how I devised the paths you'll encounter in Experiment 53-2. Let's start by looking at a small part of the Sympa docs that refers to configuring Sendmail[4] in Figure 53-1.

---

2. <SNIP>

define(`ALIAS_FILE', `(...existing value...),$SYSCONFDIR/aliases.sympa.sendmail,$SENDMAIL_ALIASES')

then recompile sendmail.cf.

Figure 53-1. *A copy of a portion of the Sympa Administration Manual showing the pseudo-variables $SYSCONFDIR and $SENDMAIL_ALIASES*

The two pseudo-variables $SYSCONFDIR and $SENDMAIL_ALIASES are not true variables as they don't work directly in the sendmail.mc file. I had to click one of these variables on the first line shown previously, and that was a link that took me to the Sympa directory layout[5] web page. That page has a list of all the pseudo-variables

---

[3] Sympa Administration Manual, `www.sympa.community/manual/`

[4] Sympa, "Configure mail server: Sendmail," `www.sympa.community/manual/install/configure-mail-server-sendmail.html`

[5] Sympa, "Directory layout," `www.sympa.community/manual/layout.html#sysconfdir`

used in the docs and the values they should have when Sympa is used with different distributions.

Just substitute the value shown in the docs for the variable shown in the configuration files. So the various configuration files like sendmail.mc should have the values in them rather than the variables.

Sympa Configuration and Integration

According to the Sympa README.RPM.md file, "A bunch of work is needed to start your Sympa service." I don't think it's all that bad, but it is a lot of work.

In Experiment 53-2 we'll perform the initial configuration of Sympa. We'll then set up the MariaDB database (MySQL) by adding a new database to the MariaDB installation we already have. Finally, we'll integrate Sympa into our web and email servers. Sympa works well with different databases, email MTAs, and web servers including the ones we already have installed.

The RPM package has already performed some of the configuration for us including creation of the initial configuration file. All we need to do is set some variables.

EXPERIMENT 53-2: SYMPA CONFIGURATION

This experiment guides us through the minimum configuration required to get Sympa up and running. Much more can be done to manage and personalize Sympa and the mailing lists created with it, but that is beyond the scope of this course.

Although it might seem faster and more efficient to deal with the sympa.conf file all at once, I think it makes sense to deal with it by task. Personally I understand the configuration better when I do it by task.

Domain and Listmaster

The first task is to set the domain name and listmaster in sympa.config. Sympa can manage lists for multiple domains, but we will only use one in this course. This domain is the primary domain whether we have one or multiple domains.

Edit the /etc/sympa/sympa.config file and change the lines as shown in the following:

```
###################################################################
# Initial configuration
###################################################################

domain        mail.example.com      #(You must define this parameter)
listmaster    student@example.com   #(You must define this parameter)
#lang         en-US
```

You may configure multiple listmasters, but we will only use one. The listmasters defined here are the administrators for Sympa and all mailing lists. Each mailing list can also have administrator(s) who only has (have) privileges to that list.

Leave this file open in your editor as we will need to revisit it in the upcoming sections.

Set Up the Database

We configure sympa.conf to specify MySQL (MariaDB) and then create the database.

We could specify "sympa" as the db_user as is shown in the Sympa documentation, but we already have the MariaDB administrator set up as the user "root," so there's really no need to change that. We could create a second user, and in a production environment, you will probably want to have different administrators for each database:

```
###############################################################
# Setup database
# See https://www.sympa.community/manual/install/setup-database.html
###################################################################

db_type      MySQL    #(You must define this parameter)
db_name      sympa
db_host      localhost
#db_port
db_user      root
db_passwd    <password>
```

Now we can create the database itself. Log into the database and enter the following lines. Don't forget the terminating semicolon (;) on each line. Uppercase and lowercase both work for the MySQL commands:

```
mysql> CREATE DATABASE sympa CHARACTER SET utf8;
mysql> GRANT ALL PRIVILEGES ON sympa.* TO root@localhost IDENTIFIED BY
'<password>';
```

Verify that the database was created:

```
MariaDB [(none)]> show databases;
+--------------------+
| Database           |
+--------------------+
| information_schema |
| mysql              |
| performance_schema |
| sympa              |
| www1               |
+--------------------+
5 rows in set (0.143 sec)
```

Create the table structure for the database. This is performed from the Bash command line, not from within MySQL. This is a good test to ensure that the configuration of sympa.conf is correct:

```
[root@studentvm2 ~]# sympa.pl --health_check
```

Verify that the tables were created:

```
MariaDB [(none)]> use sympa;
Reading table information for completion of table and column names
You can turn off this feature to get a quicker startup with -A

Database changed
MariaDB [sympa]> show tables;
+-----------------------+
| Tables_in_sympa       |
+-----------------------+
| admin_table           |
| conf_table            |
| exclusion_table       |
| inclusion_table       |
| list_table            |
| logs_table            |
```

```
| netidmap_table        |
| notification_table    |
| one_time_ticket_table |
| session_table         |
| stat_counter_table    |
| stat_table            |
| subscriber_table      |
| user_table            |
+-----------------------+
14 rows in set (0.000 sec)
```

If your list of tables looks like this, then the database and its tables were created successfully.

Testing the Log File

Sympa doesn't use systemd journals; it uses traditional log files via the syslog service. Let's do a quick test to verify that the log files are working properly.

Make /var/log the PWD. Run a Perl program that adds an entry to the sympa.log file:

```
[root@studentvm2 log]# sympa test syslog
```

And verify that the entry was made:

```
[root@studentvm2 log]# tail sympa.log
<SNIP>
Jul 17 10:55:44 studentvm2 sympa/testlogs[1843]: info
Sympa::CLI::test::syslog::_run() Logs seems OK, default log level o
```

The last line indicates that the log seems okay, so it's working as expected.

Integrate Sympa with Sendmail

Make /etc/mail the PWD. Edit sendmail.mc on StudentVM2 and change the line

```
define(`ALIAS_FILE', `/etc/aliases')dnl
```

to

```
define(`ALIAS_FILE', `/etc/aliases, /etc/sympa/aliases.sympa.sendmail,/var/
lib/sympa/sympa_aliases')dnl
```

Run **make** and then create the newaliases database. There should be two databases now:

```
[root@studentvm2 mail]# make
[root@studentvm2 mail]# newaliases
/var/lib/sympa/sympa_aliases: 0 aliases, longest 0 bytes, 0 bytes total
/etc/aliases: 78 aliases, longest 19 bytes, 801 bytes total
/etc/sympa/aliases.sympa.sendmail: 6 aliases, longest 54 bytes, 297
bytes total
```

If the Sympa aliases file is not shown in the results, you probably have an error in the Sendmail ALIAS_FILE definition, like I did. Check the line in sendmail.mc where ALIAS_FILE is defined. Look for typos and syntax.

Restart MIMEDefang and Sendmail. Remember the little CLI program we wrote in Chapter 50? Use something like that to ensure it's done in the correct order.

Testing Sendmail Integration

To test our integration of Sendmail with Sympa, send an email to the email alias we created. This email should be sent to the student email account:

```
[root@studentvm2 ~]# echo "Test of SendMail and Sympa integration" | mailx -v
-s "Simpa - SendMail Integration Test 2" sympa-request@example.com
```

Use the -v option to mailx to show the conversation with Sendmail. View the email headers using mailx as the student user on StudentVM2. The header for this email should look like this:

```
>N 44 Super User  Tue Jul 18 14:42  20/890   "Simpa - SendMail
Integration Test 2"
```

Integrating Sympa with Apache

There are two methods for integrating Sympa with Apache, but since we have already configured Apache for virtual hosts, that's how we will do this. Actually, we used virtual domain hosting in Apache HTTPD for this reason.

The best way to start this configuration is to install the sympa-httpd package that's available from the Fedora repository. This also installs the multiwatch package, which is a dependency but which is also recommended by Sympa for high-volume list sites. I added it to the command to ensure that you can see we want to install it no matter:

```
[root@studentvm2 ~]# dnf install -y sympa-httpd multiwatch
```

Installation of the sympa-httpd and multiwatch packages also creates some of the integrating configuration files that the official Sympa installation documentation would have us create ourselves. This includes three systemd unit files, sympa.service, wwsympa.service, and wwsympa.socket, in the /lib/systemd/system directory.

We also need the mhonarc package, which is a Perl mail-to-HTML converter, but it's already installed on my VM. If it's not installed, install it. Verify that it is installed on your host in the location shown here:

```
[root@studentvm2 ~]# which mhonarc
/usr/bin/mhonarc
```

Then if it's located anywhere else, change sympa.conf to reflect that location.

We need to create some files that are shown in the Sympa docs using pseudo-variables like this:

```
# mkdir -m 755 $SYSCONFDIR/mail.example.com
# touch $SYSCONFDIR/mail.example.com/robot.conf
# chown -r sympa:sympa $SYSCONFDIR/mail.example.com
# mkdir -m 750 $EXPLDIR/mail.example.com
# chown sympa:sympa $EXPLDIR/mail.example.com
```

where

```
$SYSCONFDIR=/etc/sympa
```

and

```
$EXPLDIR=/var/lib/sympa/list_data
```

Replace the pseudo-variables with the actual directory names. The PWD doesn't matter in this case since we're using the full absolute paths in the commands. Go ahead and enter them:

```
# mkdir -m 755 /etc/sympa/mail.example.com
# touch /etc/sympa/mail.example.com/robot.conf
# chown -R sympa:sympa /etc/sympa/mail.example.com
# mkdir -m 750 /var/lib/sympa/list_data/mail.example.com
# chown sympa:sympa /var/lib/sympa/list_data/mail.example.com
```

Edit the robot.conf file created and add the URL of the web page:

```
wwsympa_url http://www1.example.org/sympa
```

The FastCGI Service

Sympa requires the perl-FCGI package, but that is also installed as part of the previous package dependencies. This service enhances the capability of the Sympa list website to handle large volumes of users.

Starting the Services

Enable and start the services:

```
# systemctl enable --now sympa.service wwsympa.socket wwsympa.service
```

Verify the status of the services to ensure that no errors occurred.

The sympa docs appear to call for creation of a socket that would start Sympa only when an incoming connection occurs. However, the Fedora package included the sympa.service unit, which should be enabled instead of using a socket. I tried the socket method and it failed.

Website Integration Test

On the StudentVM2 desktop, open the web browser and enter www.example1.com/sympa in the URL field. You should see the login page shown in Figure 53-2.

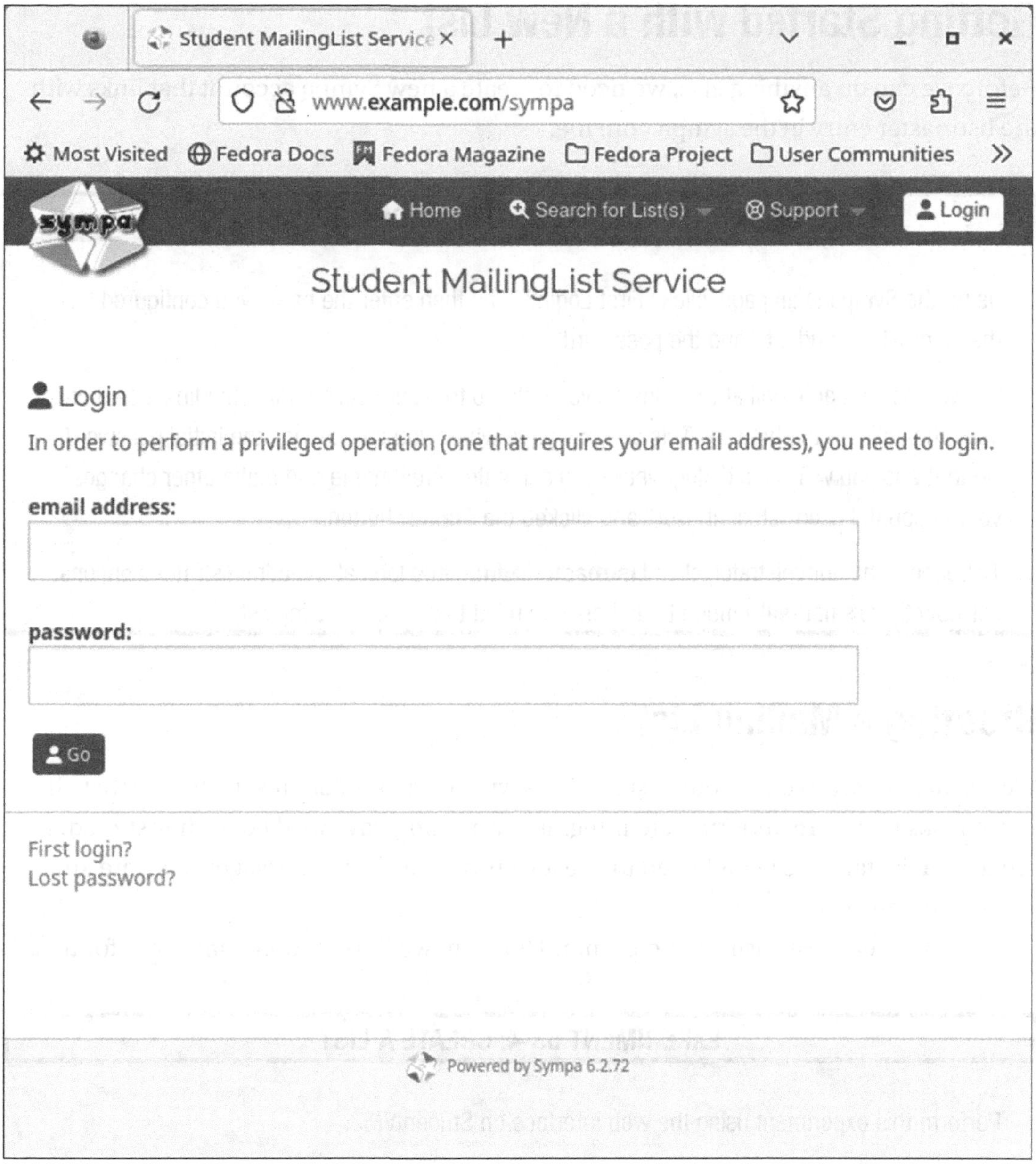

Figure 53-2. *The Sympa login page*

If you see this page, then the website integration has been performed correctly.

Getting Started with a New List

Before we can do anything else, we need to create a new Sympa account that links with the listmaster entry in the sympa.conf file.

EXPERIMENT 53-3: FIRST LOGIN AND GETTING STARTED

Using the Sympa login page, click "First Login?" and then enter the name you configured for the listmaster, "student," and the password.

You will be sent an email at the address you entered for your user ID. Click the link it sent or copy the link into the browser. This opens a page where you can change the initial password. Do that and you will see a dialog where you can enter a real name and make other changes to your account. I used "student user" and clicked the **Submit** button.

To become the administrator, click **Listmaster Admin** and look at the administrator's options. For now there's not really much to do here. We need to create a mailing list.

Creating a Mailing List

We are now ready to create our first list. This will be an excellent test to ensure that all those tasks that were performed to integrate everything have worked as they should. If creating a list fails, we would need to use log entries and error messages to locate and resolve the problem.

We can create lists using the command line, but we'll use the web interface for this.

EXPERIMENT 53-4: CREATE A LIST

Perform this experiment using the web interface on StudentVM2.

Click **+ Request a List**. Sympa displays a dialog that allows you to create the new list. Enter a list name. I used Test-List. Notice that your student@example.com ID is shown as the owner of the list.

Below that are a number of radio buttons that let you select various configuration items to define the attributes of the list. Figure 53-3 shows the topmost items in the dialog.

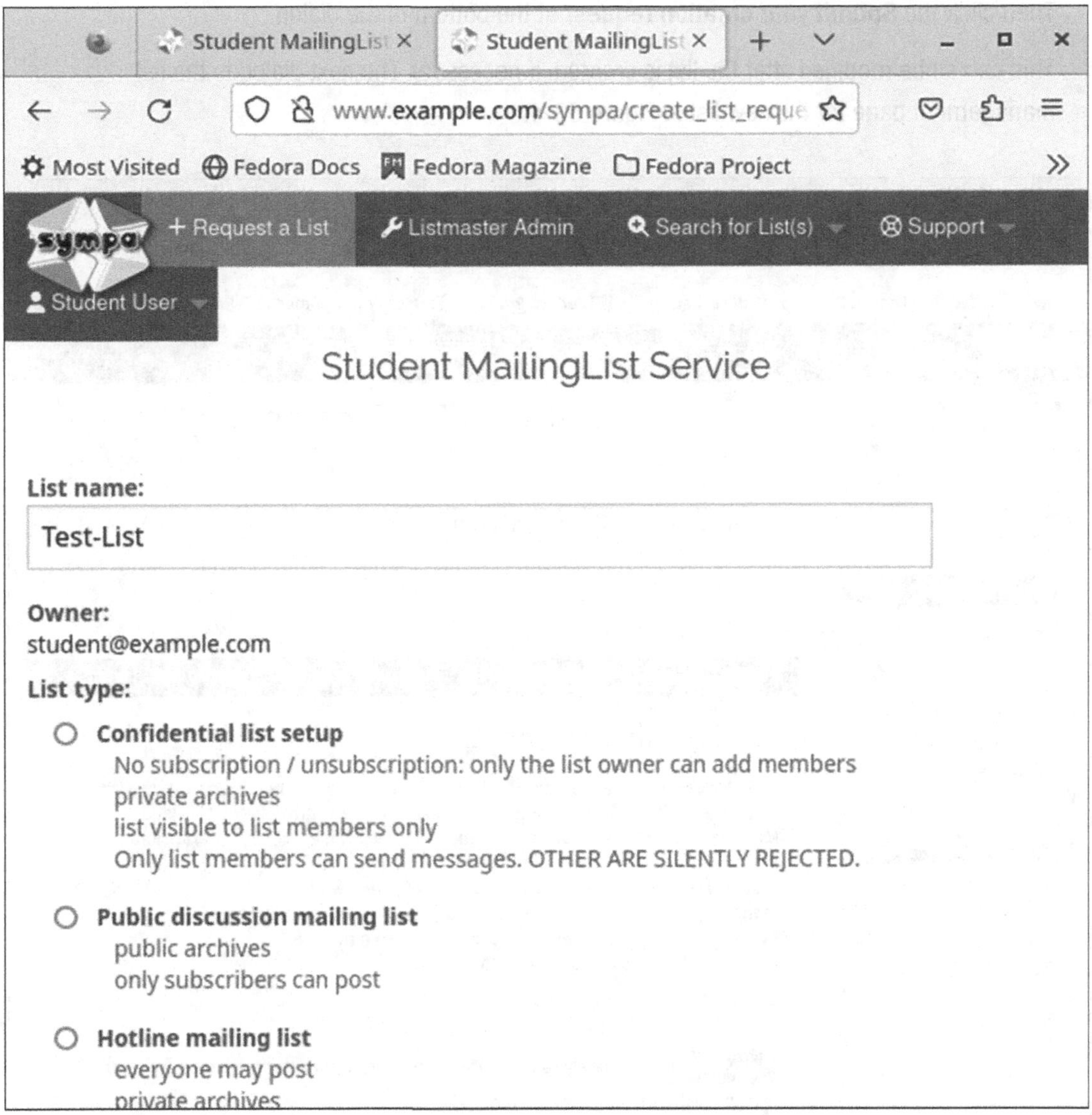

Figure 53-3. Configuring the Test-List. Choose one radio button for the list type

You can only choose one button for the list type. Take a few minutes to read the list types and their descriptions.

I scrolled down and chose the last one, **Web forum mailing list**. Subscribers can read either the emails or the web archives. Make "Test Messages" the subject and select "Computing / Software" as the audience. Add the following short description omitting the quotes:

"A list for testing the Sympa mailing list software."

Then click the **Submit your creation request** at the bottom of the dialog.

This can all be modified after the list is created, if necessary. The next dialog is the list management page for the new list in Figure 53-4.

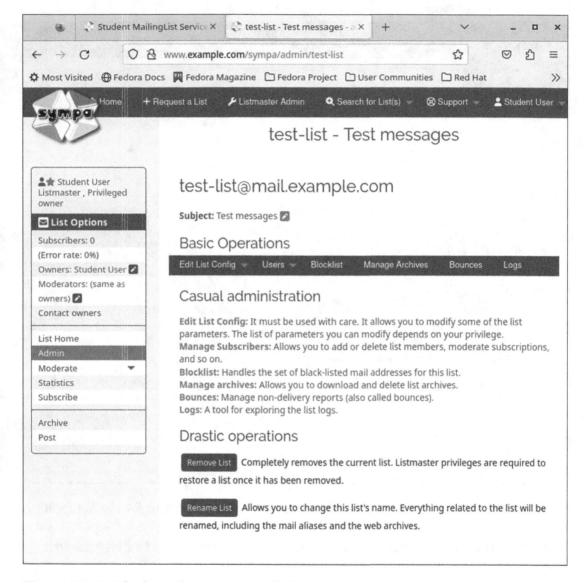

Figure 53-4. *The list administration dialog for the new list*

Although people can start the subscription process themselves, the listmaster can also add new subscribers.

The Secret Incantations

There are a few secret incantations that Linux Wizards like myself can apply to make the list work as it should.

In one of my early experiments, for example, after I added users to the list and sent a test email, the email never arrived at any of the subscribed addresses. After much thrashing about and many test emails, I began to actually *think* about what was happening. The email logs showed the inbound emails being sent to the list but no evidence of any emails being sent from the list.

I checked the archives for the first time and discovered that all of the emails were there. After some additional research, I discovered that the default mode for new lists is to send digests at a specific time on Wednesdays but not to send individual emails as they arrive at the list. So the emails were being held until the next Wednesday.

On the Basic Operations page of the list web interface in Figure 53-4, I opened the **Edit List Config** link. I then selected **Sending/Receiving setup**. In Figure 53-5 I selected the **standard** reception mode so that emails are sent to subscribers as they arrive at the list. In digest mode, emails are sent as a list of emails in a single email at regularly defined intervals. The recipient can then click the emails they want to view.

You can see in Figure 53-5 that the interval can be set by the listmaster. My personal preference is standard mode so that emails are sent as they are received by the list. This setting is the list default, but individual subscribers can use the web interface to choose standard or digest.

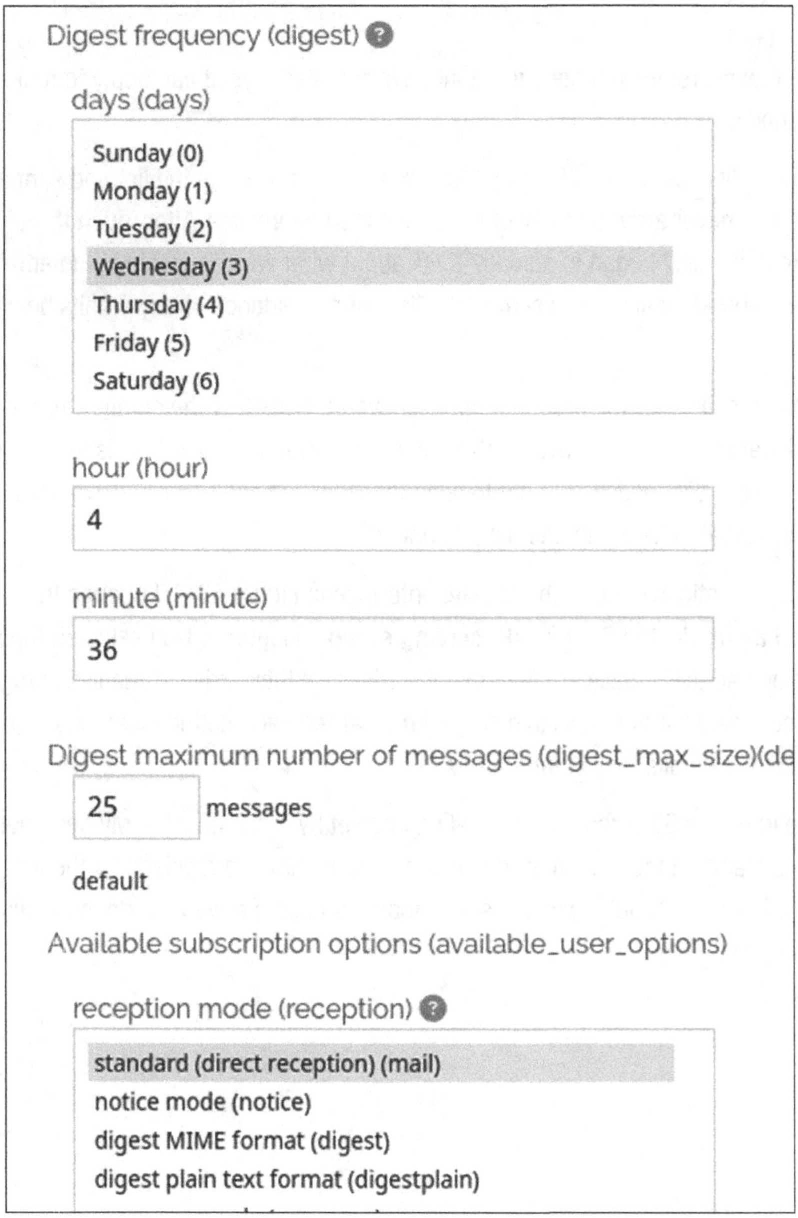

Digest frequency (digest) ❓

days (days)

Sunday (0)
Monday (1)
Tuesday (2)
Wednesday (3)
Thursday (4)
Friday (5)
Saturday (6)

hour (hour)

4

minute (minute)

36

Digest maximum number of messages (digest_max_size)(de

25   messages

default

Available subscription options (available_user_options)

reception mode (reception) ❓

standard (direct reception) (mail)
notice mode (notice)
digest MIME format (digest)
digest plain text format (digestplain)

Figure 53-5. *Select the standard reception mode for the list*

At the top of this dialog, I also verified that the list is public.

Look at the other options in this dialog because there are a lot of options here that allow you to customize the list. Each list can have a different customization.

You can explore the other tools on this page yourself, but for now let's add some members to the list.

Click the Subscribe link in the left sidebar and add yourself to the list. After completing that, the List Home dialog is displayed. You will receive a welcome email from the list, and that is a very good sign that things are working as expected.

As the list manager and the listmaster, you can manage subscribers, archives, and the list configuration. Add a couple new subscribers to your list including your real-world email address.

There is no need to restart Sympa or any other services when creating or managing lists.

Testing the List

It's now time to test the list's ability to send emails to the subscribers. If this works as expected – meaning that all of the subscribers received the test email from the list – then almost everything is working properly. But don't forget the list archives.

EXPERIMENT 53-5: TESTING THE LIST

Send an email to the list at test-list@example.com.

The email content is not important, but I always use a subject that identifies it as a test of some sort, with a sequence number when I have need to send more than one test email. This can be simple, too, like "Test email 1" or something similar.

At the very bottom of the left sidebar, the "Post" link allows a logged-in subscriber to send a post to the list. Send at least one test email using this method.

Figure 53-4 has the Archive link at the bottom of the left sidebar. Click that to view the archived emails. All subscribers can read the archive, but the listmaster can use this page to delete emails from the archive.

Global and Local Settings

After creation of the list, you set the list reception mode to send emails immediately upon receipt rather than as a digest. Although this is relatively easy, you might want the default reception mode to be standard, especially if you create a lot of lists.

There is a hierarchy of settings that begins at the Sympa default level in /usr/share/ sympa. You can explore that directory a little to see what's there, but you should change nothing there. The files in this directory are subject to change whenever a new release is installed.

The sitewide configuration files are located in the /etc/sympa directory. The file that needs to be changed is sympa.conf, which we already did when we configured Sympa for our site. Adding entries to this file overrides the ones in the /usr/share/sympa directory and ensures that any changes won't be overwritten by updates.

The Sympa website has a complete list of all possible entries for sympa.conf[6] and short descriptions of each. However you can use the man page, which provides better navigation and search capabilities:

```
$ man 5 sympa_config
```

Then search on "reception." However, this information doesn't provide a context or describe what actually needs to be done. So I signed up for the Sympa Admins list at their website, submitted an email with my question, and received an answer within 15 minutes.

The procedure is to create or copy default template[7] files into /etc/sympa and add the configuration items we want to set sitewide.

EXPERIMENT 53-6: SITEWIDE CONFIGURATION

Perform this experiment as root on StudentVM2.

Make the /usr/share/sympa/default/create_list_templates directory the PWD. Copy all of the subdirectories it contains to /etc/sympa/create_list_templates. These files will not be overwritten by a Sympa update, unlike the default files. The originals also serve as backups in case we get the copied files mangled beyond repair.

---

[6] Sympa, "Sympa Configuration," www.sympa.community/gpldoc/man/sympa_config.5.html
[7] Sympa, "Templates," www.sympa.community/manual/customize/basics-templates.html

Find the digest line in each configuration file and comment them out. For example, the line in the discussion_list/config.tt2 file looks like this:

```
digest 1,4 13:26
```

After commenting it out, it looks like this. One # would also work:

```
## digest 1,4 13:26
```

Add the following two lines to each template, which are the [template name]/config.tt2 files in each subdirectory. I suggest adding them in the location of the commented digest line:

```
available_user_options
  reception mail
```

Test this by creating a new discussion list. Then check to ensure that the list is configured as "standard direct reception."

Startup Problems

I have encountered problems with Apache and when rebooting my server. This has occurred on my physical web server at home as well as the VMs I use for this course. If you see error messages during startup – assuming you have configured Linux to show those startup messages – or if the website doesn't respond when you try to log in, it is likely that Apache has failed during startup.

I found startup errors indicating that Apache couldn't bind to the host's IP address. This is a known bug that is probably the result of the HTTPD service trying to start before the network is fully up and running so the IP address hasn't yet been assigned to the network interface.

Start HTTPD and then start all of the Sympa services with the command

```
systemctl restart sympa.service wwsympa.socket wwsympa.service
```

That will get things going again until the next reboot.

Tip   This problem only occurs when the Sympa host system is booted, and even then it doesn't happen every time. Servers aren't rebooted frequently, so you shouldn't encounter this problem frequently.

Rejections from Large Email Services

Many large email services such as AOL, Yahoo, Gmail, EarthLink, ATT, Spectrum, and more are flooded with huge amounts of spam every day. Much of the spam is from mailing lists or at least exhibits some of the attributes of email from a mailing list. Junk like joke, recipe, meme, word, quote, etc. of the day floods these services. If not controlled those services would eventually bog down and collapse under the onslaught.

To combat spam in general and spam email from lists in particular, these services have instituted some interesting but obstructive countermeasures. Much of the time these measures do not affect Sympa lists, but sometimes the email services apparently adjust the threshold at which a message from a list is considered to be spam. This is similar to what we can do with SpamAssassin.

The problem is that many messages from listservs of all kinds, even valid messages, are rejected or just dropped without any type of notification to the sender or recipient. This can occur particularly with messages sent by users with a sending email address domain belonging to one of the large mail services to a listserv that has a different domain and then message recipients with the same large email domain as the sender.

The large ISPs are trying to block spam, which can look like it originated with them. Here is what happens if the sender domain of the email user is the same as the recipient domain but the email was actually sent by a listserv with a different domain. The ISP has filters in place that compare the original sender's domain with the domain the email was resent from – the listserv. If they are different – which they always would be with a listserv – the logic applied is that any email from the original sender domain that is sent to a recipient in the same domain should never come from a mail server that does not belong to us. So it is labeled as spam and dropped or a return rejection message is sent.

Sympa has some tools on the DKIM[8]/DMARC[9]/ARC[10] dialog page that allow you to configure the list so that the emails it sends are less likely to be rejected. These are forms of authentication and identification that tell receiving email servers that the sender can be trusted – at least up to a point. The spammers can do some of this too. But it does help.

The details of this are beyond the scope of this course.

---

[8] Wikipedia, DomainKeys Identified Mail, https://en.wikipedia.org/wiki/DomainKeys_Identified_Mail

[9] Wikipedia, DMARC, https://en.wikipedia.org/wiki/DMARC

[10] Wikipedia, Authenticated Received Chain, https://en.wikipedia.org/wiki/Authenticated_Received_Chain

Chapter Summary

In this chapter we've installed the Sympa listserv software and integrated it with MariaDB (MySQL), Sendmail, and Apache. Although the Sympa documentation is quite good, it was designed for an install from scratch sort of scenario. As a result it was necessary to do a lot of experimentation for me to get the correct configuration for our simple list.

Sympa needs a database for its storage back end, and it supports MySQL/MariaDB, Oracle Database, PostgreSQL, and SQLite. Because MariaDB was already in use with WordPress, it makes sense to use it for Sympa. We learned from this that a single instance of many databases and specifically MariaDB can support multiple databases for different applications.

We also learned that the Apache web server can serve both the simple website we created and the web interface for Sympa.

We've learned about why some of the large ISPs reject email sent from a list. I also provided you a list of some tools that can be used to combat those problems.

One of my own conclusions from this chapter is that one relatively small Linux host can provide many services for a small network. This includes DHCP, DNS, firewall, email, anti-spam, router, websites, databases, and lists.

Although it's best to split the firewall and router functions out to a separate host to provide increased security for the rest of the servers, it is not necessary in a very resource-constrained environment such as those with which most small businesses are encumbered. I have one host on the edge of my network that serves as firewall and router, while a second host provides all of the other services required for my network.

Exercises

Perform the following exercises to complete this chapter:

1. Where does Sympa place its web server configuration data?

2. Create a new list. Name it whatever you choose.

3. Add a couple members to this newest list and send an email to the list.

4. Find some volunteers who have Gmail, AOL, Spectrum, or one of the other large ISPs to help you with this one. Create a list with those people. Send them messages via the list to determine if the emails are being dropped or rejected.

5. What type of list would you create if you needed the list and archives to be for private discussions?

6. Reconfigure the test list as a digest using a short interval and send several emails to the list. Review the digest email when you receive it and look at some of the emails.

7. In Experiment 53-6 we commented out the digest lines in the config file. What happens if you don't do that while keeping the two lines you added to the file?

CHAPTER 54

Remote Desktop Access

Objectives

In this chapter you will learn

- To define remote desktop access (RDA)

- To install and configure TigerVNC, a remote desktop system

- To connect to the remote Virtual Network Computing (VNC) server and perform typical desktop tasks

- To configure an encrypted VNC connection to a remote server

Introduction

Sometimes there is a need for remote desktop access (RDA) that cannot be fulfilled in any other way. This type of access connects to a remote computer using tools that enable you as the user to work on a graphical desktop as easily as if you were sitting in front of the remote host with physical access to it. VNC[1] stands for Virtual Network Computing, and it is the tool that enables use of remote graphical desktops. TigerVNC[2] is the VNC of choice for Fedora and RHEL as well as other distributions.

In Chapter 45 of this volume, we explored X-forwarding in which we used SSH to log into a remote host using the -X option and then started a single GUI application whose window appeared on our local host. The vast majority of the time, if I need remote GUI access, it is usually for a single application, so that is a perfect solution.

---

[1] Wikipedia, VNC, `https://en.wikipedia.org/wiki/Virtual_Network_Computing`

[2] TigerVNC, `https://tigervnc.org`

© David Both 2023

D. Both, *Using and Administering Linux: Volume 3*, https://doi.org/10.1007/978-1-4842-9786-5_54

However, using VNC can be useful if I need to perform multiple GUI-based tasks on a remote host. In a case such as this, I must set up a VNC server, such as TigerVNC,[3] on the remote host and then use a client to connect with that server. The result is that a GUI desktop hosted by that remote host is displayed on my local desktop.

VNC works by transmitting keyboard and mouse events that originate on the VNC client to the remote VNC server. The VNC server performs the necessary tasks and returns any screen updates back to the client so that the VNC client window may be updated.

TigerVNC

TigerVNC is a fairly standard implementation of VNC. The VNC protocols were originally developed by the Olivetti & Oracle Research Lab in Cambridge, England.[4] VNC allows multiple clients to connect to the server and is platform independent in that it allows compatible VNC clients for different operating systems to connect to the server. TigerVNC clients can also connect to compatible VNC servers on other operating systems.

The TigerVNC installation instructions are available in the Fedora[5] Documentation, specifically the "Infrastructure Services" section of the System Administrator's Guide.

EXPERIMENT 54-1: INSTALL TIGERVNC

Start this experiment as root on StudentVM2.

Install TigerVNC

We will install the TigerVNC server and the client and then configure the server and the firewall. Install the TigerVNC server with the following command:

```
[root@studentvm2 ~]# dnf -y install tigervnc-server tigervnc
```

Also install the TigerVNC client on StudentVM1:

```
[root@studentvm1 ~]# dnf -y install tigervnc
```

---

[3] Wikipedia, TigerVNC, https://en.wikipedia.org/wiki/TigerVNC

[4] Wikipedia, Olivetti Research Laboratory, https://en.wikipedia.org/wiki/Olivetti_Research_Laboratory

[5] Fedora Documentation, https://docs.fedoraproject.org/en-US/docs/

We don't need to add a rule to the firewall to allow ports 5900 through 5903 on enpOs8. firewalld provides this using the vnc-server service, but enpOs8 is on the trusted network and we don't want to open the external network to this.

There is very little configuration required for TigerVNC, but one thing you must do is to create a VNC password that the remote clients will use.

As the user student on StudentVM2, issue the `vncpasswd` command and set the password. Answer **n** for No to the question about a view-only password. That configuration would allow you to see what is happening on the remote desktop but not to interact with it. This would be useful for viewing the user's actions on the host but would prevent the remote TigerVNC viewer from interacting with the desktop in any way:

```
[student@studentvm2 ~]$ vncpasswd
Password:<Enter Password>
Verify:<Enter Password>
Would you like to enter a view-only password (y/n)? n
[student@studentvm2 ~]$
```

Warning!   This password is not encrypted. Anyone with access to your home directory on the server will be able to read this file and your password.

Testing TigerVNC

There are a couple ways in which you can test the VNC server. You can go to another host and connect to the VNC server from there, or you can connect to your own server using the client. We'll use StudentVM1 as the client.

Using the vncserver Perl Script

The vncserver Perl script is a wrapper around the VNC server, which can be run as a non-root user to start the VNC server on the remote host, that is, the one that will be logged into from your local workstation. This is a simple method and is still useful. The new method for starting the VNC server uses a systemd unit but needs some additional configuration to work. We'll use the systemd method later in this chapter.

> **Tip**   This method for starting the TigerVNC server daemon is obsolete, but it is still available and is the simplest method. In the interest of simplicity and taking things one step at a time, we'll use it for now and look at the systemd method later in this chapter.

As user student on StudentVM2, start the VNC server in the background with its simplest form. The ampersand (&) causes the server to run in the background. This allows us to log in using SSH to a remote host and start the server and then to log out:

```
[student@studentvm2 ~]$ vncserver &
[student@studentvm2 ~]$ vncserver &
[1] 4882
[student@studentvm2 ~]$
WARNING: vncserver has been replaced by a systemd unit and is now considered
deprecated and removed in upstream.
Please read /usr/share/doc/tigervnc/HOWTO.md for more information.
<Press the Enter Key>
New 'studentvm2.example.com:1 (student)' desktop is studentvm2.example.com:1

Starting applications specified in /home/student/.vnc/xstartup
Log file is /home/student/.vnc/studentvm2.example.com:1.log
```

Check the process information:

```
[student@studentvm2 ~]$ ps -ef | grep vnc
root  2099      1  0 10:19 pts/0    00:00:00 /usr/bin/Xvnc :1 -auth /root/.
Xauthority -desktop studentvm2.example.com:1 (root) -fp catalogue:/etc/X11/
fontpath.d -geometry 1024x768 -pn -rfbauth /root/.vnc/passwd -rfbport 5901
root  2104      1  0 10:19 pts/0    00:00:00 /bin/sh /root/.vnc/xstartup
root  2691   1689  0 10:19 pts/0    00:00:00 grep --color=auto vnc
[student@studentvm2 ~]$
```

We can see that the server is running and the default geometry of the screen as well as the port number and the display number. Be sure to make note of the display number assigned to the session. It should be :1. Multiple displays are possible, and if you run the preceding command again, the next display would be :2.

This invocation of the VNC server defaults to a remote screen size of 1024 × 768.

Using the application launcher on StudentVM1, open **Applications ➤ Internet** and click
the **TigerVNC viewer** icon. In the small **VNC Viewer: Connection Details** window shown in
Figure 54-1, type the name of your VNC server and the display number, that is, studentvm2:1,
and click the **Connect** button.

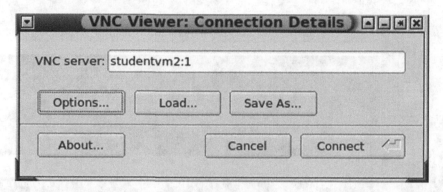

Figure 54-1. *Enter the DNS name of the VNC server and the display number and
then click the Connect button*

The VNC authentication window is displayed. Notice that it has a red band at the top with a
message to indicate that the connection is not secure. In the VNC authentication window, type
the password you previously set. The remote desktop window will open on your desktop as
shown in Figure 54-2.

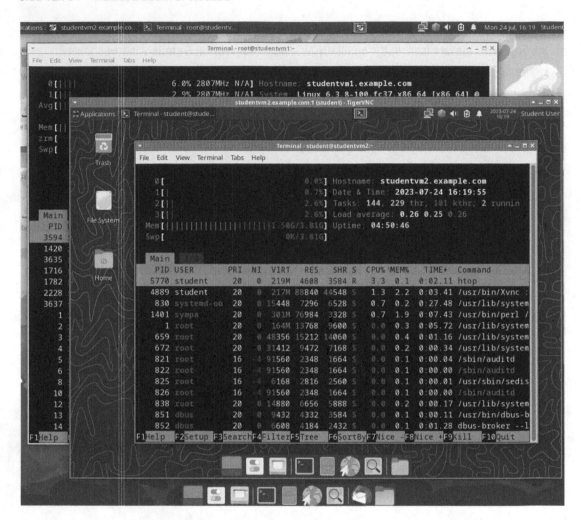

Figure 54-2. *The StudentVM2 desktop via TigerVNC as seen on the StudentVM1 desktop*

You can resize the window to the dimensions of your liking. You can use the remote desktop just as you would if you were sitting in front of the physical screen with a keyboard and mouse for the remote host.

Launch a couple programs like a terminal emulator and the file manager. You should explore the home directory a bit, and you will see that the files and directories are those of the student user. When you have finished your explorations, close all of the programs running in the TigerVNC viewer window.

Now close the remote desktop simply by clicking the "X" button to close the TigerVNC viewer window. Terminate the VNC server on StudentVM2. You must use the display number to ensure that you kill the correct display:

```
[student@studentvm2 ~]$ vncserver -kill :1
Killing Xvnc process ID 24997
[student@studentvm2 ~]$
```

As the student user on StudentVM2, start the VNC server and set the initial screen geometry for the VNC server to 1100 × 1200 with the following command. As we have seen, the screen can be resized after it is started:

```
[student@studentvm2 ~]$ vncserver -geometry 1100x1200 &
```

Back as the student user on StudentVM1, launch the TigerVNC viewer and log into the VNC server on StudentVM2 as you did earlier.

Close the TigerVNC viewer and terminate the vncserver on StudentVM2.

Using systemd

Remember that error we encountered when we ran the vncserver Perl script? It's telling us that using systemd to start the TigerVNC server supersedes the Perl script method. This will allow us more control over the configuration for multiple users. This is the preferred method for using TigerVNC.

Do this on StudentVM2.

The original systemd service must be disabled. This service was started by the vncserver script. You may run into some strange errors if you don't do this in the correct manner. First, stop the service:

```
# systemctl stop vncserver@.service
```

Make /etc/systemd/system the PWD. Then manually move the vncserver@.service file, which was used by the Perl script, to /root for possible use later. This file creates problems by interacting with the systemd processes:

```
# rm -f vncserver@.service
```

Now use `pgrep` to see if any VNC processes are running and kill them if they are. In this case 15436 is the PID of the vnc process:

```
# pgrep vnc
15436
# pkill vnc
```

Make /etc/tigervnc the PWD. Start by reading the file /usr/share/doc/tigervnc/HOWTO.md. Then edit the /etc/tigervnc/vncserver.users file and add the following line to it. Note the examples in the file:

```
:1=student
```

This assigns the student user to display number 1 regardless of which is the actual display. So we no longer need to determine which display number is being shared – that can be other than :1 – making things a bit easier when starting the client. It also prevents multiple client users from trying to use the same display. Close this file.

As the student user on StudentVM1, delete the ~/.vnc directory from your home directory. This is where your VNC password was stored. Create a new VNC password like we did earlier. This ensures that the new ~/.vnc directory and its contents have the correct SELinux context:

```
[student@studentvm2 ~]$ vncpasswd
Password:<Enter Password>
Verify:<Enter Password>
Would you like to enter a view-only password (y/n)? n
[student@studentvm2 ~]$
```

We need to configure some global settings in the same directory as the users file. Open the vncserver-config-defaults file in your editor and read the file before making any changes.

We must change the session variable because we aren't using the Gnome desktop and it's not even installed. The HOWTO.md file tells us that we can find the available session types in the /usr/share/xsessions directory. List the files in that directory. You should only have one, xfce. desktop. Add a new session line as shown in the following:

```
session=xfce.desktop
```

You might want to change the screen geometry if you have a small screen. This sets the default resolution to 2000 × 1200. For this experiment add a new session line and set the resolution to 1024 × 768:

```
geometry=1024x768
```

One of the files we need to modify is not created until we enable – but not start – the VNC unit for the user. The following command creates a unit file for the student1 user:

systemctl enable vncserver@:1.service

Here is the – as far as I could find, or rather not find – the undocumented secret to making this work. We need to edit the

```
/etc/systemd/system/multi-user.target.wants/vncserver@:1.service
```

file because it is not quite right. Change the line

```
PIDFile=/home/USER/.vnc/%H%i.pid
```

to

```
PIDFile=/home/student/.vnc/%H%i.pid
```

to provide the correct user home directory. Save the file and close the editor.

This procedure, creating the service unit for the user and editing it to provide the correct home directory, must be performed for each user, so you create a new unit file for user student2 or dboth or whatever user ID will be using TigerVNC. The unit file for each user will have the display number (:x) in its name.

Do not start any of these services. TigerVNC has a socket on StudentVM2 that listens for incoming requests and starts the appropriate service unit only when it is needed.

On StudentVM1 use the VNC viewer to connect to StudentVM2 as shown in Figure 54-1. The result should be just the same as in Figure 54-2.

The files in /etc/tigervnc set the default configuration for all VNC users. Individual users like you can override the global defaults by creating a $HOME/.vnc/config file and placing your own preferred configuration there. Do this on your client host, StudentVM1.

Security

VNC uses unencrypted connections by default. In fact, remote desktop access in general adds a security risk to your environment, but the unencrypted connection is horrible. This could result in your data being intercepted and easily accessed when connections are made to and from hosts on the Internet. We can use the **via** option of the **vncviewer** utility to create an SSH tunnel to encrypt the connection from the client to the server.

EXPERIMENT 54-2: VNC SECURITY

In this experiment we will use SSH to encrypt our connection to the server. The vncserver@:1. service file contains some comments about this procedure.

To begin, as the student user on StudentVM2, ensure that the **vncserver** is running for display :1.

As the student user on StudentVM1, create an encrypted SSH tunnel to the server using the following command. We have specifically created this tunnel to port 5901 on the VNC server:

```
[student@studentvm1 ~]$ ssh -v -C -L 5901:localhost:5901 studentvm2
OpenSSH_8.8p1, OpenSSL 3.0.9 30 May 2023
debug1: Reading configuration data /etc/ssh/ssh_config
debug1: Reading configuration data /etc/ssh/ssh_config.d/50-redhat.conf
debug1: Reading configuration data /etc/crypto-policies/back-ends/
openssh.config
debug1: configuration requests final Match pass
debug1: re-parsing configuration
debug1: Reading configuration data /etc/ssh/ssh_config
debug1: Reading configuration data /etc/ssh/ssh_config.d/50-redhat.conf
debug1: Reading configuration data /etc/crypto-policies/back-ends/
openssh.config
debug1: Connecting to studentvm2 [192.168.56.11] port 22.
debug1: Connection established.
<SNIP>
student@studentvm2's password: <Enter password>
<SNIP>
Last login: Wed Jul 26 08:46:52 2023 from 192.168.56.21
Authenticated to studentvm2 ([192.168.56.11]:22) using "password".
```

```
debug1: pkcs11_del_provider: called, provider_id = (null)
debug1: Local connections to LOCALHOST:5901 forwarded to remote address
localhost:5901
debug1: Local forwarding listening on ::1 port 5901.
debug1: channel 0: new [port listener]
debug1: Local forwarding listening on 127.0.0.1 port 5901.
debug1: channel 1: new [port listener]
debug1: channel 2: new [client-session]
```

This terminal session is now a tunnel for the student user on StudentVM1 to the StudentVM2 host. The rather lengthy output of this command shows the detail of the connection handshaking.

Tip   Don't close this terminal session until you no longer need the VNC session as it is the tunnel. If the terminal session is closed, the tunnel is also closed.

At this point you can use the VNC viewer and make the connection using localhost:1 as the target host as in Figure 54-3. This will connect to the VNC server on StudentVM2 using the SSH tunnel we created.

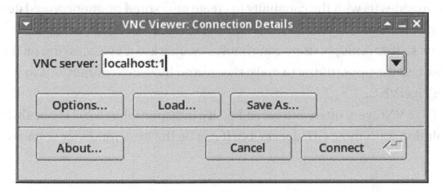

Figure 54-3. Making the VNC connection using the SSH tunnel via the localhost

These last few lines of data from the tunnel session from StudentVM1 to StudentVM2 show the connection being made:

```
[student@studentvm2 ~]$ debug1: Connection to port 5901 forwarding to
localhost port 5901 requested.
debug1: channel 3: new [direct-tcpip]
```

```
debug1: channel 3: free: direct-tcpip: listening port 5901 for localhost port
5901, connect from ::1 port 32998 to ::1 port 5901, nchannels 4
[student@studentvm2 ~]$
```

Now the VNC authentication dialog is displayed. Note that, for me at least, it still has the red banner proclaiming the connection as insecure. Type the VNC authentication password for the student user – this is a different password than the student user's Linux login password – and click the OK button.

At this point the VNC session window to StudentVM2 is displayed. Experiment with this for a bit, but the remote desktop should work no differently than it did when it was not encrypted.

When finished, terminate all VNC viewer and server sessions.

Chapter Summary

This chapter has guided us through our exploration of configuring VNC remote desktop sessions. We used TigerVNC for this, but other VNC tools are available. Some of those tools are commercial, are not free, and will cost money.

TigerVNC is the default VNC software for many Linux distributions including Fedora. It provides us with the capability to create encrypted or unencrypted desktop connections to one or more remote servers. The server also allows multiple incoming connections so that multiple users can simultaneously use a VNC desktop on the server. You've now had the opportunity to make secure and insecure connections to a remote host using TigerVNC.

I don't use VNC very often, but when I do it's indispensable. VNC is not always the correct solution for remote GUI access, but it can be the best option for some use cases.

Exercises

Perform the following exercises to complete this chapter:

1. Is the client-server terminology used in VNC consistent with its use in the standard X Window System and X-forwarding? Why do you think that might be?

2. On StudentVM2, start two VNC servers using screen :1 and screen :2. Use the TigerVNC viewer to connect to one screen from the localhost, StudentVM2. Also connect to StudentVM2 from StudentVM1 so that you have two VNC sessions running simultaneously.

3. View the TCP packet stream as you open a VNC session from StudentVM1 to StudentVM2 and perform some simple tasks.

4. Use the instructions in the vncserver service unit file, vncserver@:1.service, to create an SSH tunnel and open a VNC connection via that tunnel.

CHAPTER 55

Advanced Package Management

Objectives

In this chapter you will learn

- To prepare an rpmbuild directory structure to contain RPMs for different architectures
- To generate an RPM specification (spec) file that defines the structure of the generated RPM package and the files and embedded scripts to be included in it
- To build an RPM package that contains user-generated scripts and configuration files

Introduction

I have used RPM-based package managers to install software on Red Hat, CentOS, and Fedora since I started using Linux over 20 years ago. From the RPM program itself to YUM and then DNF, which is a close descendant of YUM, I have used these tools to install and update packages on my Linux hosts. But that was all about installing packages. The YUM and DNF tools are wrappers around the RPM utility and provide additional functionality such as the ability to find and install package dependencies.

423

© David Both 2023
D. Both, *Using and Administering Linux: Volume 3*, https://doi.org/10.1007/978-1-4842-9786-5_55

Over the years I have created a number of Bash scripts, some of which have separate configuration files, that I like to install on most of my new computers and virtual machines. It finally reached the point that it took a great deal of time to install all of these packages. I decided to automate that process by creating an RPM package that I could copy to the target hosts and install all of these files in their proper locations. Although the RPM tool was formerly used to build RPM packages, that function of RPM was removed, and a new tool, RPMBUILD, was created to build new RPMs.

When I started this project, I found very little information about creating RPM packages but managed to find a book, *Maximum RPM*, that enabled me to figure it out. That hard-copy book is now somewhat out of date as is the vast majority of information I have found. It is also out of print, and used copies go for hundreds of dollars. The online version of *Maximum RPM*[1] is available at no charge and is apparently being kept up to date. The RPM website also has links to other websites that have a lot of documentation about RPM. What other information there is tends to be very brief and apparently assumes that you already have a good deal of knowledge about the process.

Another good resource for the RPM tools that I have found is at RPM.org. This web page lists most of the available online documentation for RPM. It is mostly links to other websites and information about RPM itself. I especially like the Fedora RPM Guide.

All of the documents I found assume that the code needs to be compiled from sources as in a development environment. I am not a developer; I am a SysAdmin. And we SysAdmins have different needs because we don't – well shouldn't – be compiling code to use for administrative tasks; we should be using shell scripts. So we have no source code in the sense that it is something that needs to be compiled into binary executables. What we have is source code that is also the executable.

For the most part, the experiments in this chapter should be performed as the non-root user, student. RPMs should never be built by root – only by non-privileged users. However, we do need to work as root for a few tasks.

---

[1] Bailey, Edward C. et al., *Maximum RPM*, http://ftp.rpm.org/max-rpm/, Red Hat, 2000

Preparation

There are some things we need to do in order to prepare for building RPMs. This includes installing the rpmbuild software, downloading the tarball that contains the files we will be including in the RPM as well as the spec file used to build the RPM, and creating the build directory structure.

EXPERIMENT 55-1: PREPARATION

Start this experiment as the root user – one of few exceptions – on StudentVM1. We will install updates,[2] reboot, and then install the rpm-build and rpmdevtools packages as they are most likely not already installed. Install updates now as root:

```
[root@studentvm1 tmp]# dnf -y update
[root@studentvm1 tmp]# reboot
```

After rebooting we can install the tools we'll need for this chapter:

```
[root@studentvm1 ~]# dnf install -y rpm-build rpmdevtools
```

Now, as the student user, make your home directory (~) the PWD and download[3] a tarball that I have prepared of a development directory structure, utils.tar, using the following command:

```
[student@studentvm1 ~]# wget https://github.com/Apress/using-and-
administering-linux-volume-3/raw/master/utils.tar
```

This tarball includes all of the files and Bash scripts that will be installed by the final RPM. There is also a complete spec file, which you can use to build the RPM. We will go into detail about each section of the spec file. We installed the RPM created from this tarball in Chapter 12 of Volume 1.

---

[2] It's always a good idea to install updates. This is just a reminder in case you haven't done it recently.

[3] This utils.tar tarball is also available at my own download page: www.linux-databook.info/downloads/

As user student, using your home directory as your present working directory (PWD), untar the tarball:

```
[student@studentvm1 ~]$ tar -xvf utils.tar
./
./development/
./development/scripts/
./development/scripts/create_motd
./development/scripts/die
./development/scripts/mymotd
./development/scripts/sysdata
./development/spec/
./development/spec/utils.spec
./development/license/
./development/license/Copyright.and.GPL.Notice.txt
./development/license/GPL_LICENSE.txt
[student@studentvm1 ~]$
```

Verify that the directory structure of ~/development and the contained files look like the following output:

```
[student@studentvm1 ~]$ tree development/
development/
├── license
│   ├── Copyright.and.GPL.Notice.txt
│   └── GPL_LICENSE.txt
├── scripts
│   ├── create_motd
│   ├── die
│   ├── mymotd
│   └── sysdata
└── spec
    └── utils.spec

4 directories, 7 files
[student@studentvm1 ~]$
```

The ownership of these files and directories should be student.student. Change if necessary.

The mymotd script creates a "Message Of The Day" data stream that is sent to STDOUT. The create_motd script runs the mymotd script and redirects the output to the /etc/motd file. This file is used to display a daily message to users who log in remotely using SSH.

The die script is my own script that wraps the kill command in a bit of code that can find running programs that match a specified string and kill them. It uses kill -9 to ensure that they cannot ignore the kill message; this works much like the pkill command. The sysdata script can spew tens of thousands of lines of data about your computer hardware, the installed version of Linux, all installed packages, and the metadata of your storage devices. I use it to document the state of a host at a point in time. I can later use that information for reference. I used to do this to maintain a record of hosts that I installed for customers.

Most of the files and directories in this tree will be installed on Fedora systems by the RPM you create during this project. Some are used to build the RPM.

Now let's create the build directory structure. The rpmbuild command requires a very specific directory structure. You can create this directory structure yourself, but there is also a script to do it.

EXPERIMENT 55-2: CREATING THE DIRECTORY STRUCTURE

Let's start by creating the directory tree ourselves to see what's involved. As the student user on StudentVM1, create the following directory structure in your home directory:

```
~ — rpmbuild
    ├── RPMS
    │    └── noarch
    ├── SOURCES
    ├── SPECS
    └── SRPMS
```

The ~/rpmbuild/RPMS directory contains subdirectories for the finished RPMs based on their architecture. Here is one way to create these directories:

```
[student@studentvm1 ~]$ mkdir rpmbuild
[student@studentvm1 ~]$ cd rpmbuild/
[student@studentvm1 rpmbuild]$ mkdir -p RPMS/noarch SOURCES SPECS SRPMS
[student@studentvm1 rpmbuild]$ tree
```
.

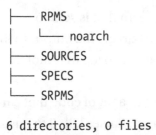

```
6 directories, 0 files
```

Here is another way to create these directories. So we can see how this works, first delete the directory tree ~/rpmbuild. Then use the following command, which is part of the rpmdevtools package, to create the ~rpmbuild tree:

```
[student@studentvm1 ~]$  cd ; rm -r rpmbuild
[student@studentvm1 ~]$  rpmdev-setuptree
[student@studentvm1 ~]$ tree rpmbuild/
rpmbuild/
├── BUILD
├── RPMS
├── SOURCES
├── SPECS
└── SRPMS

6 directories, 0 files
[student@studentvm1 ~]$
```

Note that the RPM build process will create the rest of the required directories.

We did not create architecture-specific directories such as the ~/rpmbuild/RPMS/X86_64 directory because our RPM is not architecture specific. We have shell scripts that are not specific to any CPU architecture. In reality we won't be using the SRPMS directory, either, which would contain source files for the compiler.

Examining the Spec File

Each spec file has a number of sections, some of which may be ignored or omitted, depending upon the specific circumstances of the RPM build. This particular spec file is not an example of a minimal file required to work, but it is a good example of a moderately complex spec file that packages files that do not need to be compiled. If a compile were required, it would be performed in the %build section, which is omitted from this spec file because it is not required.

As you proceed through this section, change the provided spec file as suggested to be specific for you.

Preamble

This is the only section of the spec file that does not have a label. It consists of much of the information you see when the command **rpm -qi [Package Name]** is run. Each datum is a single line, which consists of a tag that identifies it and text data for the value of the tag:

```
###################################################################
# Spec file for utils
###################################################################
# Configured to be built by user student or other non-root user
###################################################################
#
Summary: Utility scripts for testing RPM creation
Name: utils
Version: 1.0.0
Release: 1
License: GPL
URL: http://www.both.org
Group: System
Packager: David Both
Requires: bash
Requires: screen
Requires: mc
Requires: dmidecode
BuildRoot: ~/rpmbuild/

# Build with the following syntax:
# rpmbuild --target noarch -bb utils.spec
```

Comment lines are ignored by the rpmbuild program. I always like to add a comment to this section that contains the exact syntax of the rpmbuild command required to create the package. The Summary tag is a short description of the package.

The Name, Version, and Release tags are used to create the name of the RPM file, as in utils-1.00-1.rpm. Incrementing the release and version numbers enables creating RPMs that can be used to update older ones.

The License tag defines the license under which the package is released. I always use a variation of the GPL. Specifying the license is important in order to prevent confusion about the fact that the software contained in the package is open source. This is also why I included the license and GPL statement in the files that will be installed.

The URL is usually the web page of the project or project owner. In this case it is my personal web page. If you have a web page, you can change this to that URL.

The Group tag is interesting and is usually used for GUI applications. The value of the Group tag determines which group of icons in the Applications menu will contain the icon for the executable in this package. Used in conjunction with the Icon tag, which we are not using here, the Group tag allows adding the icon and the required information to launch a program into the Applications menu structure.

The Packager tag is used to specify the person or organization responsible for maintaining and creating the package.

The Requires statements define the dependencies for this RPM. Each is a package name. If one of the specified packages is not present, the dnf installation utility will try to locate it in one of the defined repositories defined in /etc/yum.repos.d and install it if it exists. If dnf cannot find one or more of the required packages, it will throw an error indicating which packages are missing and terminate.

The BuildRoot line specifies the top-level directory in which the rpmbuild tool will find the spec file and in which it will create temporary directories while it builds the package. The finished package will be stored in the noarch subdirectory that we specified earlier. The comment showing the command syntax used to build this package includes the option --target noarch, which defines the target architecture. Because these are Bash scripts, they are not associated with a specific CPU architecture. If this option were omitted, the build would be targeted to the architecture of the CPU on which the build is being performed.

The rpmbuild program can target many different architectures, and using the --target option allows us to build architecture-specific packages on a host with a different architecture from the one on which the build is performed. So I could build a package intended for use on an i686 architecture on an x86_64 host and vice versa.

Change the packager name to yours and the URL to your own website, if you have one.

%description

The %description section of the spec file contains a description of the RPM package. It can be very short or can contain many lines of information. Our %description section is rather terse:

```
%description
A collection of utility scripts for testing RPM creation.
```

%prep

The %prep section is a script that is the first one executed during the build process. This script is not executed during the installation of the package.

This script is just a Bash shell script. It prepares the build directory, creating directories used for the build as required and copying the appropriate files into their respective directories. This would include the sources required for a complete compile as part of the build.

The $RPM_BUILD_ROOT directory represents the root directory of an installed system. The directories created in the $RPM_BUILD_ROOT directory are fully qualified paths, such as /user/local/share/utils, /usr/local/bin, and so on, in a live filesystem.

In the case of our package, we have no pre-compile sources because all of our programs are Bash scripts. So we simply copy those scripts and other files into the directories where they belong in the installed system:

```
%prep
######################################################################
# Create the build tree and copy the files from the development
# directories into the build tree.
######################################################################
echo "BUILDROOT = $RPM_BUILD_ROOT"
mkdir -p $RPM_BUILD_ROOT/usr/local/bin/
mkdir -p $RPM_BUILD_ROOT/usr/local/share/utils

cp /home/student/development/utils/scripts/* $RPM_BUILD_ROOT/usr/local/bin
cp /home/student/development/utils/license/* $RPM_BUILD_ROOT/usr/local/
share/utils
```

```
cp /home/student/development/utils/spec/* $RPM_BUILD_ROOT/usr/local/
share/utils
```

```
exit
```

Note that the exit statement at the end of this section is required.

%files

This section of the spec file defines the files to be installed and their locations in the directory tree. It also specifies the file attributes and the owner and group owner for each file to be installed. The file permissions and ownerships are optional, but I recommend that they be explicitly set to eliminate any chance for those attributes to be incorrect or ambiguous when installed. Directories are created as required during the installation if they do not already exist:

```
%files
%attr(0744, root, root) /usr/local/bin/*
%attr(0644, root, root) /usr/local/share/utils/*
```

%pre

This section is empty in our lab project's spec file. This would be the place to put any scripts that are required to run during installation of the RPM but prior to the installation of the files.

%post

This section of the spec file is another Bash script. This one runs after the installation of files. This section can be pretty much anything you need or want it to be, including creating files, running system commands, and restarting services to reinitialize them after making configuration changes. The %post script for our RPM package performs some of those tasks:

```
%post
#####################################################################
# Set up MOTD scripts
#####################################################################
cd /etc
# Save the old MOTD if it exists
if [ -e motd ]
then
    cp motd motd.orig
fi
# If not there already, Add link to create_motd to cron.daily
cd /etc/cron.daily
if [ ! -e create_motd ]
then
    ln -s /usr/local/bin/create_motd
fi
# create the MOTD for the first time
/usr/local/bin/mymotd > /etc/motd
```

The comments included in this script should make its purpose clear.

%postun

This section contains a script that would be run after the RPM package is uninstalled. Using rpm or dnf to remove a package removes all of the files listed in the %files section, but it does not remove files or links created by the %post section, so we need to handle that in this section.

This script usually consists of cleanup tasks that simply erasing the files previously installed by the RPM cannot accomplish. In the case of our package, it includes removing the link created by the %post script and restoring the saved original of the motd file:

```
%postun
# remove installed files and links
rm /etc/cron.daily/create_motd

# Restore the original MOTD if it was backed up
if [ -e /etc/motd.orig ]
```

```
then
    mv -f /etc/motd.orig /etc/motd
fi
```

%clean

This Bash script performs cleanup after the RPM build process. The following two lines in the %clean section remove the build directories created by the rpm-build command. In many cases, additional cleanup may also be required:

```
%clean
rm -rf $RPM_BUILD_ROOT/usr/local/bin
rm -rf $RPM_BUILD_ROOT/usr/local/share/utils
```

%changelog

This optional text section contains a list of changes to the RPM and files it contains. The newest changes are recorded at the top of this section:

```
%changelog
* Wed Aug 29 2018 Your Name <Youremail@yourdomain.com>
  - The original package includes several useful scripts. it is
    primarily intended to be used to illustrate the process of
    building an RPM.
```

Replace the data in the header line with your own name and email address.

Building the RPM

The spec file must be in the SPECS directory of the rpmbuild tree. I find it easiest to create a link to the actual spec file in that directory so that it can be edited in the development directory and there is no need to copy it to the SPEC directory.

EXPERIMENT 55-3: BUILDING THE RPM

As the student user, make the SPECS directory the PWD and then create a link to the spec file:

```
[student@studentvm1 ~]# cd ~/rpmbuild/SPECS/
[student@studentvm1 ~]# ln -s ~/development/spec/utils.spec ; ll
total 0
lrwxrwxrwx 1 student student 41 Aug 31 11:43 utils.spec -> /home/student/
development/spec/utils.spec
[student@studentvm1 SPECS]$
```

Run the following command to build the RPM. It should only take a moment to create the RPM if no errors occur:

```
[student@studentvm1 ~]# rpmbuild --target noarch -bb utils.spec
Building target platforms: noarch
Building for target noarch
Executing(%prep): /bin/sh -e /var/tmp/rpm-tmp.QaPvYe
+ umask 022
+ cd /home/student/rpmbuild/BUILD
+ echo 'BUILDROOT = /home/student/rpmbuild/BUILDROOT/utils-1.0.0-1.noarch'
BUILDROOT = /home/student/rpmbuild/BUILDROOT/utils-1.0.0-1.noarch
+ mkdir -p /home/student/rpmbuild/BUILDROOT/utils-1.0.0-1.noarch/usr/
local/bin/
+ mkdir -p /home/student/rpmbuild/BUILDROOT/utils-1.0.0-1.noarch/usr/local/
share/utils
+ cp /home/student/development/scripts/create_motd /home/student/development/
scripts/die /home/student/development/scripts/mymotd /home/student/
development/scripts/sysdata /home/student/rpmbuild/BUILDROOT/utils-1.0.0-1.
noarch/usr/local/bin
+ cp /home/student/development/license/Copyright.and.GPL.Notice.txt /home/
student/development/license/GPL_LICENSE.txt /home/student/rpmbuild/BUILDROOT/
utils-1.0.0-1.noarch/usr/local/share/utils
+ cp /home/student/development/spec/utils.spec /home/student/rpmbuild/
BUILDROOT/utils-1.0.0-1.noarch/usr/local/share/utils
+ exit
Processing files: utils-1.0.0-1.noarch
Provides: utils = 1.0.0-1
```

```
Requires(interp): /bin/sh /bin/sh /bin/sh
Requires(rpmlib): rpmlib(CompressedFileNames) <= 3.0.4-1 rpmlib(FileDigests)
<= 4.6.0-1 rpmlib(PayloadFilesHavePrefix) <= 4.0-1
Requires(pre): /bin/sh
Requires(post): /bin/sh
Requires(postun): /bin/sh
Requires: /bin/bash /bin/sh
Checking for unpackaged file(s): /usr/lib/rpm/check-files /home/student/
rpmbuild/BUILDROOT/utils-1.0.0-1.noarch
Wrote: /home/student/rpmbuild/RPMS/noarch/utils-1.0.0-1.noarch.rpm
Executing(%clean): /bin/sh -e /var/tmp/rpm-tmp.9fGPUM
+ umask 022
+ cd /home/student/rpmbuild/BUILD
+ rm -rf /home/student/rpmbuild/BUILDROOT/utils-1.0.0-1.noarch/usr/local/bin
+ rm -rf /home/student/rpmbuild/BUILDROOT/utils-1.0.0-1.noarch/usr/local/
share/utils
+ exit 0
[student@studentvm1 SPECS]$
```

Check in the ~/rpmbuild/RPMS/noarch directory to verify that the new RPM exists there:

```
[student@studentvm1 SPECS]$ cd ~/rpmbuild/RPMS/noarch/ ; ll
total 24
-rw-rw-r-- 1 student student 24372 Aug 31 11:45 utils-1.0.0-1.noarch.rpm
[student@studentvm1 noarch]$
```

Now let's look at the contents of our ~/rpmbuild directory:

```
[student@studentvm1 ~]$ tree ~/rpmbuild/
/home/student/rpmbuild/
├── BUILD
├── BUILDROOT
│   └── utils-1.0.0-1.noarch
│       └── usr
│           └── local
│               └── share
├── RPMS
│   └── noarch
│       └── utils-1.0.0-1.noarch.rpm
```

```
├──── SOURCES
├──── SPECS
│     └──── utils.spec -> /home/student/development/spec/utils.spec
└──── SRPMS
```

Testing the RPM

As root, install the RPM to verify that it installs correctly and that the files are installed in the correct directories. The exact name of the RPM will depend upon the values you used for the tags in the Preamble section, but if you used the ones in the sample, the RPM name would be as shown in the following sample command.

EXPERIMENT 55-4: INSTALL THE UTILS RPM

Perform this experiment as the root user. First, we need to remove the utils package that we already installed:

```
[root@studentvm1 noarch]# dnf -y remove utils-1.0.0-1.noarch
```

Now we can install the RPM we just built. We will use the rpm command to install the package and not dnf. The -i option specifies an install. A -u would indicate performing an upgrade of a newer package over an older one. The -v means verbose, and -h means we want to display the progress hash marks:

```
[root@studentvm1 ~]# cd /home/student/rpmbuild/RPMS/noarch/ ; ll
total 24
-rw-rw-r-- 1 student student 24372 Aug 31 11:45 utils-1.0.0-1.noarch.rpm
[root@studentvm1 noarch]# rpm -ivh utils-1.0.0-1.noarch.rpm
error: Failed dependencies:
        mc is needed by utils-1.0.0-1.noarch
[root@studentvm1 noarch]#
```

You may have noticed that Midnight Commander was removed by the dnf remove command. The rpm command can't deal with that and just lets us know that mc is required.

This time let's do it using dnf:

```
[root@studentvm1 noarch]# dnf -y install utils-1.0.0-1.noarch.rpm
```

Check /usr/local/bin to ensure that the new files are there. You should also verify that the create_motd link in /etc/cron.daily has been created.

Use the following command to view the changelog. View the files installed by the package using the rpm -ql utils command. (That is a lowercase L in ql.)

```
[root@studentvm1 noarch]# rpm -q --changelog utils
* Wed Aug 29 2018 Your Name <Youremail@yourdomain.com>
- The original package includes several useful scripts. it is
    primarily intended to be used to illustrate the process of
    building an RPM.

[root@studentvm1 noarch]# rpm -ql utils
/usr/local/bin/create_motd
/usr/local/bin/die
/usr/local/bin/mymotd
/usr/local/bin/sysdata
/usr/local/share/utils/Copyright.and.GPL.Notice.txt
/usr/local/share/utils/GPL_LICENSE.txt
/usr/local/share/utils/utils.spec
[root@studentvm1 noarch]#
```

Rebuilding a Corrupted RPM Database

I have occasionally encountered errors that indicate the RPM database is corrupted when upgrading, updating, or installing RPMs. This can occur for various reasons, but I have found that I can cause it by breaking out of a running task such as an update or installation.

The RPM database can be easily rebuilt.

EXPERIMENT 55-5: REBUILD A CORRUPTED RPM DATABASE

Perform this experiment as the root user. We will rebuild the RPM database even though there is nothing wrong with it. We use the -vv option to display a lot of verbose output that enables you to see what is happening:

```
[root@studentvm1 noarch]# rpm --rebuilddb -vv
```

Rerun the command without the -vv option.

Chapter Summary

There are many tags and a couple sections that we did not cover in this look at the basics of creating an RPM package. Building RPM packages is not difficult; one just needs the right information. I hope this chapter helps you because it took me months to figure things out on my own.

We did not cover building from source code but, if you are a developer, that should be a simple step from this point.

Creating RPM packages is another good way to be a lazy SysAdmin and save time and effort. It provides an easy method for distributing and installing the scripts and other files that we as SysAdmins need to install on many hosts.

Exercises

Perform the following exercises to complete this chapter:

1. In Experiment 55-4 the removal of the previously installed utils package also removed Midnight Commander. Why?

2. Try building the utils package using X86_64 as the target architecture. Remove the existing version of the package, install the X86_64 version, and test the programs. Does this cause a problem? Why? Remove this version.

3. Create a short script of your own and include it in the RPM. Increment the release number and build the revised RPM.

4. Install the original noarch RPM again. Then use DNF to upgrade the RPM to the new version.

5. What happens if you make a change to the RPM spec file and rebuild the RPM without updating the release number? Is this also true for the version number?

CHAPTER 56

File Sharing

Objectives

In this chapter you will learn

- To describe file sharing and some of its uses

- To define Network File System (NFS), File Transfer Protocol (FTP), Secure FTP (FTPS), SFTP, Very Secure FTP (VSFTP), and SAMBA

- How to install and configure VSFTP

- How to install and configure an NFS server to share files to Linux and Unix hosts

- How to install and configure a SAMBA server to share files to Windows and Linux hosts

- To use Midnight Commander as a multi-protocol file sharing client

Introduction

Sharing files has always been one of the main features of networks. Although networks today can do so much more, file sharing[1] is still a staple of many networks. The idea is to make files that would otherwise be inaccessible to anyone else but the creator available on some sort of central server so that others – those people we choose – can also access the same files.

---

[1] Wikipedia, File Sharing, https://en.wikipedia.org/wiki/File_sharing

© David Both 2023
D. Both, *Using and Administering Linux: Volume 3*, https://doi.org/10.1007/978-1-4842-9786-5_56

Does this sound familiar? It should, especially if you use a service like Google Drive, Dropbox, OneDrive, or any of several others.

Apress, the publisher of this series of books, has a Google Drive set up for all three books, each with several folders such as First Draft, Ready for Author Review, Ready for Production, and more. When I finish a chapter, I upload to the First Draft folder. Later, after it has been reviewed by my development and technical editors, I download the annotated chapter file from the Ready for Author Review folder and make my revisions. Eventually the chapters go to the Ready for Production folder from where they are downloaded for processing into the production files that will be used to print this book or to create an ebook of it.

Of course we are scattered around the world. I am in Raleigh, NC; Seth Kenlon, my technical editor, is in New Zealand; Gryffin Winkler, my editor, is located in New York City; James Robinson-Prior, my senior editor, is in London, UK; production is in India and the Philippines; and so on. Yet we all have instant access to the same newly uploaded or revised files. This is a very well-defined workflow designed around shared folders and the files they contain. It is based on the simple concept of sharing files between hosts in a network.

Many organizations have a need to share files and find using their own servers to do so a better option. After all, the saying "The cloud is just someone else's computer" is true. Using someone else's computers on the Internet – regardless of what the marketing department names it – places the responsibility for the security and integrity of your data firmly on someone else's network and their security precautions – none of which you have control over and for which you will be unable to get a detailed technical description.

There are many ways to share files such as NFS, HTTP, SAMBA, and FTP or FTPS (Secure FTP), and VSFTP (Very Secure FTP). Although SCP (Secure CoPy), which is part of SSH, can be used for secure file transfers, it is not a file sharing tool. If you have SSH access to a remote computer, you can transfer any files to which you have access between those computers.

The Fedora online documentation[2] contains information in the System Administration Guide about SAMBA, FTP, and VSFTP.

---

[2] Fedora Documentation, https://docs.fedoraproject.org/en-US/docs/

Preparation

We need to create a place that we can use to share files from during many of these experiments. So we need to do a little preparation. All FTP services including VSFTP use the /var/ftp directory, and we will add files to that directory after we install VSFTP in Experiment 56-2.

EXPERIMENT 56-1: FILE SHARING PREPARATION

Perform this experiment as the root user on StudentVM2. In this experiment we create a directory named "/var/shared" for a mount point and a small logical volume to mount there to contain the data.

Create a new filesystem and mount point. Start by creating a new filesystem to export. Remember that NFS can only export complete filesystems. We intentionally left some space unallocated in the volume group vg01 when we initially installed Linux. We will use a bit of that space to create our NFS share. Verify the total amount of space left in the volume group:

```
[root@studentvm2 ~]# vgs
    VG   #PV #LV #SN Attr   VSize  VFree
  vg01   1   5   0 wz--n- 78.99g 44.99g
[root@studentvm2 ~]#
```

The remaining 21GB is more than enough space to create the new logical volume. Create a new LV with a size of 1GB and a name of shared:

```
[root@studentvm2 ~]# lvcreate -L 1G vg01 -n shared
```

Create the filesystem:

```
[root@studentvm2 ~]# mkfs -t ext4 /dev/mapper/vg01-shared
mke2fs 1.44.6 (5-Mar-2019)
Creating filesystem with 262144 4k blocks and 65536 inodes
Filesystem UUID: dba1207b-c36e-468b-82d8-666231143ef6
Superblock backups stored on blocks:
        32768, 98304, 163840, 229376
```

```
Allocating group tables: done
Writing inode tables: done
Creating journal (8192 blocks): done
Writing superblocks and filesystem accounting information: done
```

Add a label to the filesystem:

```
[root@studentvm2 ~]# e2label /dev/mapper/vg01-shared shared
```

Create the mount point:

```
[root@studentvm2 ~]# mkdir /var/shared
```

Add the following line to the end of the /etc/fstab file:

```
LABEL=shared    /var/shared    ext4    defaults    0 0
```

Mount the filesystem:

```
[root@studentvm2 etc]# mount /var/shared/
```

Verify that the new volume has been mounted.

Copy some files into the new filesystem or create a few files. You just want something in the filesystem so you can see them when the filesystem is accessed by a remote host. I copied some files from the root directory and created some text files with a bit of content. Only a couple dozen or so will be needed. I used the following CLI program to do that:

```
[root@studentvm2 shared]# cd /var/shared ; I=0 ; for I in `seq -w 1 25` ; do
echo "This is file $I" > file-$I.txt ; done ; ll
-rw-r--r-- 1 root root    16 Jul 27 08:50 file-01.txt
-rw-r--r-- 1 root root    16 Jul 27 08:50 file-02.txt
-rw-r--r-- 1 root root    16 Jul 27 08:50 file-03.txt
-rw-r--r-- 1 root root    16 Jul 27 08:50 file-04.txt
-rw-r--r-- 1 root root    16 Jul 27 08:50 file-05.txt
-rw-r--r-- 1 root root    16 Jul 27 08:50 file-06.txt
-rw-r--r-- 1 root root    16 Jul 27 08:50 file-07.txt
-rw-r--r-- 1 root root    16 Jul 27 08:50 file-08.txt
-rw-r--r-- 1 root root    16 Jul 27 08:50 file-09.txt
-rw-r--r-- 1 root root    16 Jul 27 08:50 file-10.txt
-rw-r--r-- 1 root root    16 Jul 27 08:50 file-11.txt
-rw-r--r-- 1 root root    16 Jul 27 08:50 file-12.txt
```

```
-rw-r--r-- 1 root root     16 Jul 27 08:50 file-13.txt
-rw-r--r-- 1 root root     16 Jul 27 08:50 file-14.txt
-rw-r--r-- 1 root root     16 Jul 27 08:50 file-15.txt
-rw-r--r-- 1 root root     16 Jul 27 08:50 file-16.txt
-rw-r--r-- 1 root root     16 Jul 27 08:50 file-17.txt
-rw-r--r-- 1 root root     16 Jul 27 08:50 file-18.txt
-rw-r--r-- 1 root root     16 Jul 27 08:50 file-19.txt
-rw-r--r-- 1 root root     16 Jul 27 08:50 file-20.txt
-rw-r--r-- 1 root root     16 Jul 27 08:50 file-21.txt
-rw-r--r-- 1 root root     16 Jul 27 08:50 file-22.txt
-rw-r--r-- 1 root root     16 Jul 27 08:50 file-23.txt
-rw-r--r-- 1 root root     16 Jul 27 08:50 file-24.txt
-rw-r--r-- 1 root root     16 Jul 27 08:50 file-25.txt
drwx------ 2 root root 16384 Jul 27 08:47 lost+found
[root@studentvm2 shared]#
```

We will use this directory and its contents for several experiments using different file sharing tools.

As a last bit of preparation, open a root terminal session on StudentVM1 and use **tcpdump** to monitor the data stream on enp0s3. Place the terminal session in a place on the desktop where it can be seen while performing the rest of these experiments. Be sure to monitor the data stream in this terminal session.

Firewall Considerations

Because we are performing these file sharing experiments inside the trusted network, we don't need to make firewall changes for them to work. However, if we were going to make our server available to the outside world, we would need to allow these sharing services through the drop zone. We are using the drop zone to protect our external network connection.

Using firewalld, it's easy to open the firewall to those services that need access to our server. I won't cover that in this chapter since you already know how to do that.

However, FTP and its variants have a complex design that uses separate command and data ports as well as a large number of high-numbered unassigned ports. This makes firewall configuration for FTP a bit of a challenge.

Firewall Configuration for FTP

Let's look at how FTP works in order to understand the problem it generates for configuring the firewall. FTP has two modes that can be used for file transfer: active and passive. These two modes work a bit differently, and the difference is important to SysAdmins and the configuration of the firewall. The website Slacksite.com[3] has an excellent explanation of active vs. passive FTP connections and the issues had by each. The Fedora Documentation[4] has a good explanation of VSFTP and other file sharing tools.

Note   This discussion of FTP firewall requirements is for informational purposes only. We do not need to make changes to the firewall in this chapter because all experiments take place within the trusted network. In the first edition of this course, I spent several pages explaining the requirements and creating a set of rules that could be used with iptables. I did the same for NFS because it, too, has a complex set of requirements. Fortunately firewalld has made all that easier, and we can simply add the desired service to the drop or block firewall zone.

Active Mode

The active mode of FTP is the one that causes problems. This short description will help illustrate why that is the case:

1.   The FTP client initiates a connection to the server from a randomly selected, high-numbered, unprivileged[5] TCP port – we will use port number 1547 for this explanation – to the destination port number 21 on the server. Port 1547 is the control port for

---

[3] Slacksite.com, "Active FTP vs. Passive FTP, a Definitive Explanation," https://slacksite.com/other/ftp.html

[4] Fedora 30 Documentation, "System Administrators Guide, File and Print Servers," https://docs.fedoraproject.org/en-US/fedora/f30/system-administrators-guide/servers/File_and_Print_Servers/

[5] Privileged ports are numbered from 0 to 1023 and are assigned to specific services. Ports with higher numbers are unprivileged and can be used for almost anything. However, some of these higher ports have specific services that have been used by long practice and convention and that have become de facto standards. Check the /etc/services file for specific assignments.

the client, and port 21 is the server's FTP control port. The client sends the command **port 1547** to the server to indicate the number of the control port.

2.   The server acknowledges this by sending an ACK reply to the client from port 21 to port 1547.

3.   The server now initiates a data connection from its port 20 to port 1548 on the client. The protocol always assumes that the data port is one higher than the control port. This step is the cause of the problem because the server initiates a connection to the client.

4.   If the server can reach port 1548 and initiate the connection, the client sends an ACK to the server.

Using the drop zone or the block zone prevents connections from the outside world being made to the local host – whether server or client. The ports that the client can use for the command and data connections are randomly selected from the range 1024 to 65536. This means we would need to open up all of those ports, which creates a severe vulnerability and opens our host up to attack.

Passive Mode

In passive mode, FTP works a bit differently as the client initiates all of the connections. This means that we can specify a much limited range of non-privileged ports for use by FTP when making the data connections.

Let's see how that works. For this illustration, let's assume that ports 65000 through 65534 are to be used for FTP:

1.   The FTP client initiates a connection to the server from a randomly selected, high-numbered, unprivileged[6] TCP port within the specified range – we will use port number 4048 for this explanation – to the destination port number 21 on the server. Port

---

[6] Privileged ports are numbered from 0 to 1023 and are assigned to specific services. Ports with higher numbers are unprivileged and can be used for almost anything. However, some of these higher ports have specific services that have been used by long practice and convention and that have become de facto standards. Check the /etc/services file for specific assignments.

4048 is the control port for the client, and port 21 is the server's FTP control port. The client sends the **PASV** (passive) command to the server. Note that the control port number does not need to be within the defined range and the client would not know that range in any event.

2. The server acknowledges this by sending an ACK reply to the client from port 21 to port 4048. The reply from the server contains the number of the data port from the defined range so that the client will know to where to listen for the data stream. We will use port 65248 for the data connection.

3. The client now initiates a data connection from its port 4049, the data port, to port 65248 on the server.

4. If the client can reach port 65248 and initiate the connection, the server sends an ACK to the client and the data transfer can begin.

If the server is expected to handle very large amounts of FTP traffic, the size of the range of ports defined on the server will need to be much larger than we have defined here. The key is that we can control this range and create firewall rules on the server to accommodate this. firewalld also allows us to simply add FTP as a service to access to our firewall, thus removing the need for us to consider these details.

FTP and FTPS

FTP (File Transfer Protocol)[7] is an old and insecure method for sharing files. This lack of security is because the data stream is not encrypted, and so any data transferred may be easily read if intercepted. Because of its lack of security, FTP has been upgraded with a newer, secure version, FTPS.[8] FTPS merely adds a security layer over FTP and is called FTP over SSL (Secure Socket Layer). With FTPS, one can do the same things as with FTP but in a more secure manner.

Fedora provides an FTP server written in Java.

---

[7] Wikipedia, File Transfer Protocol, https://en.wikipedia.org/wiki/File_Transfer_Protocol
[8] Wikipedia, FTPS, https://en.wikipedia.org/wiki/FTPS

VSFTP

Fedora does provide version 3.0.5 of the VSFTP (Very Secure FTP)[9] server for Fedora 29 and 30. VSFTP is the primary FTP server provided with current Fedora releases although it is not installed by default.

VSFTP is more secure because it provides encryption using SSL and it provides significant protection from privilege escalation. Developed from scratch by Chris Evans with security in mind, VSFTP minimizes the use of elevated privileges and uses unprivileged threads for most tasks. You can read the details at the website in footnote 9.

VSFTP scales up very nicely compared with other FTP servers. One user quoted on the VSFTP website says that they have a single VSFTP server running and that over a 24-hour period served 2.6 terabytes of data with more than 1,500 concurrent users at times. VSFTP, like other FTP servers, does allow anonymous downloads as well as logged-in FTP users with passwords.

Installation and Preparation of VSFTP

So let's install and configure VSFTP.

EXPERIMENT 56-2: INSTALL AND PREPARE VSFTP

Perform this experiment as the root user on StudentVM2. In this experiment we will share the files in /var/shared using VSFTP. First, we install VSFTP:

```
[root@studentvm2 ~]# dnf -y install vsftpd
```

The files served by any FTP server are located in /var/ftp. The /var/ftp/pub directory is for files served to anonymous users. These directories were created during the installation of VSFTP, so all we need to do is add some files:

```
[root@studentvm2 ~]# cd /var/ftp ; I=0 ; for I in `seq -w 1 25` ; do echo
"This is file $I" > FTP-file-$I.txt ; done ; ll
total 104
-rw-r--r-- 1 root root    16 Aug  7 21:14 FTP-file-01.txt
-rw-r--r-- 1 root root    16 Aug  7 21:14 FTP-file-02.txt
```

---

[9]VSFTP, https://security.appspot.com/vsftpd.html

```
-rw-r--r-- 1 root root    16 Aug  7 21:14 FTP-file-03.txt
-rw-r--r-- 1 root root    16 Aug  7 21:14 FTP-file-04.txt
-rw-r--r-- 1 root root    16 Aug  7 21:14 FTP-file-05.txt
-rw-r--r-- 1 root root    16 Aug  7 21:14 FTP-file-06.txt
-rw-r--r-- 1 root root    16 Aug  7 21:14 FTP-file-07.txt
-rw-r--r-- 1 root root    16 Aug  7 21:14 FTP-file-08.txt
-rw-r--r-- 1 root root    16 Aug  7 21:14 FTP-file-09.txt
-rw-r--r-- 1 root root    16 Aug  7 21:14 FTP-file-10.txt
-rw-r--r-- 1 root root    16 Aug  7 21:14 FTP-file-11.txt
-rw-r--r-- 1 root root    16 Aug  7 21:14 FTP-file-12.txt
-rw-r--r-- 1 root root    16 Aug  7 21:14 FTP-file-13.txt
-rw-r--r-- 1 root root    16 Aug  7 21:14 FTP-file-14.txt
-rw-r--r-- 1 root root    16 Aug  7 21:14 FTP-file-15.txt
-rw-r--r-- 1 root root    16 Aug  7 21:14 FTP-file-16.txt
-rw-r--r-- 1 root root    16 Aug  7 21:14 FTP-file-17.txt
-rw-r--r-- 1 root root    16 Aug  7 21:14 FTP-file-18.txt
-rw-r--r-- 1 root root    16 Aug  7 21:14 FTP-file-19.txt
-rw-r--r-- 1 root root    16 Aug  7 21:14 FTP-file-20.txt
-rw-r--r-- 1 root root    16 Aug  7 21:14 FTP-file-21.txt
-rw-r--r-- 1 root root    16 Aug  7 21:14 FTP-file-22.txt
-rw-r--r-- 1 root root    16 Aug  7 21:14 FTP-file-23.txt
-rw-r--r-- 1 root root    16 Aug  7 21:14 FTP-file-24.txt
-rw-r--r-- 1 root root    16 Aug  7 21:14 FTP-file-25.txt
drwxr-xr-x 2 root root 4096 Jul 25  2018 pub
[root@studentvm2 ftp]#
```

VSFTP is configured using the file /etc/vsftpd/vsftpd.conf. This file is well commented, so I suggest you read it to understand what can be configured with it.

The default configuration is designed to listen on IPV6 only,[10] but it will work for us on IPV4 with only a couple changes. Near the bottom of the file, locate and change **listen=NO** to **listen=YES**. This allows VSFTP to listen on IPV4. Then turn off IPV6 by changing **listen_ipv6=YES** to **listen_ipv6=NO**.

---

[10] My interpretation of the comments surrounding the LISTEN= and listen_ipv6= config items is that the default settings should cause VSFTP to listen on both IPV4 and IPV6. That is either incorrect or I have misunderstood. In any event, use the settings I described previously to enable IPV4 connectivity for VSFTP.

Start the vsftpd service and verify the result:

```
[root@studentvm2 ftp]# systemctl start vsftpd
[root@studentvm2 ftp]# systemctl status vsftpd
● vsftpd.service - Vsftpd ftp daemon
   Loaded: loaded (/usr/lib/systemd/system/vsftpd.service; disabled; vendor
   preset: disabled)
   Active: active (running) since Wed 2019-08-07 21:28:45 EDT; 8s ago
  Process: 13362 ExecStart=/usr/sbin/vsftpd /etc/vsftpd/vsftpd.conf
  (code=exited, status=0/SUCCESS)
 Main PID: 13363 (vsftpd)
    Tasks: 1 (limit: 4696)
   Memory: 496.0K
   CGroup: /system.slice/vsftpd.service
           └─13363 /usr/sbin/vsftpd /etc/vsftpd/vsftpd.conf

Aug 07 21:28:45 studentvm2.example.com systemd[1]: Starting Vsftpd ftp
daemon...
Aug 07 21:28:45 studentvm2.example.com systemd[1]: Started Vsftpd ftp daemon.
[root@studentvm2 ftp]#
```

The FTP Client

Now that the server is configured, we can install the FTP client on StudentVM1 and then test file downloads. When doing downloads the files are downloaded to the PWD that was in effect when you started the FTP client unless you specify a different download directory.

EXPERIMENT 56-3: USING THE FTP CLIENT

As root on StudentVM1, install the FTP client:

```
[root@studentvm1 ~]$ dnf -y install ftp
```

No configuration is required for the client, so we can go right to our first test. Because we are the student user on StudentVM1 and there is also a student user on StudentVM2, we can use that account for our FTP login:

```
[student@studentvm1 ~]$ ftp studentvm2
Connected to studentvm2 (192.168.56.1).
220 (vsFTPd 3.0.3)
Name (studentvm2:student): <Press Enter>
331 Please specify the password.
Password:<Enter password>
230 Login successful.
Remote system type is UNIX.
Using binary mode to transfer files.
```

Help is available if you need it:

```
ftp> help
Commands may be abbreviated.  Commands are:

!          debug       mdir       sendport    site
$          dir         mget       put         size
account    disconnect  mkdir      pwd         status
append     exit        mls        quit        struct
ascii      form        mode       quote       system
bell       get         modtime    recv        sunique
binary     glob        mput       reget       tenex
bye        hash        newer      rstatus     tick
case       help        nmap       rhelp       trace
cd         idle        nlist      rename      type
cdup       image       ntrans     reset       user
chmod      lcd         open       restart     umask
close      ls          prompt     rmdir       verbose
cr         macdef      passive    runique     ?
delete     mdelete     proxy      send
ftp> help ls
ls        list contents of remote directory
ftp> help get
get       receive file
ftp>
```

Now list the files in the remote directory:

```
ftp> ls
227 Entering Passive Mode (192,168,56,1,226,161).
150 Here comes the directory listing.
drwxr-xr-x    2 1000     1000         4096 Dec 24  2018 Desktop
drwxr-xr-x    2 1000     1000         4096 Dec 22  2018 Documents
drwxr-xr-x    2 1000     1000         4096 Dec 22  2018 Downloads
drwxr-xr-x    2 1000     1000         4096 Aug 02 12:11 Mail
drwxr-xr-x    2 1000     1000         4096 Dec 22  2018 Music
drwxr-xr-x    2 1000     1000         4096 Dec 22  2018 Pictures
drwxr-xr-x    2 1000     1000         4096 Dec 22  2018 Public
drwxr-xr-x    2 1000     1000         4096 Dec 22  2018 Templates
drwxr-xr-x    2 1000     1000         4096 Dec 22  2018 Videos
-rw-------    1 1000     1000            2 Jul 01 15:01 dead.letter
-rw-rw-r--    1 1000     1000       256000 Jun 19 12:16 random.txt
-rw-rw-r--    1 1000     1000       256000 Jun 20 12:26 textfile.txt
226 Directory send OK.
```

This is a listing of the home directory for the student user on the remote host, StudentVM2. This is the default action when doing a login on a remote host. For now let's just go with this and download a file to our account on StudentVM2.

If you have been doing all of the experiments in this course, there should be a file named random.txt in the student home directory of StudentVM2. Download that file – or another one if you do not have random.txt:

```
ftp> get random.txt
local: random.txt remote: random.txt
227 Entering Passive Mode (192,168,56,1,33,129).
150 Opening BINARY mode data connection for random.txt (256000 bytes).
226 Transfer complete.
256000 bytes received in 0.0413 secs (6193.45 Kbytes/sec)
```

Verify that the file was downloaded as the student user on StudentVM1:

```
[student@studentvm1 ~]$ ll
total 1504
drwxrwxr-x  2 student student   4096 Mar  2 08:21 chapter25
drwxrwxr-x  2 student student   4096 Mar 21 15:27 chapter26
```

```
<snip>
-rw-rw-r--  1 student student 256000 Aug  8 12:16 random.txt
<snip>
drwxr-xr-x. 2 student student   4096 Dec 22  2018 Videos
[student@studentvm1 ~]$
```

We now know that the VSFTP server is working, but we still have a few bits to work out.

Anonymous FTP Access

When logged into a remote host using a valid account, such as student, the user has access to every directory and file on that host that they would if logged in locally. This would be a major security issue if we were to give out accounts to just anyone. We need a way to limit FTP access.

Anonymous FTP access is the tool that can help with that. This is the type of access most of us are familiar with when we download files from a remote FTP server. It is called anonymous because anyone accessing the share files can do so without a unique account on the server. All that is required to access an anonymous FTP site is a generic username. Most FTP servers use "anonymous" or "ftp" for the username. No password is required. But this also opens up our public FTP directory to access by everyone on the Internet.

EXPERIMENT 56-4: ANONYMOUS FTP

We need to alter the vsftpd.conf file to allow anonymous FTP access.

As root on StudentVM2, edit vsftpd.conf. Find the statement **anonymous_enable=NO** and change it to **anonymous_enable=YES**. Then restart the VSFTPD service.

As the student user on StudentVM1, test the result by entering "anonymous" as the user account in the Name field. When prompted for the password, just press the **Enter** key:

```
[student@studentvm1 ~]$ ftp studentvm2
Connected to studentvm2 (192.168.56.1).
220 (vsFTPd 3.0.3)
Name (studentvm2:student): anonymous
331 Please specify the password.
```

```
Password:<Enter>
230 Login successful.
Remote system type is UNIX.
Using binary mode to transfer files.
ftp> ls
227 Entering Passive Mode (192,168,56,1,254,134).
150 Here comes the directory listing.
-rw-r--r--    1 65534    65534            16 Aug 08 01:14 FTP-file-01.txt
-rw-r--r--    1 65534    65534            16 Aug 08 01:14 FTP-file-02.txt
-rw-r--r--    1 65534    65534            16 Aug 08 01:14 FTP-file-03.txt
-rw-r--r--    1 65534    65534            16 Aug 08 01:14 FTP-file-04.txt
<snip>
-rw-r--r--    1 65534    65534            16 Aug 08 01:14 FTP-file-24.txt
-rw-r--r--    1 65534    65534            16 Aug 08 01:14 FTP-file-25.txt
drwxr-xr-x    2 65534    65534          4096 Jul 25  2018 pub
226 Directory send OK.
ftp>
```

Notice that the VSFTP server logs us into the /var/ftp directory. Download one of the files from there and verify that it was transferred to your PWD.

Close the FTP connection.

Securing VSFTP with Encryption

The final bit of security we can use with VSFTP is to encrypt the data while it is being transferred. For this we need to create a certificate that can be used with FTP. We have already created a certificate for email, and this will be similar.

EXPERIMENT 56-5: ENCRYPTING VSFTP

Start this experiment as the root user on StudentVM2.

Create a new directory for the key:

mkdir /etc/ssl/private

Generate a self-signed certificate. The openssl program can be used to create a certificate that we can use with FTP. Enter the requested data as shown in bold. Do this as root in root's home directory. This command does not specify a time limit for the certificate, so it never expires:

```
[root@studentvm2 ~]# openssl req -x509 -nodes -newkey rsa:2048 -keyout /etc/
ssl/private/vsftpd.key -out /etc/ssl/certs/vsftpd.crt
..............................................................+++++
........................+++++
writing new private key to 'vsftpd.key'
-----
You are about to be asked to enter information that will be incorporated
into your certificate request.
What you are about to enter is what is called a Distinguished Name or a DN.
There are quite a few fields but you can leave some blank
For some fields there will be a default value,
If you enter '.', the field will be left blank.
-----
Country Name (2 letter code) [XX]:US
State or Province Name (full name) []:North Carolina
Locality Name (eg, city) [Default City]:Raleigh
Organization Name (eg, company) [Default Company Ltd]:<Enter>
Organizational Unit Name (eg, section) []:<Enter>
Common Name (eg, your name or your server's hostname) []:studentvm2.
example.com
Email Address []:student@example.com
```

This command places the key file and the certificate in the correct locations. Edit the vsftpd. conf file and add the following lines at the bottom. My comments are intended to describe the function of each line, but are not required to be in the vsftpd.conf file. I like to keep them there so I can refresh my memory later, if need be:

```
# Configuration statements required for data encryption
# Defines the location of the certification file
rsa_cert_file=/etc/ssl/certs/vsftpd.crt
# Defines the location of the key file for the certification
rsa_private_key_file=/etc/ssl/private/vsftpd.key
# Enables SSL support
ssl_enable=YES
# We will not allow SSL used for anonymous users.
```

```
# Since this is usually the general public, what would be the point?
Allow_anon_ssl=NO
# Local data connections will always use SSL.
Force_local_data_ssl=YES
# Local logins will always use SSL. This is for the control port.
Force_local_logins_ssl=YES
# Strong encryption with fewer vulnerabilities using TLS version 1.
Ssl_tlsv1=YES
# Not secure enough so we won't use SSL versions or 3.
Ssl_sslv2=NO
ssl_sslv3=NO
# Improves security by helping prevent man-in-the-middle attacks.
# May cause connections to drop out so set to NO if that occurs.
Require_ssl_reuse=YES
# Requires stronger encryption.
Ssl_ciphers=HIGH
```

Restart the vsftpd service. First, log into an FTP session from StudentVM1 as an anonymous user, which should work normally. Now log in as the student user and see what happens:

```
[student@studentvm1 ~]$ ftp studentvm2
Connected to studentvm2 (192.168.56.1).
220 (vsFTPd 3.0.3)
Name (studentvm2:student): <Enter>
530 Non-anonymous sessions must use encryption.
Login failed.
421 Service not available, remote server has closed connection
ftp>
```

But the command-line FTP client does not support encryption. So is this encryption useless from the command line? Just wait.

Exit from the FTP connection but leave the VSFTP server running because we will use it in another experiment later in this chapter.

We now have the server set up to support encryption. The problem is that the Linux command-line ftp program does not support encryption. This means that using the FTP client from the command line is still not secure. This is one of the issues with FTP. There is a command-line solution that we will explore later in this chapter.

NFS

The Network File System (NFS) was created by Sun Microsystems to share disk resources and the files they contain among many hosts. NFS is based upon the version of the RPC[11] (Remote Procedure Call) protocol developed by Sun. One advantage of NFS as a means to share files is that the client hosts can mount the shares in the same way as they would any local filesystem. This means that files do not need to be downloaded; they can be accessed directly by file managers and application programs.

This section guides you through the tasks of exporting a filesystem and mounting an NFS remote filesystem.

NFS Server

The NFS server is designed to share filesystems of the host acting as a server to a network so that NFS clients can mount the shared filesystems and access the files contained in them. The question of where in the filesystem structure to place filesystems that are to be exported has different answers. Some SysAdmins place them at the root (/) of the filesystem, while others add them to a mount point in /var. For these experiments we will place them in /var.

EXPERIMENT 56-6: CONFIGURING THE NFS SERVER

Perform this experiment as the root user on StudentVM2. We first need to verify that some packages are installed. Check with the **dnf list** command:

```
[root@studentvm2 ~]# dnf list rpcbind nfs-utils
Last metadata expiration check: 0:00:25 ago on Thu 01 Aug 2019
03:24:12 PM EDT.
Installed Packages
nfs-utils.x86_64          1:2.6.3-0.fc38              @updates
rpcbind.x86_64            1.2.6-4.rc2.fc38            @anaconda
```

The results on my VM show that these packages are already installed. If they are not on your host, do so now.

---

[11] Wikipedia, Remote Procedure Call, https://en.wikipedia.org/wiki/Remote_procedure_call

Configure the /etc/exports file, which is empty by default. It is only necessary to add one line for each filesystem to be exported. Add the following lines to export the /shared filesystem:

```
# Exports file for studentvm1
/var/shared          *(rw,sync,all_squash)
```

The rw option means to share it as read/write; the sync option means that the directory should be synced after changes are made and before other read requests are fulfilled. This helps ensure that the most recent versions of altered or new files are available as soon as the changes are made. The all_squash option changes the shared versions of files to the anonymous user ownership of nobody:nobody. The ownership in the shared directory on the server does not change, only the apparent ownership at the client end.

Restart and start the RPC services and NFS:

```
[root@studentvm2 etc]# for I in rpcbind nfs-server ; do systemctl
enable --now $I.service ;  done
Created symlink /etc/systemd/system/multi-user.target.wants/rpcbind.service
→ /usr/lib/systemd/system/rpcbind.service.
Created symlink /etc/systemd/system/multi-user.target.wants/nfs-server.
service → /usr/lib/systemd/system/nfs-server.service.
```

And export the defined filesystem. The a option means to export all configured directories, and the v option means verbose so that we can see the result:

```
[root@studentvm2 etc]# exportfs -av
exporting *:/var/shared
[root@studentvm2 etc]#
```

Now verify that the filesystem has been shared and can be seen locally. The e option means to show the host's list of exported directories:

```
[root@studentvm2 etc]# showmount -e localhost
Export list for localhost:
/var/shared *
[root@studentvm2 etc]#
```

Now do the same as root on StudentVM1:

```
[root@studentvm1 ~]# showmount -e studentvm2
Export list for studentvm2:
/var/shared *
[root@studentvm1 ~]#
```

This indicates that a remote NFS client can access the share on StudentVM2.

Note   Like FTP, NFS also has a complex set of requirements for firewall configuration. Adding the NFS service to the drop or block zone when it's used for protecting the host from the Internet handles all of those details for us.

The NFS server is now properly configured.

NFS Client

Now we can connect to the NFS share from the client, StudentVM1.

EXPERIMENT 56-7: MOUNTING THE NFS SHARE

Mounting a remote NFS filesystem is easy. Now let's test again that StudentVM1 can see the shared directory. Do this as root on StudentVM1:

```
[root@studentvm1 ~]# showmount -e studentvm2
Export list for studentvm2:
/var/shared *
[root@studentvm1 ~]#
```

As root on StudentVM1, mount the remote export on the /mnt mount point with the following command. The t option is used to specify that this is an NFS4 filesystem that is being mounted. All recent versions of Fedora use NFS4, which is a more secure and flexible version than NFS3:

```
[root@studentvm1 ~]# mount -t nfs4 studentvm2:/var/shared /mnt
[root@studentvm1 ~]# ll /mnt
total 116
-rw-r--r-- 1 root root     16 Jul 27 08:50 file-01.txt
-rw-r--r-- 1 root root     16 Jul 27 08:50 file-02.txt
-rw-r--r-- 1 root root     16 Jul 27 08:50 file-03.txt
-rw-r--r-- 1 root root     16 Jul 27 08:50 file-04.txt
<SNIP>
```

```
-rw-r--r-- 1 root root     16 Jul 27 08:50 file-22.txt
-rw-r--r-- 1 root root     16 Jul 27 08:50 file-23.txt
-rw-r--r-- 1 root root     16 Jul 27 08:50 file-24.txt
-rw-r--r-- 1 root root     16 Jul 27 08:50 file-25.txt
drwx------ 2 root root 16384 Jul 27 08:47 lost+found
[root@studentvm1 ~]#
```

Use the **mount** command on StudentVM1 to verify that the remote filesystem has been mounted. List the contents of /mnt to verify that the files are there as they should be. What does the `lsblk` command show? Why?

Unmount the NFS filesystem. Create a mount point (directory) called /shared. Add the following line to the end of the /etc/fstab file:

```
studentvm2:/var/shared /shared        nfs4     defaults       0 0
```

Run the following command on StudentVM1 to tell systemd about the change to fstab:

systemctl daemon-reload

Mount the NFS export and verify that the mount occurred correctly:

```
[root@studentvm1 ~]# mount /shared
[root@studentvm1 ~]# ll /shared
total 88
-rw------- 1 root root  2118 Aug  1 21:11 anaconda-ks.cfg
-rw-r--r-- 1 root root 39514 Aug  1 21:11 Chapter-36.tgz
-rw-r--r-- 1 root root   469 Aug  1 21:11 ifcfg-enp0s3
-rw-r--r-- 1 root root   370 Aug  1 21:11 ifcfg-enp0s3.bak
-rw-r--r-- 1 root root   340 Aug  1 21:11 ifcfg-enp0s8.bak
-rw------- 1 root root  3123 Aug  1 21:11 imapd.pem
-rw-r--r-- 1 root root  2196 Aug  1 21:11 initial-setup-ks.cfg
drwx------ 2 root root 16384 Aug  1 21:05 lost+found
-rwxr-x--- 1 root root   272 Aug  1 21:11 restartmail
-rw-r--r-- 1 root root    10 Aug  1 21:11 testfile.txt
[root@studentvm1 ~]#
```

Adding this NFS mount to /etc/fstab means that it is mounted at boot time and that we can easily unmount and remount it if necessary.

Unmount the /shared directory.

Cleanup

Let's do a little cleanup before we move on to SAMBA.

EXPERIMENT 56-8: A BIT OF CLEANUP

Perform this experiment as root.

Unmount the NFS filesystem on StudentVM1. On your studentvm2 host, run the command

[root@studentvm2 etc]# **exportfs -uav**

to unexport all exported filesystems. Unmount /shared on your studentvm2 host.

Stop and disable the RPC and NFS services:

[root@studentvm2 etc]# **for I in rpcbind nfs-server rpcbind.socket ; do systemctl disable --now $I.service ;   done**

This completes cleanup of NFS.

SAMBA

The SAMBA[12] file sharing service provides a way to share files located on a Linux server with Windows systems. SAMBA is based on the Server Message Block (SMB) protocol. Originally developed by IBM, SMB was used by Microsoft as the primary protocol in their networking services. SMB is now known as Common Internet File System (CIFS).

We will create a scenario in which we want to use SAMBA to share some files with Windows computers. Of course Linux systems can also be SAMBA clients, so that will make our testing easy since we do not have a Windows computer from which to test in our virtual network.

---

[12]Wikipedia, SAMBA, https://en.wikipedia.org/wiki/Samba_(software)

EXPERIMENT 56-9: CONFIGURING SAMBA

Start this experiment as root on StudentVM2. First, install the required SAMBA packages. The SAMBA client should be already installed. It was on my VM, but this will ensure that it is, in addition to installing the SAMBA server:

```
[root@studentvm2 ~]# dnf -y install samba samba-client
```

Make /etc/samba the PWD. The smb.conf.example file contains comments and examples describing how to configure SAMBA to share various resources such as public and private directories, printers, and home directories. Read through this file to get an idea what is possible with SAMBA.

However, the smb.conf file is the one to which we need to add our shared directory. The smb.conf file is a minimal version of smb.conf.example. It has a few starter samples, but we need to have all of those and we need to add a stanza for our acs directory.

Edit smb.conf and add the following lines to share the /acs directory.

```
# A publicly accessible directory for ACS files that is read/write
[SHARED]
        comment = Shared Directory
        path = /var/shared
        public = yes
        writable = yes
        printable = no
        browseable = yes
```

Save the smb.conf file but do not exit from the editor. In another terminal session as root, test the syntax of the smb.conf file. It is not necessary to make /etc/samba the PWD:

```
[root@studentvm2 ~]# testparm
Load smb config files from /etc/samba/smb.conf
Loaded services file OK.
Weak crypto is allowed by GnuTLS (e.g. NTLM as a compatibility fallback)
Server role: ROLE_STANDALONE

Press enter to see a dump of your service definitions<Enter>
```

```
# Global parameters
        server string = Samba Server Version %v
        workgroup = WORKGROUP
        idmap config * : backend = tdb
        cups options = raw
        include = /etc/samba/usershares.conf
<SNIP>

[ACS]
        comment = Shared Directory
        guest ok = Yes
        path = /var/shared
        read only = No
[root@studentvm2 ~]#
```

Although it is not required in a Linux environment, the NETBIOS name service is required for SAMBA to fully function in a Windows or mixed Linux-and-Windows environment. So start both the smb and nmb services:

```
[root@studentvm2 ~]# systemctl start smb ; systemctl start nmb
```

You should also ensure that these services start on boot in a production environment, but that's not required for this experiment.

Create a user ID and password for the user "student" using the **pdbedit** command. Use a simple password for this test:

```
[root@studentvm2 ~]# pdbedit -a student
new password:<Enter password>
retype new password:<Enter password>
Unix username:         student
NT username:
Account Flags:         [U            ]
User SID:              S-1-5-21-1995892852-683670545-3750803719-1000
Primary Group SID:     S-1-5-21-1995892852-683670545-3750803719-513
Full Name:             Student User
Home Directory:        \\studentvm2\student
HomeDir Drive:
Logon Script:
Profile Path:          \\studentvm2\student\profile
```

```
Domain:                STUDENTVM2
Account desc:
Workstations:
Munged dial:
Logon time:            0
Logoff time:           Wed, 06 Feb 2036 10:06:39 EST
Kickoff time:          Wed, 06 Feb 2036 10:06:39 EST
Password last set:     Tue, 06 Aug 2019 09:02:13 EDT
Password can change:   Tue, 06 Aug 2019 09:02:13 EDT
Password must change: never
Last bad password   : 0
Bad password count  : 0
Logon hours         : FFFFFFFFFFFFFFFFFFFFFFFFFFFFFFFFFFFFFFFFFFFFFFFF
[root@studentvm2 ~]#
```

Tip   We could have used the smbpasswd command rather than pdbedit to create the password.

Now we can perform a quick test of our SAMBA share. As the user student on StudentVM2, use the **smbclient** command to display the shares on the localhost:

```
[student@studentvm2 ~]$ smbclient -L localhost
Password for [SAMBA\root]:
Anonymous login successful

        Sharename       Type        Comment
        ---------       ----        -------
        print$          Disk        Printer Drivers
        SHARED          Disk        Shared Directory
        IPC$            IPC         IPC Service (Samba 4.18.5)
SMB1 disabled -- no workgroup available
[student@studentvm2 ~]$
```

We now have the basics working.

Now that SAMBA is working, let's make a few additions to the smb.conf file. Our basic installation has caused SAMBA to use the local host's hostname for the workgroup name, and that may be incorrect. We may want to use the name of an existing workgroup or create one with a more meaningful name. We can add that information and also add some additional security to our SAMBA installation.

EXPERIMENT 56-10: CUSTOMIZING SAMBA SERVER CONFIGURATION

Perform this experiment as root on StudentVM2.

Make the highlighted changes in the global stanza in this listing to smb.conf. I originally took these from the smb.conf.example file. See smb.conf.example for a more detailed config file or read the smb.conf man page:

```
[global]
        workgroup = TESTGROUP
        server string = StudentVM1 - Samba Server Version %v
        security = user
        interfaces = lo enp0s8 192.168.56.11/24
```

We have renamed the workgroup and added a bit more information to the server string. We specified the internal network interface on which SAMBA should listen. This enhances security by limiting the sources from which SAMBA clients can connect. We could also limit connections to specific hosts.

Now check the smb.conf file again:

```
[root@studentvm2 ~]# testparm
Load smb config files from /etc/samba/smb.conf
Loaded services file OK.
Weak crypto is allowed by GnuTLS (e.g. NTLM as a compatibility fallback)

Server role: ROLE_STANDALONE

Press enter to see a dump of your service definitions

# Global parameters
[global]
        interfaces = lo enp0s8 192.168.56.11/24
        printcap name = cups
```

```
        security = USER
        server string = StudentVM2 - Samba Server Version %v
        workgroup = TESTGROUP
        idmap config * : backend = tdb
        cups options = raw
        include = /etc/samba/usershares.conf

<SNIP>

[SHARED]
        comment = Shared Directory
        guest ok = Yes
        path = /var/shared
        read only = No
[root@studentvm2 ~]#
```

We must restart the smb service or the change to the workgroup name will not take effect, so do that:

```
[root@studentvm2 ~]# systemctl restart smb ; systemctl restart nmb
```

Now let's do another quick test as the student user:

```
[student@studentvm2 ~]$ smbclient -L localhost
Password for [TESTGROUP\root]:
Anonymous login successful

        Sharename       Type        Comment
        ---------       ----        -------
        print$          Disk        Printer Drivers
        SHARED          Disk        Shared Directory
        IPC$            IPC         IPC Service (StudentVM2 - Samba Server
Version 4.18.5)
SMB1 disabled -- no workgroup available
[student@studentvm2 ~]$
```

This looks good, but there is an error that I ran into and I suspect that you did too. Internet searches discovered many references to this and similar errors, but I never found a solution to it. This does not seem to affect the remaining experiments, so you can safely ignore this message.

Using the SAMBA Client

Linux has a SAMBA client that allows us to connect with a Linux server using SAMBA to share directories, as well as providing client access to Windows systems that have shared directories. We can use this client to perform additional testing.

EXPERIMENT 56-11: USING THE SAMBA CLIENT

As the user student on the StudentVM1 host, make your home directory (~) the PWD. Then log into the remote share on your student host. The -U option specifies the user ID under which we log in:

```
[student@studentvm1 /]# smbclient //studentvm2/shared -U student
Enter SAMBA\student's password: <Enter password>
Try "help" to get a list of possible commands.
smb: \>
```

Issue **dir**, the Windows equivalent of an **ls** command, to view a listing of the files you placed in the shared directory. Try the **ls** command too:

```
smb: \> dir
  .                                   D        0  Thu Jul 27 08:50:23 2023
  ..                                  D        0  Thu Jul 27 08:48:04 2023
  file-18.txt                         N       16  Thu Jul 27 08:50:23 2023
  file-04.txt                         N       16  Thu Jul 27 08:50:23 2023
  file-07.txt                         N       16  Thu Jul 27 08:50:23 2023
  file-05.txt                         N       16  Thu Jul 27 08:50:23 2023
  file-09.txt                         N       16  Thu Jul 27 08:50:23 2023
<SNIP>
  file-13.txt                         N       16  Thu Jul 27 08:50:23 2023
  file-10.txt                         N       16  Thu Jul 27 08:50:23 2023
  file-06.txt                         N       16  Thu Jul 27 08:50:23 2023

            996780 blocks of size 1024. 927844 blocks available
smb: \>
```

We have a number of commands available in this remote SAMBA session. Use the **help** command to view them and **help <commandname>** to get more information about the individual commands.

Download one of the files from the remote shared directory:

```
smb: \> get file-18.txt
getting file \file-18.txt of size 16 as file-18.txt (15.6 KiloBytes/sec)
(average 15.6 KiloBytes/sec)
smb: \>
```

In another terminal session as the student user on StudentVM1, list the contents of the home directory. The file you downloaded should be there.

Exit from this session and stop the SMB and NMB services on StudentVM2.

Using the smbclient in this way is much like using FTP. We have a view into a shared directory and the files it contains, and we can perform a few operations including a download.

Midnight Commander

We have already explored the use of Midnight commander as a file manager. It is also an excellent client for FTP, SFTP, SMB (CIFS), and SSH. It can be used with those protocols to connect to remote hosts in one panel and to copy files from and between the remote and local hosts. It can be used to display the content of remote files and to delete them.

SSH is a powerful tool, and when used in conjunction with a file manager like Midnight Commander (MC), the pair can be used as a simple and easy file sharing system using a protocol called FISH. The advantage of this is that it uses tools we have already installed and requires no additional configuration.

This is also the most secure method I know for sharing files. The login or key-based authentication sequence is encrypted as are all data transfers. This is not just the default configuration; it is the only way in which SSH works. There is not a choice about using authentication and beginning-to-end encryption, so it cannot be bypassed.

The FISH protocol was developed by Pavel Machek in 1998 specifically for Midnight Commander. FISH stands for "Files transferred over Shell protocol." However, MC also connects with servers using FTP, SFTP, and SAMBA, so it is very versatile. I have found it needs no special configuration, unlike some other clients.

```
┌──────────────────────────────────────────────────────────────────────┐
│       EXPERIMENT 56-12: MIDNIGHT COMMANDER AND FILE SHARING            │
└──────────────────────────────────────────────────────────────────────┘
```

Perform this experiment as the student user on StudentVM1. In this experiment we will connect to the server using various file sharing protocols.

In a terminal session as the student user on StudentVM1, launch Midnight Commander. Press **F9** and then the arrow keys until the **Right** panel menu is highlighted. Then use the down arrow key to highlight **FTP link ...** as shown in Figure 56-1. Press the **Enter** key to initiate the connection.

```
   Left      File    Command    Options    Right
+<- ~ --------------------------.+-----------------------+-------------------.[^]>+
|.n        Name        | Size  |Modify t| File listing      | | Size  |Modify time |
|/..                   |UP--DIR|May 30 0| Quick view   C-x q| |UP--DIR|May 30 08:41|
|/.cache               |  4096 |Aug 10 1| Info         C-x i| |  4096 |Aug 10 12:23|
|/.config              |  4096 |Aug 10 1| Tree              | |  4096 |Aug 10 13:11|
|/.cups                |  4096 |Mar 17 2|-------------------| |  4096 |Mar 17 22:15|
|/.esmtp_queue         |  4096 |May  2 1| Listing format... | |  4096 |May  2 15:10|
|/.fvwm                |  4096 |Mar 14 1| Sort order...     | |  4096 |Mar 14 16:00|
|/.gnupg               |  4096 |Dec 22  | Filter...         | |  4096 |Dec 22 2018 |
|/.local               |  4096 |Dec 22  | Encoding...   M-e | |  4096 |Dec 22 2018 |
|/.mozilla             |  4096 |May 10 1|-------------------| |  4096 |May 10 11:28|
|/.putty               |  4096 |Aug 10 1| FTP link...       | |  4096 |Aug 10 13:03|
|/.ssh                 |  4096 |Jun 28 2| Shell link...     | |  4096 |Jun 28 22:04|
|/Documents            |  4096 |Jul  2 1| Panelize          | |  4096 |Jul  2 10:43|
|/Downloads            |  4096 |Jun  4 1|-------------------| |  4096 |Jun  4 13:59|
|/Music                |  4096 |Dec 22  | Rescan       C-r  | |  4096 |Dec 22 2018 |
|/Pictures             |  4096 |Dec 22  +-------------------+ |  4096 |Dec 22 2018 |
|/Public               |  4096 |Dec 22 2018||/Public          | |  4096 |Dec 22 2018 |
|/Templates            |  4096 |Dec 22 2018||/Templates       | |  4096 |Dec 22 2018 |
|/Videos               |  4096 |Dec 22 2018||/Videos          | |  4096 |Dec 22 2018 |
|/chapter25            |  4096 |Mar  2 08:21||/chapter25      | |  4096 |Mar  2 08:21|
|/chapter26            |  4096 |Mar 21 15:27||/chapter26      | |  4096 |Mar 21 15:27|
|/chapter28            |167936 |Apr 10 08:23||/chapter28      | |167936 |Apr 10 08:23|
|/testdir              |  4096 |Apr  2 12:45||/testdir        | |  4096 |Apr  2 12:45|
|/testdir1             |  4096 |Dec 30 2018||/testdir1        | |  4096 |Dec 30 2018 |
|/testdir6             |  4096 |Dec 30 2018||/testdir6        | |  4096 |Dec 30 2018 |
|/testdir7             |663552 |Feb 21 14:12||/testdir7       | |663552 |Feb 21 14:12|
|/tmp                  |  4096 |Jun 22 13:25||/tmp            | |  4096 |Jun 22 13:25|
| .ICEauthority        | 12444 |Aug 10 21:41| .ICEauthority    | | 12444 |Aug 10 21:41|
| .Xauthority          |    56 |Jan 30 2019| .Xauthority       | |    56 |Jan 30 2019 |
| .bash_history        | 28285 |Aug 10 14:36| .bash_history     | | 28285 |Aug 10 14:36|
| .bash_logout         |    18 |Oct  8 2018| .bash_logout      | |    18 |Oct  8 2018 |
| .bash_profile        |   186 |Jun 21 08:44| .bash_profile     | |   186 |Jun 21 08:44|
|------------------------------------------||-----------------------------------|
|UP--DIR                                    ||UP--DIR                            |
+----------------------- 3585M/3968M (90%) -++------------------- 3585M/3968M (90%) -+
Hint: Want your plain shell? Press C-o, and get back to MC with C-o again.
[student@studentvm1 ~]$                                                    [^]
 1Help   2Menu   3View   4Edit   5Copy   6RenMov  7Mkdir  8Delete  9PullDn  10Quit
```

Figure 56-1. *Select the FTP link to connect with the VSFTP server in standard FTP mode*

Type **studentvm2** in the FTP to machine field, as shown in Figure 56-2, and press the
Enter key.

```
|/Documents      +------------- FTP to machine ---------------+  |  4096|Jul  2 10:43|
|/Downloads      | Enter machine name (F1 for details):      |  |  4096|Jun  4 13:59|
|/Music          |  studentvm2                          [^] |  |  4096|Dec 22  2018|
|/Pictures       |-------------------------------------------|  |  4096|Dec 22  2018|
|/Public         |           [< OK >] [ Cancel ]             |  |  4096|Dec 22  2018|
|/Templates      +-------------------------------------------+  |  4096|Dec 22  2018|
```

Figure 56-2. *Enter the name of the host you're connecting to*

Figure 56-3 shows Midnight Commander with the student user's home directory on
StudentVM1, the local host, in the left panel and the anonymous FTP connection to
StudentVM2 in the right panel.

```
 Left     File    Command    Options    Right
+<- ~ ----------------------------.[^]>++<- ftp://studentvm2/ -------------------.[^]>+
|.n        Name        | Size |Modify time ||.n        Name        | Size |Modify time |
|/..                   |UP--DIR|May 30 08:41||/..                  |UP--DIR|Aug 10 14:36|
|/.cache               | 4096|Aug 10 12:23||/pub                   |  4096|Jul 25  2018|
|/.config              | 4096|Aug 10 13:11|| FTP-file-01.txt        |    16|Aug  8 01:14|
|/.cups                | 4096|Mar 17 22:15|| FTP-file-02.txt        |    16|Aug  8 01:14|
|/.esmtp_queue         | 4096|May  2 15:10|| FTP-file-03.txt        |    16|Aug  8 01:14|
|/.fvwm                | 4096|Mar 14 16:00|| FTP-file-04.txt        |    16|Aug  8 01:14|
|/.gnupg               | 4096|Dec 22  2018|| FTP-file-05.txt        |    16|Aug  8 01:14|
|/.local               | 4096|Dec 22  2018|| FTP-file-06.txt        |    16|Aug  8 01:14|
|/.mozilla             | 4096|May 10 11:28|| FTP-file-07.txt        |    16|Aug  8 01:14|
|/.putty               | 4096|Aug 10 13:03|| FTP-file-08.txt        |    16|Aug  8 01:14|
|/.ssh                 | 4096|Jun 28 22:04|| FTP-file-09.txt        |    16|Aug  8 01:14|
<SNIP>
|/testdir6             | 4096|Dec 30  2018|| FTP-file-24.txt        |    16|Aug  8 01:14|
|/testdir7             | 663552|Feb 21 14:12|| FTP-file-25.txt       |    16|Aug  8 01:14|
|/tmp                  | 4096|Jun 22 13:25||                        |      |            |
| .ICEauthority        | 12444|Aug 10 21:41||                       |      |            |
| .Xauthority          |  56|Jan 30  2019||                         |      |            |
| .bash_history        | 28285|Aug 10 14:36||                       |      |            |
| .bash_logout         |  18|Oct  8  2018||                         |      |            |
| .bash_profile        | 186|Jun 21 08:44||                         |      |            |
|------------------------------------------||-----------------------------------------|
|UP--DIR                                   ||UP--DIR                                   |
+----------------------- 3585M/3968M (90%) -++---------------------------------------+
Hint: The homepage of GNU Midnight Commander: http://www.midnight-commander.org/
[student@studentvm1 ~]$                                                          [^]
 1Help   2Menu   3View   4Edit   5Copy   6RenMov  7Mkdir  8Delete  9PullDn 10Quit
```

Figure 56-3. *The student user's home directory on the local host is in the left panel,
and the anonymous FTP directory on StudentVM2 is shown in the right panel of
Midnight Commander*

Copy files between the directories. Can you do it from the local host to the server?

To exit the connection to the server, enter the **cd** command. This takes you back to the student user's home directory on the local host.

Experiment. Download a file or two to your home directory. Then try uploading files to various directories on the server, such as /var/shared, your home directory, and the /acs directory. When finished you can again use the **cd** command with no arguments to exit from the remote connection.

Now connect to the server using the **Shell link** option. Use this SSH protocol to perform the same tasks as with the previous links.

Apache Web Server

We can also share files using the Apache web server we created in Chapter 51. This requires only a little additional work and no changes to the Apache configuration.

EXPERIMENT 56-13: USING APACHE WEB SERVER AS A FILE SERVER

In this experiment we will add some files to the Apache downloads directory and test the results. As the root user on StudentVM2, ensure that Apache, httpd, is running. If not, start it.

In the /var/www2/html directory, create a new directory, downloads, if it does not already exist. Then set the ownership to apache.apache. Make the new downloads directory the PWD and copy or create some new files for content. I used the following command-line program to create a few files:

```
[root@studentvm2 downloads]# for I in `seq -w 0 45` ; do echo "This is a file
for web download $I" > file-$I.txt ; done
```

As the student user on StudentVM1, open Firefox and navigate to www2.example.com/downloads. The web page should look like that in Figure 56-4. You can click the field names to change the sort although it won't make much difference since the files are all the same size and created at the same time. However, if you click the Name field a couple times, it reverses the direction of the sort. You might also want to add some files with different characteristics to try with different sorts.

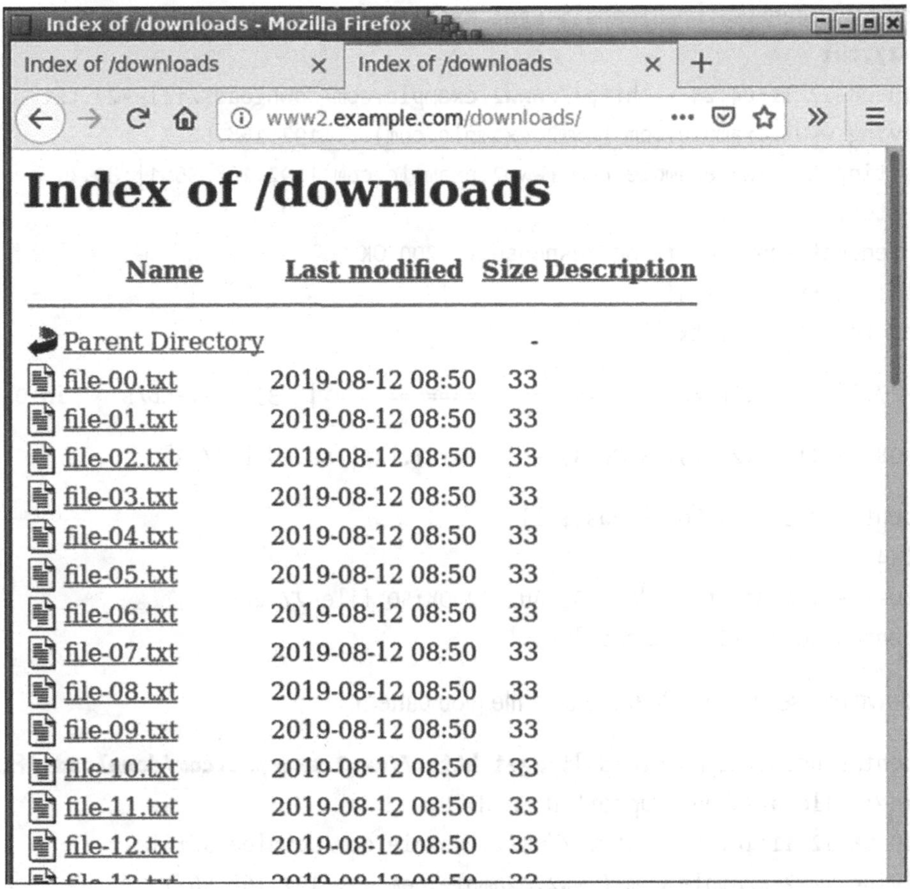

Figure 56-4. *Using the Apache web server to share files displays a sortable index*

Right-click a couple files and select **Save link as** from the pop-up menu to download them. The default directory for downloads is ~/Downloads. Look for the downloaded files there.

We also have command-line tools, **wget** and **curl**, to use for downloading files from websites. Let's look first at **wget**, which should already be installed since you've used it before in this course. We touched on the wget command briefly in Volume 1, Chapter 12, and we installed and used it to download companion files for this course from the Apress Git repository.

As the student user on StudentVM1, make ~/Downloads the PWD. Delete all of the files in this directory. Use **wget** to download a single file. Use a file that you have in your html/downloads directory; I will use file-27.txt:

```
[student@studentvm1 Downloads]$ wget http://www2.example.com/downloads/
file-27.txt
--2019-08-12 11:04:24--  http://www2.example.com/downloads/file-27.txt
Resolving www2.example.com (www2.example.com)... 192.168.56.1
Connecting to www2.example.com (www2.example.com)|192.168.56.1|:80...
connected.
HTTP request sent, awaiting response... 200 OK
Length: 33 [text/plain]
Saving to: 'file-27.txt'

file-27.txt    100%[==============================>]   33  --.-KB/s    in 0s

2019-08-12 11:04:24 (5.03 MB/s) - 'file-27.txt' saved [33/33]

[student@studentvm1 Downloads]$ ll
total 4
-rw-rw-r-- 1 student student 33 Aug 12 08:50 file-27.txt
[student@studentvm1 Downloads]$
```

Now download several files that match a file glob pattern:

```
[student@studentvm1 Downloads]$ wget http://www2.example.com/downloads/file-*
Warning: wildcards not supported in HTTP.
--2019-08-12 11:14:41--  http://www2.example.com/downloads/file-*
Resolving www2.example.com (www2.example.com)... 192.168.56.1
Connecting to www2.example.com (www2.example.com)|192.168.56.1|:80...
connected.
HTTP request sent, awaiting response... 404 Not Found
2019-08-12 11:14:41 ERROR 404: Not Found.
```

You will see the warning message that wildcards (globbing) are not supported using the HTTPD protocol. The wget utility can be used to download using FTP as well as HTTPD, and sets are supported when using FTP. Ensure that the VSFTP server is running on StudentVM2 and download some files using wildcards from the anonymous FTP site:

```
[student@studentvm1 Downloads]$ wget ftp://studentvm2.example.com/FTP-
file-1*.txt
```

The **curl** utility can use regular expressions such as sets to download multiple files for many protocols. The **curl** tool supports all of the following protocols: DICT, FILE, FTP, FTPS, GOPHER, HTTP, HTTPS, IMAP, IMAPS, LDAP, LDAPS, POP3, POP3S, RTMP, RTSP, SCP, SFTP, SMB, SMBS,

SMTP, SMTPS, TELNET, and TFTP. It can also handle user IDs and passwords, as well as certificates. As a result it can be used in a great many situations where a single downloading solution is desirable, such as in scripts. It is an excellent tool for use in scripted automation.

The **curl** utility is already installed, so we do not need to do that. Download one file using the following syntax. The -O (uppercase alpha character O, not zero) specifies that the file name used in the download, file-12.txt, is the file name to be used to save the file locally:

```
[student@studentvm1 Downloads]$ curl -O http://www2.example.com/downloads/
file-12.txt ; ll
  % Total    % Received % Xferd  Average Speed   Time    Time     Time  Current
                                 Dload  Upload   Total   Spent    Left  Speed
100    33 100    33    0     0  11000      0 --:--:-- --:--:-- --:--:-- 11000
total 4
-rw-rw-r-- 1 student student 33 Aug 12 11:47 file-12.txt
```

What happens if you do not use the -O option when doing the preceding download? The alternate form of doing a download is to use the -o (lowercase alpha) option to specify the output file name:

```
[student@studentvm1 Downloads]$ curl http://www2.example.com/downloads/
file-13.txt -o file-13.txt ; ll
  % Total    % Received % Xferd  Average Speed   Time    Time     Time  Current
                                 Dload  Upload   Total   Spent    Left  Speed
100    33 100    33    0     0   6600      0 --:--:-- --:--:-- --:--:--  6600
total 8
-rw-rw-r-- 1 student student 33 Aug 12 11:47 file-12.txt
-rw-rw-r-- 1 student student 33 Aug 12 11:53 file-13.txt
[student@studentvm1 Downloads]$
```

This requires more typing than using -O and more code in a script so, unless there is a specific reason not to, I suggest using the -O option. Note the use of the set [0-9] instead of file globs, ? or *:

```
[student@studentvm1 Downloads]$ curl -O http://www2.example.com/downloads/
file-1[0-9].txt
<snip>
[student@studentvm1 Downloads]$ ll
```

```
total 40
-rw-rw-r-- 1 student student 33 Aug 12 12:46 file-10.txt
-rw-rw-r-- 1 student student 33 Aug 12 12:46 file-11.txt
-rw-rw-r-- 1 student student 33 Aug 12 12:46 file-12.txt
-rw-rw-r-- 1 student student 33 Aug 12 12:46 file-13.txt
-rw-rw-r-- 1 student student 33 Aug 12 12:46 file-14.txt
-rw-rw-r-- 1 student student 33 Aug 12 12:46 file-15.txt
-rw-rw-r-- 1 student student 33 Aug 12 12:46 file-16.txt
-rw-rw-r-- 1 student student 33 Aug 12 12:46 file-17.txt
-rw-rw-r-- 1 student student 33 Aug 12 12:46 file-18.txt
-rw-rw-r-- 1 student student 33 Aug 12 12:46 file-19.txt
[student@studentvm1 Downloads]$
```

Download a file using FTP:

```
[student@studentvm1 Downloads]$ curl -O ftp://studentvm2.example.com/FTP-
file-02.txt
```

% Total	% Received	% Xferd	Average Speed		Time	Time	Time	Current
			Dload	Upload	Total	Spent	Left	Speed
100 16	100 16	0	0	410	0 --:--:--	--:--:--	--:--:--	421

```
[student@studentvm1 Downloads]$ ll
total 48
-rw-rw-r-- 1 student student  33 Aug 12 12:46  file-10.txt
-rw-rw-r-- 1 student student  33 Aug 12 12:46  file-11.txt
-rw-rw-r-- 1 student student  33 Aug 12 12:46  file-12.txt
-rw-rw-r-- 1 student student  33 Aug 12 12:46  file-13.txt
-rw-rw-r-- 1 student student  33 Aug 12 12:46  file-14.txt
-rw-rw-r-- 1 student student  33 Aug 12 12:46  file-15.txt
-rw-rw-r-- 1 student student  33 Aug 12 12:46  file-16.txt
-rw-rw-r-- 1 student student  33 Aug 12 12:46  file-17.txt
-rw-rw-r-- 1 student student  33 Aug 12 12:46  file-18.txt
-rw-rw-r-- 1 student student  33 Aug 12 12:46  file-19.txt
-rw-rw-r-- 1 student student  16 Aug 12 13:57  FTP-file-02.txt
[student@studentvm1 Downloads]$
```

And now do multiple files over FTP with a set:

3351334

```
[student@studentvm1 Downloads]$ curl -O ftp://studentvm2.example.com/FTP-
file-2[1-3].txt

[1/3]: ftp://studentvm2.example.com/FTP-file-21.txt --> FTP-file-21.txt
--_curl_--ftp://studentvm2.example.com/FTP-file-21.txt
  % Total    % Received % Xferd  Average Speed   Time    Time     Time  Current
                                 Dload  Upload   Total   Spent    Left  Speed
100    16  100    16    0     0    410      0 --:--:-- --:--:-- --:--:--   410

[2/3]: ftp://studentvm2.example.com/FTP-file-22.txt --> FTP-file-22.txt
--_curl_--ftp://studentvm2.example.com/FTP-file-22.txt
100    16  100    16    0     0   8000      0 --:--:-- --:--:-- --:--:--  8000

[3/3]: ftp://studentvm2.example.com/FTP-file-23.txt --> FTP-file-23.txt
--_curl_--ftp://studentvm2.example.com/FTP-file-23.txt
100    16  100    16    0     0   8000      0 --:--:-- --:--:-- --:--:--  8000
[student@studentvm1 Downloads]$ ll
total 12
-rw-rw-r-- 1 student student 16 Aug 12 14:00 FTP-file-21.txt
-rw-rw-r-- 1 student student 16 Aug 12 14:00 FTP-file-22.txt
-rw-rw-r-- 1 student student 16 Aug 12 14:00 FTP-file-23.txt
[student@studentvm1 Downloads]$
```

So we have discovered that **wget** can use file globs but not REGEXes like sets when downloading FTP. It cannot use any form of glob or REGEX with HTTPD. The **curl** utility can use REGEXes but not file globs – at least on the protocols we have tested.

The **wget** and **curl** man pages have good descriptions and examples of their many features.

Chapter Summary

This chapter has shown us some tools for sharing files on a file server. We used FTP, SAMBA, and NFS on StudentVM2 to share directories with users on StudentVM1. FTP in any form, SAMBA, and NFS all require some nontrivial setup to work in a non-secure mode. Even more work is required to provide a secure environment on those that support it.

We have also seen that tools we already have available, SSH and Midnight Commander, can work together to provide a very powerful, secure, and flexible yet easy-to-use file sharing solution that just works. Midnight Commander can be used without SSH to access FTP sites and with SSL to access VSFTP sites. MC can also be used with SSH to connect to a shell session on a remote host on which one has a user account. We have also explored `wget` and `curl` as command-line tools for downloading files with HTTPD and FTP protocols. The `curl` utility can download using many different types of protocols, and it can use regular expressions to do so.

There are a lot of options available to us to share files as well as to use for downloading those files. We have not covered all of them, but the ones we did cover should give you a good start.

Exercises

Perform these exercises to complete this chapter:

1. Monitor the packet data stream on StudentVM1 as you use FTP to connect to the VSFTP server. Examine the resulting TCP conversation and identify the components of the FTP initiation sequence.

2. As root on your student host, mount the NFS export on /mnt. Change the PWD to the stuff subdirectory and verify that the files you copied to it are there.

3. Attempt to add a new file. What message do you get?

4. Create a new mount point and an entry in the fstab for the ACS share created on StudentVM1 and mount the filesystem as a test. Reboot StudentVM1 and verify that /acs is mounted during startup.

5. Monitor the packet data stream on StudentVM1 as you use Midnight Commander as the student user on StudentVM1 to connect to StudentVM2 using various methods. Use FTP, SFTP, a shell link, and an SMB link. Observe which of these connections are encrypted and which are not.

6. Configure the VSFTP server to allow anonymous uploads.

7. Use Midnight Commander to copy files from the student account on StudentVM1 to the VSFTP server.

8. Why did you not need a user ID and password in Experiment 56-12 when using Midnight Commander to connect to the server using a shell link?

9. What directory is the PWD when you open a shell link to the server?

Be sure to shut down all file sharing client and server tools and services after completing these exercises.

## CHAPTER 57

Where Do I Go from Here?

Introduction

Wow! You made it all the way through this massive Linux course. That is impressive all by itself, but are you ready to take the next steps?

In truth, we have only just begun. I find that no matter how much I learn, there is always more. Despite the amount of material in this course, I have only introduced you to many of these subjects. How you proceed from here is up to you, but it can make all the difference in your future.

Curiosity

There is an old – and I think incredibly stupid – saying that "curiosity killed the cat." I had this used on me as a kid, fortunately not by my parents. I think this dumb saying is used mostly to stifle kids when their questions and inquisitiveness take them to places that some parents, teachers, and caregivers would rather not take the time to deal with. This is one of the ways in which the boxes were built around us.

My personal saying is that "curiosity solves problems." Following our curiosity leads us to places that are outside the box, places that allow us to solve our problems in ways that we could not otherwise. Sometimes curiosity can lead me directly to the cause of a problem, and other times the connection is indirect.

Learning never stops. Every time I teach a class or write an article – or book – I learn new things. This is all about my innate curiosity.

D. Both, *Using and Administering Linux: Volume 3*, https://doi.org/10.1007/978-1-4842-9786-5_57

I have a whole chapter dedicated to curiosity in my book *The Linux Philosophy for SysAdmins*.[1] I look at how my curiosity led me to Linux and how it helps me solve problems. I also discuss how a bit of curiosity about log entries on my firewall system led me down the path to some of the tools we explored in Chapter 41 of Volume 2.

> *I have not failed. I've just found 10,000 ways that won't work.*
>
> —Thomas A. Edison

Although the failure of thousands of specific combinations of individual materials and fabrication technologies during testing did not lead to a viable light bulb, Edison continued to experiment. Just so, the failure to resolve a problem or create code that performs its defined task does not mean that the project or overall goal will fail. It means only that a specific tool or approach did not result in a successful outcome.

I have learned much more through my failures than I have in almost any other manner. I am especially glad for those failures that have been self-inflicted. Not only did I have to correct the problems I caused myself but I also still had to find and fix the original problem. This always led to a great deal of research, which caused me to learn much more than if I had solved the original problem quickly.

This is just my nature, and I think it is the nature of all good SysAdmins to look upon these situations as learning opportunities. As mentioned previously, I have spent many years as a trainer, and some of the most fun experiences were when demonstrations, experiments, and lab projects would fail while I was teaching. Those were fantastic learning experiences for me as well as for the students in my class. Sometimes I even incorporated those accidental failures into later classes because they enabled me to teach something important.

Convert

Although I started using Linux in about 1996, I really did not start to learn it in any depth until I converted all of the computers in my home lab from OS/2 to Linux. I liked OS/2 and was comfortable with it, but I could see that I would always return to it to do those tasks that I had not yet figured out how to do in Linux. I was never going to be a Linux expert that way.

---

[1] Both, David, *The Linux Philosophy for SysAdmins*, Apress, 2018, 417

Everyone learns best in their own way. As a trainer I saw this every time I taught a class, regardless of the subject. Following our curiosity is the same – we all have that spark that leads us to discover more. Our methods may not be the same, but they will lead us all to greater knowledge and skill.

I started by installing Linux on all of my computers at home. This forced me to learn Linux and not look back. So long as I had a means to go back to my old and well-known way of doing things, it was never necessary for me to truly learn Linux. This is what I did when I decided I wanted to learn Linux, and it has taught me a large part of what I know. I had several computers and created a complete internal network in my home office. Over the years my network has grown and changed, and I have learned more with every alteration. Much of this was driven by my curiosity rather than any specific need.

I have static IP addresses from my ISP and a firewall to provide outside access and protect my internal network. I have had Intel boxes with Fedora and CentOS on them over the years. I learned a lot about using both in roles as a firewall and router.

I have a server that runs DHCP, HTTP, SMTP, IMAP, NTP, DNS, and other services to provide them to my internal network and to make some of those services available to the outside world, such as my website and incoming email. I have learned a great deal about using Linux in a server role in general. I have learned an incredible amount about implementing and managing each of these services.

All of this translated into usable skills in the job market. I learned even more in those jobs.

Tools

In this course we have looked at doing things at the command line, learning the very low-level tools for managing Linux hosts. We also created some of our own automated tools to make our administration tasks easier. I believe that it is necessary for good SysAdmins to understand the underlying tasks that need to be performed before engaging any of the more complex tools available.

There are many higher-level tools available that provide a great degree of automation and ease of use that we have not even covered. Many of these tools are also free, open source software and can be downloaded from the Fedora repositories. Most are also available for other distributions as well. You should spend some time learning about tools like Ansible and Webmin.

Ansible is an advanced tool that can automate many administrative tasks, things that we talked about automating with scripts. We have already looked at Ansible, but there is much more to learn. Webmin is a web-based administration tool that wraps around and uses many of the tools we have studied in this course. It provides a flexible, web-based center for managing Linux hosts and many of the services they provide.

There are many other tools of all kinds out there. These two will give you a starting point for advanced automation.

Resources

I have listed a large number of resources of various types throughout this course: websites, articles, and hard-copy books that you can use to further your Linux education. Many are directly related to this course, but others not so much. They will all help you learn more.

I have two favorite websites that I can count on for accurate and current information, technical as well as nontechnical. The now inactive but still useful *Opensource.com*,[2] a Red Hat website, contains technical and nontechnical articles about Linux, open source software, the open organization, DevOps, being a SysAdmin, and much more. The also inactive *Enable Sysadmin*[3] site has articles especially for SysAdmins and can be an excellent resource for all of us who do SysAdmin work. The Enable Sysadmin site has an especially good article on learning to be a SysAdmin.[4]

As I write this, many of us who contributed to those Red Hat–supported websites are in the process of working with another organization to set up a new site, Opensource. net.[5] It will be much like Opensource.com but with a wider remit that is intended to include more about distributions other than Red Hat ones.

You may also find my personal websites informative. The DataBook for Linux[6] is my technical website. It has information about problems I have found and fixed, articles covering how to do things that were difficult to find information about, and more. It is loosely structured into a book-like format, but it is strictly a reference and is not at all like

---

[2] Red Hat, Opensource.com, `https://opensource.com`

[3] Red Hat, Enable Sysadmin, `www.redhat.com/sysadmin/`

[4] Brown, Taz, "Learn the technical ropes and become a sysadmin," `www.redhat.com/sysadmin/learn-technical-ropes`

[5] `www.opensource.net`

[6] The DataBook for Linux, `www.linux-databook.info`,

this self-study course. It's fairly old, but there is still some good information there and I have embarked upon a project to bring it more up to date.

My other website is related to my published books. It is my "meet the author"[7] website, so it contains information about me and my books. I also publish errata about my books there as well as additional technical information about various Linux and hardware-related subjects.

There are many other excellent sources of information out there, both for Red Hat–based distributions as well as many of the other distributions. With a bit of searching, you can find plenty of information about Linux, almost every distribution ever created, and tens of thousands of specific problems.

Just be careful because there are many web pages with outdated or incorrect information. If you need to try out a fix or solution to a problem, be sure to do so on an expendable VM first.

And that virtual network, the one we created for this course or one like it, should also be one of your resources. Use it for testing everything you want to do on your physical network like we did in the many experiments we performed in this course.

Contribute

It can be difficult to imagine being given a completely free operating system that is the most advanced and secure on the planet – off it, too, if you count the International Space Station and the Mars rovers and helicopter. My point is that many people have been donating and continue to donate time, skills, and money to the Linux community. Because their work has made it possible for me to have this amazing and powerful operating system, I want to contribute what *I* can to help others.

There are many ways to contribute to open source, many ways to give back for what is so freely given to us. Most of those don't require us to write code. Let's look at a few.

Teaching

I have taught Linux to many people either in a classroom setting or as a mentor. Many of us have a lot of experience and knowledge. Passing that on is important to me and to the entire community. I have had some amazing mentors over the years who passed on their knowledge and expertise to me and others.

---

[7] David Both, www.both.org

The See One, Do One, Teach One (SODOTO)[8] model is used quite effectively in many teaching environments, and I have adopted it because, as I have mentioned, teaching and writing help me learn.

I was fortunate while working at IBM to have been taught presentation skills and course development. So creating training courses and other presentations and talks like I give at All Things Open[9] (ATO) and Open Libre Free[10] (OLF) is easy for me. This is a great and fun way for me to give back to the community.

Writing

Writing about something I have learned or am trying to learn helps me clarify what I already know about a subject and gives me an opportunity to expand my knowledge. Part of why this works for me is that it requires that I clarify my thinking on the subject at hand in order to be able to explain it in writing to students and readers who won't be able to interact with me in real time to get answers to their questions.

If you don't know what to write about, do what I do. I usually write about problems I recently encountered, especially difficult installations, new software I am trying out or have just adopted to replace something else, my X favorite tools to perform task Y, or whatever else piques my interest.

So write an article – or two or three – for Opensource.net or any of the other Linux-related websites out there. Most of those websites have posted information on how you can contribute your articles.

Coding and Packaging

I have done some coding in my time but don't consider myself a developer. This might be a way in which you can contribute if you are a developer. Coders and people who can assemble that code and related files and documentation into a package that can be easily installed on a Linux host are always needed on projects.

This is the manner of contribution that most people think about, but it certainly is not the only one.

---

[8] Positive Group, "What is the 'watch one, do one, teach one' method?," www.positivegroup.org/loop/articles/what-is-the-watch-one-do-one-teach-one-method

[9] All Things Open, www.allthingsopen.org/

[10] Open Libre Free, previously known as Ohio Linux Fest, https://olfconference.org/

Donate $$

Sometimes donating money to a project just makes sense to me. I have done so for more than one project – usually ones for which I can't participate in other ways. Most open source projects have links or instructions for donating on their web pages.

Skip This

Most lists of things to do ignore the bits you don't really need to do. Here is one I can suggest you skip as not being worth the time you might invest.

Compiling the Kernel

Don't bother. This might be a nice exercise if you are a developer or trying to get the last bit of CPU efficiency in a supercomputer and really want to do massive kernel mods, but most SysAdmins will never need to do this. You might also want to do this if the certification you are working on requires it, but other than that, you are pretty much wasting your time to do this.

The fact is that the kernel is compiled with a really good set of options for the vast majority of today's desktop and server needs. If you are having performance issues, you would be better off to determine whether the culprit really is the CPU and, if it is, install a bigger and faster CPU. Sometimes faster memory will help rather than a faster CPU. You just need to research it and figure out what the real problem is.

If changes to the kernel are required, altering one or more of the kernel tuning parameters in the /proc filesystem will most likely be the best way to resolve the problem.

We have already seen one interesting example of why most SysAdmins will never need to compile the kernel. Way back in Volume 1 of this course, we installed VirtualBox on a Linux host. We also needed to install some Linux development tools. The reason those tools were required is that VirtualBox compiles its own kernel module on the system on which it is installed. It does this the first time it starts on that system, and it also checks to see whether the kernel has been updated in which case it recompiles its kernel module again. The VirtualBox developers have automated that necessary task so that users do not need to know how to do it.

Of course if you are just curious …

Chapter Summary

To me, curiosity is the driving force behind learning. I can't just sit in a classroom because someone says I need to learn a particular thing and be successful at it. I need to have some interest in the subject, and something about it needs to pique my curiosity. That propensity to work harder on the subjects I liked was very evident during my school years as I did well in the subjects that intrigued me.

By using my home network lab for indulging my curiosity, I had lots of safe space in which to fail catastrophically and to learn the best ways to recover from that. And there are lots of ways to fail, so I learned a lot. I learned the most when I accidentally broke things, but I also learned a great deal when I would intentionally bork things. In these instances I knew what I wanted to learn and could target the breakage in ways that would enable me to learn about those specific things.

I was also fortunate because I had a few jobs that required or at least allowed me to take classes on various aspects of Unix and Linux. For me, classroom work is a way to validate and reinforce what I learn on my own. It gave me the opportunity to interact with – for the most part – knowledgeable instructors who could aid and clarify my understanding of the bits and pieces that I could not make sense of on my own.

Those of us who are successful at Unix and Linux system administration are by our very nature inquisitive and thoughtful. We take every opportunity to expand our knowledge base.

We like to experiment with new knowledge, new hardware, and new software, just out of curiosity and "because it is there." We relish the opportunities that are opened to us when computer things break. Every problem is a new possibility for learning. We enjoy attending technical conferences as much for the access to other SysAdmins they afford as for the amazing amount of new information we can gather from the scheduled presentations.

Rigid logic and rules do not give us SysAdmins enough flexibility to perform our jobs efficiently. We don't especially care about how things "should" be done. SysAdmins are not easily limited by the "should's" that others try to constrain us with. We use logical and critical thinking that is flexible and that produces excellent results. We create our own ways of doing things with independent, critical thinking and integrated reasoning, which enables us to learn more while we are at it.

We SysAdmins are strong personalities – we need to be in order to do our jobs and especially to do things the "right" way. This is not about how we "should" perform the tasks we need to do; rather, it is about using best practices and ensuring that the end result conforms to those practices.

We don't just think outside the box. We are the ones who destroy the boxes that others try to make us work inside. For us, there is no "should."

Be the curious SysAdmin. It worked for me.

Bibliography

Books

- Binnie, Chris, *Practical Linux Topics*, Apress 2016, ISBN 978-1-4842-1772-6

- Both, David, *The Linux Philosophy for SysAdmins*, Apress, 2018, ISBN 978-1-4842-3729-8

- Gancarz, Mike, *Linux and the Unix Philosophy*, Digital Press – an imprint of Elsevier Science, 2003, ISBN 1-55558-273-7

- Kernighan, Brian W.; Pike, Rob (1984), *The UNIX Programming Environment*, Prentice Hall, Inc., ISBN 0-13-937699-2

- Nemeth, Evi [et al.], *The Unix and Linux System Administration Handbook*, Pearson Education, Inc., ISBN 978-0-13-148005-6

- Matotek, Dennis, Turnbull, James, Lieverdink, Peter; *Pro Linux System Administration*, Apress, ISBN 978-1-4842-2008-5

- Raymond, Eric S., *The Art of Unix Programming*, Addison-Wesley, September 17, 2003, ISBN 0-13-142901-9

- Sobell, Mark G., *A Practical Guide to Linux Commands, Editors, and Shell Programming Third Edition*, Prentice Hall; ISBN 978-0-13-308504-4

- van Vugt, Sander, *Beginning the Linux Command Line*, Apress, ISBN 978-1-4302-6829-1

- Whitehurst, Jim, *The Open Organization*, Harvard Business Review Press (June 2, 2015), ISBN 978-1625275271

- Torvalds, Linus and Diamond, David, Just for Fun, HarperCollins, 2001, ISBN 0-06-662072-4

© David Both 2023
D. Both, *Using and Administering Linux: Volume 3*, https://doi.org/10.1007/978-1-4842-9786-5

BIBLIOGRAPHY

Web sites

- My personal web site, `http://www.both.org/`

- DataBook for Linux, `http://www.linux-databook.info/` My technical web site.

- FreeDesktop.org, `http://Freedesktop.org/`

- Linux.com, `http://Linux.com/`

- Opensource.com, `https://opensource.com/`

- Opensource.net, `https://opensource.net/` Many of the writers that contributed to Enable SysAdmin and Opensource.com have begun submitting articles to this new site that is hosted and supported by OSI, Open Source Initiative.

- Open Source Initiative, `https://opensource.org/`

- Raspberry Pi Foundation, `https://www.raspberrypi.org/`

- Red Hat, Enable SysAdmin, `https://www.redhat.com/sysadmin/` (No longer actively updated but still on-line.)

- Red Hat, Opensource.com, `https://opensource.com/` (No longer actively updated but still on-line.)

- WordPress, *Home page*, `https://wordpress.org/`

Web articles

- *BackBlaze, Web site, What SMART Stats Tell Us About Hard Drives*, `https://www.backblaze.com/blog/what-smart-stats-indicate-hard-drive-failures/`

- Bailey, Edward C., et al., Maximum RPM, `http://ftp.rpm.org/max-rpm/`, Red Hat, 2000

- Both, David, *8 reasons to use LXDE*, `https://opensource.com/article/17/3/8-reasons-use-lxde`

- Both, David, *9 reasons to use KDE*, `https://opensource.com/life/15/4/9-reasons-to-use-kde`

- Both, David, *10 reasons to use Cinnamon as your Linux desktop environment*, https://opensource.com/article/17/1/cinnamon-desktop-environment

- Both, David, *11 reasons to use the GNOME 3 desktop environment for Linux*, https://opensource.com/article/17/5/reasons-gnome

- Both, David, *An introduction to Linux network routing*, https://opensource.com/business/16/8/introduction-linux-network-routing

- Both, David, *Complete Kickstart,* http://www.linux-databook.info/?page_id=9

- Both, David, *Making your Linux Box Into a Router,* http://www.linux-databook.info/?page_id=697

- Both, David, *Network Interface Card (NIC) name assignments,* http://www.linux-databook.info/?page_id=4243

- Both, David, *Using hard and soft links in the Linux filesystem,* http://www.linux-databook.info/?page_id=5087

- Both, David, *Using rsync to back up your Linux system,* https://opensource.com/article/17/1/rsync-backup-linux

- Bowen, Rich, *RTFM? How to write a manual worth reading*, https://opensource.com/business/15/5/write-better-docs

- Brown, Taz, Learn the technical ropes and become a sysadmin, https://www.redhat.com/sysadmin/learn-technical-ropes

- Charity, *Ops: It's everyone's job now*, https://opensource.com/article/17/7/state-systems-administration

- Dartmouth University, *Biography of Douglas McIlroy*, http://www.cs.dartmouth.edu/~doug/biography

- Digital Ocean, *How To Use journalctl to View and Manipulate Systemd Logs*, https://www.digitalocean.com/community/tutorials/how-to-use-journalctl-to-view-and-manipulate-systemd-logs

- Edwards, Darvin, Electronic Design, *PCB Design And Its Impact On Device Reliability*, http://www.electronicdesign.com/boards/pcb-design-and-its-impact-device-reliability

- Engineering and Technology Wiki, *IBM 1800*, http://ethw.org/IBM_1800

- Fedora Magazine, *Tilix*, https://fedoramagazine.org/try-tilix-new-terminal-emulator-fedora/

- Fogel, Kark, *Producing Open Source Software*, https://producingoss.com/en/index.html

- Free On-Line Dictionary of Computing, *Instruction Set*, http://foldoc.org/instruction+set

- Free Software Foundation, *Free Software Licensing Resources*, https://www.fsf.org/licensing/education

- gnu.org, *Bash Reference Manual – Command Line Editing*, https://www.gnu.org/software/bash/manual/html_node/Command-Line-Editing.html

- Harris, William, *How the Scientific Method Works*, https://science.howstuffworks.com/innovation/scientific-experiments/scientific-method6.htm

- Heartbleed web site, http://heartbleed.com/

- How-two Forge, *Linux Basics: How To Create and Install SSH Keys on the Shell*, https://www.howtoforge.com/linux-basics-how-to-install-ssh-keys-on-the-shell

- Kroah-Hartman, Greg , Linux Journal, *Kernel Korner – udev – Persistent Naming in User Space*, http://www.linuxjournal.com/article/7316

- Krumins, Peter, *Bash emacs editing*, http://www.catonmat.net/blog/bash-emacs-editing-mode-cheat-sheet/

- Krumins, Peter, *Bash history*, http://www.catonmat.net/blog/the-definitive-guide-to-bash-command-line-history/

- Krumins, Peter, *Bash vi editing*, http://www.catonmat.net/blog/bash-vi-editing-mode-cheat-sheet/

- Kernel.org,*Linux allocated devices (4.x+ version)*, https://www.kernel.org/doc/html/v4.11/admin-guide/devices.html

- Linux Foundation, *Filesystem Hierarchical Standard (3.0)*, http://refspecs.linuxfoundation.org/fhs.shtml

- Linux Foundation, *MIT License*, https://spdx.org/licenses/MIT

- The Linux Information Project, *GCC Definition*, http://www.linfo.org/gcc.html

- Linuxtopia, *Basics of the Unix Philosophy*, http://www.linuxtopia.org/online_books/programming_books/art_of_unix_programming/ch01s06.html

- LSB Work group - The Linux Foundation, *Filesystem Hierarchical Standard V3.0, 3*, https://refspecs.linuxfoundation.org/FHS_3.0/fhs-3.0.pdf

- Opensource.com, *Appreciating the full power of open*, https://opensource.com/open-organization/16/5/appreciating-full-power-open

- Opensource.com, *David Both, SpamAssassin, MIMEDefang, and Procmail: Best Trio of 2017*, Opensource.com, https://opensource.com/article/17/11/spamassassin-mimedefang-and-procmail

- Opensource.org, *Licenses*, https://opensource.org/licenses

- opensource.org, *The Open Source Definition (Annotated)*, https://opensource.org/osd-annotated

- OSnews, *Editorial: Thoughts on Systemd and the Freedom to Choose*, http://www.osnews.com/story/28026/Editorial_Thoughts_on_Systemd_and_the_Freedom_to_Choose

- Peterson, Christine, Opensource.com, *How I coined the term 'open source,'* https://opensource.com/article/18/2/coining-term-open-source-software

BIBLIOGRAPHY

- Petyerson, Scott K, *The source code is the license,* Opensource.com, `https://opensource.com/article/17/12/source-code-license`

- Princeton University, *Interview with Douglas McIlroy,* `https://www.princeton.edu/~hos/frs122/precis/mcilroy.htm`

- Raymond, Eric S., *The Art of Unix Programming,* `http://www.catb.org/esr/writings/taoup/html/index.html/`

- Wikipedia, *The Unix Philosophy, Section: Eric Raymond's 17 Unix Rules,* `https://en.wikipedia.org/wiki/Unix_philosophy#Eric_Raymond%E2%80%99s_17_Unix_Rules`

- Raymond, Eric S., *The Art of Unix Programming, Section The Rule of Separation,* `http://www.catb.org/~esr/writings/taoup/html/ch01s06.html#id2877777`

- RPM, Documentation, `http://rpm.org/documentation.html`, This web page lists most of the available on-line documentation for RPM. It is mostly links to other web sites and information about RPM itself.

- *Understanding SMART Reports,* `https://lime-technology.com/wiki/Understanding_SMART_Reports`

- *Unnikrishnan A,* Linux.com, *Udev: Introduction to Device Management In Modern Linux System,* `https://www.linux.com/news/udev-introduction-device-management-modern-linux-system`

- Venezia, Paul, *Nine traits of the veteran Unix admin,* InfoWorld, Feb 14, 2011, `www.infoworld.com/t/unix/nine-traits-the-veteran-unix-admin-276?page=0,0&source=fssr`

- Wikipedia, *Alan Perlis,* `https://en.wikipedia.org/wiki/Alan_Perlis`

- Wikipedia, *Christine Peterson,* `https://en.wikipedia.org/wiki/Christine_Peterson`

- Wikipedia, *Command Line Completion,* `https://en.wikipedia.org/wiki/Command-line_completion`

- Wikipedia, *Comparison of command shells*, https://en.wikipedia.org/wiki/Comparison_of_command_shells

- Wikipedia, *Dennis Ritchie*, https://en.wikipedia.org/wiki/Dennis_Ritchie

- Wikipedia, *Device File*, https://en.wikipedia.org/wiki/Device_file

- Wikipedia, *Gnome-terminal*, https://en.wikipedia.org/wiki/Gnome-terminal

- Wikipedia, *Hard Links*, https://en.wikipedia.org/wiki/Hard_link

- Wikipedia, *Heartbleed*, https://en.wikipedia.org/wiki/Heartbleed

- Wikipedia, *Initial ramdisk*, https://en.wikipedia.org/wiki/Initial_ramdisk

- Wikipedia, *Ken Thompson*, https://en.wikipedia.org/wiki/Ken_Thompson

- *Wikipedia, Konsole,* https://en.wikipedia.org/wiki/Konsole

- Wikipedia, *Linux console*, https://en.wikipedia.org/wiki/Linux_console

- Wikipedia, *List of Linux-supported computer architectures*, https://en.wikipedia.org/wiki/List_of_Linux-supported_computer_architectures

- Wikipedia, *Maslow's hierarchy of needs*, https://en.wikipedia.org/wiki/Maslow%27s_hierarchy_of_needs

- Wikipedia, *Open Data*, https://en.wikipedia.org/wiki/Open_data

- Wikipedia, *PHP*, https://en.wikipedia.org/wiki/PHP

- Wikipedia, *PL/I*, https://en.wikipedia.org/wiki/PL/I

- Wikipedia, *Programma 101*, https://en.wikipedia.org/wiki/Programma_101

- Wikipedia, *Richard M. Stallman*, https://en.wikipedia.org/wiki/Richard_Stallman

- Wikipedia, *Rob Pike*, https://en.wikipedia.org/wiki/Rob_Pike

- Wikipedia, *rsync*, https://en.wikipedia.org/wiki/Rsync

- Wikipedia, *Rxvt*, https://en.wikipedia.org/wiki/Rxvt

- Wikipedia, *SMART*, https://en.wikipedia.org/wiki/SMART

- Wikipedia, *Software testing*, https://en.wikipedia.org/wiki/Software_testing

- Wikipedia, *Terminator*, https://en.wikipedia.org/wiki/Terminator_(terminal_emulator)

- Wikipedia, *Tony Hoare*, https://en.wikipedia.org/wiki/Tony_Hoare

- Wikipedia, *Unit Record Equipment,* https://en.wikipedia.org/wiki/Unit_record_equipment

- Wikipedia, *Unix*, https://en.wikipedia.org/wiki/Unix

- Wikipedia, *Windows Registry*, https://en.wikipedia.org/wiki/Windows_Registry

- Wikipedia, *Xterm*, https://en.wikipedia.org/wiki/Xterm

- WikiQuote, *C._A._R._Hoare*, https://en.wikiquote.org/wiki/C._A._R._Hoare

systemd

There is a great deal of information about systemd available on the internet, but much is terse, obtuse, or even misleading. In addition to the resources mentioned in this article, the following web pages offer more detailed and reliable information about systemd startup.

- The Fedora Project has a good, practical guide to systemd. It has pretty much everything you need to know in order to configure, manage, and maintain a Fedora computer using systemd. https://docs.fedoraproject.org/en-US/quick-docs/understanding-and-administering-systemd/index.html

- The Fedora Project also has a good cheat sheet that cross-references the old SystemV commands to comparable systemd ones. `https://fedoraproject.org/wiki/SysVinit_to_Systemd_Cheatsheet`

- For detailed technical information about systemd and the reasons for creating it, check out Freedesktop.org's description of systemd. `http://www.freedesktop.org/wiki/Software/systemd`

- Linux.com's "More systemd fun" offers more advanced systemd information and tips. `https://www.linux.com/training-tutorials/more-systemd-fun-blame-game-and-stopping-services-prejudice/`

There is also a series of deeply technical articles for Linux sysadmins by Lennart Poettering, the designer and primary developer of systemd. These articles were written between April 2010 and September 2011, but they are just as relevant now as they were then. Much of everything else good that has been written about systemd and its ecosystem is based on these papers.

- Rethinking PID, 1 `http://0pointer.de/blog/projects/systemd.html`

- systemd for Administrators, Part I, `http://0pointer.de/blog/projects/systemd-for-admins-1.html`

- systemd for Administrators, Part II, `http://0pointer.de/blog/projects/systemd-for-admins-2.html`

- systemd for Administrators, Part III, `http://0pointer.de/blog/projects/systemd-for-admins-3.html`

- systemd for Administrators, Part IV, `http://0pointer.de/blog/projects/systemd-for-admins-4.html`

- systemd for Administrators, Part V, `http://0pointer.de/blog/projects/three-levels-of-off.html`

- systemd for Administrators, Part VI, `http://0pointer.de/blog/projects/changing-roots`

- systemd for Administrators, Part VII, `http://0pointer.de/blog/projects/blame-game.html`

- systemd for Administrators, Part VIII, `http://0pointer.de/blog/projects/the-new-configuration-files.html`

- systemd for Administrators, Part IX, `http://0pointer.de/blog/projects/on-etc-sysinit.html`

- systemd for Administrators, Part X, `http://0pointer.de/blog/projects/instances.html`

- systemd for Administrators, Part XI, `http://0pointer.de/blog/projects/inetd.html`

Index

A

Address
 hardware, 150
 IP, 7, 10, 12–14, 20, 22–27, 30–33, 36, 39, 40, 43–46, 50, 52, 54–60, 62–64, 68–70, 72, 74, 75, 78–80, 82–84, 86, 87, 91, 93, 94, 96, 106, 107, 110, 113, 146, 148–151, 162, 165, 168–171, 225, 227, 235, 242, 331, 357, 405, 483
 IPV4, 55, 68
 IPV6, 55, 68
 localhost, 68
 MAC, 9, 10, 12, 13, 25, 27, 29, 31, 150
 network, 10, 40, 77
Alias
 command, 131
Alpine, 262, 267, 277–281, 283–285, 287–290, 294, 316
Apache web server
 Apache, 349–370, 388, 407, 472–477
 CGI scripting
  Bash, 366–367
  Perl, 364–366
 configuration, 357
 dynamic, 353
 index file, 353–356
 multiple websites, 358, 370
 static, 353, 369
 testing, 350–351
 virtual host, 358, 360–361, 364, 367–369

ASCII
 ASCII plain text, 22, 46, 50, 227, 229, 250, 261, 276, 314, 354
 ASCII text, 54, 152, 229, 233, 263, 269, 274, 388
Authentication, 116, 120, 133, 158, 254, 262, 263, 276, 306–314, 316, 406, 413, 420, 469
Automation
 Bash scripts, 217
 scripts, 475, 484
 automate everything, 217

B

Backup
 off-site, 205–207
 procedures, 220
 rsbu, 217, 219
 rsync, 210–217, 219
 recovery testing, 220
 remote, 131–133, 206
 strategy, 205, 209
 tar, 115, 132, 133, 200–205, 210, 221
Bash
 configuration files
  ~/.bash_profile, 124
  ~/.bashrc, 124
  /etc/bashrc, 124
  /etc/profile, 124
 shell scripts, 431

501

© David Both 2023
D. Both, *Using and Administering Linux: Volume 3*, https://doi.org/10.1007/978-1-4842-9786-5

Printed in the United States
by Baker & Taylor Publisher Services

Printed in the United States
by Baker & Taylor Publisher Services